Copy!

A life in print, Parliament, and far-flung places

by

NICHOLAS COMFORT

ISBN: 9798453112227

CONTENTS

Why "Copy"?

Before newspapers were put together electronically, every piece of a reporter's copy was processed by a long bench of sub-editors. They checked spellings, cut the story to size, marked up the type face and size to be used and wrote a headline. When they had finished, they held up the slip of paper for a messenger to take to the printers and shouted: "Copy!" That is the stage my story has reached.

Where my life has been out of the ordinary, it is in good measure due to having had an exceptional father; I have left the sweep of his life to aspiring biographers, but offer some insights of my own. As to myself, having spent 26 years to date as an obituarist I start with a possible obituary for myself to give the reader some reference points, and finish with some reflections on that craft.

To keep to a readable length I have had to be selective, and many relatives, friends and people who have influenced my life are not mentioned or given the credit they deserve. To them I apologise. My thanks for a full and happy life are due to them, and to those closest to me: my children and grandchildren, of whom I am immensely proud, and of course my wife, Jeanette.

Nicholas Comfort

Anerley, London SE20, September 2021

3

1. <u>My Story in Brief</u>

NICHOLAS COMFORT, [still alive], was a Lobby correspondent at Westminster for 20 years, nine of them for the *Daily Telegraph*. He also wrote leaders for the *Telegraph* and the *Sun*, was political editor of three other papers, and from 1995 contributed hundreds of obituaries to the *Telegraph*.

Comfort filed from more than 30 countries, being shot at covering a military coup in Uganda. From 1978 to 1987 he was the *Telegraph's* deputy political correspondent; he broke many stories as Margaret Thatcher changed the face of Britain, but his speciality was the turmoil within the Labour Party as the Bennite Left gained the ascendancy, then was driven back. He contributed a weekly parliamentary sketch to the BBC World Service, and presented Radio Four's *News Stand*.

Each of the parties tried to recruit Comfort as a spin doctor. His sympathies (at times severely strained) were with Labour, and in 2001 he went to work for the Scottish Secretary Helen Liddell, whom he had known since the 1979 devolution referendum. Comfort had first joined the party (along with his teenage neighbour Jack Straw) in 1962, but during an election strategy meeting in 2001 realised his membership had lapsed years before, and hastily renewed it. In 2014 he stood – unsuccessfully – for Bromley council.

He was the only son of Dr Alex Comfort, the anarchist, gerontologist, poet, co-founder of CND and author of *The Joy of Sex*. Publication of Comfort senior's *Sex In Society* when Nicholas was a sixth-former had its embarrassing side, as did his imprisonment with Bertrand Russell after a sit-down in Trafalgar Square.

The Joy of Sex (1973) was more a source of pride to him. It helped that the ballyhoo was confined to America, where Alex Comfort had moved after divorcing and remarrying. When after his father's death in 2000 Mitchell Beazley produced a 30th anniversary edition, Comfort himself updated the text ... insisting he was not an expert. Later, the US rights to *Joy* brought him Hollywood interests.

Nicholas Alfred Fenner Comfort was born in London on August 4 1946, the only son of Alexander Comfort and the former Ruth Harris. From Highgate School he won an exhibition to Trinity College, Cambridge to read Law, switching to History. He worked on the student newspaper *Varsity* and captained Trinity's *University Challenge* team; during vacations he worked on the *Northern Echo* and, in 1967, the *Daily Telegraph*.

On graduating, he joined the Sheffield *Morning Telegraph*, becoming its municipal correspondent. In 1974 he returned to the *Daily Telegraph* and was posted to Birmingham, covering the IRA pub bombings and the hunt for the "Black Panther", Donald Neilson.

In 1976 the *Telegraph*'s managing editor Peter Eastwood sent Comfort to Washington. He covered the Queen's Bicentennial tour and the Montreal Olympics, then concentrated on Congress, the Pentagon, energy and aerospace. He was teargassed on the White House lawn when Iranian students rioted as President Carter greeted the Shah, and was in the Oval Office when Carter met Romania's dictator Nicolae Ceausescu.

In 1978, with a general election expected, Comfort was recalled to join the Telegraph's political staff. He was with Mrs Thatcher when James Callaghan announced there would be no election, and in the gallery when Callaghan's government fell on a vote of confidence. He slept through the Brighton bombing of 1984 having been in the Grand Hotel just 20 minutes before; wakened, he found his drinking companion wandering the street in shock and swathed in a blanket.

Comfort was deputy to three *Telegraph* political correspondents: David Harris, James Wightman and George Jones. The post fell vacant early in 1986, as Conrad Black bought the *Telegraph* from Lord Hartwell; Comfort applied, but the incoming editor Max Hastings opted for new blood. Eighteen months later, Hastings made him a leader writer, joining Bill Deedes, Jock Bruce-Gardyne,

Simon Heffer and the young Boris Johnson; he wrote the occasional parliamentary sketch, and often edited the leader page.

In 1989 he moved to the new *Independent on Sunday* as political editor. The chemistry was wrong, and after six months he joined Robert Maxwell's *European*. Comfort built the paper's UK political coverage and travelled on stories requested by Maxwell, most frequently to Budapest.

After Maxwell's death, he stayed with the Mirror Group as political editor of the Glasgow-based *Daily Record*. For three years he provided its Westminster coverage and reported on elections, travelling with John Major – with whom he empathised – and covering the end of *apartheid* in South Africa. But in 1995 a lawsuit by former *European* staff against the Mirror Group reached the courts; threatened with the sack by its chief executive Charlie Wilson, he resigned.

After a spell in lobbying, Comfort returned to Westminster as a freelance, for the *Scottish Sun,* the *People* and *Scotland on Sunday;* he also wrote leaders for the *Sun*. He also began writing obituaries at the *Telegraph* (by now nearly 2,000); he once left the *Telegraph* hastily after realising he had the *Sun*'s news list in his briefcase.

Comfort formed a media training team whose clients included Royal Ordnance, trained politicians in Zambia and lectured in Kaliningrad - turning down an invitation to Chechnya.

In 1999 Mrs Liddell, John Prescott's deputy as Transport Minister, invited Comfort to be her special adviser; he had a lifelong interest in railways, aviation and the bus industry. That evening she was reshuffled to the DTI as Minister for Energy and Europe – having him recruited as a non-partisan consultant on Britain's economic reform agenda for the EU.

After Mrs Liddell's promotion to Scottish Secretary in 2001, Comfort as a SPAD handled his former colleagues in the Scottish media, ensured Whitehall departments did not ignore devolution in their policymaking, and interceded when Labour at Holyrood diverged with Westminster. He was part of Scottish Labour's 2001 general election team, and at the centre of the consultations (and blood-letting) over reducing the number of Scottish MPs post-devolution.

In 2003 he joined QinetiQ, the privatised research arm of the MoD, to develop its relations with government. He was there three years, later working for Association of Train Operating Companies, Unisys and various consultancies.

Comfort was an elder of Elmers End Free Church, a volunteer at the Bluebell Railway, a shareholder in Sheffield United and a life member of Essex County Cricket Club.

His previous books include *Brewer's Politics* (1993), *The Lost City of Dunwich* (1994), *How to Handle the Media* (2003), *The Channel Tunnel and Its High-Speed Links* (2006), *Surrender: How British Industry Gave Up The Ghost* (2012), and *The Regional Railways Story*, with Gordon Pettitt (2015).

Nicholas Comfort's first two marriages, to Deborah Elliott in 1970 [she died in 2017] and Corinne Reed in 1990, ended in divorce. He is survived by his third wife Jeanette Owens, whom he married in 2014; a son (John) and a daughter (Caroline) from his first marriage, and a son from his second (Alex).

2: Comforts and Harrises

After my grandfather Alexander Charles Comfort was widowed in 1948, he set out to research his family tree. He contacted Comforts around the world, tracing our branch to Hawkhurst in Kent, where Robert Comfort (born 1715) was a wheelwright. He found tantalising earlier fragments: a Tudor brass in Battle church, gravestones on the Isle of Grain, an abandoned Kentish village called Comport, and a mysterious Richard Curva Spina – Richard III? But there was no continuity: Hawkhurst's parish registers had been destroyed by a stray wartime bomb.

Robert, forebear also of Australian Comforts and the footballer-turned-vicar Alan Comfort, refused to marry until civil ceremonies were legitimised. His third son Humphrey Gilbert moved to London - and his third son Jabez, born 1809 and my great-great-grandfather, is the first ancestor of whom a (forbidding) photograph survives.

My great-grandfather Gilbert Humphrey Comfort was a traveller in perfume and a Plymouth Brother; he would get into furious theological arguments on trains, only to discover he had consigned a fellow Brother to damnation. He was a lonely man who found it hard to communicate with his children; the one letter my grandfather kept tried to be affectionate but was hamstrung by concerns for his soul. One of Grandfather's favourite books, Edmund Gosse's *Father and Son*, chronicled just such a relationship. Gilbert Humphrey's wife, Jane Furnish, came from Louth in Lincolnshire; they were introduced by the great Baptist preacher Charles Spurgeon. Her sister's son was Grandfather's favourite cousin, and as Sir Herbert Broadley founded the UN Food and Agriculture Organisation.

Grandfather, born on September 1 1882, was Gilbert Humphrey's youngest child. Corvine but warm, of all my family I have always felt closest to him. Ahead of him were two boys, Fred and Bert (grandfather of Angela, my only Comfort cousin), and three girls. Ella was musical and died at 21; I have her tiny rocking chair on which she carved her initials. Con worked at the Post Office Savings Bank, and Jane – with whom she shared an imposing house at Cockfosters with cut-glass doorknobs - was artistic. Their dog Jack started refusing his meals but didn't waste away; then they saw him wolfing down scraps thrown over the fence. After that, they took Jack's meals next door ....

Grandfather grew up in unassuming Cowslip Road, South Woodford. At 11 he went to the Coopers' Company school, signing apprenticeship papers which, among other things, barred him from fornication without the consent of his master; he was not expected to make barrels. He particularly enjoyed Classics; one of his masters ascribed strong views on Latin pronunciation to having been a slave in ancient Rome. A classmate's father had lost a leg at sea; asked what the stump looked like, he said: "The end of a jam roll."

From school, Alexander went to work at the School Board for London. He was soon promoted to the section building new schools; all over inner London you still see upright red-brick structures bearing the initials "SBL". He moved into County Hall on its completion in 1922, and retired soon after I was born as Assistant to the Chief Education Officer. When Labour under Herbert Morrison – whom he reckoned a "pipsqueak" – took control of the London County Council in 1934, Grandfather was asked to devise a crash school building programme; he had one waiting.

Grandfather started out a "light blue Tory", but his exposure to businessmen's greed during the Great War disillusioned him. He volunteered for the Army, but instead was sent to run the agency in Dewsbury buying the wool for soldiers' uniforms. Its first challenge was to stop wool merchants trading with the enemy. As the war dragged on, uniforms were increasingly sourced not from virgin wool but recycled "shoddy". Eventually, Grandfather told me with a catch in his voice, one track of the railway from Leeds to Goole was occupied by wagons full of bloodied uniforms from the trenches.

He often encountered the legendary Yorkshire obtuseness, minuting after one meeting: "It is impossible to explain this, or anything else, to Mr Wood of Ossett". He also witnessed the frugality; the millionaire Sir Charles Sykes routinely took an evening paper from a newsboy, scanned it for the cricket score, then handed it back saying he had no change. Half a century later, a colleague of mine called at a pub above Halifax to tell the landlord he had won the *Yorkshire Post*'s unfortunately-named "Pick the Spot" competition. Asked what he was having, Gerry ordered a pint and was told: "That will be one and threepence."

Back at County Hall, Grandfather worked closely with London's head teachers, many becoming friends. Miss Rosa Soul was the only one whose name appeared in full outside the school, to avoid her being billed as "Miss R. Soul". One of his responsibilities was distributing (then-silent) educational films. One of a surgeon at work was highly rated until shown at a school for the deaf, whose pupils collapsed laughing. The head explained that as the surgeon picked up his scalpel, he muttered: "I'm going to carve you up, you bastard!" He was also involved in referring disturbed pupils to Sir Cyril Burt, a pioneer in the field of child psychology since unmasked as a charlatan. When Burt ended a consultation with one persistent thief minus his wallet, he minuted: "Objects of value should not be left near this child."

Another interest Grandfather took on for the LCC was Coram's Fields, the children's playground and centre in Bloomsbury. This seven-acre oasis, with its motto "No adult admitted without a child", remains a very special place. He oversaw its opening in 1936, when the band of the Coldstream Guards unprecedentedly struck up *The Teddy Bears' Picnic*. But another tune caused more trouble: the National Anthem.

The Abdication crisis was brewing, and Coram's Fields was to be opened by the Duke and Duchess of York, soon to be King George VI and Queen Elizabeth. Grandfather had a worried call from the bandmaster: protocol dictated only the first four bars for the Yorks, but he had been told the Duchess would not leave the car until the entire Anthem had been played. Grandfather told him that in that case they had better play it all. When I read that the future Queen Mum was hesitant about letting her husband take the throne, I remember that phone call.

Grandfather served on the management committee of Coram's Fields up to his death aged 93. Its members ranged from "Bubbles" Harmsworth, the socialite wife of Lord Rothermere whose family had endowed the playground, to Frank Dobson, the firebrand leader of Camden Council who mellowed into one of my favourite parliamentarians. When we donated a commemorative bench, Frank dedicated it.

He was also on the management committee at St Stephen's Hospital, Chelsea (now the Chelsea & Westminster). The chairman was Admiral John Godfrey, wartime Director of Naval Intelligence and model for 'M'; Godfrey recalled an officer on his staff named Fleming scribbling in an exercise book – the genesis of James Bond. Godfrey was renowned as the rudest man in the Royal Navy, and after he took charge of the Indian Navy it mutinied. When the consultants at St Stephen's protested to Grandfather about the Admiral's manner, Godfrey's response was: "Rude to them? Called them a lot of bloody bastards, but I wasn't rude to them."

Grandfather loved music, possessing a strong baritone voice and a repertoire from drawing-room ballads like *I Am the Bandolero* to Handel. But it was his passion for cricket that he passed on to me. He had been a regular at Essex's Leyton ground from the early 1890s, and his memories were undimmed. When I asked him who were the fastest bowler and hardest-hitting batsman he had seen, he went without hesitation for C J Kortright, Essex's demon bowler whom he reckoned a yard quicker than Dennis Lillee, and Gloucestershire's double-jointed Gilbert Jessop, who broke the clock at Lord's. He had second thoughts about Jessop after seeing Ted Dexter's brutal 76 against the 1961 Australians. "You could see the fielders wringing their hands with pain," he marvelled. I wish he had lived to see Ian Botham.

His thirst for knowledge led him through evening classes to a Classics degree at Birkbeck; he was President of its Students' Union in 1910. His favourite memory of Birkbeck was arriving early for the Christmas party, whose star attraction was the janitor's non-alcoholic punch. Grandfather found him pouring in bottles of gin, rum and the like, saying of the teetotal guests: "I have to do something to cheer them up." Grandfather – who barely drank - kept schtum.

At Birkbeck he met my grandmother Daisy Elizabeth Fenner, a year his junior. Her father, Joseph, was an East End baker who moved south to Camberwell. She had a brother - Douglas - and two sisters, Maud and Gert. Douglas married Eleanor, who lived to a ripe old age; their son John died serving in the RAF. Gert stayed on in the house in East Dulwich she had shared with my grandmother; to the end, it was lit by gas.

Elizabeth was the high flier of the family. A star pupil at Mary Datchelor school, she trained as a teacher at Stockwell College, then joined its staff, teaching everything from commercial studies to PE but specialising in French. In 1909 she won a scholarship to Birkbeck, where she took a First in Medieval French, advancing her studies at Nancy University. Her great rival was Jessie Raven, later Crosland; they would live out their ambitions through their sons, classmates at Highgate. Elizabeth had a formidable intellect, with strong views on pronunciation (every word in full, every syllable accentuated), and forthright views.   When a woman collecting for the poor complained how improvident they were, Elizabeth replied: "Yes, I once heard of a family whose child was born in a manger."

Elizabeth had an elfin face topped by a mane of rich red hair. Some found her an intellectual bulldozer, but Grandfather was smitten. She, in turn, passed up the opportunity (I was told) to become the first woman to undertake research in French at Oxford.   They married one lunchtime in 1915, the year Gilbert Humphrey died, and set up home at Barnet in a new Arts and Crafts house, many of its furnishings made by LCC craft students. Havengore, with its heavy oak beams and book-lined through sitting room, was their home for 33 years; and Grandfather's for 27 more. To his dying day, he never went out without saying goodbye to her.

When I was nearly two, Elizabeth went into hospital for a hysterectomy. Two days later she was dead, through some problem with the anaesthetic. Grandfather rebuilt his life, even bottling his own fruit (there were still plums from 1949 when we cleared the house). I loved sitting in his den upstairs watching cricket, going down the garden to the (empty) beehive, playing postcard-style 78s on his wind-up gramophone and throwing paper darts along the sitting room. He took me down to Sussex to stay with his favourite retired heads, and later proudly visited me in Cambridge. Later still, he lent me his garage to store some of my furniture – fixing the roof at 90 to keep it dry.

Grandfather lived to see my father divorce my mother and marry Jane - he was a witness at their wedding - and cuddle his great-granddaughter. He only faltered in the final months of his life, after trekking up to Coram's Fields on a scorching hot day, and his death in October 1975 was a shock. I usually rang him on Sunday evenings, but that night I was on late at the *Telegraph* and didn't call him before leaving home; in the morning his neighbour Dora Tear – who for years had kept an eye on him - rang to say he had passed away, and I was left regretting that unmade call.

Going through his desk, I found letters explaining a family mystery. Back in the 1920s his elder brother Fred had left his wife and daughter and gone to Australia. Fred's letters were heartrending; he had felt he had to go, but was desperate for news of home. He settled in Adelaide with a formidable-looking woman; then, in the darkest days of the war, a firm of solicitors there informed Grandfather that Fred and his lady had died. An inquest put it down to a gas leak, but suicide could not be ruled out.

My father Alexander Comfort (he had no middle name) was born on February 10, 1920. He had a happy childhood, with holidays at Hartland in north Devon (travelling in the sidecar of Grandfather's motor-bike), and interests from train spotting to the Arkubs, formed around J F Horrabin's *Japhet* cartoon strip in the *News Chronicle*. But all my grandmother's formidable intellect was focused on him.

At seven he was sent away to St George's School at Harpenden, which he hated. He remembered his time there for the ballet classes, his parents for the day young Alex greeted the visiting Albert Schweitzer in perfect French. He moved on to Norman Court prep school at Potters Bar (now in Wiltshire), where he was encouraged by a remarkable schoolmaster, Henry Walker – to whom he would dedicate his first book - and won a scholarship to Highgate.

Highgate was an inspired choice. The headmaster, Dr J A H Johnston, had the look of a bibulous bookie but had put together after the Great War an exceptional young staff. Alex learned his Latin from "Tommy" Twidell, an ex-cavalry officer who would break off from telling boys they would never pass "that pappy examination known as the School Certificate" to show how to hold your sabre when charging, to avoid contact with an opponent breaking your wrist. Greek was taught by Charles Benson ("Charlie B"), a slight, bespectacled clergyman with a perfect voice for Evensong who seemed out of place in the classroom. Benson's observation to Dad's Classical Fifth of "Excuse me, I'm a little hoarse" or his reference in my time to "Eros in Piccadolly Circus" generated a hilarity that baffled him.

Alex had no interest in sport, but was not just a swot. He was in his own words "insufferably evangelical", refused to join the Officer Training Corps (starting a rival "Peace Society"), took up the trumpet, graduating to the longer Bach version, and became an expert on snails.

The most devastating event in his life occurred in May 1935, near the end of his year in the Classical Fifth. Alex decided to make fireworks to celebrate George V's Silver Jubilee, in the greenhouse where Grandfather propagated tiny white grapes. He had planned a cinema trip with a friend, but when his first creation left a crater in the lawn, his mother grounded him and sent the friend home. Trying again, a spark ignited the mixture, shattering the greenhouse. His left hand was mutilated, and had he not been wearing spectacles he would have been blinded. Though in great pain, he rang his friend while waiting for the ambulance to warn him not to try the same experiment.

One of his aunts left him £50, fearing he would unable to earn a living. But my grandmother used her savings with "The Co-Operative Society" to secure the finest treatment. The surgeon, Ian Twistington Higgins, pulled off a near-miracle: instead of amputating, he painstakingly rescued not only the ball of the hand but a functioning thumb. This left Alex with dexterity for essentials like tying shoelaces, despite the loss of four fingers. My grandparents were undyingly grateful to Twistington Higgins, sharing his pain when his ballerina daughter contracted polio and almost total disability; resiliently, she became a painter by mouth and was honoured on *This Is Your Life*. Alex was given an artificial hand, but seldom used it and when speaking in public he would tuck his left arm behind his back - a mannerism I unwittingly copied.

To recuperate, Grandfather took him to Buenos Aires. They sailed from Rotterdam on the tramp steamer *Pentridge Hill*, and returned on the Greek freighter *Demetrios Chandris* - the chaos aboard which contrasted with the order of the British vessel. Alex loved life at sea, returning with photos of the crew washing the ship's dog and recalling how the Greeks caught sharks, using the ship's anvil as a counterweight when the fish struck. Armed with a pass from the British Museum, he catalogued the mollusca of Madeira and Senegal, and had riotous memories (second-hand) of a fight on a tram in Buenos Aires when the crew got ashore. [It would be 2014 before I got there myself, en route for the Antarctic]. Both ships would come to grief: the Greek steamer collided with the *Empire Bunting* on a wartime convoy off Newfoundland, and the *Pentridge Hill* foundered in the Bristol Channel in 1941 when its cargo of locomotives for Iran broke loose in a storm.

The voyage started to heal Alex' emotional scars, and set him writing: *The Silver River*, an impressionistic memoir of the trip published by Chapman & Hall when he was 17. He contributed to an anthology of schoolboy verse and edited (as I would) Highgate's school magazine, the *Cholmeleian*; he upset the Head by listing among old boys' achievements the imprisonment of one for fraud.

Transcending his injuries, he won a Classics scholarship to Trinity College, Cambridge; I think he also won one to Balliol, my grandmother's preference given her own thwarted Oxford career. This alone would have been an achievement, but intent on a medical career he stayed on at school, and the next year pulled off a possibly unique double with a further scholarship in Natural Sciences.

Alex left Highgate in 1938 weighed down with prizes – a library of the Classics in gold-tooled covers, essential volumes for the naturalist and books about Amazonia. Tony Crosland won a scholarship to Oxford, but – to the annoyance of his mother - finished Speech Day with a less impressive haul.

Cambridge in 1938 was the preserve of gentlemen, and it must have been a struggle for my grandparents to finance Alex' years at Trinity. As a scholar he was allocated rooms in Great Court facing the fountain and the chapel clock beyond. P3 had a spacious bedroom and study, the latter graced by a bishop's coat of arms, but there was no lavatory and he had to cross the court for a bath. Trinity did not then provide furniture, so Grandfather ordered a bed, table and chairs, sideboard, cupboards, bookcase and more from a Jewish carpenter in Shoreditch – total cost £43 5s. They have stood the test of time.

Alex' tutor was the timeless A S F Gow, who in wartime published *Letters from Cambridge*, a collection of his writings from that oasis of civilisation to former tutees serving around the world; it became Grandfather's other favourite book. Like every undergraduate, he acquired a bicycle. After it was stolen he fitted his next with a hatpin under the seat attached to a rat-trap, to be triggered when the thief rode it away; he was its only victim, the pin being removed at A&E. He joined pacifist demonstrations, and rowdy protests when Sir Oswald Mosley visited Cambridge; a bottle of printer's ink with a firecracker in it was dropped into the basement where the Blackshirt leader was speaking.

For recreation he joined the University music society, but had to give up the trumpet when most of his teeth were extracted. His dentures developed a knack of coming loose and moving around; much later he would sneeze them out at inappropriate moments.

The family attended Barnet Congregational Church and Alex wanted to be a medical missionary; so he also joined CongSoc, the university Congregational society. There he met my uncle Stephen Harris, at Jesus a year ahead of him, and Helen Doyle, the Newnham classicist Stephen would marry – joining the CongSoc Lake District walking trips that would continue for some into the next century - and in his second year, after the outbreak of war, Stephen's sister Ruth.

Ruth Muriel Harris's background was more genteel. Her grandfather, W E Stevens (known as Cupakey) was the Pickfords director responsible for the horses that pulled its removal vans. Through the Round Chapel, Clapton Park where he was a deacon for 48 years, Cupakey supported the medical missionary Sir Wilfred Grenfell who devoted his life to wildest Labrador. He married Agnes Dyall, a stockbroker's daughter, and in 1905 moved out from Hackney to a small farm at Loughton, three years later purchasing nearby Debden House. They had four children: Percy, Ruth, Madge and my grandmother, Agnes Mabel (May) Stevens, born on February 5, 1883. The extended family was big – my mother had 26 aunts and uncles and 25 first cousins, mainly on the Stevens side – and Debden became its centre.

A rectangular white house given character by its shutters, Debden House sits in a clearing in Epping Forest; in its greenhouse, Cupakey grew pineapples until the war. An early car owner, he had a Bean (a Midlands marque manufactured up to 1929) with a boot that opened up into a seat. As his chauffeur, George Dix, neared retirement, Cupakey hoped my mother would fill the gap. Reluctantly she learned to drive, then war broke out and the Bean was put away.

For 40 years the family gathered at Debden for Christmas and major events, under his benign patriarchy. My great-grandmother died early in the war, but Cupakey survived it, dying at 87 when I was almost two. To my mother's immense sadness, Debden was compulsorily purchased as a residential centre by East Ham council. When she died in 2000 I arranged for the funeral tea to be held there, and was astonished to recognise the kitchen.

May Stevens was slight and delicate, but had a determined streak on which she would need to draw. When eight she was bitten by a supposedly rabid dog, and rushed to Paris to be inoculated by Pasteur. She studied piano at the Royal Academy of Music under Parry, Stanford and Walford Davies, and in her visitors' book Clara Butt and Malcolm Sargent jostled with missionaries. On Sunday evenings when I was small Grannie would play hymns on the grand piano while the missionary box was passed round. If we were really lucky – and usually as the result of my father persuading her – she would play items from her old repertoire, like the second, livelier portion of Beethoven's *Moonlight Sonata*.

In 1906, when 23, she travelled to Australia on the *Orontes* to visit her cousin Percy Dyall. I have her diary of the voyage, and her photograph of palm trees on the coast of Ceylon has pride of place on our wall. She went either to convalesce or to get over a broken engagement; the family's money is on the latter. Percy had emigrated in 1887 – she remembered seeing him off at the station - bought a tract of bush at Mirboo in rural Victoria and set about clearing it. My mother showed me over Christmas 1987 Percy's letter from exactly a century before describing his home - "my furniture consists of a stretcher to sleep on, made of a couple of sacks stretched out on two poles" - and his first Christmas, spent sharing a pudding he had made with the "old sodbuster" on the next plot, before weaving his way back to the cabin he had built and waking with a sore head.

In her early thirties May married Alfred Harris, a handsome Freemason 13 years her senior who ran a printing business in Leadenhall Street with his brother Leonard. One side of his family were the Booths, a big name in Congregationalism since the 18th Century; Alfred's father Booth, like Cupakey, had moved out to Loughton, becoming a pillar of the Union Church. Alfred's first wife died childless in 1907, and he and May married, like my other grandparents, in 1915, moving into Ivy Gate, a corner house facing

Loughton station. Notoriously unpunctual, he would vault over the ticket barrier to catch his train. (His son - barely three when Alfred died - inherited this trait; inconveniently for a clergyman, Stephen had a habit of being late for weddings and funerals.)

Ivy Gate was five minutes' walk from the Union Church (joint Congregational and Baptist), the imposing Regency-style chapel around which Grannie's life revolved for half a century. Her zeal against drink and gambling set her apart from the majority of affluent Loughtonians who attended the parish church, St Mary's. She had strong moral views generally; beside one photo in a late Victorian album is written in her unmistakable hand: "Elsie Smith of Stratford, Bigamist". Grannie expected her children to be teetotal - though all would drink moderately when she was not around – and she read us grandchildren stories of the evils of drink from the *White Ribbon*. When I started visiting Loughton's pubs, I discovered Mrs Gibson, who had driven Grannie for years, behind the bar at the King's Head. We each agreed to keep schtum.

My mother was born at Ivy Gate on 1 February 1917. Her middle name came from Grannie's church friend Muriel Lester, who with her sister Doris ran a mission in Poplar named after their late brother Kingsley. Muriel was one of the councillors led by George Lansbury who were jailed for "overspending" on the poor. As a missionary in India she befriended Gandhi, who stayed at Kingsley Hall in 1931. Grannie was invited to tea at their home in Loughton and my mother's sister Alison went too, recalling his luminous smile which she said Ben Kingsley captured perfectly in the film – my mother, away at school, was deeply envious. Muriel Lester hoped to take me to India, but it was not to be.

Ruth was joined by Stephen (1919) and Alison (1920), then the idyll at Ivy Gate came to an agonising end. Alfred died of throat cancer aged 50, and Grannie was left with three under-fives, no breadwinner and heavy commitments. To ease the burden, my mother was sent away on the ground that the eldest child, at four, needed her least. She spent a year with the Mobbs family at

Wickford; though she was well treated, the separation left deep emotional scars.

Grannie moved 800 yards up Alderton Hill to the more imposing Little Gables, her home for her remaining 45 years. She needed home helps, and George Preddy ("he was born when his mother was drunk") helped tend the half-acre of gardens. But she could not have managed Little Gables, or her family, without Auntie Ninnie.

Constance Winifred Gould ("Ninnie" was a child's mispronunciation of Winifred) was the youngest of the Goulds, who lived further up the hill. An old Loughton farming family and pillars of the Union Church, the Goulds reckoned themselves a cut above the Stevenses; we didn't see much of them save for Ninnie's brother Donald, who farmed pigs at Buntingford but lived round the corner from us and let us use his swimming pool. However Grannie became good friends with Ninnie, who ran the Sunday school; Ninnie looked after her parents, then moved into Little Gables, Grannie doing the delicate tasks and Ninnie, plain and sturdy, the heavy lifting. Ninnie was the ideal foil to her, bathing us, reading us Bible stories and injecting just enough fun to offset Grannie's dogmatism – though it was Ninnie who, if one of us said: "I bet", would interject: "We don't bet in this house". Grannie's children and we five grandchildren loved her, and she became one of the family.

Of her many cousins, my mother was fondest of Alfred Sadd, a few years her senior. The son of Alfred Harris's sister, he trained to be a Congregational minister – Stephen following suit – and became a missionary in the Gilbert & Ellice Islands (now Kiribati and Tuvalu). Tall, warm and personable, he had made quite an impression there by the time Japan invaded. Alf refused to leave, and stood his ground. Ordered to venerate the Imperial flag, he refused ... and was later executed. While many missionaries died in Japanese prison camps, Alf was, I believe, the only one killed in cold blood. His story was movingly told in a radio documentary, *Missing, Believed Immortal*.

There is a sequel. In Sheffield I got to know a Japanese PhD student, Kimihiko Kitamura. We lost touch, then years later met again. He was now dean at Tokyo's Gakushuin University, and had been tutor to the Emperor, Akihito. When I sent Kimi my *Brewer's Politics,* he told me he had passed it to the Emperor. This worried me, as its references to Japan concerned starting wars, corruption and ritual disembowelment.

Soon after, Akihito got a hostile reception visiting London from veterans and the tabloids. My mother had told me how several of her friends' husbands had also suffered at the hands of the Japanese, but I felt it was time to draw a line, and wrote to Kimi saying as much. Back came a note saying: "I hope you don't mind if I show your letter to the Emperor." Had I known, I would have used my best handwriting.

A more distant cousin was Valentine Dyall, who was occasionally on the *Goon Show.* Grannie considered his calling not quite proper, but reserved her outright disapproval for Kenneth Horne ("A pity, his father was such a wonderful minister"). How she would have coped had Benny Hill bought the house next door to her – he viewed it in the early 1960s - I cannot imagine.

My mother left school and, after a gap year in Switzerland, settled back into Little Gables, the only breaks with routine being the latest Fred and Ginger film and the night she, Grannie and Ninnie watched as the Crystal Palace burned to the ground 20 miles away. She was 22 and Alison 17 when war broke out and they faced being conscripted. Alison found a job at Dr Barnardo's, making appetising meals out of basic ingredients and going on to become a Cordon Bleu chef. Working later for Glover & Main menu-testing gas cookers, she met her amiable husband John Coals.

Ruth opted to work with children, but needed qualifications. She started taking a diploma at LSE, then it was evacuated to Cambridge. Her flatmate there was Jane Henderson, who was taking a degree course. Jane – slight, curly-haired and with glasses - came from a Methodist family in Kentish Town; her father was in the Indian tea trade. "Auntie Jane" became a family friend - and 33 years later my stepmother.

Ruth joined Stephen in CongSoc, and there she met my father. He was attracted by her facial profile - he created a superb likeness in plaster – and her love of music; she recognised a man of excitement and promise who could take her out of the stifling world of Little Gables. Before long she was washing his test tubes and making toast in his rooms. They were an item for the rest of his time in Cambridge – he moved on to the London Hospital to complete his training – and in October 1943 they married at the Union Church, with the reception at Little Gables and their CongSoc friend Jack Newport as best man.

Alex worked at a series of hospitals, including Chase Farm and the Royal Waterloo, where he treated air raid victims and patched up a man bottled for calling another drinker a "posthumous baby". At St Andrew's, Billericay the countryside gave him scope to forage. One outing ended in his marching home with a chicken under one arm and his air rifle under the other, having mistaken a roosting fowl for a pigeon. Another time, he was taking aim at a rabbit's ears when a US airman jumped up, shouting: "Hey, bud, don't shoot!" He was taking a nap between ops, his double-peaked cap pulled down over his face.

Throughout the war he kept up a militant pacifism, delivering broadsides in verse against Churchill (whom he branded "The Baron") and accusing his government of being little better than the Nazis; they disproved it by not arresting him. He also became an atheist (Grannie coped with this because he kept his love of church music). He befriended other opponents of the war, and kept up a formidable literary output which released the pressure of an exploding intellect. With so many expectant mothers having been evacuated, the London dispatched him to Dublin to do his midwifery ... adding yet another layer to his enthusiasms. When the V1s and V2s started falling, he went out in his tin hat to treat the victims. Ruth, meanwhile, was working as a child care officer in Bethnal Green – a V1 hit her office while she was eating her lunch in the park – and later in Rotherhithe.

My parents made their first home in a flat in Brunswick Square, Bloomsbury. They had to leave when its owners returned from the Far East, and in the autumn of 1945 bought a smallish 1930s semi in Forest Hill. And on 4 August, 1946 I was born at Guy's Hospital - within the sound of Bow Bells, so I am technically a Cockney. I shared my birthday with the then Queen - later the Queen Mother - so up to her 101st birthday I got the National Anthem before the morning news on Radio 4.

2.Early me

If I had an unusual childhood, it was thanks to my father.

Slightly built, with glasses, dark straight hair and an entirely unsuitable moustache, he habitually wore a trench coat and beret; my mother considered the outfit appalling. Coupled with his missing four fingers and his good foreigner's French, it led Parisians to assume he was a Belgian resistance hero and offer him their seats on the Metro.

At home he would sit at his typewriter with – like Tony Benn - his weaver's pint mug of tea beside him. From the machine poured books, articles, letters to editors, poems and radio talks. His correspondents ranged from survivors of Nazi persecution to Left-wing writers in the States and Australia (one, to his embarrassment, sent us a food parcel - including a tin of syrup with a double-thickness lid to keep out the termites). Over breakfast, his good hand would alternate between forking in his food and scribbling comments on the bottom of letters before posting them back to the senders.

There were invitations for radio appearances, political meetings (especially once CND got going), poetry readings and medical conferences. There were books sent for review and by fellow authors; *Tribune, Peace News* and the *Lancet* to all of which he contributed; literature from a host of campaigning groups; and the *Jewish Observer,* whose publishers thought he was Jewish. He had the *News Chronicle* delivered, and after its demise in 1960 alternated between the *Guardian* – for which he occasionally wrote – and the *Times*. How he managed to read it all, I can't imagine.

When he wasn't writing, reading or eating – and often when he was - Dad was talking and listening to the radio. My mother found the torrent of words exhausting, and once he was out of the house she switched to piano music on the Third. Yet there was an overlap between the worlds of controversy (which she did not enjoy, particularly after hearing Dad preached against in church) and of culture, where she felt at home despite lacking his intellectual firepower. Evenings at the Institute of Contemporary Arts, with the likes of Herbert Read and Roland Penrose, delighted her.

Dad was adept with a soldering iron, his missing fingers no disadvantage as he put the remaining thumb to work. He loved making things: radios from RAF surplus parts (soundproofed with Weetabix soaked in glue), our first television (in 1949, from a green and yellow cupboard), my first electric train set (converted from a clockwork one), a dinosaur suit and pirate television equipment for CND. In my teens he became a dab hand at making Appalachian dulcimers and tying trout flies; on holiday in the Lake District he was surprisingly competitive as a fisherman. On that holiday we stayed in the same guest house as Don Thompson, who had just won Olympic gold for the 50km walk; I wonder if any Olympian today would be as down-to-earth.

At Little Gables, Dad rigged up a burglar alarm triggered by a pad under the stair carpet. A length of electric fence outside the kitchen was removed after a mishap when the milkman leaned over to open the side gate. At home he left a cash box with a klaxon inside temptingly on a shelf, scaring the wits out of the daily woman when she picked it up to dust.

His love of fireworks was unabated, and we always had a marvellous display. One year he bought a five-shilling 6x6in green box, buried it in a bucket of earth, lit the fuse and waited. It fizzed for a time, then a few pink balls shot upwards; we were starting to think it was a dud when a tremendous explosion blasted the bottom out of the bucket, sending it 10 feet into the air.

Astonishingly, he started making fireworks again. His first venture was a hand-held Roman candle which deposited a molten globule on my shoe. For his next, when I was about nine, he left gunpowder in the airing cupboard overnight to dry. I was wakened by acrid smoke, with flames licking out onto the landing. My mother had a tough job explaining matters to the insurance man, and that was the end of home-made fireworks.

Then there was his love of music. Unaccountably he turned down *Desert Island Discs*; his musical knowledge was encyclopaedic and his choice would have been fascinating. Bathing me, he sang medical students' songs like *Solomon Levi* and *Riding Down from Bangor*, music-hall favourites like *She Was Only A Bird in a Gilded Cage* and *Don't Steal My Prayer Book, Mr. Burgular* and Gilbert and Sullivan's *Tit Willow*. He played Russian ballet 78s on a gramophone plugged into the light socket, and would pick out Bach's *Wachet Auf* on our upright piano. His spell in Ireland gave him a love for folk music, and he produced a leaflet of songs for the Committee of 100 called *Are You Sitting Comfortably?* He also collaborated with the great American singer-songwriter Pete Seeger, whom I met backstage at the Festival Hall; their *One Man's Hands* was recorded by the chart-topping if anaemic Highwaymen before being sung better by Carolyn Hester, and still brings in the odd cheque. He wrote another, *Go Limp*, with Nina Simone, which she recorded. I found the contract dated 1964 not long ago; the publishers claimed it had only earned him $240 in all that time.

Dad came back from his first visit to India in 1962 – sorting out the disastrously low population projections in its Five Year Plan - enthralled by its languages, its religions, its art, its food ... and its music. He brought back records from Bollywood (it wasn't called that then), and one by Ravi Shankar, saying he could become the biggest thing in pop; I, with the coolness of a 16-year-old, disagreed. In a few years George Harrison would team up with Shankar to generate a fusion that conquered the West.

He learned to drive before the war on Grandfather's tiny Morris, mastering the gearchange with his thumb, but failed his driving test; Grandfather was convinced the examiner failed him because of his disability and extracted an apology from the Ministry of Transport, but the result stood. Then, when war broke out, provisional licence holders were allowed to drive. While Dad would sound off about other motorists and confront mechanics he thought were trying to rip him off, his driving was not aggressive. He never had an accident – though he did once skid on wet tramlines at the Elephant and end up facing the way he had come. And on a trip to

Southwold, he reversed into a sign reading: "No cars allowed on this beach".

Dad bought his first car when I was about two, a pre-war Morris, keeping it in a lockup down an alley opposite our house; working under it he wore his tin hat from the war. He carried an emergency medical kit in case he encountered an accident; in those more relaxed days it included morphia and heroin. His next car was a 1937 Ford; he spent less time under it and used the crank handle less often. Then in 1952 he bought a new Ford Anglia; it was black like almost every other car then, but after seven years he had it painted apple-green.

He always carried a screwdriver, horrifying my mother in France by using it to decapitate a dead pine marten, then stirring his tea with it (at Cambridge he had posted a dead dog home to his mother to await dissection). The one thing he collected was snail shells, kept in cabinets in the spare bedroom: hundreds of every shape, size and colour; they are now in the National Museum in Dublin. The shells were supposed to be empty, but some he brought from Russia woke my aunt in the night by clanking together – she screamed, thinking they were mice.

Until I was about six he was a heavy smoker: 40 a day, plus the ends, plus a pipe. I always knew when he was coming home: his cough preceded him. He gave up overnight when Richard Doll published his research linking smoking and cancer; from his 40s he smoked cigars fairly heavily, but with no ill-effects.

Medicine he left at the London, except when dashing off another article for the *Lancet*. There were few medical books in the house; the one clue to his profession was a skull atop the bookcase whose top lifted off. Dad told me it belonged to a 19th-century Polynesian.

On Sundays, with my mother at church, he took me to watch the steam-hauled Continental Express go through Sydenham Hill station. When we went out for the day, it was usually to grandparents or my parents' Cambridge friends. I learned recently from an academic going through Dad's papers that when I was five I played with Marianne Faithfull – how could I have forgotten that? Once we drove to an outdoor swimming pool in Kent; I wandered off and jumped in – being pulled out of the deep end by a good Samaritan who reunited me with my oblivious parents.

20 Honor Oak Road stands on a steep slope, with a long flight of steps down to the gate. To the right, you walk down to the South Circular Road, Forest Hill station and the Horniman Gardens and Museum. The Horniman's star attractions were an electric eel, antique musical instruments and torture implements from the Spanish Inquisition … which amazingly survived several waves of political correctness. Turning left, Honor Oak Road leads down past Brenchley Gardens, a favourite place to play (another was Crystal Palace Park, with its dinosaurs and the last wreckage of the Palace). Past the now vanished Honor Oak station was a parade of shops where the 63 bus terminated; the butcher prided himself on his "weal an' 'am pies", and the fish shop boasted a bucket of live eels. A man with a sausage-like wen dangling from his nose lived close by; Dad longed to snip it off as a specimen, matching the huge snail-like toenail he had amputated from a pensioner during the Blitz. Once I was five, the walk continued a few hundred yards to school. Beyond lay Peckham, then a smartish shopping centre whose pride was the department store Jones & Higgins. I was once chased out by an assistant shouting: "Don't you dare do that again!" I have no idea why.

Just after my second birthday, Uncle Stephen took me to the Oval. It was the day Don Bradman played his final Test innings, needing just four for a career average of 100. Eric Hollies got Bradman second ball for a duck, but I remember nothing of that emotional day; I was later told that I threw an orange onto the pitch, disgruntling the austerity crowd to whom it was a luxury.

When I was three, I complained of pains in my bones. I was X-rayed at King's College Hospital on a huge glass sheet, but nothing showed up. At 50 a specialist told me my left knee joint was deteriorating. When, soon after, I went to a chiropractor; she took one look and asked: "Have you ever had polio?" Remembering a classmate who ended up in an iron lung I told her I hadn't, but she insisted my knee indicated mild polio in childhood. I then asked

Dad if he had considered polio when I started complaining of "bones" – and he hadn't. It seems I had a narrow escape.

One excitement in those drab years was the Festival of Britain. Under-fives weren't allowed in, but Dad argued that my age should be calculated from the date of conception; an angry queue built up, and we were admitted. We spent our day on the South Bank amid the marvels of 1951 British technology: however I can't remember much beyond an ice cream with fancy wafers. After that, it was back to rationing, which continued for sweets until I was eight.

Late that August, I started school. Friern Road Infants' was a low, elderly building overshadowed by a girls' secondary school opposite the open space of Peckham Rye; we shared the girls' ground-floor hall and gym. Some days Dad dropped me off; others I was walked there with Caroline Lambert, who lived opposite. We always walked back – quite a slog uphill, even for an adult. As I got home one February afternoon my mother told me: "The King's died".

My class - including a redhead called Karen Criddle (inevitably nicknamed Carrot), and Victor E., "born the day the war stopped" - was large, but we all sat and listened. I didn't like some of the ruder boys, but I tackled *Janet and John* without too much trouble and enjoyed singing "If you want to know the time, ask a policeman". We went over to the big school for lunch, costing seven old pence; there was a lot of stodge, but once a week we got semolina pudding with a tiny piece of fruit in it. In the playground, we paraded on Empire Day behind the Union Jack (*never* the Union Flag) singing: "Who would like to fly the flag, the flag that someone gave me?" Close by was a tiny flowerbed, where I won a certificate for growing nasturtiums.

My first Christmas, the class put on a little play. I was to hold up a giant cardboard fish when the song was reached a certain point, but brandished it upside down. The play: *Ten Little Nigger Boys*.

Starting our second year, one little girl stood out – she was black. Everything started to change with her arrival: no more Empire Day, no more *Ten Little Nigger Boys* (thank goodness), a multi-racial Friern Road, a heavily Afro-Caribbean (and for a time decidedly edgy) Peckham and eventually a totally different Britain. Even the school has now gone: replaced in 2009 by a gleaming Harris East Dulwich (not Peckham) Academy.

During my first year at school London lost its trams, and those past the end of our road were among the last to go. They burrowed under the northern portal of Waterloo Bridge and ground through the gloom to a station beneath Kingsway before emerging onto Southampton Row - where the tracks still remain - bound for Archway. I was fascinated by trams, though my cousin Andrew is the real expert. In my teens I joined the Tramway Museum Society and went on working parties to their site at Crich, and I would later have a walk-on part in the return of the trams to Sheffield.

At the end of 1952 we migrated north of the Thames as Dad moved to University College, his research there evolving from analysing snail pigments to the study of ageing. My mother's feeling of isolation in south London was the driving force as we relocated to 44 The Avenue, a 1930s detached house at the south end of Loughton, half a mile from Little Gables.

Loughton is the first town in Essex ... or the final part of London. You cross the county boundary as you leave Woodford on the A121; the houses stop at the top of Buckhurst Hill and you descend through a glorious half-mile of forest, coming into Loughton at its foot. The Central Line runs between open fields on one side, and continuous development on the other.

Up to the war Loughton had a population of 10,000, its growth curbed by the campaign in Victorian times against the clearing of Epping Forest, which borders it to the west. The marshy Roding valley bounds it to the east, but farmland to the north became a soft target for London's overspill. Building the Debden estate, stretching almost to Debden House, in the post-war decade tripled Loughton's population. The old and the new have only gradually merged.

The forest was an ideal place to play. It was close, it was exciting, and to me and my friends – Giles Hollingworth opposite and John and Glen Coyle down the road - it was safe (though you heard of the occasional body being found). There were open spaces where we charged around in the Cubs. There were thickly wooded areas you could hide in, and lots of bracken. There were ponds where we fished (without success), sailed boats or rode bikes round the sandy edge. There were tracks for horse riding along which we took family walks. Fallow deer would occasionally charge across the road in front of your car. And beyond the "horse pond" at the foot of Buckhurst Hill was a long, sloping, tree-lined ride which made a perfect toboggan run in the two snowy weeks of winter. Dad had kept his steerable sledge with steel runners, from the Empire Exhibition of 1924, and it went like a bomb. The run petered out safely in a bed of leaves; trying a steeper run the other end of Loughton as a teenager, I flew off and cut my head open.

Bordered by forest and with pockets of forest land among its houses, Loughton felt insular, and slightly rural. The shops along the High Road were still "the Village", though the Goulds had given up their forage yard. Our meat, delivered by bicycle, came from Miss Grimsley, who had taken over the Sunday school from Ninnie. I saw more of Miss Giblett's sweet shop, Dolan's with their sixpenny cones of what tasted like home-made ice cream, the toy and record shops, Boots (where we got discount because Dad was a doctor), Smith's at the station – for whom I briefly delivered papers – and Warnes the outfitters, with a barber's in the back where a young man on leave from the RAF ripped your hair out with blunt scissors. There was also the Century cinema; when Disney's *The Lady and the Tramp* opened in 1955 after relentless plugging on the BBC, the queue was several hundred yards long. It was at the Century (and the Majestic, South Woodford) that a crowd of us would take in a black-and-white war film or British comedy on a Saturday afternoon - and as we neared 16 con our way into X-certificate movies. The Century closed in 1962, just as a modernistic Co-Op supermarket was opening opposite – a rare change in the face of the Village.

We usually only left Loughton for the dentist's at South Woodford (a Scottish lady who used as little anaesthetic as she could get away with) and to lay up Grannie's furs at Puddicombe's in Leytonstone, then a smart shopping centre. Occasionally my mother and Auntie Alison, always the more adventurous, would take me shopping in Oxford Street, with an hour in a cartoon theatre (always Disney, never Warner Brothers).

Moving meant a new school: Essex House (now Avon House), at Woodford Wells. I caught the bus on my own (aged six) to the Horse and Well; the conductor announced it as "'Orse 'n' Wells", so I grew up thinking Orson Welles was a pub. My first term saw London's worst smog ever; with visibility just a few yards, the conductor had to walk in front of the bus to guide it.

Essex House was run by Mrs Huntley, a firm but pleasant lady from Dunster in Somerset, about which she claimed *All Things Bright and Beautiful* had been written. She was succeeded by Miss Molyneux, tall, slim, a little severe and a convert to Moral Re-Armanent. My first class teacher was Mrs Aldridge; with the frankness of a six-year-old, I told her one day: "My Daddy says you're an old cow." Next came Mrs Bishop; trying on shoes at Gorringes, a long-gone department store in Buckingham Palace Road, she was allowed to wear "Queen Mary's slippers", kept for Her Majesty's visits.

Our classrooms were in the house and a small block behind it; from the playground a path led down to the sports field, whose pavilion doubled as the music room. On one side was our small garden; down a slope on the other the tennis club, where Christine Truman was training for junior Wimbledon; her sister Nell was in my class, breathlessly telling us one day that "Dingleby" had come to interview Christine. One spring day, several of us tried to move a small but heavy roller parked beside the garden; it shot across the path, down the slope and through the netting. When the entire school went to see the film of the Coronation, we had to stay behind. Coronation Day, 2 June 1953, was a great experience, though in our neighbourhood street parties were unthinkable. The Union Church was so full for a special service that they uniquely had to open the gallery upstairs. We were the only family members with a television, so elderly relatives crowded into our sitting room. The weather was filthy, and you could see dignitaries from the hottest parts of the Commonwealth getting soaked. In subsequent days the Queen toured London; we stood for hours to get a glimpse of her passing Whitechapel station. I was given a paper Union Jack to wave, but by the time the crowd surged forward to see her I had eaten it.

For my ninth birthday I was given a cricket scorebook, and for several Saturdays I sat under the scorebox at Loughton's charming cricket ground, religiously recording each ball. The season over, I devised matches with marbles on the floor between the world's great players, and they took over the scorebook. Then I started going to watch Essex, armed with cucumber and Marmite sandwiches. During Ilford Week Valentine's Park was abuzz with 5,000 spectators; when I went back in 1999 during the very last, there were barely 500 people there – most my age or older - and only a handful of schoolboys.

Ilford was one of several grounds Essex used for a week each season, with an aged bus converted into a scoreboard and toilets. I spent a day at Romford in soaking rain without a ball bowled, at Chelmsford saw Cyril Washbrook play almost his last innings, and with John and Glen Coyle watched the 1961 Australians at Westcliff. But I came to watch most of my cricket at Leyton; there I bagged Frank Tyson's autograph.

Essex then meant the great England all-rounder Trevor Bailey. His finest season was the hot summer of 1959, when he scored 2,000 runs and took 100 wickets with his fast-medium pace. Too often he was anchored to the crease trying to hold a collapsing innings together, earning with England the nickname "Barnacle." Eventually, at Brisbane, he overdid it with 68 in seven hours. Years later when Bailey was summarising on *Test Match Special* there was talk of the greatest ever ducks; I couldn't resist writing in that I had never been able to stay long enough to see him dismissed for nought. To my delight - and embarrassment - they read my postcard out.

Cricket is more intimate than football; supporters get closer to the game, and most of the players respond. My son John's support for

Essex has led to his becoming almost an unofficial mascot ... despite his penchant for telling a player when he is having a bad game. Graham Gooch and Mark Pettini have been supportive, but I owe special thanks to Ryan ten Doeschate. When John told him I'd missed Essex's Lords final in 2008 after detaching a retina, Ryan commiserated and sent me one of his Essex shirts. It's players like Tendo who make cricket the king of sports.

At nine I moved on to St Aubyn's, a prep school a mile nearer London. I spent four happy years there, learning more than I did anywhere else. Our caps were baggy like an Australian cricketer's, and navy coloured, with red piping and a pewter badge which – rougher elements claimed – made a handy weapon. St Aubyn's – known to its rivals as St Dustbin's – was started by two Victorian ladies, but for decades had been owned by Lieutenant-Colonel Colley, a Great War veteran who had played rugby for Cumberland. The Colonel – "Skit" to us – was getting on, and the school was increasingly run by his son Harold, once of the Palestine Police.

Harold Colley's beatings were to be avoided, but he was devoted to bringing us on. He made fun of my father's politics, but included me in a group who stayed after school to listen to music and made yearly outings to D'Oyly Carte. As scoutmaster, he encouraged me in pursuits I'd never imagined I would take to. Most of my knowledge of historic London comes from his scout trips, and I took to camping with enthusiasm, spending soaking weekends on the sports field and a marvellous ten days in Switzerland. I left with a First Class Scout badge - after a 24-hour hike near Bishop's Stortford with a classmate - and a scar on my left hand caused by a fellow scout waving a knife while buttering rolls.

At St Aubyn's I was put into the third form, where I was the oldest. After a fortnight I was moved up, and at the end of term up again to the fifth form, as the youngest. There I made three good friends: David Roberts, John Bellamy and Peter Thwaite. David's father installed radio masts around the world after a hairy war as a civilian technician flying in bombers, and his mother was delightful; they became family friends. David and John were bus spotters, and inducted me into the hobby. Peter's father played good rugby, and his mother's death when we were 12 shook our secure little world. For two or three years we did a lot together; I kept up with David, and 50 years on we teamed up with Peter again. Sadly, David only just reached his 70th birthday.

The Colonel despite his age taught Latin well, and his son headed a team of mainly exceptional teachers. The best – for English - was J S Tudsbury, a chunky northerner rumoured to have played Rugby League, and I benefited from his gruff encouragement. He was inspirational out of class too, persuading us to attend school matches by claiming they would be on ITV. I felt it unfair that St Aubyn's only awarded prizes for sporting prowess: though top of my class, I was never going to win one. Also outstanding was our geography master, Mr Eastwood; I passed Geography O-Level three years after leaving St Aubyn's, having received no tuition in the meantime. Mr Higgins, known as "Whisky", was less impressive. We began reading our set history book, *The Whig Supremacy,* at the start of the year, restarted it 14 times and only once got halfway, leaving me knowing everything about Walpole and nothing about George III. The only master I disliked was Mr Singer, who taught maths – my weakest subject – while telling us what a holy man Pope Pius XII was. Despite Mr Singer being Irish – normally a plus with him – my father shared my assessment, and when Mr Singer suggested extra tuition, told him he should be teaching me properly in the first place.

My great hobby until introduced to Ian Allan's *ABC of London Buses* was I-Spy, in the *News Chronicle*. I collected the books, ticked the box whenever I spotted an item illustrated, and when I had enough points sent off for another feather for my Indian head-dress; I had 13 altogether. I mastered the codes, went with Dad to the I-Spy Rally at Olympia (a deaf aunt thought it was a "nice pie rally") and joined the mob around the Big Chief's car. I won a couple of their competitions (one prize was a glider kit), being disqualified in the first for "parental assistance" until Dad insisted to the Big Chief that it was all my own work.

Loughton was on the Underground, but still had steam trains which I could hear in the small hours. A trip to Ongar before the line beyond Epping was electrified was a treat; otherwise I would pause at Loughton yard to watch an elderly loco, No. 65464, shunting (my e.mail address is named after it) – or watch the trains at Stratford station, then quite unlike the modernistic hub of today. In the spare bedroom I built up my Hornby Dublo layout, with friends' locomotives making guest appearances.

On Sunday mornings – it sounds amazing in these nervous days - I would go out and roam. From age ten I would leave around 7 am; sometimes I would catch the first train to Ongar, sometimes the bus to Ilford where they had trolleybuses with tinted windows diverted from Johannesburg in wartime. Once I had a bike I set off most light and dry Sunday mornings for the country, the climb up Buckhurst Hill discouraging trips toward London. I headed for Debden Green and Theydon Bois, then through Abridge to a green my mother said had inspired the poem "Under the spreading chestnut tree the village smithy stands", and when really energetic to Ongar - a 26-mile round trip on almost deserted roads.

I had a series of pets: two goldfish, a tortoise, two budgies and finally a tabby-Siamese named Trotsky. Acquired from my economics master Fred Fox he was a magnificent creature, fierce to humans generally but devoted to my mother. She once went out calling for him, only for a bearded dustman to ask: "Were you referring to me, madam?" He first cat, a Persian called Beauty, had been stolen when she was 17, and when Trotsky was run over aged 11, she could not bear to replace him.

When I was small, Grandfather inherited a bungalow at Hassocks, just behind Brighton; he rented it to Mollie Rowlands, a retired head teacher friend. Mollie had a passion for music, and when Jacqueline du Pre's iconic recording of Elgar's concerto was released we sat in the garden listening to it. Mollie died weeks after Grandfather; I would love to have taken over the bungalow, but by then I was in Washington. Only recently has an owner expanded it into a house, and whenever I hear the Elgar my mind goes back to that garden, with the Downs beyond.

Staying at Hassocks, I got to know the Bluebell steam railway, which enthusiasts had recently reopened. I was there the day in 1963 when its main line connection at Horsted Keynes closed, leaving the line isolated. Decades later, John got involved with the Bluebell and I started going again; before long I was a volunteer booking clerk/porter at Kingscote station, and later at a reopened East Grinstead, and editing the staff newsletter. I love the railway and its people, and getting to meet our visitors.

I never really minded being an only child; I had friends, and was good at occupying myself. There were also my Harris cousins, Andrew, Elizabeth, Graham and Clare. When I was five, Uncle Stephen – then Congregational minister at Bury St Edmunds - contracted meningitis; Andrew came to stay at Little Gables, going to school in Loughton and reorganising Ninnie's chickens, and Elizabeth stayed briefly with us. Staying later with them, I loved being part of a larger family; Auntie Helen seemed as able to cope with four children as my mother could with one.

My favourite older visitors were Grandfather, Auntie Alison – who planned midnight feasts, which I invariably missed – and Jane. She lived for a time in Canada, sending me funny letters from places she visited. We stayed with her in Leicester, she once went with my parents to Yugoslavia, and eventually we all holidayed together in Ireland. A few months after that, Dad mentioned that they had met for dinner, she didn't visit any more and just after I left school my mother told me he was dividing his time between them.

My friends were promised new bikes for passing the 11-plus, but I was expected to. I won a place at Buckhurst Hill County High School - today a Sikh academy - but my parents agreed with Colonel Colley that I should try for Highgate. Just before Christmas 1958, I sat the scholarship exam there with 80 other boys, some with uniforms even more garish than mine (as one of three School Praepostors, I now had yellow piping round my blazer). A call came through days later that I had won a scholarship – the only time I remember my mother hugging me.

For the rest of that school year I was one of a class of two marking time, along with Roger Spearing, whose mother took us to the cinema in a tiny three-wheel car that lost traction if driven uphill with anyone in the back. In the wider sixth form was Paul Ebblewhite, whose father had a music shop in the City and was the starter at the Crystal Palace racetrack, where they would crash-test the Minis in *The Italian Job*. It was a serious venue, with races up to non-championship Formula 1 and the lap record set by Jochem Rindt and Mike Hailwood. Paul's mother drove us there, shooting through the park gates with an inch to spare, and we had grandstand seats by the finish.

It was over 30 years before I went back to St Aubyn's, for Harold Colley's retirement. It felt strange going into the gloomy Sixth Form classroom overlooking the duck pond, looking through photos of our scouting trips, and revisiting the sunroom where he had played us Gilbert & Sullivan. Purging my conscience, I confessed that I had come top in a French exam after not owning up to talking during it; those who did had had to start afresh. Harold Colley never married, but put his heart into his school. At the height of the 1980s property boom, Tesco offered him millions; he sent them packing and turned St Aubyn's into a non-profitmaking trust. The school survives, hopefully with pupils as happy as I was; we owe Harold Colley a lot.

Highgate School, atop the Hill, is a north London landmark; the view from the top-floor classroom where I struggled with Chemistry is awesome. Big School, where we met for assembly, dominates the approach from Hampstead, and behind the chapel Coleridge is buried. Founded by Sir Roger Cholmeley in 1565 (Highgate boys – and now girls – are known as "Cholmeleians") the school was tiny until Victorian times when it was transformed by the great Dr Dyne. The main, island site was filled, then round the cricket field down Hampstead Lane a second campus developed: boarding houses, the junior school and, just before my arrival, the dining hall (boys previously lunched in the houses).

The Highgate I joined in September 1959 had changed little since my father's time; indeed for English, French, Greek, Latin, Maths, Physics and Politics/Economics I had masters who had taught him, and most found me wanting. They ranged from Charlie Benson and Tommy Twidell to the florid "Gubbo" Gibbon, who in algebra lessons would produce a chair leg from his desk and tell errant boys in a booming but not unfriendly voice that he would "do the same to both sides". Parker, teaching French, was the only teacher to work out what made me tick, saying apropos Dad's latest book that I was suffering from "too much Darwin and not enough naked lady". School House - today an arts centre - was a large Victorian building which housed the headmaster and his family at one end and 56 boys at the other, with two masters and Matron. The Head was Alfred Doulton, an Oxford classicist with a prominent nose and eyes that bored straight through you, hence his nickname of "Beady". He had an uncanny knack of knowing what was going on at the other end of the house, at the back of assembly or simply behind him. Our housemaster was George Sellick, a bachelor physics master in his fifties, who recalled Noël Coward shocking the wartime troops in Iraq with the coarseness of his stories. George was benign and down-to-earth, leaving discipline to a younger master who would burst into the dormitory after lights-out and beat any boy he thought had been out of bed (I escaped the cane at Highgate, but incurred a sackful of PCs: penal copies of a page of calligraphy).

Boys in the third and fourth forms were in dormitories of 18, arranged in bays of three. Fifth-formers had a smaller dorm, and senior boys shared "dens". We chatted after lights-out, before the prefect allocated to our dorm retired to bed. My dorm-mates curbed my early loquacity by suspending me upside down from a rafter with a pyjama cord – an episode the prefects lampooned at the annual house supper. I was picked on in other ways, but kept quiet and was highly embarrassed when the Head told a house assembly that it had to stop. (More seriously, he cracked down on "queer" activity in another dorm, and expelled two persistent thieves).

The long school evenings meant pop on the Common Room radio before lights out ... and under the bedclothes afterward. Usually we listened to Radio Luxembourg – programmes like *Jack Jackson's Jukebox Show*, sponsored by the record companies with saturation adverts for the H Samuel Ever-rite watch and Horace Batchelor's Infa-Draw Method for winning the pools. Why Batchelor hadn't made his pile and retired somewhere more exotic than Keynsham I could never understand.

My first Sunday at Highgate, I surprised my parents by coming home. More often I would go to Barnet and see Grandfather, sometimes taking a housemate. When I stayed in School House all weekend, there was little to do apart from Sunday chapel – with robust Victorian hymns and an excellent choir – and reading through a library whose most recent acquisitions dated from about 1930. In my fifth term I was poorly for several weeks; my parents asked if I'd like to start afresh at Buckhurst Hill, but I was determined to see Highgate through, becoming a weekly boarder.

Highgate was predominantly a day school. The day boys were generally brighter than the boarders and many were Jewish, their number supposedly limited by quota (the school was firmly C of E). My response to mild anti-Semitism among some boarders was occasional attendance at the pre-school Jewish Circle. Usually this consisted of prayers and an Old Testament reading, but once we were shown Alain Resnais' shattering film *Night and Fog*, about the Holocaust (a term then little used). Saturday morning school has since been discontinued "because Jewish parents wouldn't stand for it" but I can't recall anyone minding then; maybe, in this post 9/11 world, all cultures have become more assertive.

After St Aubyn's where I always finished in the top two, Highgate was a challenge. I started in Form 3A, one of two top streams out of five, and was expected to excel at classics, but I had gone off the boil at Latin and never really got into Greek, despite scraping an O-Level pass. My maths remained shaky (though I managed Advanced Maths O-Level) and my performances at Physics and Chemistry ruled out a scientific career, so I settled at A-Level for History, English – where apparently my O-Level short story won top marks nationally – and Politics and Economics with Fred Fox. My favourite master after Fred was Alan Palmer, an authority on what he called the "beachtly Balkans" who became a respected historical author; I shall never know why I only just scraped through History O-Level, but his teaching (with Fred's) got me into Cambridge.

Fred was the perfect foil to Doulton's muscular churchmanship, which culminated in an appeal to the leavers never to visit prostitutes. He was marvellous at getting us to think, bringing in provocative guests. One week it was a cheerfully irreverent Denis Healey, another Martin Gilbert, Palmer's former star pupil who would be Churchill's biographer. Gilbert was severe on Neville Chamberlain and Rab Butler for not standing up to Hitler; 40 years on he told me his subsequent research made their conduct appear even more culpable. I was less strong at English, but responded well to Cyril Hartley, a flamboyant younger master who brought John Donne to life.

Gradually I began to enjoy Highgate, becoming one of the crowd on a pre-O-Level trip to Menton. The best friend I made was Paul Grayson, one of twins from Harlow. Despite a withered arm, Paul went on to join the Army and lecture at Shrivenham before sadly dying in his thirties; his sister Anna and I remain friends. I also teamed up with John Roberts, who started boarding when his banker father was transferred to Manchester, and at the height of Beatlemania stayed with him in Southport. We spent a day in Liverpool, savouring the NEMS record shop and the Cavern - cramped and sweaty, but with an atmosphere like no other. Just 18 months before, John, Paul, George and Pete Best – soon to be dropped for Ringo – had been regulars there.

We also made a pilgrimage to Anfield. Bill Shankly's Liverpool had just come up from the Second Division, *You'll Never Walk Alone* had recently topped the charts, and the Kop had found its voice. The atmosphere was fantastic, though John did alert me to "use my *Footie Echo*" (rolling it up into a cylinder); there was no chance of reaching the Gents. Outside, I saw the famed sandwich boards urging supporters to repent; to one reading: "What will you do when the Lord returns?" a Scouser retorted: "Move St. John to inside-left." I returned home on cloud nine ... to be told my great-aunt Con had died.

Highgate set rigid bounds, one contemporary being absurdly punished for going to the American Embassy to collect A-Level material. Maybe it was as well boarding ended in 1995; London's fleshpots were just too close. However those unseen boundaries did increase my sense of isolation. Nor could I easily ring home: I had to dial the exchange and wait to be put through to Loughton 629, and one lunchtime I gave up after 45 minutes. Subscriber Trunk Dialling reached Loughton in my final term, Grannie having to give up her pre-war phone with its mouthpiece hanging from a stand.

My Highgate days have become a series of vignettes: watching the masters play cricket as we did our prep; fainting during a rehearsal for the school unison competition; raking through my dandruff in an English lesson; dancing classes with masters' daughters as partners; hitting a golf ball with a broom handle straight through a window, which shattered into a fortunately empty swimming pool; the bitter early months of 1963 when there were no games for a term; managing to finish the annual cross-country race round Hampstead Heath with eight schoolmates behind me (and 209 in front). Highgate was, and is, an excellent school, and in the end I got a lot out of it.

When I started at Highgate my mother went back to child care, with Essex County Council (later Waltham Forest borough). Needing to drive, for the first time since before the war, she bought a new A40 Farina and settled into a demanding job she would persevere with for some 20 years. She made new friends, and later joined the group of expert needlewomen who restored the Tudor hangings on the state bed at Hatfield House.

Life at home became less austere. My parents were already supporters of Joan Littlewood's Theatre Royal, Stratford, and the State Cinema art house in Leytonstone. Now Dad developed a passion for ballroom dancing, bringing home dance music LPs I can remember every note of and practicing in the sitting room. His new levity caught my mother on the hop and while she tried to keep up, I could tell it was a struggle. It was probably no coincidence that within a year or so, he had taken up with Jane.

By now I was a regular visitor to Dad's lab in the Zoology department at UCL, housed (as now) in an old furniture repository. He was one of a dazzling team: the explosive Marxist JBS Haldane, the courtly Sir Peter Medawar, GP Wells (son of HG), JZ Young, and Donald Michie (nicknamed Duckmouse). Dad saw Haldane as an anarchic role model, but quietly respected Medawar. Half a century later, researching Michie's obituary, I discovered that he and Alan Turing had been friends at Bletchley Park. I have often wondered if Dad knew this; many of the Bletchley set took their wartime secrets to the grave.

I admired the tank of axolotls (endangered Mexican cave salamanders) in the lobby before climbing the stairs to Dad's small office and lab overlooking a courtyard. The lab was filled with tanks of guppies; he monitored how putting them in larger or smaller tanks or giving them varying amounts of food affected their longevity: those eating less and in a smaller space lived longer.

The highlight of the day was lunch in one of the Euston's numerous Indian restaurants. Dad was in his element here, even before his two-month secondment to the Indian Statistical Institute in Calcutta that led him to curry our 1962 Christmas lunch. In the Agra, the Shahi or the Noor Jahan he would run me through the strange-sounding dishes; Rogun Gosh became my favourite. Decades later I would return with Frank Dobson, the local MP and a true curry man.

My teenage memories of home are of the weekends: Perry Mason on Saturday nights and *The Billy Cotton Band Show* at Sunday lunchtime; the explosion of *That Was The Week That Was* onto the screen; having our record player stolen (a policeman neighbour saw the thief but did nothing as he looked a lot like me); and cricket with John and Glen. When I made new friends they came in a rush, after I joined Buckhurst Hill and Loughton Young Socialists and, a year or so later, the Congo Coffee Club at Buckhurst Hill Congregational Church. Congo plugged me into the Swinging

Sixties; one of the minister's sons was in a band on *Ready, Steady, Go!*

Hugh Gaitskell was Labour's leader when, in September 1962, I joined the YS. In an upper room at Loughton Hall (a 19th-century replacement for a more interesting pile), I found a dozen or so late teens and early twenties holding a business meeting that turned into a political discussion. The branch secretary was Joan Underhill, a perky Brummie who worked at Transport House – then Labour's headquarters - and whose father Reg Underhill became the party's national agent; as Joan Stocks, she would chair Nottinghamshire County Council. Joan was firmly on the Right, but her fiancé Eddie Fennell, a bearlike and amiable blacksmith at Beckton Gasworks, was well to the Left. Bob Edwards was a rugby playing future physics teacher who at Sussex University became a key figure in the Militant Tendency. Selling *Militant* outside the station, Bob came up with the spiel: "All the winners! All the winners! Marx! Lenin! Engels! Trotsky!" - selling twenty before commuters realised they weren't getting the racing results. There were a computer engineer just out of the RAF, a passionate rock fan who worked in a pharmacist's (Brian Smith, a friend today), two entertaining telephone engineers, an art student who wore floppy felt hats, and a voluptuous girl from a prefab whose sister in California dated Stephen Boyd, Charlton Heston's adversary in *Ben-Hur*.

An occasional attender was Jack Straw, a boarder at Brentwood School, whose family lived in a maisonette where Loughton merged into the estate. When our MP, John Biggs-Davison, temporised at a meeting in the Lopping Hall about Rhodesia's UDI, Jack asked him: "Do you support Ian Smith? Yes or No?" Identifying the YS as a political dead end, Jack at Leeds University concentrated on student politics; he won a national reputation as president of the NUS and went on to be Home Secretary and Foreign Secretary. Jack's sister Susan, blonde and exuberant, came to the YS more often; she and her boyfriend were suspended from Keele University for disrupting a service broadcast from its chapel by playing *Leader of the Pack*, which the BBC had banned.

It was a good time to be Labour. The wounds over unilateralism were healing, and Harold Macmillan's government was tired. Gaitskell's death early in 1963 was traumatic – as John Smith's would be – but it enabled Harold Wilson to give the party a new drive; I proudly stuck on my school folder the *Time* cover featuring him. Then came the Profumo affair, Macmillan's retirement and the "emergence" of Sir Alec Douglas-Home. We couldn't believe our luck, though Home would come close to keeping Labour out at the 1964 election despite the talk of "thirteen wasted years".

Our weekly meetings fired off resolutions to Transport House, who must have quaked in their boots. Increasingly they were about Vietnam; we hoped Wilson could influence LBJ to pull out, but in reality he was resisting American pressure for Britain to go in. We had guest speakers, from the Movement for Colonial Freedom to a representative of Sir Oswald Mosley (costing us a couple of Jewish members). We held weekend schools at the Clarion Youth Hostel near Tonbridge (a vestige of HN Brailsford's Clarion movement, though I suspect we drank more than those early Fabians), helped at elections and held a poorly-attended dance and a jumble sale where inadvertently I sold a friend's coat for sevenpence. A lot of our time was spent in the pub putting the world to rights - often, ironically, in the Sir Winston Churchill (which would be demolished just 50 years after his death).

The YS – during the holidays at least - took up a lot of my life till I left Cambridge (they came up to see me and we demolished an Indian – five meals and ten plates). I became a delegate to the constituency party's General Committee, and learned how party organisation works from our full-time agent Harry Biggs, left completely bald (then a rarity for a younger man) by his proximity to a wartime searchlight battery. The future TUC general secretary Len Murray (known locally as Lionel) lived round the corner, but astoundingly I never met him; when, years later, I rang him from the *Telegraph* he was less than helpful.

Once I graduated and moved to Sheffield, I was a bird of passage at The Avenue. My parents lived there until their divorce in 1972. My mother nearly bought a seafront cottage at Aldeburgh, then took over Auntie Alison's house near ours when she and John moved to the other end of Loughton. She stayed there 25 years – even longer than at The Avenue – until she checked into a nursing home in 1998. She thought she was suffering from anaemia, but was actually in the early stages of myeloma, and dementia.

She died a month after my father, and is buried in Loughton Cemetery with her father and his first wife; I added an inscription to Grannie, who had been cremated in 1968. I am also responsible for Dad and Jane's forest grave near Cranbrook, and the Comfort plot in Chingford Mount Cemetery, unnervingly close to the Krays'.

The friends from my teenage days have now all moved away from Loughton. The landmarks are the same, but few shops in the Village sell what they used to – save for the chemist and the dry cleaners, whose art deco façade was tragically ripped out a few years ago – and most of the pubs have had damaging makeovers. It's easy to accept the myth that Loughton has been taken over by bling merchants; look hard, though, and its charm survives.

4. Cambridge

Going into my A-Level year I applied to Southampton, Exeter, Hull and Nottingham universities to read Law; I wanted to be a solicitor. I was offered places at Southampton and at Exeter, then Highgate upped the ante. Customarily, the Oxbridge scholarship exams were taken a term after A-Levels, candidates staying on in an Upper Sixth, but a dozen of us were entered a year early. This was a challenge: I was going for a Cambridge scholarship in History, just four terms after coming within one mark of failing History O-Level. My first choice of college was easy: Trinity. In mid-November I was summoned for an interview and nervously located the rooms of Alan Ker, my prospective tutor. Short, dry and civilised, he probed my interests; I talked about psephology (the study of elections and opinion polls) and left feeling out of my depth. Weeks later in early December, I was back for the exam. University Term had just finished, so I could stay overnight in a student's room between taking the history and general papers. I can't remember the questions, but I do remember writing the pretentious phrase "Socrates drank the hemlock".

I missed the last two weeks of term at Highgate (including the House Supper where I was no longer a target in the monitors' song) to help with the Christmas mail - my second year of six working from Loughton sorting office. I remember vividly two homecomings from there. One was on Christmas Eve 1967. Dad had broken his false teeth in Czechoslovakia and fixed them temporarily; that evening he restuck them with Araldite and put them in the oven with the mince pies to bond. Belatedly he remembered them – and was confronted with a pink sticky puddle dotted with white gravestones. The other was just before that Christmas of 1963: as I walked round to the back door, Dad threw it open with a cry of "Congratulations - you've got an exhibition!" Ringing my classmates, I found that eight out of ten had won scholarships or exhibitions (a lesser scholarship) and the rest had places.

Highgate saw no point in my taking my A-levels - and I was not convinced I would do well in them. I spent one more term at school - trying to learn basic German and Spanish - then left at Easter, surprised by the tear in my eye as we sang the school song *Fifteen Hundred and Sixty-Five*. I spent the summer with the *Guardian*, then at the end of September 1964 went up to Trinity.

As an exhibitioner I could spend my first year in college, rather than in digs which could be some way out. I was actually in a hostel in Sidney Street, over a sports shop opposite Sidney Sussex College; I had a large first-floor living room level with the top decks of passing buses, and a small bedroom above. In charge was the formidable Mrs Deas, who lived upstairs with her much smaller husband and their young son who would join the Navy.

There were ten freshmen in the hostel, plus graduate students from India, Pakistan and Japan. Next to me was Trevor Derry, a

Rhodesian reading Natural Sciences, and we became firm friends. Trevor had been as apprehensive about Britain under a Labour government as I would have been enrolling at university in Rhodesia with Ian Smith in power, and we spent long evenings finding out what made each other's country tick. Trevor went on to Witwatersrand University, Johannesburg, where researching the refractive properties of diamonds he became a professor of nuclear physics.

My first invitation was to the Matriculation Dinner, whose purpose, with hindsight, was to see how we coped with alcohol. Trinity does events superbly, as befits a college whose wealth was multiplied when a farm it owned in Suffolk became the site of Felixstowe Docks. After drinks with the president of the Junior Common Room (JCR) came dinner in Hall with the Fellows. I sat next to the historian George Kitson Clark, one of several dons from my father's time; our conversation took off when he mentioned that Thomas Bouch, designer of the ill-fated Tay Bridge, had been his great-uncle. Six tiny courses followed, with copious wines, as Holbein's Henry VIII, founder of the college, looked down on us magisterially. Port followed, then drinks with our directors of studies – for me the agreeable Law don Gareth Jones, early in a distinguished college and Cambridge career. The Law intake worked its way through a crate of Greene King audit ale, then it was back to our rooms before the gates were locked at 11pm. Another Sidney Street resident invited me to share a bottle of peach wine, and unwisely I accepted. Just one glass, and my dinner came up. I shot into the corridor, and spotted an open window in the room of a rocker from Wolverhampton (later a consultant paediatrician). I rushed to it - and my dinner precipitated onto landed on a man on the pavement below. He said something I was too drunk to take in, then disappeared, spattered, into the night.

My peach wine friend began leaving two empty sherry bottles in my bin every morning, and my bedmaker alerted Alan Ker that I was drinking heavily. When, later that term, I was rushed to the old Addenbrooke's Hospital with stomach cramps, his questions at my bedside were tactful, but pointed. Appendicitis was suspected before I was diagnosed with hepatitis; I was put in a room for 48 hours with a pigman from Saffron Walden receiving enemas from a nurse he christened "the bumshandy queen", then sent home. I was ordered not to drink for six months; when I told the college GP, who doubled as president of the Boat Club, that I hadn't touched a drop, he replied: "Good God, man, I didn't mean don't drink, I meant don't DRINK."

The first weeks were a whirl: meeting my supervisors - including Leon Brittan, newly called to the Bar, for criminal law - buying textbooks, my gown (compulsory at lectures, in Hall and after dark), crockery from Woolworths and a record player; getting my bike registered; and getting into the rhythm of lectures - a solid four hours most mornings. Checking out the societies, I joined the Union (speaking just once), the Labour Club (until I realised it was to the Left even of the YS) - and CongSoc.

CongSoc was friendly with a streak of irreverence, heavily Home Counties with a leavening of Yorkshire, with 100-odd members. I immediately felt at home, and two fellow freshmen I met - Norval Lyon and Julian Maw – became lifelong friends. Two of my parents' crowd were still around: Jack Newport, by now principal of Cheshunt, the Congregational theological college, and Max Walters, curator of the Botanical Gardens, whose nephews were contemporaries of mine.

We met at Emmanuel Church on Trumpington Street over a bread-and-cheese charity lunch after a Sunday service which – as you expected in Cambridge – was special for its sermons; the best, from an American professor, tackled the difference between knowledge and belief. We held weekly "fellowship groups" in members' rooms, an Easter walking holiday/work camp in the Welsh mountains and a May Week punt breakfast. We even went out occasionally to lead services in small village chapels. I took one in Hemingford Grey, later John Major's home village; expecting only a handful in the congregation, I had prepared to speak on the text from Matthew "Where two or three are gathered together in thy name...", only to find the place packed.

With England's Presbyterian and Congregational churches about to merge as the United Reformed Church, CongSoc amalgamated with the university Presbyterian Association (Cupa), based on St Columba's Church, which had a slightly smaller and mainly Scottish, Welsh and Northern Irish membership. "Prong Soc", of which I became treasurer, was thriving then; astonishingly in the mid-1980s it would fold. Recently St Columba's and Emmanuel themselves have merged, with Emmanuel's imposing building sold to Pembroke College.

After a year in CongSoc, I joined Buckhurst Hill Congregational Church. For much of my life I would attend Anglican churches, yet my roots remained in the URC: my membership passed from Buckhurst Hill (where I would return for my mother's funeral, she having joined well after my time) to Westmoreland Congregational in Washington DC, to Wanstead URC and eventually to the exceptionally welcoming Elmers End Free Church.

I also joined the student newspaper *Varsity*. A well-produced weekly tabloid, *Varsity* was read by almost everyone in the university (and – we hoped – Fleet Street) and was put together in a rickety building in Bridge Street, 200 yards from my rooms. The editor my second term was Richard Whiteley, later of *Countdown* - known to all as "Spritely" - and the staff a mixture of wannabe hacks, talented types with no long-term interest in journalism, the odd serious writer and the occasional masochist who wanted to sell advertising or make the paper break even.

The top floor comprised a cramped newsroom and the editor's tiny office; below were a bigger commercial office and a meeting room full of badly stuffed chairs and abandoned coffee cups. One winter day Robin Wight, later a giant in advertising, arrived wearing a long faux fur coat and sat down with his back to the electric fire; a large hole melted in it before anyone noticed. In my first year the stars of those meetings were Clive James and the formidable Germaine Greer, postgrads whose worldliness made a freshman feel hopelessly gauche. One week Germaine - also a star of the Footlights - wrote a column decrying the virility of Cambridge men;

at the next meeting she read out a postcard from one affronted male reading: "Let me f*** you for Queen and country!"

I started as a reporter along with Julian Maw, and made another friend in Keith Reader (later Professor of French Literature at Glasgow University), who formed a deadly partnership in cinemas and Indian restaurants with Trevor Derry. As with CongSoc, most *Varsity* friends came from outside Trinity; Tony Pickering, who eventually edited the paper, was the one exception. When the staff baulked at Tony's efforts to take *Varsity* upmarket I shared their concerns, and when he agreed to a U-turn he was very forgiving of my part in the episode. One of my few contemporaries to go into provincial journalism and stay there, Tony now runs a company selling Sudoku to the media.

Varsity attracted future Fleet Street stars: Simon Hoggart; Peter Cole; David Bell (later a Washington colleague and head of the *FT*); Valerie Smith (now Grove); the film critic Brian Gibson; Suzy Menkes, who caused a sensation with the first Courrèges boots in Cambridge; Phil Graf (later chief executive of the Mirror Group); Patrick Eagar, the groundbreaking cricket photographer. Other colleagues found fame elsewhere: Matthew Robinson in television, Paul Whitehouse as a chief constable. Jonathan King was already a pop star when he started writing for us.

Over time I gained my own page - interviewing a don each week - and became deputy news editor, then news features editor, particularly enjoying the page I put together for the 1966 election. Some of my ideas didn't work, through lack of research, lack of time, lack of imagination or the fact that we laid out our own pages, requiring me to learn sub-editing from scratch. One that did come off was charting the tortuous course of the A11- my own road home -from Cambridge to the outskirts of London, discovering in the process that a motorway (now the M11) was planned. So did a spread on life on a North Sea gas rig (no oil then), being choppered out from Great Yarmouth and spending 24 hours with the roustabouts. No sooner had my photographer, Mike Carter, and I got to our cabin than an alarm sounded; we had no idea where our emergency gear was or where to assemble. When next I visited a rig - eleven years later in the Gulf of Mexico - I knew what to do.

Putting the paper together culminated in four of us taking a taxi early on Friday to supervise the compositors making up the pages. First we went to the sleepy *Bury Free Press,* then when production moved to the printing works at Peterborough which was the genesis of Emap we felt part of a serious newspaper, acknowledging this with a Berni Inn lunch on expenses. It was fascinating watching a process that had changed little since Caxton's day as rows of type were shoehorned into a metal frame, headlines and rules added and pictures inserted, with lines of text removed with tweezers if a story wouldn't fit, or strips of lead inserted if it was too short. Once a papier-maché impression - or flong - had been taken of the finished page, we read through the proofs for literals (misprints), then metal plates were cast from the flongs and the presses rolled. We taxied back to Cambridge clutching the first of the 7,000 copies of *Varsity* that would hit the streets next morning.

Most of us took producing *Varsity* very seriously. There were, inevitably, deliberate double entendres, but the most celebrated trick was played on us, by a rugby player who told one of our sportswriters that he was off to tour South Africa with the Old Assolians. However the dons who ultimately controlled *Varsity* were reluctant to let Simon Hoggart become its editor. Simon's ability was obvious, but their fears that he would let rip were confirmed one Friday when he took the paper to press. He and Peter Cole had done a profile of Ernest Brauch, a pillar of the Student Representative Council, studded with crossheads of cats (Brauch's flat was full of them). Great care had been taken to keep on the right side of legality, and there was consternation when *Varsity* appeared with an item in the Stop Press headed: "Ernest Brauch Arrested." Anyone reading further discovered that Brauch had (allegedly) said he was "arrested" by the success of his SRC handbook, but the damage was done and Simon had to make do with a lifetime of success on the *Observer* and the *Guardian.*

I covered one story for *Varsity* - interviewing an American postgrad named Mike Meeropol - totally unaware of its deeper significance. It was 40 years before I learned that his parents had been Julius and Ethel Rosenberg, executed in 1953 as Communist spies at the height of McCarthyism. What a legacy to carry, particularly as doubt persists over whether both the Rosenbergs were guilty.

Our coverage polarised between serious(ish) news, features and sport and monitoring the "luminaries" blazing their way across the student firmament. A number would star in later life: Norman Lamont, Vince Cable, Germaine Greer, Clive James, Anne Mallalieu, Robert Lacey and Robin Wight, to name a few. For others, the bravado and eccentricity which set them apart at Cambridge would not suit the adult world, though one Spanish grandee I assumed to be a howling snob turned out, when I finally met him 40 years later, to be utterly charming. There was plenty of scope to be silly, and it was easy to succumb; I got sucked into a Welsh nationalist movement that was challenging General de Gaulle over his treatment of the Bretons. But those who would thrive used their time at Cambridge to grow up.

Varsity was time-consuming, and near the end of my third year, with my Part I exams looming, I baled out. I did agree to be circulation manager, but apart from devising a few slogans and organising extra sales for a 27-mile sponsored walk to Bishop's Stortford (I was too stiff to stand up the next morning) I let the connection lapse. In my final year I turned down an invitation to edit a special supplement; David Taylor took it on, gaining worldwide headlines by getting Prince Charles to write a piece complaining about the dustmen banging and clattering in the lane below his room.

The Cambridge our *Varsity* chronicled was the Cambridge of the - almost - swinging Sixties. CND was in eclipse and the student unrest post-1968 was in the future. As for sex, drugs and rock'n'roll, pop dominated our lives, at parties, in the pub, when we collected in each other's rooms and as background when we worked - though I preferred jazz in the small hours typing up my lecture notes on my Smith Corona portable. When the exam question "Can we stand too much reality?" came up, I cited *Eleanor Rigby;* my director of studies told me the examiners were staggered to receive so many answers based on pop, and good ones, too. There was a fair amount of sex, most of it happening to other people. And of drugs there was little sign, unless you hung around one dodgy pub where grass was on sale. One idiot told *Granta* that LSD was being manufactured in the Chemistry Labs, then was surprised when the police raided them. A friend who tried LSD saw his wallpaper turn into tigers.

One night a gang of us, after a few pints and a seething curry, went to see *The Sound of Music*. We felt the audience weren't being properly entertained, so Trevor and Keith produced sound effects that led a Pole in front to hiss: "Vorse than peegs you are!" And when the Mother Superior told Maria: "Every time a window in your life closes, a door will shortly open", a voice interjected: "Shut the door, they're coming in the window!"

Heckling, and worse, in a cinema is a Cambridge tradition. But Trevor added a deafening colonial laugh that kicked in after any obscure double-entendre; a few seconds later, the entire audience would collapse. I first experienced it in *Goldfinger*, when Sean Connery awakes to find Honor Blackman bending over him:

> *Bond:* Who are you?
> *Blackman:* My name is Pussy Galore.
> *Bond:* I must be dreaming.

Trevor's laugh proved even more deadly for live theatre, where it not only convulsed the audience but halted the performance. Other outbreaks of mirth - one in the Arts Cinema during, of all things, a vintage railway short on the delights of the Peak District - were generated by current events. David Steel was taking through his Abortion Bill, and the line: "It was here that Izaak Walton conducted his first experiments with string and a bent knitting needle" brought the house down.

After our exams came May Week (in June), with the "bumps" to watch and a strenuous round of parties. Most memorable was "Armageddon", held after our 1967 exams in Cheshunt College as it closed to merge with its Presbyterian counterpart, Westminster and hosted by myself, Julian Maw and our ProngSoc friend Steve Gregory. Jack Newport was alarmed when *Varsity* carried quotes from the invitation, including "Sheep will be sorted from goats at midnight". We had none of the gate-crashers Jack feared, but the party went like a bomb and one guest had to be fished (alive) from the Cam. Fifty years on to the day, 40 of the participants would reconvene, sedately, in York – Cheshunt, now an A-Level college, being unavailable.

The morning after another party, several of us took a tiny cabin cruiser to Ely; there is nothing worse for a throbbing head than 80-degree heat and an equally throbbing engine. Rounding off May Week was each college's May Ball. I went to three at Trinity, staying up all night for the first time in my life but flaking out late the following afternoon. The first year, my partner crashed out as the champagne triggered her hay fever medication. Though legend has it that the great groups of the Sixties played at May Balls just before hitting the big time, I don't remember any. But with cabaret acts in a marquee, a group in another and a disco, no-one was complaining. Cambridge wasn't one long party. There were periods of introspection, angst and downright depression. Our romantic lives had their ups and downs - mainly downs - in a city were male students outnumbered females five to one. Some contemporaries found their studies too demanding; a handful did not complete the very first term. And a few took overdoses.

For many, May Week is what they remember best: the trees newly in leaf, the long warm evenings, the carefree punting after the exams. But for me, Cambridge will always mean a foggy November evening during a Law supervision in Clare with the hedgehog-like Dr Lipstein - whose elegant wife, I discovered years later, had been at LSE with my mother. It is dark outside and a damp chill hangs in the air, the bell tolling from one of the college chapels a reminder that Cambridge is an island, cut off from the rest of the world, and from time.

Trinity is Cambridge's largest college: you are bound to find people you have plenty in common with, but you won't get to know everyone. I envied friends in smaller ones, until they pointed out that they couldn't get away from people they didn't like. But taking subjects where my supervisor was often in another college and belonging to university, rather than college, societies, I had the best of both worlds.

At one of our Trinity reunions, Bob Reiss – then rector of Grantham – described the intakes of 1964 and 1965 as nondescript - and he was right. The year before, there had been Rajiv Gandhi; the year after, Prince Charles, who had rooms above a friend of mine in New Court. We did produce a bishop, a general and a Lord of Appeal and some of the scientists went on to do dazzling things, but we were a good, solid and socially mixed bunch and none the worse for that.

We were at Cambridge to study, but you could spend most of your time on other things despite the discipline - absent in Oxford - of exams at the end of each year. It was also easy to forget that we were living amid history, becoming blasé that Newton had rooms in Trinity, that Byron kept a bear in his, and that, not long before, Wittgenstein had been a fixture.

To locals, Trinity was the pinnacle of privilege. Before the advent of high-tech industries, Cambridge was a low-wage city with the University and the colleges the largest employers, and resentments were inevitable; we must have looked carefree and arrogant as we hurried between lectures in our gowns. Students didn't worry about money then; your tuition was paid for and your grant gave you enough to live on, unless your parents refused to contribute (as some did). The whole Town v Gown issue crystallised for me in Hall one evening. A young waiter was serving soup when a begowned student thrust his arm backwards and inadvertently sent a loaded plate flying. The waiter paused for a second, then exclaimed: "F*** you, Sir."

Elections for the JCR Committee came round in my second term, amid a feeling that it was time for modest change. The reformers asked me to stand as freshmen's representative, and to my surprise I got in. Colin Ravden, our chairman, was a Communist but docile and constructive, unlike the hardline CPers the YS had debated with. Our reforms were limited, and only pursued after a great deal of unstructured discussion. But a backlash set in, and in the second-year elections I was ousted. During my year in office I found a niche as "kitchen representative", trying to diversify Trinity's menu which relied nightly on braised celery and mixed vegetables. I was also deputed to round up a team for *University Challenge*, selecting four far brainier contestants than me but naming myself as reserve. I was not to know this would line me up for the captaincy three years later ... by when I would have expected to have left.

Lawyers faced a continual grind of compulsory lectures, many of which sounded like a textbook being read out and which had to be learned by rote. My neighbour in lectures, an amiable Northerner with Buddy Holly glasses, retained his sanity by drawing horses playing electric guitars; Geoff Bowman went on to become First Parliamentary Counsel, retiring with a well-merited knighthood. I enjoyed Criminal Law and Legal History, getting good first-year marks for both, and was still committed to Law when I returned for my second year after a summer with the *Northern Echo*. But after a few weeks of Contract and Tort I gave up. My moment of truth came during a lecture on Roman Law - which I otherwise quite liked - from Tony Weir, one of Trinity's young stars. As he set out a hypothetical case involving a camper van full of dwarves being driven over a cliff, it dawned on me that the law and the real world had precious little to do with each other. I have not had cause to change that opinion.

History was the easiest subject to change to, having got me into Trinity. Alan Ker, just before his sudden death, persuaded the college and then the University, from which a special "grace" was required, to let me change, and by mid-November 1965 I had done it. As both Law and History involved a two-year "Part 1", I had to start again with three years to complete, making four in all. It was the best thing I could have done, as only in that fourth year would I get full value from Cambridge. I spent my first three trying to enjoy myself, doing enough work to get by, but in my fourth I worked really hard – and enjoyed myself much more.

History offered a wider range of lectures from which you could pick and choose. Sir Jack Plumb's boisterous take on the 18th century I found engaging, Sir Geoffrey Elton's studious approach to the Tudors less so. The great Walter Ullman, whose son Ralph I studied alongside, lectured on the Medieval Papacy in an unnerving combination of English, German and Latin. The pioneering social historian Peter Laslett did his best to teach me Economic History, bemoaning my inadequate grasp of economics.

In my catch-up year I discovered the Merovingians, the post-Roman kings of France, and the Europe of Charlemagne. My third year Part I involved digging deeper rather than covering new ground, and my 2:2 led to Trinity not renewing my exhibition. But the final-year options caught my imagination: a course on Franco-Italian relations during the *Risorgimento* taught by an approachable veteran don from Christ's, and one on Nazi Germany whose highlight was Owen Chadwick's lectures (intended for theologians) on Hitler's relations with the churches.

Above all, I revelled in the new post-colonial option of African History. Even the massive University Library, where I belatedly became a regular, contained little to flesh out our lecture notes and the handful of set books. The map changed every few months as colonies became independent, and tensions over UDI and apartheid overshadowed the challenges of migration to Africa's cities as rural populations exploded, the struggle against hunger, and the resurgence of tribalism as colonial structures broke down. I specialised in eastern and southern Africa; their history then was of the colonial period, the upsurge in African political consciousness and South Africa from Shaka Zulu to Verwoerd. Studying the subject today, with apartheid in the past and Nelson Mandela – in jail then – a great historical figure, would be even more interesting. But we were the pioneers.

I was supervised by John Lonsdale, who the next year directed Prince Charles' studies. His teaching sparked an interest in Africa that would commend me to the *Daily Telegraph* and eventually take me back there. Lonsdale had taught in Dar-es-Salaam, where his students most wanted to hear about the execution of Charles I, the guillotining of Louis XVI and Marie-Antoinette and the murders of Tsar Nicholas II and his family. Yet Tanzania has turned out one of Africa's most peaceful countries.

I stayed two years at Sidney Street, then for my third came into college. The 1950s Angel Court, to the left of Trinity's Great Gate, is a strange mixture of the contemporary and the pre-existing; my bed-sitter was strictly functional. It was in D9 Angel that I heard of the Aberfan disaster, and revised for my unspectacular performance in Part 1.

As a fourth-year undergraduate – one of only a dozen at Trinity – I became eligible for "unlicensed lodgings". I teamed up with three friends who were staying on to do PhDs, and we found a detached house on the Huntingdon Road, most of the way to Girton. It was a handy introduction to adult life: we ordered anthracite for the stove instead of anthracite nuts (it fell through the grate), and when not dining in hall lived on canned Australian stewed steak and boiled potatoes, after which we sat around groaning. Cleaning was a challenge, until we persuaded the girl next door to take it on.

The lesson I learned at Huntingdon Road was that your friends may not get on with each other; indeed only Geoff Jones, a sporty geographer from Wrexham and today a professional photographer, survived the year with me. One housemate left after a few weeks to go home to Wales. His replacement, a middle-aged white Rhodesian fundraiser, departed leaving an outsize and unsaleable folding bed. A third – a good friend today - fortunately survived an overdose. We turned down one applicant as too boring, only to realise that was just what we needed, and ended up with a quiet Irish maths teacher. We rounded off the year – and my Cambridge career - with a bigger party than we could have held in college.

Having gained a 2:1 which my director of studies sniffly reckoned "the most you had been trying for", I returned weeks later to take my degree. We went up in fives, each clutching one of a proctor's fingers as the Vice-Chancellor awarded us our BAs (you buy your MA three years later for £5). Next to me as we knelt was Jonathan King, and the proctor was, fittingly, Jack Newport. When that autumn I went back for parties, I found my contemporaries inhabiting a world now closed to me.

In those days the colleges didn't keep up with their alumni. You had a standing invitation to dinner at High Table, a privilege I have exercised just once, and every ten years Trinity laid on a "gathering" for your intake and the one before or after it. I missed the first because I was in Washington. At the second, as we turned 40, one of our number confessed to being a grandfather; he was taken outside and spoken to. For the third, I was allocated my old room in Angel Court, where every coffee cup mark recalled some half-forgotten trauma. By the fourth, one third of my contemporaries had retired (by choice or otherwise), a third were on the point of packing up and the rest including me were still working like beavers, or trying to. By my fifth, in 2013, and sixth, in 2019, we were gathering more often as the numbers thinned out, but with long-unseen contemporaries reappearing.

Colleges now take a genuine interest in their alumni – and not simply to raise funds. With John Lonsdale in the lead, Trinity a few years ago held an alumni lunch in Nevile's Court. The response was such that the the Master, Martin Rees, invited graduates from various walks of life to dinners in the Lodge, from which developed a series of Trinity associations: for the Law, the City and, in my case, Arts and the Media. The Trinity Arts and Media Association involved at the outset such diverse talents as the sculptor Anthony Gormley, Andrew Burns, our former ambassador to Israel, John Tusa, who has run the BBC World Service and the Barbican, Nicholas Coleridge, head of Condé Nast, and Richard Charkin of Bloomsbury, who published *Harry Potter*. With organisational backing from the college we held several successful events, but TAMA has struggled to achieve critical mass.

5: Catching the news bug

Fleet Street in the 1960s housed the world's greatest concentration of mass-circulation newspapers: their reporters were despatched all over the globe, and their presses printed millions of copies each night. From the proprietors in their penthouses to the hacks and printers who thronged its pubs, the thousands who worked there inhabited a world of their own, with its own legends, its own caste system - and Byzantine working practices that would contribute to its downfall. Working in Fleet Street was the goal of almost every young journalist, and I was no exception.

My first experience of national journalism came before I had that ambition: at the *Guardian,* between school and Cambridge in 1964. I had found a job with a travel agency, but it lessened in scope as the start date approached. Meanwhile I joined an Isle of Wight walking party led by Theodore Mallinson, one of Highgate's most inspirational teachers. "Mally" had joined the staff on the outbreak of war and taken charge of just about every activity, remaining part of the school as its roving ambassador until his 100th year. He only taught me in my final term, when I tried my hand at Spanish, and he persuaded me to join his annual trip. It was strange spending a week with schoolmates I might never see again, but I enjoyed even our marathon hike from Freshwater to Carisbrooke and back.

Soon after, a letter arrived from Theodore, the first of many: Gerard Fay, London Editor of the *Guardian,* needed a messenger and was I interested? I was, and late that May I started work. Only two years before, the paper had rebranded itself from the *Manchester Guardian* and moved its expanded London staff into the *Sunday Times* building in Grays Inn Road. It was striving, on a limited budget, to increase its circulation from just under 200,000 by winning southern readers without alienating its traditional base in the North-West.

My work for Gerard Fay was confined to fetching bacon sandwiches. In practice I was the newsroom factotum: opening the mail - including an agonised letter from a nurse in Cambridge seeking a then-illegal abortion - managing the petty cash (float: £5) and every Thursday collecting the weeklies, from the *New Statesman* to the *Police Review*. One such Thursday I negotiated Holborn tube station behind my double, who was even dressed like me; I have always wondered who he was.

Working alongside talented and hard-bitten journalists, the magic of newspapers rubbed off on me. The *Guardian*'s staff was small: perhaps ten reporters and as many specialists. I shared a table with Jean Stead, Eric Clark and Tony Geraghty, who would make his name with a book about the SAS. Harry Jackson and John Cole - future political editor of the BBC and then with an even richer Belfast accent - made up the news desk, with the genial future

Today presenter Brian Redhead; Mike Hides (later my editor in Sheffield) headed the subs' table. Most of the executives shuttled to and from Manchester, where the leaders were still written. Presiding over it all was Alistair Hetherington, donnish but with a shrewd journalistic brain; on my final day I was allowed into his editorial conference and I still have the schedule for the next day's paper.

Snippets from that summer - a hot one - stick in my mind: Harry Jackson dismissing a BBC news bulletin as "straight PA"; Jean Stead questioning a hapless official about bucket toilets at Moggerhanger school; monitoring the wires as England took on the Australians; and watching the *Guardian's* Communist affairs expert (an elderly refugee) cull items from Eastern bloc newspapers. I got a couple of pieces into the diary column, then turned in my first news story - about the fate of town halls rendered surplus by the creation of the London boroughs. Seeing it in print was a thrill, even if it was headed "By our own Reporter". I would wait a decade for my first national byline.

In the canteen I met a *Sunday Times* van driver who previously worked for the *Daily Mail*. The *Mail* had bought a machine for bundling papers into quires of 26 for loading into the vans, leaving a dozen well-paid men without jobs. The print union Natsopa threatened to "black" the machine, so one man was rehired to count the bundles coming out of it, another to intercept every 12th bundle, a third to cut the string, a fourth to throw the papers onto the floor, a fifth to pick them up and a sixth to stuff them back into the machine again, alternating with the other six redundant men.

I left the *Guardian* hooked on journalism, and the next summer found a job in Darlington with the *Northern Echo,* under Harry Evans - now Sir Harold - who had made his name as a fearless and enterprising deputy editor of the *Manchester Evening News*. The staff was again small, with the *Echo*'s reporters - and a handful for the *Evening Despatch* - one side of a corridor and the subs on the other with Harry's office beyond. Next to the newsroom was our news editor, Mike Morrissey. Every so often Morrissey, wearing a headset, would beckon through a hatch: "Would you come here, Mr Er, Er ... ?" The day the contract to build the motorway through south Durham was let, Morrissey prematurely despatched me with a photographer to find the diggers at work, and he once told the York district man: "Christ has been seen walking the streets of York. Get quotes from shopkeepers." But after he was fired as news editor Morrissey's persistence as a reporter generated story after story until his notice expired.

Importantly for my future, the *Echo*'s chief reporter was Mike Corner, the perfect big fish in a smallish pool who would decline to follow Harry to London. He was a marvellous storyteller, and while there was a hint of elaboration most likely he did play football for Manchester University, once facing a nearly full-strength United team. It's probable, too, that he was a tenpin bowling international. It was certainly Mike who found a Ferryhill man who had changed his name from Jack Shufflebottom ... to George. It was Mike, too, who realised the woman judging cakes at a local show had been on a TV commercial saying she couldn't tell Stork from butter. And it was certainly Mike who, covering Stanhope magistrates' court, heard the young policeman who had arrested a farmhand for offences against sheep describe how he found a pair of waders in the man's car. When the copper quoted the defendant as saying he wore them to stop the sheep kicking, the chairman of the Bench interjected: "They do, y'know." Yet Mike had his serious side, conducting a risky investigation into the payment of "luck money" at local agricultural marts.

Mike gave me a formidable grounding in how to track down the news, deliver it in adverse conditions and thwart the opposition. He would send you to cover a story at night, filing from a remote telephone box minus its light bulb; you soon learnt to extemporise yet get the facts right. Mike also posed the question: "There's a tanker on fire in the Tees. You and your photographer find two boats. What do you do?" His answer: "Take one each - then we get the exclusive picture."

I was sent to review Nat Jackley's end-of-the-pier show, fresh from Llandudno, with the *Despatch*'s Philip Norman, later the biographer of John Lennon. We found an audience of just five, despite our heavy promotion of the show; this was before the Beatles showcased Jackley in *Magical Mystery Tour*. Troupers to the last, the cast not only went ahead but prevailed on Phil and me, in the front row of the circle, to join in the chorus. It was possibly the most embarrassing moment of my life. A close second was being stuck in a coroner's inquest with rip-roaring hay fever and no handkerchief. I also found some local accents challenging. When I rang a cinema at Whitley Bay for the week's programme, the manageress told me they were showing *Genius Korn*; it took me some time to realise she meant *Genghis Khan*.

Deputising for reporters on holiday, I covered league cricket at Redcar, council meetings at South Bank, Middlesbrough's stipendiary court where most cases were either riotously funny or unreportable because of the language, a council by-election and, tragically, the death of a five-year-old Middlesbrough boy in a road accident. The news desk (Morrissey was off) told me to ask the boy's mother for a "pick-up" photograph. She was not on the phone, so I caught the bus desperately hoping to find no-one in. The boy's aunt sat me down with a cup of tea and fetched his mother, who was ready not only to talk about her wonderful son but lend me a treasured photo. When I got back to Darlington, I was told I had done a good job - but should never have been sent. On a lighter note, I marvelled at the shop in Middlesbrough where a cake baked for George V's Silver Jubilee was still on display.

I also became notorious, for something I didn't do. A highlight of the year in Middlesbrough was the Corpus Christi procession, and Morrissey, a devout Catholic, gave it the full treatment. The colleague sent, David Francks, colourfully wrote of beggars crying in the street, and Catholic readers' subsequent protests made it the stuff of legend. Unfortunately the myth spread that I wrote it - it was actually the month before I arrived - and as David died soon afterward there was no-one to contradict it. Thirty years later a prominent Teesside journalist greeted me with: "I've always wanted to meet the man who wrote that Corpus Christi piece."

The *Echo*'s staff were typical of a regional paper. Most were young and enthusiastic; a few much older and cynical. Most had joined from school; a few were graduates. Most were men, but talented women were coming through. Some were desperate to work on a national; others happy to stay. There were a stranded aesthete (Stan Hurwitz), a writer attuned to local traditions (George Lambelle), a fragrant female reporter (Judy Allinson) and a languid young man in manifestly the wrong job (David Francks). There was also one much older trainee: Ken Calcutt, recently retired from the RAF. He proved his value dealing with Vaux Brewery, whose owner staffed its press office with officer types. When one ex-lieutenant tried to pull rank, Ken replied: "Yes, and I'm Wing-Commander Calcutt of the *Northern Echo*. Now tell me what I need to know." He never had any trouble again.

My time at Darlington had its downs; there are always things you learn the hard way. But I left with Harry Evans assuring me: "You'll walk onto a national", and weeks later I was no longer a law student.

I took other work during the World Cup summer of 1966, but having extended my time at Cambridge I had one more summer to fill, which I spent in Fleet Street proper. I owed this start to a connection with the *Telegraph* that to date has lasted 52 years to the paper's City Editor Kenneth Fleet, who was Grannie's next-door neighbour. The negotiations were conducted at that level, and to my shame I never thanked Ken properly; I was rather in awe of him. In June 1967 - as *Sergeant Pepper* was released - I reported for work at 135 Fleet Street. The marble entrance hall reminded me of a bank, but Goldman Sachs, its present occupant, can't have the traffic of drunks, men in boiler suits and no-hopers seeking justice who then passed through it. Climbing the stairs, you passed the library on the mezzanine, then reached the modestly sized newsroom; it had a lowish ceiling and long desks at which some 20 reporters could sit, plus a rostrum for the news editor, his deputies and a bright support team who were the offspring of print workers. Next door was the Foreign Room, smaller and less pressured except during an international crisis; across the corridor was the subs' room where the copy was processed, and beyond it the "back of the house" where you ventured at your peril lest you inadvertently spark a walkout by one of the 51 union "chapels" at the paper.

Upstairs, with a manicured lawn on their balcony, were the proprietor, Lord Camrose, and the editor-in-chief, his brother Lord Hartwell, who was the real driving force. Intensely shy, we saw little of him, but his "wanted points", communicated daily through the managing editor, were exhaustively followed up. Behind Lord Hartwell was his formidable wife Lady Pamela Berry, daughter of the legendary advocate F E Smith. Throughout the post-war decades, the *Telegraph's* Paris and New York bureaux kept her supplied with currency in excess of the £25 to which every Briton going abroad was restricted.

The management left each night well before the paper came off the presses, and seemed to consist of just two people: Hugh Lawson, a Berry cousin, and H M Stephen, who looked after the finances. When I was sent to Washington I asked Stephen for a loan; he replied sorrowfully: "How can we lend you money when the paper has an overdraft?" When he died, Hartwell's tribute began: "Although Mr Stephen had been with us 37 years, I did not know him well."

Back in 1967, the *Telegraph* seemed simply to happen. There was no daily editorial conference, and indeed no editor in the conventional sense. The titular editor, Maurice Green, controlled only the opinion pages; everything else was the province of the managing editor, Roy Pawley (or by the time I joined the paper permanently, Peter Eastwood.) With this lack of structure which continued until Conrad Black took charge, the paper relied on a highly experienced team, each of whom knew what needed doing.

In the newsroom there were a few reporters in their late 20s, but most were middle-aged or more. Almost all could produce a faultless story after consuming prodigious quantities of alcohol. Fights were frequent, most involving the estates correspondent John Armstrong, who had lost his hands in the RAF and had a hook crafted to hold a G&T at lunchtime. After several, he would return and pick on the young reporters - though once he targeted

Paddy Travers, a tiny, timeless Irishman, who pinioned John and attached his hook to the desk. His behaviour was tolerated until he accused the recently-bereaved news editor Jack Hill of having murdered his wife. There were also specialists in hutches and garrets all over the building; some never mastered a typewriter and telephoned their stories to the copytakers a couple of floors below.

At the behest of Jack Hill and his less forbidding deputy Bill Tadd, I wrote up the pollen count and the Top Ten, and covered events that didn't merit a top-notch reporter. These included the crowning of the forces' first serving beauty queen, a protest by Cheyne Walk houseboat owners against plans for a motorway through their moorings (they won) and the 90th birthday of a Hassocks man who had played cricket with W G Grace.

One morning Bill called me over and said: "I've something here about an Australian pop group who are going to be deported. Sounds a good thing to me, but you'd better go along." Half an hour later I was sitting in a Marylebone mews house ... with the Bee Gees. The Home Office had given the Gibb brothers and Vince Melouney notice to quit for outstaying their permits. They sat there shyly, leaving most of the talking to their manager Robert Stigwood. I got a few paragraphs into the paper, the Home Office gave way and within months the Bee Gees had a number one with *Massachusetts*. Occasionally I glimpsed the archaic machinery on which the *Telegraph* was produced; the most recent of the presses dated from 1912, and when a Japanese paper took an office in the building its staff were forbidden to view them. I was also introduced to the Ludgate Circus Lyons', one of a rapidly diminishing chain and with good reason; the tea was purple.

Then there were Fleet Street's legendary pubs, most of which were awful. This had much to do with the clientele, as journalistic drunks have a deterrent effect on business and many of the print workers had almost nothing else to do. A few had redeeming features - my favourite was the Hoop and Grapes round the corner in Farringdon Street - but the very worst was the Kings and Keys, next door to the *Telegraph*. It was gloomy, smoky, filled with nasty drunks and the beer wasn't great. Bill Deedes, then editing the diary column, would sit there apparently oblivious to how vile the establishment was; a connoisseur of beer and pubs, I suspect he took a perverse delight in its sheer awfulness. More salubrious if touristy was the Cheshire Cheese, a haunt for younger *Telegraph* and *Standard* reporters. If we headed for Wolsey's Wine Bar, home of a cheap, sweet Austrian wine called Schluck and a red christened "the infuriator", things could go downhill, but usually we went back after a couple of drinks. Such was the reliance on alcohol that the *Telegraph* itself had a top-floor bar nicknamed the Starlight Room, next to its rudimentary canteen.

Despite its Dickensian feel I liked the *Telegraph*, and while no promises were made, returning there was a possibility. I had been in Sheffield five years before a feeling that the time was ripe led me to contact Bill Tadd. I also had an interview at the *Financial Times,* who would offer me a job on their industrial staff a couple of weeks after I joined the *Telegraph*. I wonder how my career would have panned out had their letter arrived first; as it was, it was 2012 before I received my first byline in the *FT*, for an obituary of Norman St John-Stevas.

In March 1974 the *Telegraph* recruited me, to be its reporter in Birmingham. The timing was not ideal: Deborah was seven months pregnant and the move entailed not just relocating but spending an initial two months in London. We sold our Sheffield house, expecting to leave in mid-May once the baby had arrived with me starting at the *Telegraph* soon after. Dad and Jane offered us their flat in Tufnell Park for the short term. The arrangement was convenient for us, but to visit her new grandchild my mother had to come to the flat her husband had shared with his mistress; it must have hurt.

The pregnancy went on and on, and our Sheffield friends Richard and Heather Cousins were kind enough to take us in. Eventually doctors at the Jessop Hospital induced, and on Saturday 1 June 1974 Carrie was born. On the Monday I started at the *Telegraph*, covering the IRA's attempt to blow up Westminster Hall. The next weekend I brought Deborah and Carrie down to London.

The Conservative Party was in disarray after Edward Heath's defeat in the "who governs Britain?" election, and with a further election likely its backers in Fleet Street were out to discredit the minority Labour government. Eastwood sent me to Companies House to dig for dirt; I discovered several small companies founded by Lewis (later Lord) Silkin, an influential figure in Attlee's government ... one of which had been donating to the Tories. The *Telegraph* ran the stories to embarrass Silkin's sons John and Sam, by then in Wilson's government; they had in no way been involved, but this did not stop Sam Silkin's constituency party giving him a hard time. I consoled myself that I had not, like counterparts on some other papers, been despatched to harass Tony Benn over fake stories that his children had had private medical treatment.

The newsroom was a happier ship than seven years before, as the most disruptive elements had given way to younger reporters. It was still not a place of refinement, as canteen meals left outside on the window ledge for months could testify. The assignments handed out were still pretty quirky. Eastwood sent me to investigate the decline of Methodism in Yorkshire - staking out a supposed seance at the home of a council engineer in Barnsley - and the Met's refusal to admit that mugging existed for fear of being accused of racism. Bill Tadd got me investigating the porn industry, maybe because *The Joy of Sex* was in the best-sellers. The highlight was interviewing the blue movie star Mary Millington in a freezing shop in Manor Park, she fully clothed and with a hot water bottle between her knees, sipping Beechams from a Basil Brush mug.

Occasionally you were sent out of London, but most of the work was in the office and around town. Many stories broke on the Press Association teleprinter; the desk checked successive editions of the *Evening Standard* and the increasingly dire *Evening News,* and monitored news bulletins to make sure we didn't miss anything. Most stories were put together in mid- to late afternoon, in time for the desk to read through, then - unless further work was required - pass to the back bench who decided which to run and at what length; a fair number always went unused.

Late in the afternoon the managing editor handed over to the night editor, and the smaller night news desk team took over, with a veteran foreign correspondent home from their final posting on the "piano" to check agency copy and call local "stringers". The evenings were usually quiet until around 10 pm when the other papers' first editions appeared. Following up their stories often involved ringing important people late at night, but it had to be done. After that, it would take a major disaster for us to be busy, but that happened just often enough for the 9 to 4 turn not to seem a complete waste of time.

After midnight the swivel chair derbies began and a nifty-fingered reporter would open the news editor's confidential files. One colleague had befriended a nymphomaniac Swedish Page Three girl, and she would ring around 1 am; if he wasn't there she would pester whoever answered the phone to tell her "what you would do next", with the switchboard almost certainly listening. At 4 am having stayed sober paid off and I could drive home, in midsummer getting back in broad daylight. One heavy-drinking colleague habitually fell asleep on the train, missed his stop at Reading and woke up in Swansea. The one time I was obviously the worse for drink - after a protracted lunch with a bibulous Canadian diplomat - the night editor Harry Winslade deputed a colleague to put me on the right train home.

With the poisonous elements weeded out, colleagues would make a point of letting you know you were "doing well". Sometimes their interest was not helpful; when the schoolmistressy Kate Welsh asked an interviewee in regal tones: "Have you any birds?" the reply was drowned out by second-rate bird impressions. In one corner R Barry O'Brien, our investigative reporter, would be researching a 263-page memo to Eastwood on a dodgy building firm in Cheshire; I don't think he ever got a fact wrong. Our top reporters Ken Clarke and Jim Allan (unless they were abroad or in Belfast) would be working on the day's big stories, with Tony Hopkins, Gerda Paul, Amit Roy, Brian Silk and Vic Swain, an Arctic Convoy veteran and a rugby writer in his spare time, tackling "wanted points". One required Amit to ring Spike Milligan; the conversation ran:

> Amit: "I'm Amit Roy from the *Daily Telegraph.*"
>
> Milligan: "Boy, what a memory!" (Hangs up)

It fell to me to cold-call the boxer Joe Bugner about some trivial matter; he was courteous. Victor Lownes of the Playboy Club was downright unpleasant. These things stay with you.

Amidst it all was Guy Rais. Moustachioed and with a touch of Sam Costa, Guy had come to the *Telegraph* from the Army via a short spell working in Brighton. Court reporting was his speciality, and he became a Fleet Street legend for his stage whispers of "What's the old fool saying?" as a judge was summing up. Buoyant and unfailingly helpful, Guy was a joy to work with, because he could get away with anything; I can hear him now picking up the phone and asking: "Mr Justice Weaselbag?" But no-one ever took offence.

I was also inducted into the mystery of Fleet Street expenses. The golden age of implausibility had passed, but creative claims still gave reporters a lifestyle way beyond their salary if they worked the system; if you didn't, you were letting the side down. Within the office there was a steady trade in blank taxi and restaurant receipts; a couple of *Express* hacks even considered setting up a phoney restaurant called "L'Addition".

During the Falklands War the wife of our reporter with the Task Force called Accounts to ask where his expenses were, explaining that he habitually banked his salary without touching it. A *Mirror* contemporary returning from Pakistan concocted a restaurant receipt from his airline sickbag, impressively lettered in Urdu. Weeks later a subcontinental voice from Accounts asked him: "About this receipt from Mr Sickbag ... "

I was often sent down to the front hall to "get rid of" callers bringing tales of woe. Some handed over encyclopaedic letters in green ink, but a few had genuine grievances and had exhausted every other channel. I remember one man facing deportation because he was stateless, despite having spent years working in Egypt for the RAF who accepted him as British. I set out the story to Mike Green, Bill Tadd's deputy; he could see there might be something in it, but couldn't afford to devote a reporter to it for two or three days.

Guy Rais had a problem when French accident investigators turned up unannounced. He had covered the crash of "Concordski" at the Paris Air Show, and quoted an eyewitness in some detail. Going through the coverage, the investigators realised that only Guy's "M. Dupont" had noticed certain things, and were anxious to interview him. They returned to Paris wondering whether Guy's source existed.

Equally elusive was the Gloucestershire landowner Raphael Dunvant, who appeared sporadically in stories from the Bertie Woosterish Godfrey Barker. Dunvant showed solidarity with striking Bunnies, had his tin leg struck by lightning while umpiring a cricket match, and repelled marauding hippies at a rock festival. His crowning act was to fend off drunks with a salmon rod on the sleeper from Inverness. Unfortunately for Godfrey, John Junor of the *Sunday Express* had been on that train and witnessed none of the scenes so lovingly described. A barbed column from Junor sent Godfrey scurrying to extract Dunvant's cuttings from the library; the librarians anticipated this by creating a duplicate file.

The librarians – one of whom joined me for a 1967 Pink Floyd overnighter at Alexandra Palace - cut the paper daily to fill thousands of personal and subject files. Many of these were kept on the mezzanine, more in the basement and a nearby warehouse, and others in Lord Hartwell's barn in Buckinghamshire. The files were encyclopaedic (and still are, though no new cuttings have been taken since 2004 and they are now stored inconveniently at Wigan), but also quirky. Researching mugging, race and gangs, I was given the cuttings on a betting coup involving a horse called Gay Future.

Other oddities stemmed from the *Telegraph*'s style book. This remarkable tome, since rewritten more sensibly by Simon Heffer, lays down the correct use of English for a conservative newspaper. Reporters and subs were reminded that "only Malays run amok." Taiwan had to be referred to as Formosa, Iran as Persia, Tony Benn as Anthony Wedgwood Benn, and Cardinal Tomas O Fiaich as Cardinal Fee, because Eastwood believed it would annoy him.

The *Telegraph* of the 1970s had an umbilical relationship with the 1.2 million Middle Englanders who bought the paper, a circulation achieved despite limited space (extra pages would have involved unaffordable payoffs to the unions), abysmal picture quality, a lack of feature articles (everything had to be dressed up as a news story) and at times downright barmy opinions. All this under the radar, as well into the 1980s the *Today* programme often ignored the *Telegraph* in its review of the papers; at the BBC they read the *Guardian*. Yet it exerted a formidable influence - whose full extent I only realised after getting something wrong.

My greatest mistake - if it was such – earned me three days before a High Court judge for contempt of court. I had taken a call from a Pakistani solicitor's clerk whose under-age daughter had been taken into care and made a ward of court, only for social workers to reunite her with the boyfriend who was the problem. At the parents' home near Heathrow I ran through the details with them, reading the paperwork with what I thought to be care; as I left, her father told me the wardship had ceased. I got back to the office convinced he had a watertight case, tried and failed to get a comment from social services, banged out the story and went home. I arrived next morning to find that the Official Solicitor had rung to say we had committed contempt by naming the daughter, who despite what I had been told was still a ward of court, and that we should be at the Law Courts at eleven. The paper, not I, was the defendant, so Peter Eastwood and Bill Deedes came with me to face the music. After a brief hearing to set a date for a full trial we repaired to the pub; at no point did my bosses utter a word of reproach. The Friday before the three-day trial, Eastwood insisted on my writing the front-page report of Peter Hain's acquittal on bank robbery charges (trumped up by South African intelligence) so the judge trying our case would know I was a serious journalist; I wasn't in court for the Hain case, and it would be 18 years before I met Peter, in Johannesburg.

The prosecution's argument was simple: the girl was a ward of court, there was an absolute ban on naming wards of court, *ergo* we were guilty. They did not challenge my account of events supplied by our QC, the former Conservative Attorney-General Lord Rawlinson, in part because the *Slough Evening Mail* had repeated the story and were also up before the judge, no doubt cursing the *Telegraph*. Representing them was Leon Brittan; he couldn't resist coming over and saying: "We didn't get this far in the syllabus, did we?" Leon put stronger and more imaginative arguments than Rawlinson, but both papers were convicted - though the judge waived his power to send Bill Deedes to jail, fining the *Telegraph* instead.

Rawlinson saw no point in appealing, but Leon insisted and when the Slough paper appealed, so did we. By now I was in Washington, so I missed the chance to see the formidable Lord Denning, one of the three appellate judges, in action. The argument revolved not around what I had done - one judge said that if I'd read the documents more carefully I might have realised the girl was still a ward of court - but whether the law made sense. Denning observed that as things stood, if a ward of court won a scholarship to Oxford, the *Times* could be prosecuted for reporting it. I heard that the Court of Appeal had quashed the conviction when I rang in from Chicago. I was mightily relieved, and very grateful to Leon.

One summer day in 1975, protesters against the conviction of the East End criminal George Davis for armed robbery dug up the pitch on the eve of the Headingley Test match. I was despatched to Bow alongside the rest of the media to track down the culprits, and spent the day in a block of council flats trying to interview people who knew a lot more than they were letting on. There were plenty of determined looking women to tell us Davis couldn't have done the robbery, plus a character called Mickey Ishmael, who told me: "You're trying to make me say I done it", and an American social worker who seemed on the locals' side. My own suspicion was that Davis hadn't done it, but had paid the price for other crimes the Met knew he had committed but couldn't prove. (Freed by Roy Jenkins, he would be caught red-handed on another job, but finally cleared of the original robbery in 2011). Back in the office I pulled together what I knew and went home.

Next morning I got a shock. My story was leading the paper, but it was evident from the radio (and the other papers) that there had been loads more going on which no-one had thought to add. Most woundingly, the *Mail* had a story from Peter Birkett, later a good colleague at the *Telegraph,* questioning what "American Anne" was up to. I set off for work wishing the ground would open up, but the desk didn't seem bothered. They told me Colin Dean, one of the protesters, was stark naked on an island in an East London park, and I should capture the moment when the police moved in. There was nothing to see by the time I got there, so I returned to Fleet Street ... to find the police waiting, to find out what I knew. The answer: humiliatingly little.

I joined the *Telegraph* at a time of industrial friction. Most of the staff belonged to the National Union of Journalists, though a few took pride in staying out and some belonged to the rival Institute of Journalists; management encouraged the IoJ reckoning it less militant, only to be disabused later. With the unions having agreed a maximum £6 a week increase with the Labour government, our arguments revolved around exceptions and fringe issues, and our pursuit of a "house agreement" covering all aspects of our employment.

With the *Telegraph* campaigning to stop Michael Foot as Employment Secretary turning Fleet Street into a closed shop for journalists as well as printers, management saw a house agreement as a step in that direction. Negotiations deadlocked, and in the summer of 1975 several one-day strikes were called. Though we knew we were the only workers in the building who couldn't stop the paper coming out, pickets were mounted to make our point. I was given the rear entrance, but our veteran (and strongly Tory) political correspondent H B (soon to be Sir Harry) Boyne courageously took the front door so he could speak to Lord Hartwell. This cost Harry dear; retiring soon after, he was awarded the basic Telegraph pension (a pittance) and not the larger discretionary sum given to the paper's loyal servants. Harry supplemented his pension as an usher at Bow Street magistrates' court until Conservative Central Office put him in charge of its press office.

At the back of the house, the Inland Revenue had belatedly stopped casual workers coming from their other jobs to sign on as "D. Duck" or "M. Mouse" and collect a day's pay tax-free for doing nothing. But other practices continued verging on the criminal, and managements connived at them. One night, Natsopa started picketing the *Express* over some grievance, real or imagined. Management paid them £15 a head to go and picket the *Telegraph* next door; our printers refused to cross the line, and the paper didn't come out. Another episode ended in tragedy. Security men at the *Mirror* noticed men in boiler suits in the loading bay who appeared, suspiciously, to be working, and the alarm was raised. The "workers" were in fact robbers after the *Mirror*'s payroll; shots were fired and a security guard was killed.

This Fleet Street culture survived well into the 1980s. The pace and nature of daily journalism were very different then, with no 24-hour television news, let alone a website to be updated. So were mobiles and pagers - which meant you could disappear for hours if you chose, at the risk of missing the big story. There were no papers on Good Friday, so you knew you could book theatre tickets for the evening before.

We were still using typewriters, and every line of copy was set by a "linotype" machine from a bath of hot metal. Photographers still sent film to a darkroom for processing, with the positives engraved on plates whose poor quality made pictures in the *Telegraph* look as if they had been taken through an old sock. Our printers, highly skilled in their craft, still managed to get the paper out against the clock as the circulation topped 1.4 million, and at night the building came alive with the throb of the presses. We could not imagine things any other way – but change had to come.

6. Six years in Sheffield

I loved living in Sheffield. My flat above Broomhill looked down into the city centre, and with binoculars I could read the cricket scoreboard at Bramall Lane. From the office there was a panorama of 18th-century streets, and beyond them Parkwood Springs - where some of the funniest scenes in *The Full Monty* were shot - and the Woodhead railway, with initially a multi-coloured boat train to Harwich. One day the interior was more interesting: a showman brought in a cuddly lion cub.

Seeking a job in newspapers, I had applied first to Westminster Press, publishers of the *Northern Echo,* I ruled out the *Oxford Mail,* having finished with universities, and Barrow because I had heard the chief sub had to take copy as there was no teleprinter. Their other papers didn't want me. I was also interviewed by Sir Alick Jeans, proprietor of the *Liverpool Echo,* in its awe-inspiring Victorian offices. His opening question was: "We have 200 graduates wanting to work here. Why should I choose you?" I stammered out something about enthusiasm and loyalty, but didn't impress.

One application - to Michael Finley, editor of the Sheffield *Morning Telegraph* - brought no reply. Then, just before finals, I got talking with Brian Holroyd, a mature theology student and pillar of ProngSoc. It turned out that Brian had been at school with Finley, and he was a terrible correspondent. I wrote again - and was called for an interview. Mike Corner, my mentor in Darlington three summers before, had just arrived as deputy news editor, and urged Finley to hire me.

Arriving for my interview, I was impressed by the modern city centre around Castle Square, its subterranean concourse lined with tanks of massive fish. (I would amuse city councillors by offering a prize to anyone who could tell me which of them the largest resembled.) Castle Square was created when the tramlines were torn up; three decades later it was filled in so they could be relaid.

This interview went well: Finley was youngish, enthusiastic and authoritative. I went home, bought a second-hand Singer Chamois, got my stuff together and late in August 1968 reported for work. I found digs, in a house at Totley owned by a sub on the *Star,* but only stayed a month as it was falling down. I moved on first to a ground-floor bedsitter in Nether Edge – where there was a daily race for my newspaper between me and an art student's cat, for very different reasons – then that spacious attic above Broomhill.

As the *Sheffield Telegraph* under its previous editor David Hopkinson, the paper had won a sackful of awards exposing the "Rhino Whip scandal" involving abuses by the city's police force, subsequently amalgamated with Rotherham's. It had been a broadsheet with a touch of the *Express*: urgent, populist but literate, but Finley concluded that with Sheffield's industrial base eroding, it had to broaden its appeal. There were already readers outside the city, served by reporters in Rotherham, Barnsley,

Chesterfield and later Doncaster and Worksop, with a scattering as far as the Lincolnshire coast. In 1966 Finley relaunched the paper as *Morning Telegraph*, with a less urgent typeface and greater out-of-town coverage. In the short term the revamp slowed the gentle slide in circulation, picking up a few distant readers at the expense of some Sheffielders who reckoned the paper was no longer for them. It also brought some American bloodstock advertising, through confusion with an eponymous New York racing paper. But the "Sheffield region" was not middle-class enough to sustain such a paper, and Finley's successor Michael Hides curbed the "Town and Country" page – with its photos of worthies with glass in hand - and adopted a punchier masthead.

Circulation continued to drift, and in 1986 the paper would fold. Three years later, the *Sheffield Telegraph* was reborn as a weekly, built around the Saturday property pages that had kept the morning paper afloat. For my first year I specialised in property: covering auctions (once being roped in as a pretend bidder), getting to know the city's estate agents and welcoming them one Friday night when they came to see the presses roll and take their pages home.

Our offices in York Street were newer than the *Northern Echo*'s: the newsroom covered an entire floor, and we shared it with our evening counterpart the *Star* which, with a circulation of 225,000 to our 65,000, was the dominant force. Again we had our characters, from the cynical, stranded in-house intellectual (the Anglo-Irish wordsmith Ian Sainsbury), to the fount of local knowledge: Peter Harvey, regarded throughout the city as a family friend. Peter was a tremendous mentor when I took on his old municipal beat, and when we re-established contact just before he died he was as calm, funny, insightful and modest as ever. Peter, Stuart Machin (the chief sub), and Keith Farnsworth (senior sports reporter) were all Sheffield born and bred, with little desire to ply their trade elsewhere.

Mike Corner became news editor, went on to edit the *Star*, then set up a PR firm in Sheffield, dying in harness in his early sixties. My graduate reporter contemporaries Paul Allen, who became a Radio

Four arts presenter and adapted *Brassed Off* for the stage; John Turnbull, an archdeacon's son who, with the BBC, would work alongside me in the Lobby; John Wyles, future Brussels correspondent of the *FT;* and Bob Bennett, our red-bearded Bristolian education correspondent. One afternoon Bob got a mysterious summons to the Students' Union. He hesitated ... but went, to be thrilled by Paul McCartney's first tryout of Wings, his new band after quitting the Beatles.

Brian Wesley, a zany young Boltonian who had come to Sheffield by way of Wolverhampton and went on to produce ITV's top variety shows, was our most enterprising reporter. Also destined for television was Clive Jones (now Sir Clive), who rose to be chief executive of Carlton – and David Cameron's boss - and chair the Disasters Emergency Committee.

Our cartoonist was Ralph Whitworth; a teddy bearish ex-Royal Marine with an eye for the absurd. After a professor declared that there was no such thing as being accident-prone, Ralph depicted a newsvendor with a placard telling the story ... and an elephant about to land on him. His finest moment came when Enid Hattersley, chairman of the Libraries & Arts Committee and mother of Roy, spoke so long in the city council that the meeting had to be abandoned. Next day's Whitworth showed a costermonger with a three-legged donkey shouting: "Oi! Mrs 'Attersley!" She did not appreciate the joke, but everyone else did.

On the sports desk we had the veteran tipster Len Ellis ("Fortunatus"), who at 77 topped the *Sporting Life* naps table. Collapsing in the office; he was carried out exclaiming: "Blue Flash for the 2.30!" - and it came in at 7-1. When Len's death was confirmed Benny Hill, our most cynical sports reporter, grunted to his boss David Jones, with whom he had never got on: "That's the first leg of my autumn double."

There were also several mountaineers, attracted to Sheffield by the Peak District's rockfaces. Tim Brown, killed years later when he slipped during a harmless clifftop walk, was the most extrovert, his irreverent wit upsetting our advertisers. The *Guardian* took Tim to task for having – according to the theatre's advertisements –

claimed that the comedy *Pyjama Tops* was "more sexually arousing than *Oh! Calcutta*". Outraged, Tim pointed out that he had in fact described *Oh! Calcutta* as "even less sexually arousing than *Pyjama Tops*".

The Telegraph & Star building boasted a high concentration of really attractive women. When the Lord Mayor put on a reception for the women of Sheffield she asked me to recommend which of the female staff to invite; I sweated at producing a cross-section of deserving (rather than stunning) employees, taking in the lower-profile departments, and in the process made myself very unpopular.

On the *Star*, I was close to Richard Redden and Gordon Ducker, passionate exiled Charlton supporters. Richard was in my very first digs, and went on to write Charlton's unofficial history; 45 years later we would fight parallel council elections in Bromley. Gordon went to the *Express* and as a reservist ran the RAF's press operation during the Gulf War. The congregation at his funeral was one-third Charlton red, one-third RAF blue and one-third civvies.

Although we competed with the *Star,* relations were civilised. One exception came the weekend of the first Moon landing. Working our skeleton Saturday shift, I couldn't help overhearing that they were onto something. After lunch, with their people gone apart from the *Green 'Un*'s sports desk, I answered the phone and realised the caller was filling in gaps in the story. And what a story it was.

A 14-year-old Sheffield schoolgirl had been accused of not paying a fine for soliciting in Middlesbrough, leaving the girl and her parents dumbfounded. It turned out that a classmate had run away to Teesside, gone on the game; and when arrested claimed to be her (until then) friend. The police made no checks as the other girl was prosecuted, and this innocent teenager found herself with a sleazy criminal record. I confirmed the details and wrote up the story with gusto; it led the back page, and but for the moon landing would have been the splash. The date on that historic edition was changed to 'Moonday', at the suggestion of an elderly messenger.

Sensing my frustration, Peter Harvey told me of the night he returned from a Watch Committee meeting about the Rhino Whip affair. He rushed in, panting: "I've got the splash. They've sacked the chief constable." Without missing a beat, the night editor replied: "No you haven't. Kennedy's been shot."

To clean up the force, Edward Barker, a military man, was brought in as chief constable. Soon after, a committee of MPs came to Sheffield to take evidence on relations between the police and the (then small) immigrant communities. Asked how he would sum things up, Barker replied insouciantly: "You can take it they get a fair crack of the whip."

Our own relationship with the Sheffield & Rotherham Constabulary - and indeed with Colonel Barker - survived one episode of strain. Shortly before I arrived, a Press Club opened in a city centre office block. It wasn't glamorous: two rooms with a bar (presided over by a formidable German lady), decorated with blown-up photos of England winning the World Cup and featuring a juke box which only seemed to play *Private Number* by William Bell and Judy Clay. It was a brave venture giving the finite number of journalists and their hangers-on in Sheffield (though we did have a few who commuted to Manchester) and before long the club, observing licensing hours that forced it to shut before many members finished work, ran into difficulties.

The committee, headed by Mike Corner, went to see the chief constable. They explained the club's dilemma, and his reaction was civilised: it was a gentlemen's club, and provided no other offences were committed he was prepared to turn a Nelson's eye. The club stayed open past midnight and business improved, as solicitors, clergy from the Cathedral and the occasional coachload of coppers returning from a rugby match swelled the numbers. Soon after the deal I became club secretary, but when I got married I decided to resign. There were no takers, so when the police raided the club one Saturday night late in 1971 my name was still on the letterhead. The Licensing Squad had been watching the club for some time; a colleague had been tipped off, but didn't pass on the hint. They went in to find 15 people nursing drinks; names were taken, and a few days later the committee, plus the drinkers, were invited to West Bar police station and charged. Mike alerted the arresting officers to his conversation with the chief constable, but they were unmoved.

One morning in February 1972 a dozen journalists, a couple of solicitors and several upright citizens crammed into the dock at Sheffield magistrates' court to answer charges of permitting alcohol to be served after hours, or of consuming it. Prosecuting us was Gerry Bermingham, an Irish-born solicitor who would become an incident-prone Labour MP. Gerry's brief was to get us convicted with minimum fuss; he produced policemen who testified that after permitted hours they had found drinkers consuming "an amber-coloured liquid that, on analysis, proved to be beer". Our solicitor, Adrian Molloy (a Labour councillor who sadly died young), called Mike and a colleague to swear that the chief had said he didn't give a monkey's what time we drank till provided we behaved ourselves. Eventually the magistrates fined the drinkers £5 each, and the committee £6 each with a conditional discharge. As we left, the head of the Licensing Squad muttered: "Bang goes my promotion."

Sheffield Newspapers Ltd took me on under indentures, a kind of three-year apprenticeship; in the event I stayed nearly six. My training involved a two-month course back in Darlington and a refresher at Richmond College, Sheffield, which was run like a school. The goal was the Proficiency Test, which I sat in Bradford. As a graduate I was illogically exempted from the papers on British Constitution and local government, but I did have to master newspaper practice, law for journalists and shorthand. Struggling with Pitman I switched to Teeline, a then new system designed for journalists, and secured my 100 words per minute certificate. Teeline has stood me in pretty good stead; 100 wpm is adequate for most purposes, but reporting the Commons I had to go a little faster.

My routine as a general reporter included producing "Today's Diary": meetings of the Non-Destructive Testing Society, talks at libraries on "Glorious Devon" by Mrs V M Wibberley, and Worksop Priory's Rayton Spur service; I imagined this a knightly ritual until

I discovered Rayton Spur was a housing estate. On late, I did the "calls" - ringing the region's police, fire and ambulance control rooms in case a story was developing. If one was, it usually involved a road accident and my next call was to a hospital, to be told the victim was "as well as can be expected" - a phrase devoid of meaning. Our need to cultivate the blue light services gave them an entree to the pre-release cinema showings put on for the film critics. The biggest turnout was for *Girl on a Motorcycle* starring Marianne Faithfull; 40 years on, I would discover we had been childhood playmates.

At the end of 1969, the paper invited readers to name their "Man of the Decade", and Enoch Powell, soon after his "Rivers of Blood" speech, emerged the likely winner. We were encouraged to vote for Bobby Kennedy in the hope of preventing this, but I bridled at thwarting the wishes of our readers, deplorable though they were.

There were only about four homicides a year in Sheffield, but they all seemed to happen on a Friday night. We had two editions, one that came off the presses soon after 10.30 and another around 1 am. There was usually just time to put a story together for the later edition, concentrating on the crime scene with a canvas awning over it and lighting powered by a generator. Another Friday night produced a man up a crane on a city centre building site. We got there as an officer with a loud-hailer called out: "Mr Simmonite, we've got your wife here." From way aloft, a voice came back: "Put the old bag underneath and I'll jump on her."

My first front-page lead was the collapse of the ITV mast at Emley Moor, halfway to Huddersfield, leaving thousands of viewers without programmes. My next caused me some heart-searching. My mother had invited Wilfred Hyde, son of the former minister at the Union Church, to Christmas lunch. Wilfred was a senior official at the Home Office, and I asked him why there wasn't a prison in the Sheffield area. He told me they were thinking of building one, and when I got back I rushed into print. It was years before the prison eventuated; in the meantime I rued a broken confidence.

There were always the little absurdities that make the British local paper a delight to read. Some were deliberate, like the photograph of a vine at Wath-Upon-Dearne which enabled one sub to fulfil a life-long ambition with the headline: "The Grapes of Wath." Some less so, like this paragraph in the *Star*: "Julie Smith, 23, of Pitsmoor was fined £5 by Sheffield magistrates yesterday for stealing an orange from the Sheaf Market. It was a Jaffa." Others betrayed a lack of local knowledge by new arrivals: Manor Top appeared as "Mannertop", and there was an occasional reference to the Coal Board's Minestrone Executive. A few were downright Rabelaisian. One resident was quoted complaining about the sewage works: "We had relations last week, and the smell was terrible."

Sheffield attracted minimal interest from the national media, football and - later - the rise of Seb Coe (to us "Sebastian Coe of Tapton School") apart. The nationals' Manchester editions shared the BBC's view that Northern news meant a pensioner run over in Oldham. Occasionally one of them would stage a circulation drive with a page of local news; the *Daily Express* did this with a month-long Wakefield promotion only to discover that every copy had been thrown into a canal by a disaffected van driver.

Nevertheless even in its prime, Sheffield's morning paper had been heavily outsold by the nationals, and we had to fight for readers. One boon for us was the appalling industrial relations in Fleet Street, and to a lesser extent in Manchester. When we suspected one of the nationals wouldn't be reaching us, one of our reporters would ring its circulation department, posing as a newsagent from Lincoln, and if they confirmed it we would put thousands of extra copies into fringe areas of Nottinghamshire and Lincolnshire, hoping a few readers would stay with us.

Later deadlines than the nationals, handy if a local story broke late on, were not always an advantage. On the night of the 1972 Munich Olympics massacre we went to press just as it seemed momentarily that the hostages were safe; the nationals, printed hours before, had a gloomier story matching the outcome.

In the summer of 1969 the nationals made hay as British Rail lost a series of dogs in its charge. Eventually a local boy returning from a family holiday in Margate had his pet mislaid. BR's Sheffield press officer rang to say the dog had been found and was on the train, and a photo opportunity was arranged. A local freelance filed – in advance - a story affectionately detailing the reunion, which the nationals duly carried. I went down to the station with a photographer to capture the moment: the train pulled in, and the guard brought out a dog the boy had never seen before.

While the national dailies were our competitors, we kept an eye open for stories we could sell to the popular Sundays – and once I thought I had one. A veterinary nurse friend told me how a male baboon had been brought in for minor surgery. When its anaesthetic wore off it made overtures to the vet, chasing him round the room until it could be tranquilised. I sent off the story to the *News Of The World*, to be told: "If only it had been a female baboon ... ".

One event I covered simply because I was there. The Rolling Stones' free concert in Hyde Park on 5 July 1969 marked the last crescendo of the innocence of the '60s. People crowded on the grass as far as the eye could see – 300,000 on some estimates - with not a trace of commercialism, just music. The concert was overshadowed by the death 48 hours before of Brian Jones, who had recently quit the group. Jagger dedicated it to Jones, whose replacement Mick Taylor was playing for the first time, and recited a poem by Shelley in his memory (not that we could hear it). Then we almost forgave an interminable support act and an abysmal sound system as Jagger launched into *Midnight Rambler*. Luckily it didn't rain.

For some reason I was despatched to interview the Beach Boys when they appeared in Sheffield. I asked why they had never released *Here Today* as a single (there had been a catchy Robb Storme cover) and Brian Wilson said it had never occurred to them. Then I told them we were organising a charity football match for Bangladesh flood relief (the press against the City Council) in one of the city's parks, and to my surprise two of them came along. The weather wasn't great and the attendance small, but they were friendly and signed a lot of autographs. I didn't see much of them as I was playing (wearing John Flynn's No. 4 United shirt), and, off the field, trying to keep a mother and daughter who were both dating one of my colleagues from meeting.

My final general news assignment, at the start of 1970, was the last scheduled passenger train through Woodhead tunnel. It reached Manchester too late to go back to Sheffield, and I and another passenger organised a sit-down in the stationmaster's office until a return train was provided. Just as well; at the moorland halt of Dunford Bridge we picked up two shivering Kiwi hikers unaware they had missed the last train to call there, ever.

My fellow troublemaker was the rumbustious Peter Fox, who went on to be a Lib Dem city councillor, and to found *Today's Railways*. I spent decades failing to get articles published in railway periodicals, and when in 2003 I had an idea for one, I e.mailed it to this new magazine. I got a friendly reply from Peter, reminding me of that night in Manchester, and have written for them ever since; sadly Peter died before his time in 2011.

When Mark Pickering succeeded Peter Harvey as municipal correspondent I became his deputy, concentrating on Sheffield City Council and its activities: housing, education, social services, buses, recreation, markets, libraries and arts, highways, refuse collection, public health, water, public works and much more. Before contracting-out and privatisation, the council employed 27,000 people. Heading this mighty organisation was an impressive team of chief officers, answerable to 81 councillors and 27 aldermen (elected by the councillors). And covering it was ideal preparation for a career in the Lobby ... not that I had one particularly in mind.

Sheffield is an overwhelmingly working-class city, and Labour had been in power since 1926. In 1967 the city had absorbed a sliver of north Derbyshire to build new council estates; this triggered an "all in, all out" election, each ward electing three councillors instead of the usual one, and Labour squeaked back. The next year was the nadir of the Wilson government's fortunes, and the Conservatives took control.

Any organisation under the same management for 40 years has weak spots, and the Tories found some. No outright corruption surfaced - though one committee chairman was surprised by the Christmas gifts that arrived - but quite a few absurdities came to light.

The Conservatives' leader was the genial but forceful Harold Hebblethwaite, but the sharpest Tory was Irvine Patnick, the builder son of a Jewish general dealer who was an institution in the city. As deputy chairman of the Housing Committee Irvine attracted more headlines than more senior colleagues, bursting into the Town Hall press room with a cry of "Sapristi!" to unveil some new daftness; he would go on to lead the opposition in what he termed the "Socialist Republic of South Yorkshire", and become MP for Hillsborough and a junior environment minister. When briefly off the council, Irvine was a star witness at planning inquiries, pointing out that some feature that technically rendered an ageing house unfit had been incorporated by the council into a prizewinning new development.

With no experience of office, the Tories made mistakes. Most costly politically was their decision - which today would be unavoidable on health grounds - to end free baccy for old folk in the council's homes. Labour played on this relentlessly, and regained control against the national trend in 1969 – going on to rule for 30 years until the Lib Dems briefly took control.

Two of the Tories quit the party and sat as Liberals. One, Mike Swain, spoke memorably in the debate on replacing the tiny Playhouse with the new theatre eventually named the Crucible; nobody then imagined it would become the Mecca of professional snooker. The Crucible's controversial feature was its "thrust stage", compared with the Playhouse's conventional proscenium arch; Swain told the council he was "not going to pay eight and sixpence to see Hamlet's backside."

Sheffield's imposing Victorian town hall housed the council chamber, committee rooms, several departments and the Lord Mayor's parlour. Once a month the council met in formal session, punctuated by high tea. Before it were the minutes of the month's committee meetings, on each of which the Lord Mayor would ask for "questions ... amendments ... observations." Tight control of the voting and of its members' participation was exerted by the ruling group, meeting beforehand; consequently the proceedings seldom dragged on, and most of the best copy came from the Opposition. The afternoon start of the session - and of all committee meetings – enabled members to miss as little work as possible, councillors then being unpaid. Fortunately for me, this meant that almost all decisions were reached after the *Star* hit the streets.

The council's "bible" was a small black diary listing the councillors, membership of committees and the monthly cycle of meetings. It noted each member's length of service (despite a shakeout of geriatric aldermen, one had been in harness since before the war), which ward they represented, their address and their occupation. With a horizontal borer, a universal miller and a centreless grinder, this underlined what made Sheffield tick, skilled manual workers outnumbering housewives, solicitors, accountants and salesmen. The few teachers, including the Education Committee chairman Peter Horton, worked outside the city as they could not serve on the council that employed them.

Sir Ron Ironmonger was the council's Labour leader, and the very best of his kind. He combined a gruff manner with a twinkle and led by consensus (the only time the group split was over whether to hold out to the last against the Heath government's legislation forcing up council rents). Although the most powerful man in the city, he matched his considerable presence with a complete lack of ego. He and his wife Jessie kept their unassuming house and he carried on working at GEC, though management moved him from a milling machine to a tiny office so he could deal with urgent business. But he never minded being rung at home, and when you heard his bark of "Ironmonger!" you knew he would be straight with you. When my *Star* counterpart Paul Potts and I left Sheffield, we took Ron and Jessie out to dinner with our wives, feeling we were leaving two friends behind. Ron went on to lead South Yorkshire County Council, but suffered a severe stroke soon after I joined the Lobby. He died in his fifties - a terrible loss.

David Blunkett saw Ron Ironmonger as his mentor. I first met David - then a Methodist local preacher - when he was a council candidate, and even then you could tell he was special. Quite apart from overcoming his blindness - with help from his then wife Ruth and his guide dog - David had authority, ability and a way with words that marked him out. Successful politicians are adept at remembering names and faces, but David had to memorise tones of voice; he has recognised mine in the unlikeliest places. We had an enjoyable evening with the Blunketts in that Broomhill flat; other guests included Francis Butler, the council's first elected Liberal since 1920. Another Labour councillor, Alf Meade, helped rewire the house we bought at Millhouses despite commuting to Dover; I never adequately compensated him.

Dominating the council were a group of aldermen who had overseen the city's post-war transformation. Patience Sheard, Lord Mayor when I arrived, chaired Social Services; she was the first to equate the ponderous Sidney Dyson with the giant fish in the Castle Square aquarium. Sidney, who had done away with the trams and privately regretted it, chaired Public Works; Isidore Lewis, finance director with Spear & Jackson, oversaw Finance; Harold Lambert, a pillar of the Co-op, handled Housing; Jim Sterland, a director of Sheffield United, had charge of Planning; and Jock Sturrock, a younger Scot, chaired Recreation.

Every committee met behind closed doors except Mrs Sheard's Clean Air Committee which included Sheffield's neighbours, and even this went into private session. She only had to say: "It is at this point ..." and we press filed out. During committees, we waited in the press room for anything up to three hours, before first the Conservatives came past to flag up anything controversial and then the Labour chairman – some more forthcoming than others - took us through the agenda. We emerged with plenty of copy, but the minutes when published often included major items we had not been told about. In 1974 the law changed to allow us in for all discussions not commercially sensitive. Even then, the real debate often took place in the Labour group.

The press room was tiny, with a shelf along one wall and three or four chairs. Occasionally both the *Telegraph*'s municipal staff would wait there, but generally one plus our counterpart on the

Star - Bob Poulton, a Norfolk man a little my senior, or Paul Potts. Paul, a Wednesdayite through and through, had joined straight from school. A tremendous colleague who at times acted as my conscience, Paul had a gift for getting on with people, on top of his manifest ability. It is a tribute to his professionalism and good nature than in more than four years competing against each other, with the dice loaded against the *Star* because of the time most council stories broke, we never had a cross word. Things didn't gel for Paul when he followed me to the *Daily Telegraph,* but he bounced back at the *News of the World*, going on to be deputy editor of the *Daily Express* and for 15 years editor-in-chief of the Press Association, probably the most prestigious job in the business. Radio Sheffield's Bob Simpson, later an outstanding BBC foreign correspondent, and the veteran *Yorkshire Post* reporter Roy Macleod, from the "holy city" of Rotherham, also came in. Roy was always worth listening to. I remember Paul asking him how as a Catholic he contemplated death; Roy unnervingly replied that it terrified him.

The Town Clerk, Denis Harrison, seemed a remote figure until we were thrown together on a town twinning visit to Donetsk. John Aldhous, who ran the massive Housing Department, came across as aloof until you realised his creative genius; he once allocated an "impossible-to-let" house next door to highly disruptive tenants to a family of deaf mutes. I particularly liked Jan Kot, the chief architect. When the Poulson affair broke, I asked him how Sheffield, almost alone in the region, had not fallen for the corrupt Yorkshire architect. He told me Poulson had tried, but "We gave him ze two fingers." As for the city treasurer, if he had anything to say he went to the *Star.*

Someone who usually rang me was the enthusiastic Peter Wigley, hired to sell Sheffield as a forward-looking city ripe for investment. Peter commissioned a promotional film, *Sheffield: City on the Move,* which decades later reached a global audience as the opening sequence in *The Full Monty* - which ironically highlighted the decline of Sheffield's heavy industries.

My contacts stretched from the council's time and motion man who would tell me over lunch of fresh absurdities he had uncovered, such as blind tenants having to pay for receiving television, to Brian Norfolk, tenants' chairman on Sheffield's most deprived estate. Brian's family home became my base for eye-opening tours of the Wybourn, from houses where door frames had been burnt for firewood to those where operatives from the prizewinning Public Works Department had signed off repairs not done - something I reported to an embarrassed Sidney Dyson.

Sidney may have got rid of Sheffield's trams, but I played a small part in their return. When Sheffield and Rotherham councils commissioned a Land Use Transportation Study, I kept close to the consultants and emerged with the exclusive story that the trams were coming back. Decision-making being what it is in this country, it took 21 years for the first Supertram to run.

The council was still trying to replace "unfit" terrace housing with modern developments, though no longer gargantuan ones like the Park Hill and Hyde Park flats. New roads were also planned, notably the Parkway linking the city centre with the M1. I became a regular at public inquiries, coming to realise which aspects of a scheme – say, a slip road - had been included so they could be sacrificed to objectors to get the project through. A local named John Tym began delivering copious objections; with an "e" added to his surname, he would disrupt inquiries into road schemes up and down the country.

For new developments, I regularly checked the Town Hall register of planning applications. There I discovered a proposal to replace Viners' cutlery works, then very much a going concern, with an office block. Paul Potts and I went to see the Viner family, who assured us the application must have been lodged by a speculative third party. Soon after, Viners switched production to Korea.

My first ceremonial assignment for the paper was to accompany Patience Sheard when she called on the city's oldest resident. As she pecked him on the cheek, the frail old gentleman went into an apparent seizure; momentarily I envisaged the headline "Lord Mayor's kiss of death", but he recovered. A colleague was less fortunate: arriving at an old folk's home in Nottingham where a record third resident had just had their telegram from the Queen, she was told: "Sorry, duck, we're back to two again."

My DJ came in for heavy use attending civic dinners. During one at the Cutlers' Hall, the Conservative Lord Mayor Kenneth Arnold launched an intemperate attack on the press for some perceived slight. They got their own back when he was caught watering his lawn during a hosepipe ban. On the plus side, Arnold was up for it when Mike Corner suggested he challenge the mayor of Rotherham to a round of golf, with me and my Rotherham colleague Colin Birch as caddies; it made an excellent picture story.

Of the numerous civic receptions, two stick in my mind. One was for United when they clinched promotion, the players warily sipping orange juices on one side of the room and starstruck local worthies something stronger on the other. The other was for civic leaders from Bochum, Sheffield's twin city on the Ruhr (the other being Donetsk). When one Bochum councillor asked Jock Sturrock if he had ever been there, Jock managed not to reply that he had flown over it in a Liberator.

While the Lord Mayor changed yearly, the macebearer, Stan Cooper, was a fixture, immaculately uniformed and ready to bellow: "Pray silence for his/her right worshipful the Lord Mayor!" at the right moment. He was marvellous at finding people for the press to talk to and became a celebrity in his own right; but when one new Lord Mayor felt overshadowed, he went.

One plum assignment was the council's annual tours of inspection. The Water Committee inspected reservoirs, the Transport Committee bus garages, and the Markets Committee the civic abattoir. This was clean and efficient but not for the squeamish, and as we lunched afterwards at a Peak District hotel, one councillor fainted. The chairman asked: "Is there a doctor in the house?" forgetting that the Medical Officer of Health was present. Dr Clifford Shaw was one of two medics I dealt with, trying to extract news from his annual report excitingly titled *Aspects of Prophylaxis.* The other was Alan Usher, the Home Office pathologist; when his lab was demolished for road widening, the subs sadly rejected my suggested headline: "Fall of the House of Usher".

At the end of 1972 I took over from Mark Pickering as municipal correspondent, inheriting a weekly column. This was a challenge, but the spread of the council's activities and the rich canvas of personalities gave me plenty of material. And my scope broadened as reorganisation hove into sight.

Local government then was an archaic patchwork. Sheffield, Barnsley, Doncaster and Rotherham had all-purpose county borough councils, the areas between being covered by borough, urban and rural councils (some extremely small) with the West Riding County Council providing social services, education, police and fire services. The county covered a vast area resembling a string vest, having no responsibility over the cities and larger towns within it.

Whitehall decided a structure was needed combining economies of scale with an ability to plan strategically, rather like the Greater London Council formed from a similar ragbag in the 1960s. (Toward the end of my time in Sheffield I applied for a job in the GLC press office. My ambition to work in Grandfather's County Hall evaporated as my interviewer patronisingly explained that experience of a city of a mere half-million inhabitants was irrelevant where London was concerned. In the end, I deliberately blew the interview.)

Edward Heath handed the task of reviewing the structure for England outside London to Peter Walker. Early in 1971 I attended a Department of the Environment briefing in Nottingham where, to my astonishment, a senior official virtually read out Walker's yet-to-be-published White Paper - and as the only daily reporter there, I had the story to myself. I broke it next day under the headline "Yorkshire to have South Riding". The south of the West Riding, centred on Sheffield, was to have a GLC-type metropolitan council, with the smaller units merged into metropolitan districts based on Barnsley, Doncaster and Rotherham. Sheffield would lose to the county its fire service, social services, waste disposal, and water and buses to separate new authorities, but would gain a necklace of neighbouring communities, notably the growing Derbyshire commuter town of Dronfield.

The main objections came from the Dronfields, which resented being swallowed up, and cities like Nottingham which would lose more powers than Sheffield and become districts under a "shire" council. Dronfield stayed out after Sir Ron decided absorbing it would be more trouble politically than it was worth, but the basics stuck.

With elections set for May 1973 and the new authorities taking over the following April, I started covering neighbouring councils to ascertain who might matter in the new set-up. My visit to Doncaster identified several heavy hitters; my evening at Stocksbridge brought a protest from our correspondent there. Mike Corner told him with relish that if he depended on us for his income, he should apply for National Assistance. I already covered Nottinghamshire County Council meetings , and was co-opted onto its advisory panel on explaining the new set-up to the public.

When the new councils were elected, Labour took a stranglehold on South Yorkshire and its four districts. The first decision taken, to site County Hall in Barnsley, was pushed through the Labour group by councillors who did not want power concentrated in Sheffield. After that fait accompli I made a regular 16-mile trek to Barnsley for council and committee meetings as the county prepared to take on its powers. The new South Yorkshire Metropolitan County Council launched a public information campaign and I was asked to help. A pamphlet I drafted included the inaccurate statement that Ralph Vaughan Williams had been born at Hooton Roberts, near Rotherham; he had only lived there for a time, and there was some uncomfortable comment in the *Guardian*.

This new order – which would be abolished by the Thatcher government in 1986 - brought big changes for Sheffield. Sir Ron moved to the county council and was replaced by George Wilson, an amiable but shambolic upholsterer. The abolition of aldermen removed wise old heads as well as dead wood. And the further "all in, all out" election at the nadir of the Heath government's popularity brought in a flood of young Labour councillors reflecting the militancy that was starting to pervade the party grassroots and would culminate in the hard Left's capture of the council, and internecine warfare nationally.

The handover in April 1974 went smoothly, apart from the new Passenger Transport Executive changing the numbers of several bus routes without warning. Sheffield City Council held a moving final meeting. with a vote of thanks to the press for its coverage over the years. The one messy area was planning: the split between tiers was not clear-cut, and costly duplication in staffing occurred. Nationally, the merry-go-round of chief officers as councils were abolished and new ones created pushed up salary costs.

By the autumn of 1973 I had been in Sheffield five years. I loved the city, but knew I would have to move on. Bill Tadd at the *Daily Telegraph* suggested I wait until after my assignment to Donetsk that autumn, then send him my cuttings. I had barely done this when I found myself on strike.

Relations between the NUJ chapel and *Telegraph & Star* management had been deteriorating for some time, because of tightening control over costs and poor chemistry between Tom Watson, the former *Star* editor who ran the company, and the father of the Chapel, Mike Bower, industrial correspondent of the *Star* and a future city council leader. I was active in the union myself - and am now a life member, though I have despaired at times at the NUJ's posturing over trendy causes when it should have been protecting its members. Mark Pickering - whose mild manner masked a pretty radical mindset - served on the union's national executive, and I became chapel clerk, keeping minutes of our meetings. These were held in the office during working hours; only if they dragged on did management term them "disruptive".

I cannot remember what the strike of November 1973 was about, or how it began. With tension rising, we had imposed some restrictions. One was a ban on reporters taking copy, to protect the copytakers' jobs - on the face of it a sensible move. I fell foul of it myself: calling from Donetsk after waiting ages for a line to find the copytakers had gone, I asked a colleague to take down my story so it would get in the paper, and on my return was given a reprimand.

Soon after, I returned from holiday to find pickets outside the building, and the chapel in session in the T&G union office next door. Messages went off to management and were sent back. Labour councillors staged a demo when some of us appeared in the gallery during a council meeting, Ken Arnold rebuking all concerned. Clever things were said and attitudes struck, but the papers kept coming out. The printers carried on working, and so, ironically, did the firm's drivers who belonged to the T&G – though the smaller United Road Transport Union did back us. We thought we had cut off the supply of newsprint, then found it was being delivered to a barn owned by a friendly judge and brought in by Land Rover one reel at a time.

Two weeks into the strike, we were getting lukewarm support from the NUJ, and more critically not getting paid. Our meetings grew tetchier, then we discovered that a dozen colleagues were planning to go back. To me that settled things: all we could do was try for face-saving concessions, then return with the "dirty dozen". A hard core wanted to hold out, but we told management our intentions and secured minimal concessions; when it became clear these would not be fully honoured, I abstained on the return to work.

We worked hard to win back readers as the three-day week kicked in, with a giant generator installed in the loading bay, but it was clear grim times lay ahead. Early in 1974 Bill Tadd wrote offering me a job, and on 3 June I reported for work in Fleet Street ... as Carrie's birth announcement appeared in the paper.

Happily, my connection with Sheffield didn't end there. I came back on stories, surprising former colleagues. I was ordered out of the Hallam Tower hotel at 7 am because of a bomb scare - only to receive an alarm call when I got back. I was at the McDonald's Games at the Don Valley Stadium when Jan Zelesny broke the world javelin record, and more recently have come up for meetings at *Today's Railways*, and caught up with old colleagues not seen for decades. Then there's the football.

Sheffield Wednesday traditionally drew its support more from workers at the city's big steel and engineering firms, Sheffield United from the "little mesters", whose workshops were closer to Bramall Lane. Wednesdayites predominate in the north of the city, and United's supporters in the south. Stories abound of the Unitedite lorry driver who always closed his eyes passing Hillsborough, and Wednesdayites who won't eat bacon on match days because of its red and white stripes. I once met a Wednesdayite builder devastated after finding a dead owl in a fireplace; days later the Owls (named after the ground's location near Owlerton, not the bird) were relegated. But my favourite tale was of how Wednesday's goalkeeper threw himself in front of a bus after a bad game ... and it went under him. Yet while the passions run deep, the banter is good natured and at derby matches there is rarely any trouble.

I arrived in Sheffield with memories fresh of the 1966 World Cup matches at Hillsborough. Wednesday were then the city's top dogs so I watched them first, impressed by the huge, seething open-air Kop, topped by an electronic scoreboard where United's score flashed up every 15 minutes to a predictable reaction. The club's greatest legend, Derek Dooley, had lost a leg after an injury at Preston in 1954, but fought back to become Wednesday's manager until being sacked, on Christmas Eve of all days, as the club was hit by a mystery virus. Dooley would cross over to United, take on its commercial side and eventually chair the club: a modest man and a fine advertisement for the game.

I sensed that something else at Hillsborough wasn't right when I stood in a swaying crowd at the Leppings Lane end. There were steep steps up from the back, a narrow crest without any crush barriers, then terracing down to the pitch; it seemed inevitable someone would lose their footing and get trampled. Twenty-six years later, at precisely that spot, a surge of Liverpool fans let into an already packed terrace by negligent policing would bring disaster.

It was March 1969 before I went to Bramall Lane, seeing recently-relegated United lose 3-2 to Blackpool (50 years later I was there to see us lose to Bristol City by an identical score). Arthur Rowley had been brought in as manager and the long-serving John Harris moved upstairs, but the team seemed listless. Wearing my property hat I lunched John Hassall, a housebuilder and United's chairman, who told me Rowley would have to go. Weeks later he did - and Harris returned to build the side that won promotion in 1971, and for a dizzy autumn topped the League with a breathtakingly open style of football built around Tony Currie.

I knew at once that Bramall Lane was the place for me. The ground was more workaday than Hillsborough and the open fourth side with its cricket pavilion an anachronism, but the atmosphere on the Shoreham Street kop was keener. Catching the United bug threw me together with my Catweazle-like *Star* colleague Mike Burnham, an outstanding graphic artist in the days when it was all done the hard way. Mike designed United's programme for a decade, and was close to the players without breaking confidences. His sense of humour was invaluable as we travelled to Blackburn, Derby and even Portsmouth – on the day of the Ibrox disaster, which we heard about on an interminable train journey home.

United had exciting players: John Tudor, a Shearer-like striker (in looks rather than finishing, as Newcastle fans would discover); the stylish Colin Addison, who would mastermind Hereford's epic defeat of Newcastle; and the late Alan Woodward, a winger who scored direct from corner kicks. But Currie was the star, with his long blond hair and his shirt outside his shorts, blowing kisses at the crowd as they chanted "Currie for England!" Tough in the tackle, he was a master of the inch-perfect long pass. His greatest goal was against Liverpool; Len Badger took the ball up the right to the halfway line, then passed to Currie in the centre circle; he trapped it, then fired in a shot Ray Clemence hardly saw. Close second came a solo effort against Leeds, when he ran half the length of the pitch to shoot past Gary Sprake. It was tragic to read years later that Currie played when unfit because he was so keen to get on the pitch, and that he made no money out of the game. His aching limbs forced him to retire after spells at Leeds, QPR (whom he captained in the 1982 Cup Final replay) and Torquay; but

United staged a testimonial match for him, then took him back as an ambassador. At a pre-match lunch a few years back, TC nudged me in the ribs and asked if there was a dumpling left.

Promotion to the top flight was clinched against Cardiff on 27 April 1971. Over 43,000 crammed into the Lane to create an atmosphere I can still taste. Billy Dearden scored early on, but Cardiff equalised and it took a rare header from Currie to give us a 2-1 lead. Roared on in the second half, United took Cardiff apart. John Flynn powered in a header and Dearden would add a fifth, but the goal of the night came from Gil Reece: the little Welsh winger ran twenty yards sidestepping two defenders to crack the ball into the net.

On an August night at Highbury, we faced the side that had won the League and Cup double. Woodward scored in the seventh minute and the defence, superbly marshalled by Eddie Colquhoun, held out. Next day Mike Burnham produced a cartoon of a smouldering artillery piece with a shattered barrel. And the national press began to take notice.

After ten games we were still unbeaten, and five points clear at the top. Then came our biggest test: at Old Trafford. We streamed over the Snake Pass to experience a real sense of occasion. The Stretford End was being rebuilt and 20,000 people were locked out, with young lads standing on walls keeping them up with play; there would be a roar in the ground ... then seconds later another outside. We matched Manchester United in every department until the final ten minutes, when George Best destroyed us. He took the ball down the right, forced wider and wider, then just as his chance seemed to have gone fired in an unstoppable shot. Alan Gowling scored a second, and we at last had been beaten.

Next, we lost 3-2 to Stoke at home, with the decisive moment a rare penalty miss from Woodward, overawed by facing Gordon Banks. From then on, it was a roller-coaster. We trounced Ipswich 7-0, then lost 5-1 at Crystal Palace. Arsenal won their return fixture, Alan Ball taunting Currie by sitting on the ball, and Cardiff got their revenge in the Cup. We had come down to earth, but we had made our mark and still finished tenth.

Subsequent seasons brought more unforgettable moments: Peter Osgood blasting over from two feet out, and a return fixture with United: a 1-1 draw before 45,045 on an Easter night with the entire Kop chanting:

> "Georgie Best, superstar
> Carries a handbag and wears a bra."

The evening before, I had taken Deborah to dinner at the Hallam Tower; we had barely sat down when in came Busby, Best, Charlton and the rest.

Players came and went, and Ken Furphy succeeded John Harris. During the 1972 miners' strike some matches were played on weekday afternoons, before half the normal crowd. I stood on the terracing with Norman Cole, local secretary of NALGO, putting the world to rights.

Despite my lack of footballing skills, I played in two charity matches - both on park pitches, with the enjoyment greater than the proceeds. The first, the Beach Boys came along to. The other, between the Telegraph & Star and Radio Sheffield, made other waves. The secretary of Sheffield and Hallamshire FA was walking his dog when he happened on an unregistered match involving the FA's regional coach and the future Wednesday manager Howard Wilkinson - who marked me out of the game - with a League referee in charge. Several people were given a warning.

By 1975 Bramall Lane's pavilion had gone, a new stand obliterating the hallowed Yorkshire square. Defeats set in and I flew out to Washington with United relegated; in seven years they would slide all the way to the Fourth Division. Though I seldom got to Bramall Lane in those days, I was there the emotional Saturday after the sinking of HMS *Sheffield* – the "Shiny Sheff" – during the Falklands War.

Dave Bassett took us back to the top flight in 1990; one glorious day we thumped Leicester 5-2 at Filbert Street as Wednesday were relegated (and Essex scored over 700). And three years later came a Cup semi-final against Wednesday.

After protests over staging a Sheffield derby at any ground where thousands would have been locked out, the FA switched it to

Wembley and, armed with the *Daily Record*'s press ticket, I headed for the Twin Towers. Wednesdayites were blasé about the walk up Wembley Way, but I was just thrilled to be there. I collected my box lunch, then sat at one of a row of slanting desks, taking notes in case the *Record* wanted a piece (they didn't) and doing my best not to appear a "fan with typewriter", the damaging epithet that has haunted reporters following Scotland's national team. We lost 2-1, and I was left wondering if this was the nearest to a Cup final I would get. So far it has been – though I was at the new Wembley for our 5-3 semi-final defeat by Hull City in 2014.

Our founder-membership of the Premier League ended traumatically in 1994. Ten minutes from time at Stamford Bridge we were winning 2-1 and set to finish 16th. Then Chelsea scored twice, Everton turned the tables on Wimbledon in a game that would interest a libel jury, and I emerged from a friend's wedding to the cruellest of disappointments.

It took Neil Warnock to rebuild the team around Phil Jagielka, as I bought shares in the club. In 2003 we reached the semi-finals of the League Cup and FA Cup, but choked in the play-off final against Wolves. Promotion took three more years, and John and I were at the decisive match against Hull.

We went ahead against Liverpool in our first game back in the Premier League, then Stevie Gerrard won a dodgy penalty. We beat Arsenal at home and Newcastle away – but missed two penalties against Blackburn, gave away silly home points and went through the motions away to the top sides. We still looked safe, but West Ham were gaining on us thanks to Carlos Tevez, whose controversial signing a League tribunal had refused to penalise by deducting points, assuming they were down anyway. And on the final day we needed a point at home to Wigan to stay up.

Months before, I had a vivid dream. We were playing Wigan, and David Unsworth – who Warnock had let go after missing one of those penalties against Blackburn – scored the winner for them. On the day I searched for a betting shop to put £200 on Wigan; strangely, my local Ladbroke's had closed for good the night before. I watched transfixed on a friend's computer with a party going on around me as we fell behind, equalised ... then went down to a penalty from Unsworth.

Since then we have tumbled into League One, then fought our way back to the Premier League under Chris Wilder, holding sixth place when Covid struck, then crashing out again the following season. But my hopes are undimmed.

7: Carnage in Birmingham

Birmingham in 1974 seemed tired. Big names like BSA and Triumph were on their knees. British Leyland was about to go bust as one strike followed another. The city's ethnic diversity – a Brummie being "an Irishman with a leek in his turban" – had yet to be seen as a strength. And unnervingly the IRA had embarked on a bombing campaign.

Yet the seeds of revival were being sown with the imaginative National Exhibition Centre, promoted in the face of indifference from Whitehall. Its success would create a climate for redevelopment of Birmingham's canalside, the promotion of Symphony Hall and the revival of the Jewellery Quarter. No sane person would have suggested staging a global summit in the Birmingham of 1974. But by 1992 when John Major welcomed

European leaders and, still more, 1998 when Tony Blair hosted the G8, the city could be credible on the world stage.

However Brum was an important centre for the media. The BBC had a large operation at Pebble Mill, and ATV - fiefdom of the one and only Lew Grade - was a strong creative force. BRMB was among the best of the new commercial radio stations (though I did once hear a conversation between its "agony uncle" and a man contemplating suicide interrupted by a commercial for High Speed Gas). The *Birmingham Post,* with its evening and Sunday counterparts, occupied a confident modern tower, and almost all the national papers had a reporter in Brum. Though always out for exclusives, members of the "ring" worked together on many stories, meeting every lunchtime in the Bodega Bar unless there were major developments out of town.

One August morning, I parked my Avenger on the disused platform at Snow Hill station - since reopened - and made for the *Telegraph*'s office in the *Post* tower. Its main role was commercial; there was an avuncular advertising manager, Chris Brown, a sales rep, Dave Robinson, and an excellent secretary, Fiona Daly. Chris had been in the Scots Guards; when I asked when he had been most in danger, he replied: "After D-Day, with the French shooting at us because they were upset the Germans had gone." Dave had a marvellous turn of phrase; when a hot air balloon crashed in sight of his window, I had to quote his comment that it "fell like a sausage".

My priorities were to join the Ring - who made me welcome - get my office functioning, bone up on issues I would be covering and start making contacts. I also had to charge out on stories, learning as I went. Early on, the desk despatched me to Long Lartin high-security prison in Worcestershire, after two inmates tried to escape. Having filed, I was ordered back to find out more and was physically removed from the jail - surely a first, though my reworked story did read better.

I joined the media huddle outside Longbridge - usually because of a strike, once to view the upgraded Allegro production line - toured the Meriden motorcycle co-operative with Tony Benn, and stood at the back as Benn and Roy Hattersley addressed BSA workers facing redundancy. I came out to find a yellow wire protruding from under my car, and as there were two Cabinet ministers nearby I alerted a policeman. The Bomb Squad screeched up, and presented me with ... a length of yellow wire.

Before driving in to work, I went through the *Post* and a dozen national papers to spot stories worth following up. On a rare quiet day I would go to WH Smith's and buy a sheaf of local weeklies, checking for stories I could develop. One, tucked away on an inside page, told how the new stand at Worcester racecourse had everything except a proper view of the track. Another concerned escapes by baboons and sealions from the West Midlands Safari Park at Bewdley. Having infiltrated the park with a photographer for a "tourism feature", I described how council workers encountered sealions in a trench they were digging, and baboons staged a mass breakout by sneaking round a lorry at a checkpoint. I couldn't resist adding that locals were expecting a card from Switzerland saying two of the baboons had made a successful "home run". The baboons can't have liked the story: when over 20 years later I revisited the park, they stripped the rubber trim from my sun roof.

Weeks after I arrived, Harold Wilson called an election and I had to juggle breaking news with constituency profiles. But nothing during the campaign matched the furore surrounding Sir Keith Joseph's speech at Birmingham's Grand Hotel nine days after the Conservatives' defeat. I found him in the lobby, trying to explain to a growing number of hacks that it wasn't as provocative as the advance headlines - that he would call for the feckless poor to be sterilised - suggested. He then delivered the speech, declaring that "our human stock is threatened" while apologising once more for saying it. Then, as we queued for the payphone to file our stories, Sir Keith came out again to insist he was being misunderstood. The next morning's headlines were just what he had feared.

Next came (though I didn't let on) my first major court case: a two-week obscenity trial in a packed Birmingham Crown Court. It concerned films (no DVDs then) seized by police in

Wolverhampton, and the defendants ranged from market traders to John Lindsay, a former *Glasgow Herald* photographer who had shot them. One had been filmed in a school locker room; police spotted a towel lettered GHAM ED and showed a clip to every head teacher in Birmingham and Nottingham; the astonished head of Aston Manor school identified his janitor and a former head boy among the cast.

The evidence was given added flavour by the deadpan yet censorious tone of prosecuting counsel as he quoted the movies' highly explicit sales material. We learned quite a lot, one defendant explaining that he was a "stand-by" in case another male performer ran out of steam.

I quickly realised that representing the *Telegraph* gave me the edge over my rivals: as long as the language was deadpan, I could get the most lurid details into the paper. While our Page 3 might not match the *Sun*'s for pictorial content, it could get away with a far more riveting read. Even so, it was the *Sun*'s photographer who nursed a groin injury after snapping one of the accused leaving court.

Mr Justice Wien, a dry Welshman, decided that the jury should see the films. The public was admitted too - two members of the Mothers' Union - and the press. Led (I forebore from reporting this) by W G Wanklyn of the *Birmingham Post,* we filed into the Grand Jury Room to find a police inspector working the projector. The films, though amateurish, were certainly explicit. After viewing three of the seven, the judge called an adjournment and drew hard on his pipe. Halfway through the fifth, entitled *Anal Rape,* I reported, "the judge was seen to remove his wig". This phrase so delighted Peter Eastwood that he had me hauled out of court to give me a £700 a year pay rise.

Into the second week, a psychiatrist testified that the films featuring only women were particularly therapeutic. Wien could maintain his stony facade no longer, asking: "Dr Hayward, am I to understand that you prescribe lesbianism on the National Health Service?"

The jury disagreed over some charges, acquitted some of the accused and left those who pled guilty wishing they hadn't. Months later, the Met prosecuted Lindsay over the same films, but Wells Street magistrates threw out the charges on the ground that he had already been tried. Before that hearing, I had a friendly interview with Lindsay and his wife in their Hampstead flat.

That November, one of the most extraordinary political stories of modern times broke with reports that John Stonehouse, a former Labour Postmaster-General just re-elected for Walsall North, had drowned off Miami; his clothes were found on the beach. The Ring smelt a rat, and so did Stonehouse's colleagues, not least Walsall South's Bruce George who had a flat in the same Westminster block. The cleaner told Bruce: "Isn't it a shame, and him with that lovely young dark-haired wife too." Stonehouse's wife, though attractive, was middle-aged and blonde, but his secretary Sheila Buckley was indeed young and dark-haired, and in on the plot. Speculation in the Bodega mounted; one colleague suggested Stonehouse might be in La Paz, and astonishingly it turned out he did have contingency plans to go there. But on Christmas Eve, five weeks after his disappearance, Stonehouse was arrested in Australia. He was charged with fraud over his business activities and eventually sent to jail, in the meantime embarrassingly turning up at the Commons to make speeches on penal policy.

One December Sunday I was despatched to Edwalton, outside Nottingham: an old people's home had burnt down overnight, with heavy loss of life. Barbara Castle, the Social Services Secretary, came to tour the charred ruins, meet survivors and review the situation with civic leaders, several of whom I knew. The scale of the tragedy guaranteed front-page coverage, but we all missed a further story, revealed only when Mrs Castle published her diaries: her flaming red wig caught on a dangling wire, and she managed to slap it back on before anyone noticed.

Intrusion into private grief could be unavoidable. I faced it covering the inquest at Banbury into the suicide of Patrick Crossman, the schoolboy son of Richard, who had died of cancer months before. Crossman's *Government and the Governed* was one of Fred Fox's essential texts, but my opinion of him fell after he raised NHS charges on the day of the 1969 council elections, costing Labour hundreds of seats. All such feelings evaporated as I saw Anne Crossman arrive, devastated by the loss of her husband and now her son. Thirty-three years later I would write her obituary for the *Telegraph;* she was a woman to admire.

I experienced another family's heartache after the kidnapping in January 1975 of 17-year-old Lesley Whittle from her home at Highley, Shropshire. At a late-night police press conference we were briefed that Lesley had been abducted and a ransom demand for £50,000 received. DCI Bob Booth, heading the investigation, told us what we could and could not report if they were to get Lesley back alive. We filed, then a couple of us mounted what we hoped was an unobtrusive watch on a phone box in Kidderminster where a further call was expected. I did wonder whether Lesley's abductor might have spotted us and aborted, but in fact her brother Ron, owner of a local coach company, missed the rendezvous. For several days the Ring operated from the pub at Highley as Lesley's family hoped against hope for her safe return. I never spoke with them, but one colleague returned from the house with a moving appeal from Mrs Whittle to be left alone, only for us to find after we had filed that it was an embroidering of less dramatic quotes obtained at second hand.

As the hunt continued, Lesley's captor was christened the Black Panther, on account of his balaclava and his commando-like ability to move around undetected. Identikit pictures bore a passing resemblance to Ron Whittle, who the police knew was not implicated as he had been with them when the ransom demand was received. They urged us not to mention the likeness, as it was impeding the inquiry. An *Express* reporter new to the story went big on it, and I was hauled out of bed by the news desk. They agreed we shouldn't follow the *Express*; so instead I filed a story saying Ron Whittle had offered to take part in an identity parade, but the police had declined.

After a couple of weeks we moved on to other stories, knowing we would be back - and in early March Lesley's body was found in a storm drain at Kidsgrove. It was December 1975 before Donald Nielson was arrested after a post office shooting in Mansfield; he was given five life sentences and died in jail in 2011. The police had known everything about him except his name; the moment he was in custody it was obvious he was the Black Panther. The Whittles were left with their grief; years later Ron Whittle was elected president of the Omnibus Society - well-earned recognition for the progressive business he ran.

My final day in Birmingham, I was instructed to "get over to Grimsby" as we had been tipped off about an imminent fishermen's strike. I got there around 6 pm in drizzle and fading light, not a soul around and nothing about it on the radio or in the evening paper. Telling the desk I couldn't stand the story up wasn't an option so I headed for Cleethorpes, reckoning the sea air would clear my head. Parking on the seafront, I picked out in the gloom a solitary figure walking his dog ... who turned out to be the chairman of the strike committee. By seven o'clock I was dictating my exclusive to a copytaker, and next morning I was part of a media throng as the fishermen tried to blockade Immingham docks.

The IRA's bombing campaign took advantage of Birmingham's large Irish community, into which an active service unit could disappear. Initially it only seemed intended to frighten, though the wife of the Sports Minister Denis Howell was lucky to survive an explosion when she started her car. Then, on the evening of 14 November 1974, Belfast-born James McDade blew himself up trying to bomb Coventry telephone exchange.

The Archbishop of Birmingham refused to allow the funeral, so McDade's remains were flown to Dublin, baggage handlers in Belfast having blacked it. In the coffin were 32 plastic bags, McDade having been identified only by his thumb; one police officer joked that when his head was found, he still had his fingers in his ears. And on the evening of 21 November - having moved into a bigger house on the Bournville estate that day because we couldn't get Carrie's pram through the door of the first - I drove to Birmingham Airport to cover the departure.

No sooner had the plane taken off than an assistant chief constable told us: "Bombs have gone off in the centre of Birmingham. There are bodies." I alerted the office and headed for the scene. At 8.17 pm, six minutes after a warning telephoned to the *Birmingham Post*, two bombs had exploded in bars packed with young drinkers: the Mulberry Bush, on the ground floor of the Rotunda close to New Street station, and the Tavern In The Town cellar bar. Their impact was heightened by the confined space: 19 people were killed outright - two dying later in hospital - and nearly 200 injured, many horrendously; one barman had a chair leg driven straight through him.

I arrived soon after ten. Passing the police headquarters, I saw teams of grim-faced detectives bursting from the revolving doors. Heading for the police cordon around the Rotunda, the steady stream of ambulances was my first indication of the scale of the carnage; what I had picked up on the car radio did not prepare me. Astonishingly New Street station was still open, and inside I found a row of telephone boxes. I had barely got through to the office and heard that my colleague Ken Clarke was on the way up (by taxi, his car having been boxed in) when a soldier appeared. "I wouldn't stay here if I were you, Sir," he said. "We're looking for another one right over your head." I hung up. There was indeed a third bomb, but two miles away; made safe by a controlled explosion, it was similar to the pub bombs - and seven others planted in Birmingham, Coventry and Wolverhampton over the previous fortnight. I filed from somewhere safer, then headed for a midnight police briefing, giving the location of the targets and a first guess at casualties. I linked up with Ken, and around 2.30 am, with our last copy away, brought him home – to sleep among unpacked boxes.

Next morning the enormity began to sink in; after the Islamist London bombings of 7 July 2005, the Birmingham pub blasts remain the worst terrorist atrocity on the British mainland, and the IRA's deadliest attack anywhere (the Omagh bomb of 1998 was the work of dissidents).

I had three stories to work on: the suffering of the victims and their families, the outrage of the community, and the hunt for the bombers. The hospitals held a graphic press conference, civic and community leaders coupled demands for a crackdown on pro-IRA activity with appeals to the public not to take the law into their own hands, and the police appealed for evidence.

Well before sunset that second evening, a tangible darkness hung over the city centre - a darkness of the soul. Home Secretary Roy Jenkins, a Birmingham MP, was greeted by demonstrators chanting "Bring back the rope!" and there were a handful of attacks on Irish-owned businesses; but the vast majority came together in their grief. Hundreds turned out for the funerals – Catholic (several of the victims were Irish), Protestant, Hindu, Sikh – and thousands for a memorial service organised by motor industry shop stewards. Prince Philip visited, with compassion and dignity. Pubs imposed tight security, with every drinker frisked - a few women too enthusiastically.

Weeks later an all-star variety benefit for the bomb victims was staged at the Birmingham Hippodrome. Morecambe and Wise were invited to top the bill, but their agent feared the show would be a target, so into the breach stepped Frankie Vaughan. I hadn't reckoned him my kind of entertainer, but he gave it everything: singing, dancing and wisecracking, Frankie put on the show of a lifetime and left the stage with the audience roaring for more.

Nineteen years later, I would be backstage in Warrington with Colin Welland before he compèred a similar show, after IRA bombs there killed two young boys. It seemed we were getting nowhere, but Warrington was almost the Provisionals' last hurrah; talks behind the scenes were under way, and five years later the Good Friday agreement was signed. Hopefully peace in Northern Ireland will stick, despite both lunatic fringes.

Late on the night of the bombings, five Irishmen from Birmingham were arrested at Heysham as they boarded the Belfast ferry en route to McDade's funeral: Patrick Hill, Gerard Hunter, Francis McIlkenny, William Power and John Walker. They had caught a train at New Street 22 minutes before the explosions. A sixth, Hugh Callaghan, was arrested later in Birmingham. Aged 29 to 44, four were unemployed, one was a millwright's mate and one a crane driver. These men would become known as the Birmingham Six, and their case a cause célèbre - for either they were guilty of England's greatest ever mass murder, or they were the unluckiest men imaginable.

On the Sunday night, a weary Assistant Chief Constable Maurice Buck told the most crowded police press conference I have ever attended: "I am satisfied that we have captured the men primarily responsible." Next morning, amid the tightest security, the Six appeared, one by one, before the stipendiary magistrate. Walker was starting a black eye; the others appeared dazed but unharmed. Three days later they were back in court, having clearly undergone a serious beating. They had been transferred to Winson Green prison, and the first big question about the case presented itself: had the police beaten them to obtain confessions, or had warders laid into them in revenge? I felt it prudent to write that the Six "are thought to have been attacked by other prisoners while taking exercise, despite efforts by staff to keep them away". That same day the inquest opened into 20 victims; one had yet to die.

Finding an impartial jury in Birmingham would be impossible, so the Six stood trial in June 1975 before Mr Justice Bridge at Lancaster Crown Court: the great hall of the Castle keep, with walls feet thick and easier to secure than a city centre courthouse. Nine other men were in the dock, accused of other bombings in Birmingham; the evidence against them overlapped. The trial would last nine weeks; I attended the first fortnight to hear the prosecution's case, came back for the opening of the defence, then again for the closing speeches, the judge's summing-up and the verdicts. I stayed initially in the fading art-deco Midland Hotel at Morecambe, since magnificently restored, then joined my counterparts in the Elms at Bare, closer to Lancaster.

I was also finishing the "backgrounder" which in the event of convictions would tell a fuller story than came out in court. I had talked to people in Birmingham, but needed to see the British Transport Police at Heysham. Inspector Peter Featherby briefed me and BRMB's Colin Palmer on the nuts and bolts of the arrests, then talked around the case a bit.

The Belfast passenger ferry had recently been taken off (it has now resumed), leaving just a vehicle ferry which was less of a headache to police. An IRA sympathiser aboard had been stealing cash and cheques from mailbags, the theft coming to light when empty envelopes washed up on the Isle of Man. Then there was the throng of Manchester United fans who came over every match day. Traditionally a sergeant and three constables policed the boat, but escalating drunkenness and violence led to each crossing tying up an inspector, three sergeants, a dozen Pcs, a WPc and a dog handler – a big strain on limited resources. The bar on the ferry remained a battle zone until one policeman had a brainwave: a direct line to the bridge. Next time the fans started bottling each other, the skipper gave the order: "Pull in the stabilisers!" and they tumbled into a sea of broken glass and puke. By the time the ferry came off, a sergeant and three Pcs again had the upper hand.

The trial opened imposingly, then slipped into a routine; despite the heat outside, the courtroom remained chilly. Details were outlined, as coldly as only a QC can, of the injuries caused by the blasts, and of the prosecution's timetable alleging how the Six - in part through admissions by some - had set up the explosions, then (with one exception) headed for Belfast. Particularly telling was how Hill had conned £15 out of a nun for his fare. Forensic evidence was produced that their hands had tested positive for explosives; this residue was later reckoned to have come from the cards they played with on the train. With details of the pro-IRA fundraising some had undertaken and their links to the other defendants, known as "the Nine", the evidence looked damning.

Counsel for the Six did their best, but didn't have much to go on. On the train south at the end of the week, they told us they were having a problem mounting any kind of case: the prosecution held all the aces, their evidence of rebuttal was thin and some of the Six were too unreliable to put before a jury. All this said over a bottle of fine claret, put on the train at Carlisle to reach room temperature as it pulled into Lancaster. We reporters had not heard anything to suggest the Six were innocent, though the *Guardian*'s Peter

Chippindale, operating separately from the pack, became sceptical after talking to their wives.

Weeks into the trial, the judge became ill and had to adjourn - though not before making, then retracting several statements that forced me twice to rewrite my backgrounder; this did not endear me to the *Telegraph's* subs and printers, as my copy was to take up an entire broadsheet page and all the type had to be reset. As the judge summed up, it became clear that of all the defendants he had a special regard for Michael Murray, a works foreman eventually convicted only of conspiracy. He treated "Big Mick" as their leader, complimenting him as "a soldier" and saying the jury might accord him a "grudging measure of respect"; this left us wondering if he knew something we didn't. He also accused Kenneth Harwood, the prison doctor at Winson Green, of lying to protect the warders, and as the jury retired, those accusations led my story.

On the final night, our hotel was taken over by policemen singing *Green Grow The Rushes, O!* So a group of us went into Morecambe, ending up at a club whose star turn was a man with a clairvoyant hen. First he asked members of the audience to take out banknotes, with Florence (the hen) clucking their "numbers", which were correct. Next, he broke an egg Florence had laid earlier, which turned out to contain a sliver of paper. He asked another punter to tear up a newspaper, until just a tiny piece remained - and the words on it matched the words from the egg. We hacks thought we knew the magician's secret. You can buy "advertising blanks", dummy newspapers on which the same phrase is repeated over and over again. That would explain the two identical slivers - but how did one get into the egg?

After the 43-day trial (then the second longest in English legal history), came the verdicts - guilty on all the main charges - and the sentences: life imprisonment 21 times over for the Six.

There seemed no reason then to think the Birmingham Six were innocent. To the critics who later emerged, the two who confessed had done so under duress and all were convicted on manufactured evidence in a climate of such hostility that they never had a chance.

The Six were certainly not helped by being tried with others charged with less devastating bombings against whom the evidence was stronger. Over time, some crucial evidence against them was discredited, as were some police officers and experts involved in the prosecution. The Court of Appeal twice confirmed the convictions, then finally in 1991 it quashed them, after the Crown withdrew the forensic evidence and the confessions. The Six were released, receiving substantial compensation for nearly 17 years served in prison.

Chris Mullin - the one-time acolyte of Tony Benn and author of *A Very British Coup* who became an outstanding Labour MP - once told me I was the last person who was prepared to say publicly that they were guilty. And it is largely down to Chris that they are free today. While no-one in court apart from Peter Chippindale doubted their guilt, Chris put together some years later a *World in Action* documentary challenging important parts of the evidence, and a book, *Error of Judgement,* which put the case convincingly. Not only did he give credence to the Six's own account of events, he reckoned to have met the real Birmingham bombers in the Irish Republic. This was not a factor considered by the Court of Appeal, but if the people Chris met were telling the truth, the Six had to be innocent.

I wasn't convinced, though Chris marshalled his arguments with skill and passion. I had heard what I had heard in court, and it was hard to unhear it. But I was having doubts myself, and in 1988 I went to Derry to take the mind of Bishop Edward Daly. Daly was best known as the priest waving a bloodied handkerchief who brought out the dying on Bloody Sunday, the most shameful episode in the recent history of the British Army. Despite that experience, he had no time for the IRA and after one atrocity declared from the pulpit that the terrorists had excommunicated themselves. Yet he had visited many Provisionals in prison, including Bobby Sands whose life he tried to save, and he had been to visit the Six. I explained my dilemma to him, and his reaction was categorical: he could never pronounce on guilt or innocence, but he could say the Six were quite unlike any other group of convicted bombers he had met. They lacked the commitment, and they lacked the brains.

I am not now convinced that the Six carried out the Birmingham pub bombings, and not just because they could sue if I said they had. It was probably their sheer bad luck to have boarded a train at New Street for an IRA funeral in Belfast just before bombs went off a stone's throw away. Some were not the sharpest tools in the box; it was hard to imagine Paddy Hill, in particular, organising anything. The recent fresh inquest into the bombings uncovered little new, and the only way the truth could ever be conclusively established would be through a retrial, and far too long has elapsed for this; witnesses have died or their recollections become clouded. My hunch is that if a retrial did take place, the fact that the Six alone were in the dock, and not alongside others who unquestionably were IRA footsoldiers, would result in their acquittal. I leave it at that.

8: Ireland, South and North

A nurse who worked with my father at the Royal Waterloo during the war told me he talked of writing two definitive books: about sex and about Ireland. The first is history; the second never happened, but would have been tremendous. It might seem strange for an atheist to feel so at home in a strongly Catholic country, and for a pacifist to appreciate the "terrible beauty" of Irish nationalism. Yet he loved Ireland deeply: its people, its mountains, its culture ... and its contradictions.

My first memories of Ireland are of family holidays at Mullaghmore, Co. Sligo, watching Earl Mountbatten, whose wife owned Classiebawn Castle nearby, netting for shrimps in the harbour with his trousers rolled up. In 1979 Mountbatten would be assassinated by an IRA bomb just offshore; but when I went back in 2012, I found the magic undiminished.

I cannot claim Irish roots, though Gilbert Humphrey Comfort travelled in perfume in Ireland in the late 19th century and a Fenner great-aunt lived twenty years at Whitehead, finding the Ulster resort starchily unfriendly. So when my father, newly married, had to gain his midwifery experience at the Rotunda in Dublin because few babies were being born in wartime London, he was starting from scratch.

He loved the Rotunda, whose dean was a Jewish ex-boxer and where (he told me) babies separated from their paperwork were tagged "Baby Murphy". He debated in the *Irish Times* with Myles na Gopaleen (Flann O'Brien), and struck up a lifelong friendship with Robert Greacen, a Protestant poet from the border country. When four decades later the Irish government banned *The Joy of Sex*, Greacen wrote to the papers attacking such treatment of "a good friend of this Republic". (Despite the ban, Dad considered retiring there until a visit reminded him how chilly and damp it could get. I enquired whether he would be *persona grata* through my Irish diplomat friend Richard Townsend, and the reply came back that he would be welcome.)

Drawn by Yeats and his description of "Ben Bulben's craggy brow", he caught the train across Ireland to Sligo, then the bus north to Mullaghmore, on a headland at one end of a long, curving strand with mountains cresting behind it. There were two bars with rooms above, and the one he chose – Hannon's – was run by a 90-year-old ex-Gaiety girl from Dublin who had twice received the last rites, only to wake and holler for a glass of porter. Now, as the Beach Hotel, it is in much younger hands but the welcome is as warm as ever. In the other – the Pier House - he found furniture made from ammunition cases from the previous Troubles.

Mullaghmore exuded song, the thing he loved most about Ireland; we once heard a deckhand on a fishing boat singing *The Hills of Donegal* through a tin funnel. It was the northernmost port of call for the crab and lobster boats from Brittany, and when the Bretons came ashore the bar of the Pier House reverberated with Celtic song. Nowadays the lobsters are trucked out twice a week, and the Pier House is a smart spa.

There was also a convent, whose nuns bathed from the strand in the costumes from when they joined the order. Children from Belfast and Derry came for a holiday – and for refuge when the Troubles erupted again. In front of the convent is a green, bisected then by the remnants of a railway from a bauxite quarry in the mountains, and the delightful harbour.

Mullaghmore was the perfect antidote to the obscenity of war. Energised by plentiful food and pure air, Dad scrambled up Ben Bulben and its neighbour Ben Whiskin collecting mollusca; he took home all he could carry, and decades later donated his collection to the National Museum in Dublin. He spent hours in Mullaghmore's post office and bars (though he scarcely drank) absorbing locals' views on the state of the world and the Church. And when he finished at the Rotunda, he came home with a slight Irish brogue and a sackful of stories.

His favourite he did not hear for another 30 years. Moving to California, he got to know the science writer Ritchie Calder, who had been the *Express* man in Dublin in the '30s when there was bloody rivalry between the IRA and the neo-Fascist Blueshirts. Warned to leave by the IRA, he ordered a taxi to the boat. The driver boasted that he was a Blueshirt, but that his brother-in-law was a senior figure in the IRA. Surprised, Calder asked him: "If the two of you meet across the barricades, which of you will die for Ireland?" Without a pause, the driver replied: "That's a damn silly question. The one that gets shot, of course." That line could have come straight out of Brendan Behan.

I have found Dublin taxi drivers just as entertaining. One told me how a Texan walks into an Irish pub and brags: "My ranch is so huge, it takes me two days to drive across it." One of the locals commiserates: "I know how you feel. I had a car like that meself once." Another, taking me to a meeting between John Major and *Taoiseach* Albert Reynolds, told me what happened when, supposedly, Major, Ian Paisley and Dr Casey, the disgraced Bishop of Galway, are aloft in a small plane with three nuns. The engine sputters, and there are only three parachutes.

"Let's give the nuns the parachutes", says Major, chivalrously.

"F*** the nuns!" replies Paisley, unwilling to save Papists.

"Have we got time?" asks Casey.

To return to my childhood ... There were no drive on, drive-off ferries: our car was craned into the hold at Fishguard, and hoisted out at Rosslare onto railway wagons, hauled by an elderly steam engine to a point where we could drive off, handed a road atlas of Ireland by a promotions girl from Caltex. Returning home, it was searched by the Garda for pornography; all they found were snails, and LPs by the magically-voiced Mary O'Hara and the raucous Clancy Brothers.

We drove up to Dublin before heading west, pausing at towns like Mullingar, where in a shop a brass cylinder containing receipts and cash whizzed on a wire just above my head) and then-gloomy Boyle. We detoured to Belturbet to see the Cavan & Leitrim Railway with its engines' Wild West cow-catchers, then found the main road to Cliffoney, beneath the mountains, and beyond it Mullaghmore.

Ireland in the 1950s was a far cry from today's modern nation: Victorian, conservative, depopulated, poor, yet always friendly and intensely proud. By our last holiday new cars were appearing, driven at speed by terrified rustics. The only signs of investment were the turf-fired power stations, the glistening Sweepstake Hospitals which contrasted with the villages' long rows of single-storey cottages, and the ultra-modern salmon leap bypassing Ballyshannon power station. Yet much of 1950s Britain was equally drab.

The countryside provided a backdrop for Dad's stories of the Easter Rising, the notorious Black and Tans and his hero, Michael Collins. Burnt-out police barracks testified to the violence that preceded partition; little was said of the vicious Civil War that followed, save that it cost Collins his life. One of my lasting regrets is that, having been captivated on a flight to Zambia by Liam Neeson's portrayal of Collins, Dad's death came too soon for me to show him the DVD.

One of our visits coincided with an election, with everywhere the slogan "Vote for Dev!" – Eamon de Valera, who broke with Collins over partition, resorted to arms and brought about his death, then ended Fianna Fail's boycott of the *Dail* to become prime minister. (In Strasbourg thirty years later, I would meet his granddaughter Sile after her election to the European Parliament). The IRA was then regarded with an amused tolerance. Occasionally "the boys" would blow up a telephone box, and the one time Dad suggested crossing the Border (to visit the Belleek pottery); we found the road closed after an explosion.

On those holidays I dug in the sand, swam in a sea perfect save for giant poisonous jellyfish, spun for mackerel from a motor boat and tried to catch anything I could in the harbour. We picnicked among the ruins on the holy isle of Inishmurray, inhabited until 1947, and took in the Yeats Festival in Sligo, with its baffling dramas modelled on Japanese Noh plays.

For our third Irish holiday, in 1961, Jane joined us. I did not sense that she and Dad were becoming a couple, but did pick up tensions. The adults spent more time in their rooms, and we didn't do as much together. Yet as we boarded the ferry at Dun Laoghaire, I could not have imagined that a dozen years later Dad and Jane would be married, or that it would be 17 years before I returned to Ireland, as a reporter.

I only had a walk-on role in reporting the gory madness that bedevilled Northern Ireland during the Troubles. But in Birmingham and Brighton I came close to the IRA's campaign of terror, and I talked daily with the politicians who were wrestling with it. The official line was always that things were improving, but they would sometimes admit otherwise. Peter Eastwood reckoned that if any of his reporters came back from Belfast thinking there was a solution, there was something wrong with them. Certainly I could never see an obvious way forward ... and would have been mightily relieved had I known there would ever be an agreement involving Sinn Fein and the Loyalists, even in 1998.

The contradictions that run through Irish life spilled over to Westminster. Frank Maguire, the nationalist MP for Fermanagh, arrived at the gates at the height of an IRA bombing campaign. A Royal death had been announced and the attendant asked him: "Did you hear the Duke of Gloucester had gone?" His mind on other things, Maguire replied: "To be sure, I never drank there much meself."

Nor were the hard-nosed Loyalists immune from paradox. One day they occupied Stormont, pledging to stay until the Government dropped some proposal to engage with the Republic. Then they remembered there was a Barry McGuigan fight on, so they struck a deal with the RUC: if carried out, they would only appear to resist.

The gathering storm in Ulster first registered with me when, on 4 January 1969, a Paisleyite mob attacking a "People's Democracy" march from Belfast to Derry made the television news. That summer my *Morning Telegraph* colleague Brian Wesley returned from covering the rioting with graphic tales of bigotry and brutality against Catholics. The IRA's violent response, first in the North, occasionally in the Republic and eventually on the British mainland, became a nightly fixture on the news, but had no personal relevance until I moved to London - when things changed overnight.

As I started at the *Daily Telegraph* on 3 June 1974, there was an explosion in an anteroom of Westminster Hall. The bomb was tiny, and exploded before MPs and staff had returned after the weekend. But when I interviewed Tam Dalyell and David Steel, fresh from the sleeper, they were concerned both that things could have been much worse and that the IRA had been able to breach supposedly tight security. Throughout a campaign lasting more than two decades, this was the only time the bombers got into the Palace of Westminster; when Airey Neave was killed there, the device had been attached to his car before he left home.

A year later, I returned to Fleet Street hardened by the bombings in Birmingham. To my relief, I was not sent to Belfast. I did, however, spend a night in my car outside the police cordon during the Balcombe Street siege; I saw nothing, and left hours before the IRA unit surrendered in the mistaken belief that the SAS were moving in.

When I went to Strasbourg to cover the European Parliament after Britain's "Yes" vote in the 1975 referendum, Ireland held the presidency of the EEC, and the Republic's President, Cearbhall O Dalaigh, paid a visit. An eminent judge, O Dalaigh insisted on speaking Irish when he met Irish journalists; those with rusty language skills had to hide behind a pillar when he briefed us Brits. He came across as a 24-carat pedant, and I was not surprised when he resigned claiming the Republic's defence minister Paddy Donegan had insulted his office. Angered by his delaying anti-terrorist legislation as "unconstitutional", Donegan was quoted as calling O Dalaigh a "thundering disgrace", but everyone knew he had used the F-word.

By then I had moved to America, where a propaganda war under way between IRA supporters, keen to influence and raise funds from the 20 million Americans claiming Irish origin, and the British government and, up to a point, that of the Republic. London was desperate to prevent the Provisionals winning over Congress and the media, while Dublin was concerned lest terrorism in the North and Britain's response to it destabilise the South; the IRA was, after all, pledged to overthrow not the British Government but that of the Republic.

I arrived in Washington in 1976 with the Provisionals winning the battle for hearts and minds. My role was to report on the extent of pro-IRA activity and fund-raising, the degree to which American politicians and the media were accepting the Provisionals' narrative, and the efforts made by British diplomats and visiting ministers to counteract it. This involved getting to know the relevant people in the British and Irish Embassies, meeting key players in the Administration, Congress and the Irish-American community and checking the register kept by the US government of donations to

Noraid, which claimed to help political prisoners in Ulster but was assumed to be funding the IRA. Hundreds of thousands of dollars were declared, no doubt the tip of the iceberg.

To my relief, I was not expected to penetrate the murky world of wanted terrorists on the run and the virulently anti-British minority of Irish-Americans. A colleague emerged reeling from a taxi in Philadelphia after the driver blamed him personally for the potato famine, but I never encountered discourtesy from any Irish-American for being British. Provided you respected Ireland and its culture, you were welcomed.

While colleagues cautioned that the Republic's interests were not quite the same as Britain's, its diplomats did their utmost to damp down the anger over events in Ulster without appearing to be London's poodle. This could only credibly be done by distancing Dublin from British actions which would alienate Irish Americans; in explaining this to *Telegraph* readers I once unwisely used the word "atrocities", and was taken to task by my Irish contacts.

Developing this relationship, I got to know Richard Townsend. Strangely we had not met before, despite being Cambridge contemporaries and my mother being a friend of his aunt. There had also been a curious episode when the British Standards Institute, where Richard was then working, asked me to write its official history, called me in for a meeting, then went silent. Our paths would cross again when he was posted to London and permitted by his superiors to marry Eiriol, a charming lady who worked at the Foreign Office (marriage between different countries' diplomats is usually forbidden). He went on to be Ireland's ambassador in the Hague, and in retirement a generous host to us in Dublin.

The British Embassy kept in touch with the Administration and with Congress, monitored pro-IRA activity, did its best to rebut its propaganda and hosted British politicians in America to put the case for a regime widely perceived as repressive. One reason for Peter Jay's controversial appointment as ambassador was David Owen's quest for one who would actively sell British policy on Ulster in the American heartland. Jay did prove quite effective, but all the ground gained in a year could be lost if one day's headlines put Britain in the wrong ... as would happen during the hunger strikes of 1981.

I first went back to Ireland in the autumn of 1978, with Lobby colleagues as a guest of its government - one of several such trips combining a chance to question senior politicians (on this occasion *Taoiseach* Jack Lynch) and enjoy Irish hospitality. One included a pitch from the Irish Development Authority, whose world-beating salesmen had reputedly been trained by the Mormons in Salt Lake City, in a darkened basement after an excellent lunch with Foreign Minister Michael O'Kennedy. Waking with a start, I hurriedly asked an incoherent question – then was told by the *Guardian's* Ian Aitken that I had been snoring.

Our hosts were keen to bend our ears about developments in the North, insisting the Republic had to be involved if terrorism were to be put back in its box. They also stressed their fast-modernising nation's role in Europe, and explained their differences with Britain, notably over the Common Agricultural Policy. I found Lynch an agreeable if opaque old fox (as in a more academic way was Garret FitzGerald) and O'Kennedy able and persuasive, but I gained my greatest insights from an Irish politician, in the bar at an EEC summit in Luxembourg, from the Agriculture Minister Brian Lenihan, whose baggage as a Fianna Fail machine politician would deny him the Presidency.

The next year saw Margaret Thatcher's coming to power, the IRA's killing of 18 soldiers at Warrenpoint ... and the tragedy at Mullaghmore. I was geared up for a party conference that would be the nastiest in Labour's history when Peter Eastwood despatched me to cover Pope John Paul II's visit to Ireland. There was not only the prospect of an active new pontiff promoting peace, but the risk of his presence triggering a bloody response from Loyalists. The *Telegraph* also sent my Sheffield friend Paul Potts, who had good Catholic connections – notably Cardinal Hume's press secretary, an entertaining Jesuit who warned me not to get carried away and convert. I later made the *faux pas* of inviting him to lunch during Lent.

The Pontiff was in Ireland just three days, but what an impression he made. After centuries when the successor of St Peter was always an Italian and often charmless, Cardinals had the year before chosen Karol Wojtyla, a Pole with virility, charisma and intellectual firepower. The part he would play in the collapse of Communism in his own country and throughout the Soviet bloc is still being assessed. But during his brief visit to Ireland, I knew I was witnessing true greatness.

I got closest to him when he blessed the travelling media from a balcony at Maynooth. He spoke with kindness and authority, making us feel we really mattered among thousands he had met during a gruelling tour. He had earlier given ordinands troubled about not being able to renounce their vows and marry the nearest I have heard to a convincing reason, telling them: "If married couples who are having difficulties come to you for help, how can you advise them to stay together if you cannot also accept the permanence of your marriage with the Church"?

On 29 September 1979 1,250,000 people – one-third of the Republic's population and more than twice the number who would turn out for Pope Francis in 2018 – flocked to Phoenix Park for an open-air Mass. I was moved by their enthusiasm as the Popemobile moved among them, and the dignity and joy of the service, with *St Patrick's Breastplate* sung again and again. The media operated from a tented enclosure, relying on TV monitors for a view of the ritual hundreds of yards away across a sea of humanity and filing from the customary bank of telephones. My abiding memory is of the long walk to the park in the company of thousands, and the walk back – which seemed shorter - among people whose hearts had been lifted. This would be the last manifestation of Ireland's deep, unquestioning Catholicism, before revelations of sexual abuse of children by priests broke the trust of many in the Church.

The Pope went on to address a crowd of 200,000 at Drogheda, just south of the Border. It had been decided that an appearance in Ulster would pose risks not only to himself but to every Catholic attending; as it was, tens of thousands safely crossed the Boyne to hear John Paul appeal "on my knees" to the men of violence. Ireland held its breath to see if the IRA, which claimed the allegiance of Ireland's Catholics despite a strong Marxist strand in its ideology, would respond. But soon the bloodshed resumed.

Paul went with the Pope to Drogheda, and the next day to Galway, Knock and Limerick prior to his departure for the United States. I stayed in Dublin, based at the press centre created in Dublin Castle for a forthcoming European Summit – which I would again use covering EU and Anglo-Irish meetings over the next 15 years.

The Church laid on free Guinness, and as we finished our stories on the first two evenings, a large and convivial group of hacks gathered. I caught up with Paddy Clancy, a former *Telegraph* colleague who had rebased to his home country. Paddy was famed for repeatedly missing his train home from Waterloo after getting caught in the bar there. When he missed a parents' meeting, he got home to find a note from his wife reading: "Your supper's in the oven". Inside were the charred remains of a salad.

The talk turned to Liam Kelly, the *Mirror*'s legendary man in Dublin. Kelly was a fine reporter, but not always appreciated by head office. Once he was asked to locate the text of *Macnamara's Band,* for a story about an eponymous large family who always holidayed at the same boarding house in Blackpool. After much difficulty he came up with the words, rang the copytakers and began: "Kelly, Dublin. Band, one [The catchline that identifies any piece of copy]. Me name is Macnamara, I'm the leader of the band ..." At which point the copytaker interjected: "You're pissed again, Kelly!" and hung up.

Kelly's greatest moment came after the IRA's Kevin Gallagher and Marlene Coyle kidnapped a Dutch businessman, Tieder Herrema. The Garda traced them to a house at Monasterevin just west of Dublin, and Kelly was instructed to report their first exchange with the kidnappers. He rushed to the phone, got through to copy and began:

"Kelly, Dublin. Add siege, one.

"As the Garda moved in, Chief Inspector O'Flaherty raised a loud-hailer and roared colon quotes: Come out, Gallagher, you're outnumbered, close quotes point paragraph.

"There was a pause, then a curtain twitched and Gallagher shouted back colon quotes: F blank blank blank off comma, you cunts. Close quotes. Ends."

I also got talking to some working-class ladies of a certain age who had arrived in their Sunday best. They said they had something to show me and – dismissing any thought that they were on the pull – I followed them through a concealed door and up a narrow staircase. At the top was a second door ... into King George V's State apartments, kept exactly as they had been on the day of Partition and maintained by these self-same ladies. The apartments, with their rich hangings, were their pride and joy, and I got the impression this was one of the very few opportunities they had had to show them off. It would be another 31 years before the Queen paid a visit.

The moment His Holiness took off from Shannon and we had got our stories away, the bar switched to the hard stuff. That evening I saw more fights in a confined space than at any other time in my career.

Though I was only to stay in Belfast two or three days, I was nervous about my first visit to the North. On the train, the jovial CIE ticket collector disappeared as we neared the Border and a slim, dark Ulsterman took over. That was the only formality; when years later the Home Office argued for a massive presence on Eurostar to guard against terrorism, I couldn't help recalling that at the height of the Troubles they took no interest in cross-Border trains in Ireland.

Beyond Dundalk lay "bandit country", where bombings frequently disrupted the trains and every station nameboard evoked some atrocity. Passing Lisburn, the first major town in the North, the Catholic areas proudly sported yellow and white Papal flags. I left the train feeling jittery and headed for the Europa Hotel, glancing anxiously around for bombers and snipers.

I stayed at the Europa (now the Forum) several times over the next 12 years – considerably more often than it was bombed - and after a few hours of that first stay I seldom felt edgy. I heard no explosions and precious few sirens, and while the Europa could never feel like home, the staff did make you welcome. One morning I was with the Press Association's legendary Chris Moncrieff when he rolled into the bar and ordered a Guinness. "I'm sorry, we're closed", the barmaid told him. "But you can have a drink while you're waiting."

Chatting with shoppers from Ballymena or Bangor who came in for a coffee left the Troubles seeming a long way off. Mind you, a short taxi ride away (reception would find you a Catholic or a Protestant firm depending on where you were going) they talked of little else. I particularly remember a visit to the constituency office in the Shankill of Peter Robinson (more recently First Minister), an able if chilling man who shared Paisley's prejudices despite not being chiefly motivated by religion; he gave me the Loyalist line in an office full of case files just like those of any other hard-working MP.

John Reid summed up Ulster's communal tensions when he said that all the time they were building the *Titanic* in Protestant East Belfast, they were building the iceberg in the Catholic West. The division is not confined to the cities; a friend with a country house in Co. Fermanagh told me that when they held a fete, the Protestants arrived through one gate and the Catholics through another. You learned to pick up the signs: on an internal flight the stewardess betrayed her background by referring to "the North of Ireland"; no Protestant would say that.

The *Telegraph* had a Belfast staffer, Colin Brady, renowned for his gigantic coat, and colleagues went over to back him up and keep him sane. Belfast reporters had to develop thick skins, and their humour was not always appreciated back home. A *Mirror* man was covering a particularly grisly bombing when the women's editor rang to say a lady from Belfast had been named Slimmer of the Month. Without missing a beat, he replied: "Did she lose an arm or a leg?"

After that first visit I usually went over with Lobby colleagues, to be told by ministers, security chiefs, civil servants and others how the fight against terrorism was being won, new political initiatives launched and jobs created. Invariably we were told that cross-Border security had been bloody awful six months ago, but now the Republic was doing its bit. Some things we were told, particularly about security, turned out to be simply untrue.

The dangerous world of intelligence-gathering in Ulster impinged on me in the unlikely surroundings of a drinks party in Welshpool. I was chatting to an articulate but guarded woman in her late 20s who had something to do with the military; I later learned she was on leave from her regular job of sitting in pubs in Ulster's "bandit country" passing herself off as a local. One false move, and she would be dead. Looking back, I realised that while she had pleasant blonde looks, her face was, in the nicest way, forgettable, enabling her to vanish into the crowd. We owe a lot to people like her.

My recollections of Ulster are a colourful jumble. There were the gala reopening of Belfast's Grand Opera House - sharing the lift with Rowan Atkinson - and the RUC's diamond jubilee tattoo, with a bizarre combination of pipe and mounted bands. There was a delightful boat trip along Lough Erne followed by the mother of all carveries at a country club. There was an unproductive salmon fishing session near the Bushmills distillery, where I developed an attachment to the Old Black Bush. Even the knowledge that most places I visited had suffered from terrorism or were subsequently bombed did not dispel the magic.

Humphrey Atkins, Mrs Thatcher's first Northern Ireland Secretary, was particularly helpful to me. Over lunch at Westminster six months into his posting, he explained his lateness by telling me he had had to stop off to buy a pair of underpants, such was the pressure on his time. Observing an Orange parade from an RUC lookout, Humphrey was fascinated by the banners of the Temperance and Total Abstinence Lodges. "What's the difference?" he asked the inspector in charge. "It's simple," came the reply. "By tonight the temperance boys will be well away, but the total abstainers will be f***ing paralytic."

Jim Prior didn't want to jeopardise his rocky relationship with Mrs Thatcher through contact with hacks who might spin his words into rebellion. Tom King was more open, but I got on best with John Major's Ulster supremo Peter Brooke. Appearing at a forum on Northern Ireland and Europe in Belfast as political editor of the *European*, I was embarrassed when he hailed me as a cricketer of note on the strength of one appearance for the Lords and Commons a decade before.

Some Northern Ireland ministers thrived on the pressure; others didn't. Labour's Roy Mason clung to his Special Branch escort far longer than his predecessor Merlyn Rees - partly because he liked his status symbols but also because having hit the IRA so hard, his life was genuinely in danger. John Stanley, an outgoing PPS to Mrs Thatcher in opposition, was so petrified that he would only leave Stormont Castle if there was an RUC man posted at a set of traffic lights where he felt at risk. Jack Hermon, the chief constable, put a stop to that. Stanley had not been over-popular at the MoD, and when he moved his private office dialled Stormont so his new officials could hear the corks popping.

It was 1989 before I made it to Derry, to ask Bishop Daly about the Birmingham Six; I left wishing I had gone there earlier. Thereafter most of my visits were to the Republic, to cover European summits and the contacts between John Major and Albert Reynolds as Sinn Fein gradually came on board the peace train. I monitored the situation from Westminster into the Blair years, and pulled together the *People*'s coverage of the Omagh bombing. A mid-afternoon atrocity comes at the worst possible time for the Sunday papers, as almost all resources are geared to processing football reports. But pages were cleared for the story, headlines written, pictures sized and an editorial written (by me) in time for the first edition. Despite the horror, challenges like this bring out the best in any newspaper production team.

8. Letters from America

Despite his politics, my father was always welcome in America. He first went over in 1958 on the *Liberté* - flying home because he couldn't cope with the liner's abundance of food. He started visiting California in the late 1960s, and even before *The Joy of Sex* was a regular on chat shows there. At the height of the Vietnam War one host asked if LBJ was a "happening"; his reply, "No, he's more of a bad trip", broke up the camera crew. By the mid-'70s, he was almost a household name on the West Coast.

When Dad and Jane moved to California in 1973, I little imagined that within three years I, too, would cross the Atlantic, but after less than two years on the *Telegraph* I was appointed to its Washington staff. The manner was characteristic: Peter Eastwood appeared beside me in the Gents and offered me the job.

I had just two months' notice of the move: quite a challenge. Dad sent advice about living in the States, my future boss Steve Barber wrote encouragingly, and Alex Faulkner, just retired as New York bureau chief, invited Deborah and me to dinner. Gentlemanly and distinguished-looking, Alex reminded me instantly of Alistair Cooke; it transpired that he had spent his entire career being mistaken for his BBC and *Guardian* counterpart, and it rankled.

I flew to Washington at the start of May 1976. Staying at Steve's house near the Cathedral, America seemed rather like home, but I only had to turn on the sports news to know I was in a foreign country. Every Briton arriving in America discovers this in a different way. A friend of Grandfather's married an artist with the National Geographic; at her first Washington party she mentioned having "a cough right down to my diaphragm", perturbing ladies who thought she was referring to a contraceptive coil. Our own social faux pas came when neighbours brought round a "dessert", and we failed to grasp the complex etiquette connected to it.

I rented a comfortable, squarish colonial-style house in Sherrill Avenue, Chevy Chase from my predecessor Nigel Wade; overlooking parkland and with a rampant bamboo, it was home throughout our time in Washington and for over a decade housed my successors. Nigel had, uncannily, been born in Australia on the same day as me. Brought up a Kiwi, he had worked his way to Fleet Street via Vietnam, covered Watergate with verve and was now off to Beijing, where he would break the news of the arrest of the "Gang of Four" as China began breaking with Maoism. Nigel left me his hire car; only when I returned it a fortnight later did I discover it had been posted missing, believed stolen. I bought a car of my own – a second-hand Plymouth Valiant – from a salesman personally decorated by George VI for clearing mines from the Normandy beaches before D-Day.

Steve was a generous boss – he financed my car purchase himself after the office refused to, and lent us his cottage in Suffolk for a holiday - though his gout could make him snappy. When not under pressure he was immensely entertaining; a devotee of W S Gilbert, he would describe some story as "adding an air of verisimilitude to an otherwise bald and unconvincing narrative." Totally committed, he expected as much from his team, ideally preferring "young men who have just been divorced".

Stocky and bespectacled, Steve had started in journalism as a teenager in Cairo when war broke out (his family having been ruined in the Depression), been wounded covering the war with US forces, and gone on to a distinguished Fleet Street career with the *News Chronicle* - for whom he retraced with an elephant Hannibal's crossing of the Alps - and the *Sunday Telegraph*. For the latter he covered Kennedy's visit to Dallas, telling his wife as he left: "I'd better go, somebody might shoot him".

It smarted with Steve that the Washington Establishment acknowledged only one London paper: the *Times*; he also had an animus against the *Sunday Times*'s veteran correspondent Henry Brandon which prevented me getting to know him until years later, when I found him charming. But his counterparts admired Steve for his honesty and courage; he had told the visiting Margaret Thatcher she couldn't make Reggie Maudling Foreign Secretary as he would be arrested the moment he touched down at Dulles over of his connections to the fraudulent Real Estate Fund of America.

After my return, Steve was in line to succeed Peter Eastwood when his heart gave out. It was an immense loss to the paper, but no surprise to colleagues. While working full-time in Washington for the *Telegraph*, he also filed to the Johannesburg *Sunday Times* and the *Far Eastern Economic Review* from a telex machine in the bedroom. Despite this, Steve and his formidable but kindly wife Deirdre were very close.

Steve's other work brought a stream of South Africans through the office, almost all white and mostly liberal. On the rare occasion a minister arrived from Pretoria, he would open doors for them in Washington, otherwise closed because of their government's racial policies. This did not stop them complaining: one Sunday morning I picked up Steve's phone to receive a Force 9 tirade from Foreign Minister "Pik" Botha, a relative moderate, about something in that day's Johannesburg paper.

Washington was a three-man office, and Steve's deputy was the highly experienced Richard Beeston. Dick was happiest in the world of espionage; the former CIA man James Jesus Angleton was a prime contact. Miles Copeland (father of Stewart, drummer with the Police) was another; at one of his parties I met the young and then slim-ish Nick Soames, then an aide on Capitol Hill. Once a year Dick took a swing through the Caribbean, returning with spine-chilling stories of growing Communist influence.

Where Steve was hyperactive, Dick was laid-back. His mid-morning announcement "I'm off to the State Department" meant he was going downstairs to listen to a briefing piped through to the National Press Club. To Steve's amusement, Dick had a propensity for writing his own intro to a story and clipping the rest from an American newspaper, handing the cutting to Sam, our teleprinter operator; every so often an American usage or spelling would spark irritation in London. Dick – whose son Richard became a distinguished foreign editor before dying tragically young - left late in 1977 for Moscow, and Jim Wightman – my future boss at Westminster - took his place.

Three secretary-researchers - working in part for Steve's other strings - completed the team. Betty was a sparky and motherly Aussie. Karin was a Dane married to an American diplomat. Stephanie had been a girlfriend of Dick Holbrooke, who would be Bill Clinton's key man on Bosnia. Applying to be a *Washington Post* cookery writer, she was surprised to find an ingredient missing from her test recipe and let the paper know; the omission was deliberate, candidates who pressed on regardless being ruled out.

Each *Telegraph* staffer had a room, and the researchers shared a large one where in 1978 a primitive fax machine appeared. Our suite also housed John Hamilton of the *Melbourne Herald* and Jim Srodes, who wrote for half a century on gold and commodities. As a youngster in Florida Jim had been in a group playing on the same bill as Buddy Holly; when later Neil Kinnock visited Washington, I made a point of introducing them.

There was also a wire room, where we monitored machines for the news agencies: AP, UPI and Reuter. There was no 24-hour television news then and while there was all-news radio, we only listened in our cars unless there was something major to follow. To alert subscribers when a story broke, each agency had a code of bells. One afternoon they all sounded: two jumbo jets had collided on a runway in the Canary Islands in what remains the deadliest air crash ever. Another time the UPI bells went berserk to announce the death of President Tito - only for a grovelling apology to follow, his obituary having been mistakenly transmitted as a test. The wires also suffered heavily from literals. UPI advised reporters wishing to cover a visit by Rosalynn Carter to apply for "press pusses" - hurriedly corrected to "press asses". And Reuter listed Bristol Rovers as 'Bristol Aortas' – all heart, presumably.

We had a teleprinter for Sam to send our copy, and a flimsier Telex, which we could operate. This was our normal link with London, though urgent matters were handled on the phone. Each morning a message arrived for "Gluson New York, onpass Washington" (Gluson was a former tenant of our office in the Rockefeller Center) telling us where our stories had appeared in the paper and what items were wanted. Steve would acknowledge, listing the stories we were working on. From late morning till mid-afternoon - deadline for all but the most urgent news given the time difference - Sam would transmit copy to New York for forwarding to London; after that, we filed it ourselves.

Our office was on an upper floor of the 1920s *Daily* Planet-like National Press Building, recently given a characterless makeover; three blocks from the White House and a taxi ride from the Capitol and State Department, it housed most of the foreign media, though the BBC were some way up Pennsylvania Avenue (all distances in Washington look convenient till you try walking). It also housed the National Press Club.

Presidents and visiting statesmen spoke at NPC lunches, a fellow guest once telling me of a South African attempt to discredit Harold Wilson. More intimate "Newsmaker Breakfasts" gave us a chance to meet speakers from "Israeli dove Arie Eliav" to a voluptuous Hispanic undercover drugs agent. The Club staged an annual chili cookout dominated by Texans, and was home to a bureaucrats' club whose emblem was a pencil with an eraser at each end. It also had a restaurant staffed by dignified elderly black men, to which Steve, Dick and I would repair for soup with tiny saltine biscuits and a burger around 2 pm (7 pm in London) when we had got our copy away. On our return we handled late-breaking stories and worked on features.

The *Telegraph's* two-man New York office covered North American news plus boxing, but not Wall Street over which Jim Srodes kept watch. Ian Brodie, a former *Express* man who would take over Washington after Steve died, looked after California and Hollywood. We covered the capital: the President, Congress, politics, diplomacy and defence, rarely travelling except with the President or during elections, and seldom taking on stories outside the Beltway. I handled the areas that least interested Steve and Dick, or they didn't have time to cover. I boned up on oil and gas, going on a press tour of rigs in the Gulf of Mexico; in New Orleans we went to see *Deep Throat,* the projectionist switching off after 20 minutes out of boredom. The aviation brief gave me a grounding that would prove valuable in the Lobby and later at QinetiQ. I covered the Bermuda II negotiations which came within hours of halting BA flights to America, revelled in a visiting Freddie Laker's attacks on the big airlines, and was deafened at the end of the runway at Dulles as its first Concorde took off.

My coverage of American support for the IRA led to my invoking the Freedom of Information Act to see the files on fund-raising by Noraid. FoI is handy provided you already know what to look for, but most outstanding political stories will always come from good, old-fashioned leaks.

My first Sunday, working alone, was a baptism of fire. There were seven story requests, one for a speech Hubert Humphrey had supposedly made about Rhodesia. There was nothing in the *Washington Post, Washington Star* or *New York Times* - we had to plough through them all, no mean task on a Sunday when supplements proliferated - or on the wires. New York knew nothing about it. Neither did the Senator's press secretary when I plucked up the courage to ring her. I didn't like to ask London where the story had come from, and having filed the other six I telexed that I had drawn a blank. Months later, I found that Humphrey had indeed said something, out of earshot of any of his staff; how the office got to hear of it remained a mystery.

While I enjoyed the *Washington* Post's revelation that a veteran Congressman, Wayne Hays, had hired a former beauty queen for services that did not involve typing, I was so bogged down meeting Gluson requests that I didn't try to follow it up. Eventually London - seeing the Hays story on agency - requested copy; I scrambled something together, but it wasn't very good. Next day Steve explained to me (1) why Wayne Hays mattered and (2) that it was a rattling good story even if he didn't. Hays' "typist" Elizabeth Ray had the last word: "He did to me what Nixon did to the country."

On Saturdays, we took turns to cover for the *Sunday Telegraph*. I had seen enough of the *Sunday* to know that from Friday teatime onward, many of its decision-makers were paralytic. It was hard to influence matters from across the Atlantic, witness the fate of two first-rate stories.

One I obtained when the Queen toured Jefferson's home at Monticello as the Marxist government in Angola was threatening to execute some British mercenaries. A group of us buttonholed Tony Crosland, who as Foreign Secretary was accompanying her, and asked whether she would be appealing to the Angolans for clemency. Crosland caught up with Her Majesty, then gave us her response; we commandeered the press bus and filed from nearby Charlottesville. I could raise no-one on the *Sunday* to alert, and nothing appeared.

The other was a world exclusive. You may remember Joyce McKinney, the obsessed former beauty queen who followed Kirk Anderson, a young Mormon missionary, to Britain and kidnapped him. Kirk went to ground after being freed, but I managed to locate his parents in Salt Lake City and coax an interview out of them. Again I filed to the *Sunday,* only to find no-one lucid there. When around 1984 I was offered the political job on the *Sunday*, I turned it down; matters only improved there under Conrad Black.

My first weeks were a blur of new experiences, from obtaining a White House pass from the Secret Service (surprisingly easy) to passing the Maryland driving test (less so). Fleet Street was strikebound, so Steve told me to get in my car and discover America. Excellent advice it was: with the Starline Vocal Band's *Afternoon Delight* on the radio I headed beyond the Beltway into a different world. Two days driving through the glorious Virginia spring, staying in cheap motels, stopping at village drugstores and old-fashioned diners, listening to talk radio and chatting with locals opened my eyes: their priorities were not those of the Washington village.

The Foreign Office used to rate Washington a hardship posting. While spring and fall were mild and the colours beautiful, the winters could be bitter; one crisp, still morning the temperature at my bus stop was -11° Fahrenheit. Luckily there was not the wind chill they experience in Chicago. But the sticky, debilitating summers were the trial. Washington almost shut down for July and August, those having to remain sending their families to the beach. I have never experienced humidity like it; taking a shower, I was often as damp after drying myself as before.

Life in Washington was good. We had an agreeable house, though the garden bolted after summer rains. My salary would not have gone far, but I received an untaxed "foreign living allowance". We had two handy shopping malls, a convenient bank - on Saturdays you had to drive-through as it was closed to pedestrians - and a sandwich shop (still there) called Booeymonger: favourite item, the Patty Hearst. At her nursery, Carrie hugged a boa constrictor found in Rock Creek Park by one of the parents and memorised the Pledge of Allegiance; when John was about six months old we found her trying to teach it to him, pinning his hand to his chest.

Next door were a Swiss Embassy family whose sons practiced flag-waving on the lawn. Beyond were a Congressional aide married to a painter, and their growing children. On the other side was a gracious octogenarian who was convinced Roosevelt had orchestrated Pearl Harbor. Round the corner were the Kiaries, a Kenyan diplomatic family of whom more later, and two scientific journalists; Carrie was suspected of having eaten a praying mantis that vanished from their conservatory.

We found a congenial church - Westmoreland Congregational - and through friends there got to know Rick Lidinsky, a (Catholic) Baltimore maritime lawyer, his wife Dusty and their son Ricky, who would marry the shoe designer daughter of George W Bush's ambassador in London; they adopted a second son, John. Rick and I have stayed close for 40-plus years; he became a vice president of Sea Containers and eventually chaired the Federal Maritime Commission for Barack Obama.

Westmoreland combined a stately building, a large, friendly and liberal congregation and musical excellence. There were some cultural surprises: I was baffled by the concept of liturgical dance, with diaphanous women swirling in front of the altar, in which some American universities were bizarrely offering degrees.

I drove in to work at weekends when parking was possible, locking my doors along 14th Street to keep out the hookers (among them freelancing off-duty vice squad members). On weekdays I took the bus from Friendship Heights on the District Line (the DC/Maryland boundary). The buses were packed, the journey took ages, and it was doubly frustrating that the Metro along the same route belatedly opened just after we left.

My irritation with the buses boiled over after mine was stuck for two hours in a jam caused by an Iranian Embassy party, the DC Police waving through equal numbers of vehicles in each direction despite 90% heading out of town. My letter to the *Post* brought plaudits from neighbours, and a defence of the police's lack of imagination from its local government reporter. For me this was one of several incidents proving the crassness of low-level American bureaucracy. I once went into the post office at the US Treasury to buy some Captain Cook commemorative stamps. There were two types of stamp on the sheet, and when I asked the clerk to tear me a strip down the middle to give me a set of pairs, she told me Post Office regulations obliged her to tear across, not down.

Dad and Jane were living at Montecito, a smart suburb of Santa Barbara whose best-known resident was Ronald Reagan. I pictured their home in Oak Grove Drive as a mansion, and was disappointed when eventually I visited in 1992 to find essentially a large packing shed. Dad had joined the Center for the Study of Democratic Institutions, a think-tank headed by Robert M Hutchins, a distinguished academic who had advised Roosevelt, and to avoid UK taxes had made over the royalties of *The Joy of Sex* to it in return for a salary. Then he fell out with Hutchins; a bad-tempered lawsuit got him the rights back, but the judge wasn't impressed.

They stayed at Montecito until they returned to Britain in 1985. Dad worked as a geriatric psychiatrist at a veterans' hospital, but could not practise medicine as California doesn't recognise British medical degrees; eventually Saskatchewan gave him the necessary qualifications. They came to stay when Dad had business on the east coast, but we were never invited to Santa Barbara. Life was too busy for this to seem strange; only later did I realise how deep they had been into the West Coast swinging culture.

This was a period of relative calm in America, but close to our office the Willard Hotel, gutted in the riots that exploded in 1968 after the assassination of Dr Martin Luther King, stood charred and forlorn. The Washington I arrived in was also recovering from the twin traumas of Vietnam and Watergate. The scars from the war took longer to heal; our church had split over it with the hawks seceding. America lacked self-confidence, and when Jimmy Carter articulated this mood, as with his warning that the energy crisis was "the moral equivalent of war" (cruelly abbreviated by the

Boston Globe to MEOW), Americans didn't like it. What they wanted was certainty, for which they would turn to Ronald Reagan after the fiasco of the American hostages in Tehran. A sign of this yearning was the runaway success of *Star Wars,* the ultimate saga of good overcoming evil; it was six months before we could get in.

My time in Washington covered the last eight months of the Ford administration and the first 18 of Carter's. Gerald Ford never shook off his image as a man who, in LBJ's words, "can't fart and chew gum at the same time". You could hardly switch on the news without seeing him fall down the steps of an aircraft or trip on a pavement. Ford was still being pilloried for pardoning Richard Nixon, having realised the last thing America needed was continued bloodletting over Watergate.

I didn't see much of Ford in the flesh as he was on the road much of the time campaigning for re-election, and the one trip of his that I set off to cover was cancelled. I did, however, meet a Navy officer's wife who was high school counsellor to Ford's daughter Susan. When she asked Susan's Secret Service agent what happened if a date got too hot, he replied: "I'm there to save her from other people, not from herself."

When Carter moved into the White House, the first Southerner in generations, a patronising media recalled Andrew Jackson's inauguration in 1829, when drunken hillbillies trashed the place. In fact the occasion was highly civilised, a light note coming from the *Sesame Street* team I found outside the White House inaugurating the Cookie Monster.

Carter benefited from the weakness and disorganisation of the Republican Right, who were only just starting to rally around Reagan; for a rare moment in American history, the flat-earthers and isolationists did not have a cause, save for blocking the Equal Rights Amendment for fear it would give women the upper hand. Even Carter's handover of the Canal Zone to Panama, lambasted by conservative columnists, didn't really get them going.

Watergate had established Washington as the Mecca of investigative journalism. Bob Woodward and Carl Bernstein had not only made their names (and prompted scores of imitators) by bringing down Nixon; they had made the *Washington Post* the most talked-about newspaper in the world, and its editor Ben Bradlee a demigod. The *Washington Star* I found easier reading, but the *Post* was authoritative and I got to know several of its staff.

Foreign correspondents in Washington had their own furrow to plough and didn't see much of the giants of political reporting away from White House briefings. But Steve Barber knew them, James "Scotty" Reston being his favourite, and alerted me to a couple whose output should be treated with caution. I was unimpressed by columns from the legendary Jack Anderson, and disliked the output of his closest rivals, Evans and Novak, based on whinges from brasshats and bureaucrats whose advice had been ignored.

The British correspondents had a definite pecking order: Steve, Henry Brandon and a veteran *Economist* correspondent were at the top, along with - ex-officio - the *Times* man (Fred Emery) and the BBC's bureau chief (John Humphrys). Having watched an apparently-toupeed John reporting on America's attempts to keep out Concorde, I couldn't resist telling him I was relieved to discover his hair was his own. Through shrewd deployment of his expenses John had acquired a magnificent home at Potomac, where he was a generous host. I saw less of Martin Bell, who worked largely for BBC Radio; he then wore a raincoat rather than the white suit that became his trademark reporting from Sarajevo. Latterly ITN's Mike Brunson arrived, stunning American counterparts with the size of his technical retinue demanded by Britain's broadcasting unions; I would work with him more closely in the Commons.

Of our newspaper correspondents, I saw most of the *Mail*'s Bill Lowther. Bill had interviewed a former Wehrmacht infantryman who - transfixed by the skirl of the pipes – had been bayoneted by an advancing Jock, and during Vietnam had discovered a route into Canada for draft evaders run by two elderly Welsh editors who communicated in their native tongue. When Bill took a holiday, his replacement from London filed total fiction.

I spent time on the Hill - mostly in committee hearings - and sampled the legendary bean soup in the Congressional restaurant; press facilities in the Capitol were pretty basic. Getting to know American politicians wasn't easy. One Congressional aide explained that as the *Telegraph*'s readers couldn't vote for his boss, there was no mileage in his talking to me, but when it mattered I could get through to several Congressmen and the odd senator. My most interesting conversation was with Senator Henry 'Scoop' Jackson at a White House Correspondents' dinner. Jackson – whom I had always reckoned an unreconstructed Cold Warrior - happened to mention that his forebears came from Orkney, a place I know and love.

Plugging into the Administration proved easier. It wasn't difficult to get a White House staffer out to lunch; I struck up a friendship with Richard Whitworth, an Aussie academic who became Carter's deputy education secretary, and the cliffhanging Bermuda II aviation talks made me a frequent caller to David Jewell, spokesman for Transportation Secretary Brock Adams. I got to question Chief Justice Warren Burger in the Supreme Court's imposing chamber, and meet Griffin Bell, Carter's attorney-general. Later I would become good friends with Bob Gray, who as Under-Secretary for Defense wrote the still-classified instructions on firing Cruise missiles.

Steve made sure I got into the White House. Occasionally I went to the daily briefing in the press room, where only American reporters asked questions; I was once in there on my own when Jimmy Carter stuck his head round the door, said "Hi!" and disappeared again. I flew with Carter to West Virginia and the UN (not on Air Force One but the accompanying "zoo plane"), and was in the Oval Office as he greeted Romania's President Ceausescu, misguidedly reckoned a friend of the West. I also covered welcoming ceremonies on the White House lawn – unbearably sticky in summer - and the welcome for the Shah proved unforgettable.

Initially a reformer, the Shah by 1978 had become supremely arrogant. To boost his visit, his secret police rounded up Iranian students from America's universities and bused them to

Washington. The exercise backfired, with hundreds rioting on the Ellipse, throwing tear gas canisters to leave the President, the Shah and us spectators coughing and spluttering - save for one black photographer who produced a gas mask. As the fumes abated, he explained: "I was in 'Nam, and you gotta be ready." I can't imagine anyone getting a gas mask through White House security nowadays. I picked up the resentment of veteran White House reporters that neither Ford nor Carter lived somewhere interesting, like Nixon's San Clemente. One reason they were slow to go for the jugular on Watergate was that they could fly to California with Nixon for $50 return. One took his girlfriend, ditched her there and didn't see her again till he checked into a hotel in Rome to find she was the receptionist. He did not get the best room.

Dick Beeston handled most State Department business, but I often went to its briefings. These consisted of a spokesman repeatedly fielding the same question from reporters apparently schooled by the Jesuits, the slightest change of inflexion being treated as a reversal of policy. Yet they did produce occasional stories, mainly involving Korea. The South Korean government was desperate for influence in Washington, and when the Korean CIA was caught suborning members of Congress, Henry Kissinger told the Korean ambassador that while he was sure the KCIA had done nothing of the kind, if they did it again they would be thrown out.

American foreign policy was dominated by the Cold War, and generally the only countries to feature in its politics - apart from the Soviet Union - were Israel and South Africa. In those days the Democrats would support whatever the Israeli government did and the Republicans would the occasional question; nowadays the Democrats are fractionally less unquestioning, while Republicans see Israel as the fulfilment of a Biblical prophecy.

London was preoccupied with how Britain in the troubled 1970s looked from America. Early on I covered a visit by Harold Lever, tasked by Harold Wilson with securing support for sterling; he got a dusty answer. Labour's loss of its majority weakened its hand; I first met Denis Healey in a Washington lift the morning after a humiliating by-election defeat.

Hot potatoes affecting the "special relationship" ranged from how far the vocal Irish-American lobby was influencing US policy to the supposedly environmentalist campaign by anti-British politicos in New York to keep out Concorde. In between came tricky issues of defence procurement (we hoped for more orders after selling them the Harrier, but the much vaunted "two-way street" never materialised), and the ongoing efforts to end UDI in Rhodesia. I was astonished when Britain's UN ambassador Ivor Richard briefed us that David Owen wanted to incorporate the guerrillas into Ian Smith's army – but that is almost what eventually happened. Such issues required close contact with visiting British ministers, and above all made us keep alongside the Embassy.

Any correspondent in a foreign capital needs the Embassy, both as a source of news and to find out where you can buy Marmite and real sausages. The quality of Britain's missions abroad varies, depending on whether the Foreign Office believes they will ever have a crisis to deal with. Most I have found excellent, but I did wonder how some of our diplomats in 1980s Nairobi would have fared in a more demanding post.

The Washington embassy is our most important, and postings there are coveted. The Lutyens building up Massachusetts Avenue is the nerve centre of Britain's day-by-day relationship with our dominant ally. If the Ambassador and the embassy are doing their job, they have an inside track to the administration; if the chemistry is poor, they become bystanders. Much of the work is unglamorous, and some embassy staff are doing an essentially Whitehall job. That didn't prevent their being interesting to know; one couple broke the ice at dinner parties by recalling how in Kampala Idi Amin had been their babysitter.

Initially the ambassador was Sir Peter Ramsbotham, an old-school diplomat endeavouring to maintain Britain's credibility despite economic decline; his crowning moment was to play host to the Queen. He was nobody's fool, but Callaghan and David Owen decided someone more attuned to Carter's younger team was needed. One morning in 1977 I got an urgent summons to the embassy. The first person I saw was Ramsbotham's secretary

Jeremy Greenstock, much later our ambassador at the UN; on a sheer hunch I asked him: "Have you got us here to tell us about the new ambassador?" only for his face to fall. There was, indeed, to be a new ambassador - Peter Jay, Callaghan's son-in-law - and Greenstock momentarily feared a leak. When the news broke at Westminster, there was a storm over claims that Number 10 had branded Ramsbotham a "fuddy-duddy".

Ramsbotham became governor of Bermuda, and Peter and Margaret Jay moved in. They brought a more proactive style, with Jay particularly adept at countering IRA propaganda. Margaret too made an impact, though her affair with Carl Bernstein would leave wreckage.

On 4 July 1976, America reached its Bicentennial. The country needed something to celebrate, and there were fewer murders in New York that day than anyone could remember. In Washington hundreds of thousands turned out to watch the fireworks on the Mall between the White House and the Capitol. When the display ended no-one alerted Metrobus to start running again, and there were a lot of very sore feet.

Days later, the Queen arrived to show there were no hard feelings, and I covered her visit. It began in Philadelphia, and I travelled up by train to join the press party: Fleet Street Royal correspondents, US-based British reporters, and baffled American hacks. From Philadelphia – where as a pool reporter I angered colleagues by failing to notice whether the Queen actually touched the Liberty Bell - she travelled to Washington, to be greeted by President Ford.

At the Embassy's royal garden party, I introduced myself to Tony Crosland; he talked of having sat next to my father at Highgate, reflecting: "We both had very forceful mothers." Seven months later he was dead; his widow, Susan, would recall that the day he suffered his fatal stroke, he had put aside an article about Dad to read.

That evening the Queen gave a dinner for the President. The VVIPs dined inside, Elizabeth Taylor meeting Ford's Navy Secretary John Warner who became her sixth husband. The rest of us were exiled to the Embassy garden - no hardship on a slightly sticky evening. I patrolled in my burgundy dinner shirt, getting mistaken for one of the Grimethorpe Colliery Band. Several guests I half-recognised, then round a bend in the path I ran into Muhammad Ali. The Greatest, then at the height of his powers, looked lost; I couldn't understand why he wasn't indoors with the highest and mightiest. I asked if he had any words for the occasion; he quietly told me he hadn't, then wandered off into the dusk. The evening ended in style: Steve had arranged a limo to make sure Sally Quinn, the hottest name in the Washington media after Woodward and Bernstein, got home OK. Overawed, I dropped her at her door; she went on to marry Ben Bradlee.

New York I did not look forward to; it was then a byword for squalor, crime and rudeness, and the prospect of skyscrapers terrified me (I suffer acutely from vertigo). My first visit didn't change anything: the crowd to greet the Queen on Wall Street jostled until an irritated voice shouted out: "Can't we behave like human beings, instead of New Yorkers?" and later I had my pocket picked. Briefing in a hotel suite, the Queen's press secretary Ron Allison was dumbfounded when an American hack asked if Her Majesty was left-handed. "What makes you think that?" asked Ron. "Well," came the reply, "at the White House banquet she held her fork in her left hand ..."

After a day in Virginia visiting Monticello it was on to Boston, where expected pro-IRA demonstrations didn't materialise. Boston seemed more English (or Irish) than New York, with shorter distances to cover on foot. There was a whiff of home about the Old North Church where the Queen attended a service ... spoilt by a cameraman who grunted loudly at every instruction on his headphones. The tour ended in Newport, Rhode Island, where Ford gave her a farewell dinner we didn't get close to. On the bus back to Boston Airport, one American reporter announced: "The real tour begins tomorrow - and this time we're gonna get it right!"

For the Canadian leg, the Americans and US-based Brits mostly gave way to reporters from London - and the Canadian media. I headed down to the quayside at Halifax to meet the Royal yacht; it was damp and miserable, then out of the mist marched a band playing *Hearts of Oak*. I can't remember when I've felt prouder to be British. After an unceasing diet of Sousa from bands including, naturally, a sousaphone, this band had a good, old-fashioned tuba. The Royal party had had a rough passage; when I reminded Prince Philip – who joked with us about it - decades later, it was an experience he hesitated to relive.

The Queen toured the Maritimes on a Canadian military aircraft, with our press bus hosted by an Airborne officer who goodnaturedly counted us off like a stick of paratroopers. When she signed the visitors' book at Government House in Halifax, a duplicate page lay ready in case of bombardment by seagulls. I could understand why Scots felt at home living under the Saltire in craggy Nova Scotia; the local paper was even suggesting the province could break with Canada to join an independent Scotland. New Brunswick to the west was greener, less wind-blasted but still totally unspoilt, locals compared it to Maine in the 1950s.

The press, even in a confined space, distanced itself respectfully from the Sovereign, but in Halifax she gave us an informal garden party. The Queen has a reputation for putting people at their ease, but while Prince Philip steered us into a relaxed conversation we all felt nervous with her as we stood in a circle with our tea and cucumber sandwiches. I, for one, broke the golden rule of not speaking till you're spoken to.

Britannia's doctor invited me aboard while the Royal party was ashore, and I had a fascinating tour: from the chart table at the stern where the Queen could sit on a high chair to study the ship's progress to the kitchens where Palace pastrycooks were hard at work. In the NAAFI with its stocks of underpants and deodorant, I purchased the ship's crest, which still hangs on my wall.

Next came Montreal. Quebec separatism was at its height, and not long before, militants had kidnapped a British diplomat. There were fears that the massacre of Israeli athletes at Munich four years before could be repeated, and British papers on sale in Canada were comparing Montreal with Belfast and Beirut. This assignment didn't look like being fun - but it was.

The Olympics in 1976 were far less of a media circus than today. Coverage for Canadians was wall-to-wall, but globally there were far fewer media outlets, no 24-hour or all-sport networks, no professional athletes and, above all, less hype. Montreal hosted only a fraction of the 22,000 media accredited for London 2012. The *Telegraph* sent four staffers: Jim Coote, our athletics correspondent; Donald Saunders, our veteran chief football writer; Alan Smith, who covered several sports including equestrianism; and myself; freelancers looked after niche sports like swimming. My role was to cover the Royal involvement in the Games and look out for news stories, freeing the sportswriters to do their job.

I was in the Olympic stadium - a massive white elephant Montrealers took decades to pay for - for the opening and closing ceremonies, and saw Brendan Foster win bronze in the 10,000 metres – Britain's only track and field medal. Sitting by the trackside, I found myself thinking; "This is the Olympic Games. It ought to feel more special." (London 2012 did). More of my time was spent in the press centre, with each country's sporting hacks celebrating triumph or lamenting failure.

Inevitably, there were glitches. The American network screening the opening ceremony failed to realise the teams were entering the stadium in French alphabetical order and cut away for commercials as the athletes from Spain (Espagne) marched in - missing altogether the arrival of the USA (États-Unis). And when on a rest day the Olympic flame went out, an enterprising handyman used his cigarette lighter, only for a po-faced International Olympic Committee to demand a formal re-lighting ceremony. When the *Telegraph* produced its 150th anniversary brochure, this was one of my two stories used, along with the vandalising of the display of bricks at the Tate the year before.

For the first week, I followed the Queen as she visited the Olympic pool and reminisced - in French - at a dinner about watching ice hockey in Montreal in 1951. I realised how deeply the Royals were embedded with the Canadian establishment when I overheard Prince Philip greet one of their generals with: "Jack, you know the Trudeaus, don't you?" After they flew home, I covered Princess Anne competing in the three-day event at Bromont, well outside the city. Eventing isn't my favourite sport: one Canadian hack compared dressage to watching paint dry, and you can't see the cross-country from a fixed position, which leaves only the showjumping to enjoy. I experienced a surreal minibus journey with Jackie Stewart at the wheel, and further disappointment from the *Sunday Telegraph.* On the Saturday, Princess Anne was thrown on the cross-country circuit. I tracked down the team doctor, who declared her fine apart from the odd bruise; I filed, only for the paper to carry a lurid account of injuries she had never received.

One morning, the foreign desk woke me at 5 am. They had proof that an international terrorist - Abd Al Wahab Syed Al Kiali - had infiltrated Canada under diplomatic cover to blow up the Games; the story would appear whether I could stand it up or not, but would look better with a Montreal dateline. My brain was spinning on the bus to Bromont; only when I got there could I call the Mounties' press officer. When he returned my call, it became evident they were checking out the same story. He didn't exactly confirm it, but corroborated it to the point where, under continuing pressure from the desk, I wrote that he had.

When the paper hit the streets, the solids hit the fan. The IOC, then the Mounties, called press conferences to rubbish the story. I compiled a follow-up which tried not to discredit what I had written, dwelling heavily on the ongoing investigations. And the foreign desk discovered the story had been planted on us by Israeli intelligence to keep the Canadians up to scratch. Worse followed: Mr Kiali turned out to be not only a respectable Syrian diplomat, but a subscriber to the *Telegraph,* and he sued for libel. Astonishingly, I was never involved in the proceedings despite the story carrying my byline. London asked me for a detailed explanation, then my New York colleague Harry Miller was sent up to Montreal to talk to the Mounties. They too had been suckered by the Israelis, and were surprisingly understanding. Harry got me off the hook, but the episode cost the *Telegraph* £8,000 in damages, plus costs.

Any Olympic city goes into carnival mode, and so it was in Montreal for locals, visitors, the media and competitors whose events had finished. Some evenings the *Telegraph* team ate together, others I struck out on my own, sampling the thick Quebec pea soup, served whatever the temperature outside, and getting to meet a charming Lebanese family and an Estonian refugee social worker supporting athletes who had cracked up. As the Games neared their end, I had less to write about, even covering a mutiny on a freighter in port at Halifax.

After the closing ceremony I caught the Super Continental to Ottawa to join Deborah and Carrie, who were staying at nearby Petawawa with her sister Glenys, matron of the base hospital. Petawawa would hit the headlines in 1995 when Canada's defence minister David Collenette disbanded the Airborne Regiment after the torture and killing of a teenager in Somalia; a sign on the main street read: "I'd rather eat shit with the Airborne than steak with Collenette."

A year on, I went back to Montreal reporting on Quebec separatism and renewing acquaintances, then stayed at Glenys's A-frame on one of the Thousand Islands in the St Lawrence before looking up family friends in Toronto. There I met an old lady who boasted of having lived 20 years in a French-speaking village in Quebec without learning a word of the language; this made me understand why many Francophones wanted to get even.

One quiet Washington Friday in 1978, I went over to the Canadian Embassy for lunch with a military friend. On my well-lubricated return a message was waiting: Canada had renounced nuclear weapons, we were splashing the story and as I had Canadian military contacts could I come up with some elaboration? My colonel was by now on his way to the mountains, and I couldn't contribute a sausage.

Over time, I adjusted to Washington life and found American attitudes rubbing off on me. There were family trips to Colonial Williamsburg and New Orleans, but after John was born, almost all the travelling was for work – notably to the Appalachians covering a miners' strike.

In the small town of Welch, West Virginia I checked into a motel where a tide mark on the walls testified to recent flooding. The owner was the Sheriff, Clark Belcher. He told me Carter had invoked the Taft-Hartley Act ordering the miners back to work, and he was going up to the mine at dawn. Then he asked: "Can you handle a gun?" "Only a rifle", I replied, remembering my mushroom-blasting days in the CCF. "In that case you'd better lie on the floor", he said. In the event he snuck off without waking me, returning to tell me over breakfast that there hadn't been any trouble.

I drove on through rural Kentucky and Tennessee, ending up at the Virginia mining town of Norton. I passed several mines with pickets outside; they were often just holes in the rock, beneath dangerous-looking tangles of concrete and rusty metal.

We had a choice for the summer of 1978: tour the Grand Canyon or go home and see the family. We had only been back a few days when Peter Eastwood called me in. A vacancy had arisen at the Commons, and with an election imminent it had to be filled at once. With hindsight it would have made more sense to recall Jim Wightman from Washington, as he would head the Lobby team within a year anyway and had not been able to move his family to the States. But for me the move was a promotion. I went back to Washington to pack and mind the shop until Steve returned from his holiday; in the meantime John, back in England and just 12 months old, contracted measles which would leave him with brain damage, before he could have his jab.

It was six years before I returned to Washington, with Neil Kinnock, and on the drive in from Dulles I realised how much I had missed America. On the flight over Neil was at his most mischievous, recounting how the Lebanese Druze leader Walid Jumblatt had told him: "Your Michael Heseltine, he is - how you say it? - a pryke." I followed Neil and Glenys round Washington and introduced them to a completely changed *Telegraph* team. At the Embassy they overlapped with Norman Tebbit; Neil claimed that each night he hung a clove of garlic on their bedroom door.

The Reagan White House wasn't interested in a British opposition leader with suspect policies; Margaret Thatcher was flavour of the month. But Neil did meet Reagan's Secretary of State, George Shultz. With my deadline close, I camped out in the State Department foyer with a handful of other reporters. Neil eventually emerged, confirming that he and Shultz had not seen eye to eye on nuclear policy, and I went off to file.

Next morning I was woken by the foreign desk demanding to know why I had missed the story. They read me a quote from Neil on the BBC that Shultz had "got out of his pram" defending US policies. I was nonplussed: the BBC hadn't even been at the State Department, and Neil had said nothing like that to us. It turned out that, having missed the rendezvous, Martin Bell had contacted Neil at the Embassy and been given the explosive phrase that would damn the visit as a failure. My crime was having done my job; had I spent the afternoon schmoozing with old colleagues and rung Neil later, he might have said those words to me. There again, he might not.

In New York, we stayed at the UN Plaza Hotel, which to my alarm had one corner overhanging the street dozens of storeys below. I kept as close to the door of my room as possible. Neil was there to visit the UN - where the *Telegraph* over three decades had had a buckshee office whose use was discouraged because the paper disapproved of the organisation. He also called on Mayor Ed Koch. Frustrated with trying to pin Neil down on Northern Ireland, Koch eventually interjected: "Yeah, but what's your position?" Nothing in that visit to the Big Apple made me want to live there, and when months later Peter Eastwood offered me New York I turned it down.

I was on the point of leaving the *Telegraph* for the *Independent on Sunday* when I next visited America in the autumn of 1989 - and I was on holiday. I started in Dallas, visiting Ethan Stroud, a distant Comfort relative. Ethan was a rugged lawyer of old Texas stock - the independent Republic of Texas - and a lone Democrat among conservative Republicans. He lived at prestigious Turtle Creek in a mini-Roman villa, with his charming third wife Mimi. Missing my connection at JFK, I arrived after midnight. But I was made unfailingly welcome, and taken to the ranch that doubled as South Fork in *Dallas;* their country club - Mimi's daughter had a horse named Maserati; the *Dallas Morning News;* the Texas School Book Depository from which Lee Harvey Oswald shot JFK; and the grassy knoll from where many claim someone else did.

Ethan gave a dinner for me and twenty of his friends, all of them worth millions. The talk was not of oil - most wells around Dallas had run dry - but of silver, the billionaire Nelson Bunker Hunt having gone bust after failing to corner the market. Ethan, who himself wrote knowledgeably on gold, had once shared the school run with Hunt. "Dammit", he told me. "They even distrained his Rolex."

Next stop was Lancaster, Pennsylvania, where Bob Gray had invited me to lecture at Franklin & Marshall on developments in Europe. I skirted the Amish country with its grain silos and neat picket fences, toured the Hershey chocolate factory, and in a small town drugstore obtained a coffee for a nickel (5 cents). Starbucks put paid to prices like that.

Then I did Washington, in style. The *Telegraph* travel desk had conjured up, from its "broody file" of untaken free trips, three nights at the Four Seasons in Georgetown. I used the hotel's stretch limo to tour the sights I hadn't seen while living there, starting with the Lincoln Memorial. I took the Metro to Friendship Heights for a nostalgic visit to Sherrill Avenue where another *Telegraph* staffer was in residence, and caught up with my old neighbours.

Final port of call was Baltimore, where I stayed with Rick and Dusty Lidinsky. Rick showed me how the city (of which his father had been Comptroller) was regenerating; despite what you saw in *The Wire*, real efforts have been made. We ended with oysters beside the Inner Harbor, close to the Civil-era warship

Constellation; I still prefer Maryland's other delicacy of crab – enjoyed again when I went back with Jeanette 30 years later.

I accompanied John Major to Washington for meetings with George Bush senior and Bill Clinton, but have since seen more of the rest of America. Two visits to California were necessitated by Dad's first stroke in 1991 and Jane's subsequent death. In 1992 Corinne and I headed for Santa Barbara with a host of financial and practical loose ends to resolve. Dad said we could stay in the "garden house" he kept on as a bolthole, but we found a lean-to full of insects, intruding vegetation and a rotting fridgeload of food – and checked into a hotel. I shuttled between lawyers, accountants and banks amid the Spanish-style delights of Santa Barbara, arriving at one bank to find Dad's account had that very day gone into the red - a serious matter in America. A year later we rented a convertible in Los Angeles and drove up the coast via Santa Barbara to San Francisco and beyond, then inland to Crater Lake, Portland, Mount St Helen's - still desolate 13 years after the eruption - and Seattle. In one Oregon village store I saw a sign that summed up the battle between environmentalists and loggers: "World paper shortage - wipe your ass with a spotted owl."
Returning to California since. in Palm Springs in 1998 I just stopped Alex, then four, falling from a fourth-storey window. A piece I wrote for the *Telegraph* after visiting a rather tired Disneyland brought a formal protest, plus several "readers' letters" that turned out to be from Disney employees. And in 2004 I stayed at Oceanside, outside San Diego, with Norval Lyon and his Californian wife Lynn after a bruising year for all of us. A Mexican illegal immigrant on speed had driven into Lynn at 100 mph while she was stopped at traffic lights; by then out of hospital, she was having intensive physio. Norval had worked wonders adapting the house and recovering the costs of her treatment from their insurance company. We visited old Spanish missions and the hotel where *Some Like It Hot* was filmed, and I filled gaps in my wardrobe, carrying everything home in a suitcase purchased at

WalMart. Ten years on, Jeanette and I would hit the red carpet in Hollywood, but you will read about that later.

10: Westminster

Most political stories, whatever their apparent subject, are about the great game: who's up, who's down, who's in, who's out, who's going to lead the party and, above all, who will win the next election? One exception - expenses apart - is stories about Parliament itself.

The Palace of Westminster may be historic; I would suddenly realise I was in the room where Parnell had fought to save his career, or Tory backbenchers had mutinied in 1922. But it is an exasperating place to work, hopelessly out of date and until recently without office space for every MP. Being privileged to serve your constituents is all very well, but there is no excuse for the archaic procedures, the shambolic way the building has been administered, or the way security until recently bumbled along in the hands of the "men in tights": the semi-Royal functionaries whom Parliament seemed powerless to influence.

I had been primed on these shortcomings by Sir Barnett Cocks, a former Clerk to the House and an Oxford friend of Deborah's stepfather Conrad Miller-Brown. Barney's history of the Palace, *Mid-Victorian Masterpiece,* is scathing about the way it was run – drawing richly on his own experience of its more asinine traditions as enforced by a succession of indifferent Serjeants at Arms. One of the first sights to greet me was a door atop the stairs from the Members' Lobby to the Committee Corridor, outside which two empty milk bottles appeared each morning. It served the Deputy Serjeant at Arms' official residence, which occupied valuable space at the heart of the building until around 1990 when it became the office of the leader of the Liberal Democrats.

The way the place is run has improved, particularly since 1997 when a huge and younger new intake – mainly Labour but more importantly heavily female – decided things had to change, starting with the working hours. Tam Dalyell in the 1960s began a long-running campaign to secure for MPs the numerous empty rooms he found, but only in the last 25 years have real changes been made: in working hours, in procedure, in simplifying documents and, above all, in injecting an element of common sense.

Security has been the last bastion to crumble; it took repeated incursions by Fathers 4 Justice for the police and security services to gain any real say. Yet it was an astonishing lapse by the Commons itself that brought protests to Parliament Square, instead of the traditional rallying point of Trafalgar Square. Every year MPs passed the Sessional Orders, which banned demonstrations in Parliament Square under the guise of guaranteeing access to the House. One year in the late 1990s the Orders were not put, and within weeks gay rights campaigners and the Countryside Alliance were storming the building. When Parliament tried to find a way of reintroducing the ban, it found itself accused of violating human rights.

Back in the 1970s security in and around the Palace of Westminster was almost non-existent, despite the threat from the IRA and the many experienced police officers deployed to sit in its corridors. The only concerted police action was a nightly patrol on the corner of Whitehall which stopped motorists who were black.

As a political reporter, you have to get to know a representative cross-section of people at Westminster to leave no issue or viewpoint uncovered: ministers, backbenchers, peers, party officials, special advisers, MPs' research assistants and secretaries and Whitehall press officers. And by the mid-1980s I must have been on familiar terms with 200 MPs out of 659, and on a nodding acquaintance with most of the rest.

There were a few I never got to know, either because others covered the same ground or they didn't seem to have much to contribute. I remember one colleague lunching a senior Labour MP, only for each to realise they had absolutely nothing to say to each other. There were also a few – Geoffrey Robinson and Jonathan Aitken come to mind – who were preoccupied with matters away from the House or too grand for mere hacks. Alan Clark, surprisingly, was approachable, because – as his *Diaries* would reveal - he pored over what we wrote for clues as to whether he was on the way up or out. He was not alone in that.

The long hours spent patrolling the lobbies, corridors and bars had their compensation in stories unearthed, politicians understood better … and simply being at the centre of things. The regime is slightly less damaging to home life today, with a "family friendly" Commons, than when you had to be there by lunchtime and couldn't leave till midnight. But after the 1997 election, I no longer felt like spending long hours getting to know the new intake; time to hand over the baton.

Most of the MPs I've known have worked an even longer day, and been public spirited and financially honest. There have always been a few on the make, but most in the 1970s, '80s and '90s came to Westminster expecting to live frugally. MPs' expenses were never controversial until the *Daily Telegraph* published its breathtaking catalogue of abuses, nor should they have been. Traditionally the average MP feared the Fees Office's strictness about what could be claimed. But somehow, around 2003, the brakes came off allowing the venal to take advantage, and sadly the number who cashed in was nearer 50% than the 10% I would have expected. The expenses tap was not turned on by a decision of the House, but by officials answerable to a committee chaired by Speaker Michael Martin.

I first visited the Commons in 1963 courtesy of Tam Dalyell. Richard Crossman asked Tam, his PPS (Parliamentary private secretary), to find out what scientists would want from a government committed to harnessing Harold Wilson's "white heat of technology", and one day Tam called at my father's lab. Dad gave him a few thoughts to mull over, then told him: "My son is fascinated by politics – could he have a look round the Commons?" Tam said he would be happy to arrange this, and soon afterwards I secured an afternoon off from school.

Tam was a courteous host, as well as, in Andrew Marr's immortal words, "possibly the only member of the Socialist Campaign Group to keep peacocks". He gave me lunch, then installed me in the Strangers' Gallery to hear the debate on the Beeching Report. The only speaker I can remember was Labour's Leslie Spriggs – not for what he said, but for his bombastic style which simply didn't work in the House. My other recollection from that day over half a century ago is of the glass splashbacks in the parliamentary urinals.

I returned occasionally, with Fred Fox's encouragement. One evening early in 1964 I got back to school, switched on the radio and heard that twenty minutes before I arrived in the gallery, Sir Winston Churchill had left the Chamber for what would be the final time. I would have given anything to see him, having put ten shillings into a school collection toward his statue on Woodford

Green. My parents begrudged it, largely because Grannie, a constituent of Churchill's, had disagreed with him passionately over India ... not surprising as she had met Gandhi.

At the start of September 1978 I returned to the Commons as number two in the *Telegraph*'s Lobby team. I had been rushed back from America because Peter Gill had left to join ITV and Jim Callaghan was expected to call an election. Parliament was deep in the summer recess (and its annual ordeal at the hands of the builders). I stood in the archway where you catch the lift up to the Press Gallery wondering which of the besuited men passing by were MPs; in those days they did not have to display their passes except on arrival, and we did not need them at all.

Then as now, the *Daily Telegraph* operated from Room 10 of the Press Gallery, two floors up and midway along a corridor – separated by a metal grille from the Speaker's wing - whose rooms housed much of the national and regional press. Room 10 has a magnificent view over Parliament Square; below is New Palace Yard, whose catalpa trees still thrive four decades after being condemned. There were long desks topped by typewriters, a phone booth in the corner and a teleprinter across the corridor which transmitted our copy to Fleet Street. Along the walls were shelves laden with cuttings books for each of the staff; I filled one about every five months. Near the door was an annunciator, one of the television screens all over the building which since the mid-1960s have shown what is being debated, who is speaking and how long they have been on their feet.

There were ten of us in the room. David Harris, the Political Correspondent (a title that now denotes the Number 3), was in charge. Deceptively mild-mannered and immensely kind, David managed to be both a conscientious political reporter and an active Conservative; his pre-conference questioning of Tory grandees was rigorous. David gave me valuable party contacts, though I did wonder what he'd been told about my politics when he asked during *Land of Hope and Glory* if I knew what the tune was. Soon after I arrived, David became a candidate for the first European elections; after a spell at Strasbourg he would be MP for St Ives. Had I been at Westminster longer when he left I would have been in the running to succeed him, but I was only six months into the job so Jim Wightman returned from Washington to take charge. Jim and I would work at close quarters for nearly seven years.

Being a number two in the Lobby isn't easy. You have to know everything that's going on, and write authoritatively at a moment's notice on anything from defence to social security, from foreign affairs to council finance. The *Telegraph*'s specialists came down to Westminster sometimes, but usually you simply had to get on with it. Equally you must allow your political editor to shine. If he is taking the day off, you must be ready to give up the day's main story at an advanced stage of preparation if he bustles in at teatime. But equally you have to be ready to fight not only your corner but that of others in the team.

Unless there was an obvious main story Jim – who among other things had excellent Palace contacts - would look after the Government and I took care of Labour, but the arrangement was fluid and we had to know people in every camp. There was nearly always enough going on to keep us all fully stretched; even deep in a recess, there was hardly a day I didn't find something to write.

Our number three was Tony Conyers, a tabloid veteran and a former correspondent in Moscow and Paris (where he could pass for a *Marseillais*). Tony's speciality had been debriefing Brits who claimed to have been in the Foreign Legion. If suspicious, he would shout one word at them: "Balox!" Those taking a swing at him failed the test: Balox was the beer specially brewed for the Legion. Politics wasn't really Tony's thing, but he was a joy to work with, sharing with me not only his knowledge and experience but his contacts in Annie's Bar. Over the years, several other agreeable colleagues held the number three job, among them Graham Paterson (who became foreign editor of the *Times*), Valerie Elliott, a bubbly Welsh blonde who also went to Wapping, and David Millward, a mad-keen Chelsea fan who is now the *Telegraph*'s correspondent in Maine.

Into the 1990s, the *Telegraph* carried a daily account of the debates from both Houses, from a team of four experienced gallery reporters with excellent shorthand led by Peter Pryke; Tony Looch, a camp South African, was its most colourful member, though his inability to keep quiet when others were under pressure once prompted Conyers to threaten to kill him.

There was also our sketchwriter: the theatrical reviewer of the day's proceedings. Being original and funny about Parliament against the clock isn't easy, as I would later discover when I wrote the sketch myself. In the 1970s our *enfants terribles* Frank Johnson and John O'Sullivan were compulsory reading, not least because of their unflattering treatment of Mrs Thatcher's performances in the House. As I arrived, a new generation including Edward Pearce and Stephen Glover was taking over.

Our secretary, Sally Hallam, organised our lunches, parried readers and lent a sympathetic ear during personal crises. She took the future MP Julie Kirkbride, a later *Telegraph* team member, under her wing when Julie's former boyfriend, the Conservative MP Stephen Milligan, was found dead in highly embarrassing circumstances. A Liverpool doctor's daughter who had played a nurse in *Emergency Ward 10*, Sally came to the Commons by way of the *Daily Telegraph* Information Bureau. Her theatrical background manifested itself in her refusal to turn over the calendar ahead of time (bad luck), her decidedly un-Merseyside accent and her enthusiastic adoption of the late '70s fashion for see-through blouses. She also had a passion for cricket, watching Test matches in Australia with Mrs Richie Benaud.

We also had a teleprinter operator, and a messenger who brought mail from Fleet Street and took slips of copy through to the operator as we tore them from our typewriters. We typed a top copy and a carbon of everything, kept on a spike; if mistakes crept in later, it was handy to have proof.

Except on Fridays when the Commons sat in the morning, the tempo was slow before lunchtime. There might be the odd call from Fleet Street - usually to relay "wanted points" - but while there were occasional morning committees and press conferences, things only got busy once we were all in and writing. Unlike nowadays when most stories are immediately put online, there was no point in filing if further developments were likely, but by around 4.30 the subs needed copy. I often had several stories to hammer out, punctuated by calls to contacts and trips down to the Members' Lobby (a good five minutes' walk away) to catch one last source or tie up a loose end.

The pressure was greatest late on Thursday afternoons, when we had Prime Minister's Questions, Business Questions (always good for a story) and briefings by the Leader of the Opposition and the Leader of the House. As these not only set the agenda for the week ahead but enabled us to probe on the big story of the day, you couldn't start writing till they had finished, so from around 5.30 you produced an avalanche of copy. With typewriters clacking and all of us trying to drag the right words, or a recalcitrant fact, from our brains the pressure was acute, but raised voices were the exception; we usually just blocked out the noise. All along the corridor, reporters on other papers were doing the same. Though we were fiercely competitive, we made sure no-one missed a fact everyone else had, and compared notes on the implications and weight of a story.

Unless something big came up, there was little contact with the production team headed by the night editor. It's a tribute to the patience and professionalism of the back bench at Fleet Street that they could sense which of the many stories we sent should be given prominence in the paper.

The first edition came off the presses at 10.30 pm and, even with old technology, you could at a push get a story in at 8.30, but we tried to clear the decks well before then. Next there were evening meetings to doorstep, a further search for "intelligent life" downstairs, then a hurried canteen meal. Once the other papers' first editions were out, we would chase up stories they had. Some of our counterparts would alert us so we could get started without having to get anyone out of bed. And the *Mail*'s Gordon Greig liked to share a story he was not quite sure about; if his editor asked for corroboration he could say: "Well, the *Telegraph* has it too."

I started finding my way around as the builders cleared away their props (including one year a piece of sacking lining our lift that had apparently been marinaded in stale urine) - though it would be several years before I discovered the quickest route to the House of Lords at the far end of the building. After a security guard locked me in one night, I even found another way out of the Press Gallery, via the boiler room.

The press facilities at Westminster were more generous than in the US Capitol. By the lift at the end of our corridor, up a few steps, was a heavily-used cafeteria offering meals until late, and beyond it a reasonably-priced restaurant, handy for entertaining when there was no time to leave the building. Opposite the lift was the press bar, presided over by a gay Ulster Prod named Sam. Here hacks unwound after getting their copy away (before mobiles and pagers, the Gallery switchboard would Tannoy for us). Sometimes MPs came up; the young Neil Kinnock regularly drank there with the *Guardian*. Occasionally a colleague overimbibed. One Burns Night, a veteran *Express* gallery man returned to his seat and heckled Jonathan Aitken; as Aitken's family owned the paper, this was a bad career move.

Beyond the bar was a sizeable library, useful for reference though the books were long in the tooth; as Gallery librarian I freshened it up, encouraging colleagues who published books to donate them. Beyond were two flights of stairs, up to the *Times* room and down to the room where I would spend 3½ years with the *Daily Record*. Today the cafeteria's hours are limited, the bar has been rolled into it, the restaurant has gone and the library houses reporters.

One level down was the Upper Gallery: the preserve of the usually absent foreign press, whose doors to the press seats were only opened for a crisis or set-pieces like the Budget. Until quite recently it was adorned with yellowing pictures of "Parliament Houses of the Empire", from Gothic monstrosities to the Isle of Man parliament (an open-sided tent). Off the Upper Gallery was the

Commonwealth Writing Room, little used but with a television, then one of the few on the premises.

Beneath was the much busier Lower Gallery. On one side were the doors to the seats overlooking the Chamber, locked until daily Prayers were over (they are always held in private). My seat for the first nine years was the third from the right in the very front row, looking down directly on the Government front bench; later I was at the far end round the corner, next to Matthew Parris. On the other were cubicles with telephones to every newspaper's head office; when a story broke in the Chamber, reporters rushed out to brief their editor and secure space. In the centre was a long table divided into boxes, for the day's written ministerial answers from each department – useful sources of news now circulated online in their hundreds. Press releases from Whitehall and the parties went on a smaller table at the end; at a desk by the Gallery's only window attendants issued passes for visiting leader writers and the like. Off the Lower Gallery was a large room occupied by the BBC, with probably a tenth of the staff they have now, and a smaller one for the Press Association. There was a further small office for Reuters, later shared with GMTV, which became my base during my attachments to the *People,* the Scottish *Sun* and *Scotland on Sunday.*

The Lords provided simpler facilities: two good-sized rooms just with desks and phones. Only a handful of reporters, one from the *Telegraph*, based themselves at that end of the building, but when a Government defeat was in prospect we would surge over.

The other essential locations for us were the Members' Lobby, where you could catch MPs unless there was a vote in progress and talk on a not-for-attribution basis (Lobby terms); the Lobby Room high in a turret where we met on Friday mornings and every afternoon (and with the Leader of the House on Thursdays and sometimes the Leader of the Opposition); the Vote Office off the Members' Lobby where we picked up the Vote, the daily bundle of information including the Order Paper (the Lords still printed the date on theirs in Latin); and the Terrace where from Whitsun to the Summer Recess we could mingle with unwinding MPs until

Michael Martin barred us. Before MPs' expenses became front-page news, convivial members would raise their glasses to passing sightseeing boats and shout: "It's all free!" There was also a dubious episode when two Labour MPs dangled a kissogram girl over the edge.

Then there was Annie's Bar. Annie's identity is long forgotten, and the bar has had a fitful career, only reopening postwar when Ted Heath came in for a pint as prime minister, and being shifted in the 1990s from under the Chamber to a less convenient location. As its purpose was for politicians and hacks to converse off-the-record, the whips were never happy about it. Moreover, several MPs who propped up the bar at Annie's were deselected for alleged lack of effort.

Annie's circa 1979 spawned the Sir Frank Barlow Memorial Award. Frank, secretary of the Parliamentary Labour Party for a generation, was a tremendous raconteur. On his death just after retiring, the denizens of Annie's instituted an annual award for the most tasteless story. Frank's widow got to hear of the Award – though thankfully not its nature - and asked if she could be at the ceremony; it took a lot of diplomacy to dissuade her. The Barlow Award – won most years by a policeman from the Central Lobby - ran for a decade, being superseded by a competition for the most repulsive tie.

The most popular bar for MPs was the Strangers', better known as the Kremlin, again below the Chamber and handy for the Terrace; we could only drink there by invitation. Packed and claustrophobic, it was heavily used by Northern Labour MPs, their staff and constituents, and the late night decibel count made conversation impossible. The staple drink, as in all Commons bars then, was Fed: the Northern Clubs Federation beer, which reminded "Red Wall" MPs of home.

While 70 or so journalists held Lobby tickets in 1978 (it is far more now) and the Galley's total membership approached 200, the number of active reporters was less; many tickets were held by editors and the like. Moreover Sunday paper journalists only surfaced toward the end of the week. The explosion of electronic news outlets (and of staffing levels at the BBC) had yet to kick in, and at a push one person from each organisation could still cram into the front room at Number 10 for the 11 am briefing. The political big beasts knew most of us to stop and chat to, though they often dealt mainly with the reporter from their own regional paper.

The Lobby was then - and probably still is - a mixture of old-timers, younger but experienced reporters who would graduate to senior jobs, and newcomers finding their feet. Quite a few colleagues had covered Attlee and Churchill; having seen it all, they had a feel for what might happen next. There were also high-flyers for whom the Lobby - or even journalism - was a stepping-stone: Jim Naughtie on the *Scotsman* and *Guardian* before finding his niche at the BBC; Robert Harris, a fish out of water as an *Observer* lobby man before writing superb thrillers; David Davies with the BBC before becoming a football grandee; and Alastair Campbell with the *Mirror* before joining Tony Blair.

Relatively few had been to university; for much of my time in the *Telegraph* room I was the only graduate. The number of women in the Lobby was increasing, but it was galling when ministers invited "number ones and women" to their parties, or when a tabloid sent a woman to Westminster reckoning she would get more out of male politicians. Women proved themselves in journalism long ago, and such treatment was demeaning.

The Lobby and Gallery are organisations based on professional convenience, with a very limited social side. I was aware of an active Masonic Lodge; occasionally the chairs in the Lobby Room were left in a strange arrangement, and Lobby elections seemed predetermined. The Lobby in 1986 held a centenary dinner at the Savoy, with Sir Robert Armstrong, head of the Civil Service, at the *Telegraph* table; the *Spycatcher* affair, which did his reputation great harm, was about to break, and only when I met Armstrong again years later did I discover another side to him as a friend of Vaughan Williams. The Gallery held monthly lunches with a guest speaker; these were handy for inviting a politician you didn't know well or to whom you owed a favour. At one Roy Jenkins spoke of the "experimental aircraft" that became the SDP; another hit the headlines when Labour's Eric Heffer, brought as a guest, heckled the TUC chairman Tom Jackson.

Ministers often invited us to drinks parties in their departments, but unfailingly at 6.30 pm, when we were busiest. Once lobbying firms mushroomed in the 1990s, they entertained in the lead-up to the summer recess. One party we all tried to attend was at the Irish Embassy, where the drink flowed free - leading one Bishop of Southwark to disgrace himself.

The one internal social event was the children's Christmas party, held in the Gallery restaurant with the furniture pushed back or in a Commons dining room. My first was by far the best: with Roger Hargreaves - whose brother was in the Lobby for ITN - drawing and narrating his Mr. Men, and Mrs Thatcher in attendance. To my last, when Alex was a toddler, Cherie Blair brought two of her children, very much keeping a back seat.

The Lobby's greatest character was Chris Moncrieff, the Press Association's senior political reporter. With a "lived-in face and slept-in suit", the rumpled Moncrieff frequently overnighted in a corridor rather than go home to Chingford, convinced his wife he was allowed only two weeks' holiday a year and worked on decades after supposedly retiring. Chris had a unique gift for getting politicians to say more than was prudent; his endearingly familiar manner (even the most distinguished statesman was "Old Fruit" to Chris) broke exclusive after exclusive, even if some concerned the froth of politics. It was Chris who encouraged a Labour MP to denounce Michael Foot for wearing a "donkey jacket" at the Cenotaph, but it was also Chris who lured Sir Geoffrey Howe into revealing his displeasure at the Vestey family's tax avoidance. It is a tribute to Chris that his sources never minded when they saw their indiscretions in print; the only time I heard one rebuke him was when a tipsy Lena Jeger told him with a twinkle: "Don't call me a silly girl. I'm chairman of the Labour Party."

Then there was the *Guardian*'s Ian Aitken. Known universally as "Uncle", Ian personified the judgment, facility with words, ability to muffle his own opinions and care for young reporters that makes an outstanding Lobby man. Ian's roots lay in the Bevanite Left, but over three decades - initially with the *Express* - he had earned respect across the spectrum. As a busy day wound down, he could be found in Annie's or the Press Bar with a Bell's, always worth listening to.

Ian memorably accompanied Jim Callaghan to the Guadeloupe summit early in 1979; it was the one returning from which Callaghan almost said "Crisis, what crisis?" During one of the interminable waits that typify such gatherings, he went for a swim ... and lost the glass eye he had worn since a bout with cancer. French security men dived for it unsuccessfully, and Ian had to make do with his spare. When next he strolled into Annie's, Stan Crowther was ready for him. I knew Stan as the Rotherham freelance who became the town's mayor and Labour MP, but he was also a handy folk singer. Stan struck up *Island In The Sun*, adding the chorus:

> *But please, Oh please, do tell to me:*
> *How did my eye land in the sea?*

Geoffrey Parkhouse ran Ian close; a man of refinement tasked by the *Glasgow Herald* with getting close to the Tory hierarchy, he developed (for professional purposes) a lifestyle rooted in clubland. It was tempting to write Geoffrey off, but he was the only reporter to pick up the late swing to the Tories that won John Major the 1992 election. Geoffrey had his foibles - such as hurling an alarm clock through his bedroom window without checking that it was open. But he was an unselfish colleague - it was he who introduced me to Jeffrey Archer - and his early death was much lamented.

With us an even shorter time was the *Sun's* Chris Potter, taken in his mid-forties. Chris was my favourite colleague, but then he was everybody's. A teddy bearish South Walian, he had a generous heart and an infectious sense of humour. It was Chris who, encountering a routine written answer about dog licences, came up with the headline "Ruff Justice for Rover", then solicited quotes from a bemused Jim Pawsey, MP for Kenilworth, to drag in every possible pun. Chris survived a liver tumour only for cancer to strike;

the *Sun*, supposedly a monster of an employer, sorted out his tax affairs (discovering the Revenue owed him a fortune) and found a handy ground-floor flat for Chris and his magnificently supportive girlfriend Sue, whom he married. At his funeral outside Cardiff, the church was packed to the doors with people whose lives Chris had touched.

Lobby work involves alternate spells of boredom and pressure. In quiet times you hang around the Members' Lobby hoping to encounter an MP with a tale to tell; I put my varicose veins down to long hours standing on that cold tiled floor. Yet the sheer pace of events and volume of work can make it a struggle to keep up, particularly in the late afternoon.

Political reporting is cyclical, reflecting the parliamentary sessions and recesses, set-pieces like the Queen's Speech and the Budget, the party conference season and of course general elections. Each sitting week had a rhythm of its own, with Prime Minister's Questions, the Parliamentary Labour Party each Wednesday, the next week's business and party briefings on Thursday, the 1922 Committee every Thursday evening and the Lords' briefing every Friday. Each day there were the morning Lobby at Number 10 (at the Commons on Fridays), morning press conferences or committees (far fewer then), maybe lunch out with a politician, Questions at 2.30 (earlier on Fridays), the 4 o'clock lobby, then hopefully a chance to get writing. At 10 pm came the main division, after which – if it mattered – one of us collected from the Clerks' office a division list on which the Ayes and the Noes were ticked off in pencil, and combed it for rebels for a late-edition story. Then came a flurry of catching up with other papers' stories, and unless there was a late sitting on something really controversial, the last train or a minicab home.

The most challenging day for me was Budget Day - not because of the economic and political importance of the Budget, but because in the 1980s the public spending White Paper was released at the same time. I had three hours to "gut" this weighty document and make sense of its plethora of tables to produce a single coherent story - and I don't think I ever got anything wrong.

The high point of the parliamentary week is PMQs, now half an hour on a Wednesday but prior to 1997, when Tony Blair combined them, two 15-minute sessions on Tuesdays and Thursdays. At PMQs, Parliament - and nowadays the nation - gets to see how the Prime Minister measures up against the Leader of the Opposition, and vice versa. I was reared on sketch writers' accounts of Harold Wilson baiting Harold Macmillan, then of the tussles between Wilson and Ted Heath. I arrived to see Mrs Thatcher hectoring Jim Callaghan, and after a few months Mrs Thatcher hectoring Callaghan again but now as prime minister. Generally the protagonists charge past each other like jousters, only occasionally landing a blow. The one thing the PM does not do - except when given a friendly prompt - is answer the question. When John Major succeeded Mrs Thatcher, he did so for the first few weeks, and there was a tangible sense of shock.

I watched from the Gallery duels between nine pairs of leaders: Thatcher/Callaghan, Callaghan/Thatcher, Foot/Thatcher, Kinnock/Thatcher, Kinnock/Major, Smith/Major, Blair/Major, Major/Blair and Hague/Blair. Mrs Thatcher lacked a relationship with the House, preferring to bludgeon it, but there is no doubt she was the most dominant at PMQs; Kinnock felt himself at a particular disadvantage, confiding frustratedly: "How will it look if I'm rude to a woman?" Even that superb parliamentarian Michael Foot never rattled her; she had too much self-belief. When Callaghan complained that her exchanges with the TUC's Len Murray were "a dialogue of the deaf", she responded: "I did not know Mr Murray was deaf." Just as it took members of the public to get her rattled when experienced television interviewers had failed, the rare punches landed on her came from backbenchers.

John Major had a fairly easy ride until Blair became along, though Kinnock scored some points off him in the run-up to the 1992 election. John Smith was a brilliant debater, but not quick enough on his feet to get the better of Major with his permitted question and two supplementaries, but in Blair Major met his match, and became prickly. This was partly because his government was running out of steam and credibility, but also because Blair, like Wilson, took a righteous zeal to those exchanges.

In power, Blair in his second and third terms exerted a dominance reminiscent of Mrs Thatcher. His first was another matter. Despite the Conservatives' crushing defeat, William Hague acted from his first question time as though Blair had been discredited. His approach was not pretty, but it rattled Blair - and helped rescue Tory morale.

I was present in the Gallery for events historic, poignant and farcical. The most momentous was the night of 28 March 1979, when Callaghan's government was defeated by one vote on a no-confidence motion. Labour was floundering after the "Winter of Discontent" and the abortive referenda on devolution; indeed it was the SNP, not the Tories, who initiated the motion. But Mrs Thatcher took it forward.

The House was packed and the debate electrifying, Callaghan warning the SNP they were "turkeys voting for an early Christmas". Of many fine speeches, the best came from Michael Foot, scorning David Steel for having metamorphosed from "boy wonder to elder statesman". The Conservatives, Liberals and SNP would all be voting against the Government, but Roy Hattersley was wooing Ulster Unionists with the promise of an undersea gas pipeline. Gerry Fitt, a Nationalist who normally voted with Labour, was holding out because of Roy Mason's tough security policy; the other Nationalist, Frank Maguire, was in the bar to make a "positive abstention". The House divided with the result impossible to predict. For a moment Labour MPs thought they had hung on, then came the announcement from the tellers: "The Ayes to the right, three hundred and eleven. The Noes to the left, three hundred and ten." For the first time in well over a century, and by the narrowest margin, a government had fallen on a vote of no-confidence. Mrs Thatcher rose to ask Callaghan's intentions, and he replied robustly: "We shall take our case to the country." We rushed out and pounded our typewriters.

Only in the morning did I discover the Labour leadership had turned down one more vote, which would have tied the outcome and obliged Speaker George Thomas to declare the motion not carried. "Doc" Broughton, MP for Batley, was seriously ill, but ready to come to the House and be "nodded through". Foot and Michael Cocks, the chief whip, honourably decided not to send for him; within three days, he was dead.

I missed the emergency Saturday session after the invasion of the Falklands, listening to it frustratingly at home. Nor was I there for Mrs Thatcher's final speech as prime minister, the only really good one she ever made. I was, though, when John Major won the respect of many Labour MPs by crossing the chamber to shake the hand of the dying Eric Heffer.

On the evening of 10 February 1983, I was in the cafeteria when "sitting suspended" flashed onto the annunciator. That meant trouble, so I shot downstairs - to find that the Welsh Office minister Michael Roberts had dropped dead at the Despatch Box in mid-speech. Frenzied efforts were made to revive him, and as I phoned the office Roberts was rushed to an ambulance, only to be declared "dead on arrival" at hospital. This could not be taken at face value, as it is an absurd fiction of the Palace of Westminster that no-one can be said to have died there.

Several moments of farce involved the rotund and incorrigible Tory Geoffrey Dickens, who once mentioned at the end of a press conference exposing "phaedopilia" that he had left his wife for a nurse he had met at a tea dance - then was surprised at Mrs Dickens' reaction. It was Dickens also who, followed round his constituency by a woman who wanted to see her MP at work, sent her a framed photo of himself but undid the effect by addressing it to "Horseface".

Geoffrey's defining moment came when he rose to ask Mrs Thatcher a serious question about rape. He began: "Mr Speaker, I should like to do every woman in the United Kingdom a favour ... ", then paused. The entire House – except Maggie – collapsed. After a minute or so of uproar, Speaker Thomas suppressed his own laughter to declare: "I am not here to save Honourable Members from themselves."

Another parliamentary boffo was at Mrs Thatcher's expense. At the time of Nelson Mandela's release in 1990, some sycophant asked: "If the Prime Minister, like Mr Mandela, had been in prison for 27 years ...", only for Labour's razor-sharp Gerald Kaufman to interject: "As she should." Again, it took time for order to be restored.

Every generation laments that the great days of parliamentary oratory are over, and certainly in today's managerial Commons the rhetorical conceits of Disraeli or Lloyd George would be entirely out of place. Yet there is still room for a well-honed argument, and for wit, and there have still been speakers who could fill the Chamber: Enoch Powell on his day, though I heard him make bad speeches too; Tony Benn (as when he convinced backbench Tories their rights were at risk during the Zircon affair); Michael Heseltine, for sheer nerve; and John Smith, uncomfortable at Question Time but magnificent in debate. Tony Blair reserved his finest speeches for party conferences. More recently the one parliamentarian you had to listen to was William Hague; he could present a threadbare argument with such skill and presence as to give it the full force of logic.

In my time the finest speaker of all has been Michael Foot. My colleague Edward Pearce observed – without exaggerating - that Foot could bring an audience to its feet with the single word "And!" He could captivate MPs on the benches opposite, lead them hypnotically to hover above a political dung-heap, then effortlessly release them into it. He once wrongfooted Tory backbenchers by suddenly saying: "Hands up all those who agree with the Government's economic policies!" A few reacted instinctively, and under taunts from Foot more raised their hands. But he left everyone else in the Chamber – including the Tory whips and an unhappy Sir Geoffrey Howe – with the clear message that support for those policies was less than wholehearted.

I saw him at his finest winding up a debate on Sir Keith Joseph's handling of British industry, telling a packed House of visiting a

Plymouth music-hall in his youth. The magician had invited an "aldermanic" figure up from the audience and asked for his watch. Foot told theatrically how the magician produced a hammer and smashed the watch to smithereens. Then, he recalled, the magician looked blankly at his victim and announced: "Oh dear, I've forgotten the rest of the trick." Joseph's stewardship, he declared, had been no different. What a performance.

The Speaker is judged by how well they control the House: responding to its mood, calming post-prandial fervours around the 10 o'clock vote, knowing when to be firm and when to allow latitude. In 1972 Selwyn Lloyd sat transfixed as Bernadette Devlin crossed the floor to assault the complacent Reggie Maudling after Bloody Sunday; other Speakers have ejected members for the mildest transgression. In my time those most frequently ordered out have been Dennis Skinner and Tam Dalyell - the latter once for an attack on Mrs Thatcher over the sinking of the *Belgrano* that included almost every word termed "unparliamentary" by Erskine May.

George Thomas was the first of four Speakers I saw in action. On his watch regular sound broadcasting of the Commons began, and his call of "Order, Order" became a catchphrase. Most successful Speakers evoke an element of showmanship, and this elderly, slightly mischievous Welsh preacher had a touch of the pantomime dame. Thomas was out of the Chair for a break when Labour's Reg Race became the first MP to utter the F-word in the Chamber, during a debate on licensing sex shops. Next day he reprimanded not only Race but, unfairly, the editor of *Hansard,* who had inserted a row of dots.

Thomas's greatest moment came in the twilight of the Labour government when Jim Callaghan, baited by the Tories, made a passing reference to Churchill sending troops to break a miners' strike at Tonypandy. Winston Churchill, the great man's grandson, demanded an apology, which on the facts he was entitled to. Then Thomas observed from the Chair: "As an old boy of Tonypandy grammar school, I never imagined that the final word on this would rest with me."

Bernard Weatherill was less theatrical, but largely overcame misgivings about his ability to control the House. The head of a Savile Row tailoring firm, he lived down the story that when he arrived, one landed Tory observed: "Can't think what this place is coming to. They've even elected my tailor." Weatherill was highly approachable, with an impish sense of humour: when I interviewed him as Michael Dobbs' *House of Cards* was being screened, he kept replying: "You might say that, but I couldn't possibly comment", the hallmark response of Dobbs' villain, chief whip Francis Urquhart. During Weatherill's tenure (1983-92) the Speaker's House was restored to its former glories and reunited - by his wife - with examples of Pugin's original design; the Speaker's ceremonial purse turned up in the Lords being used as a firescreen, and the State Bed was recovered from Wales.

As an ex-Tiller Girl, Betty Boothroyd had pizazz, and her presence carried her through when other Speakers might have struggled. She maintained a dignified silence when her successor came under fire, but was overly quick to criticise when John Bercow abandoned the fancy-dress side of the Speakership for a simple black gown. The authority of the Chair comes from the values it represents, not the flummery surrounding it.

Michael Martin was the first Speaker since 1695 to be forced out, over his handling of the expenses crisis of 2009. He struggled at times, but was the target of appalling snobbery from preening sketch writers and did not deserve their epithet of "Gorbals Mick". However the press had never forgiven him for booting them off the riverside Terrace a decade before, despite an appeal from a deputation including myself. Martin did his best to maintain the standing of the Chair and the House, but when the expenses scandal broke, it was a sign of how out of touch he was that his instinct was to fight back. He deserved to be its most prominent casualty: he did nothing to stop the abuses when they came to light, and some of his own expenses - and his wife's – set a poor example.

Almost all our contacts with the machinery of government were through departmental press officers, mostly friendly and helpful. For several years I even lectured to them on the nexus between Whitehall and the media. Yet of the civil servants who actually ran the country, we saw little. There was almost a phobia in Whitehall about such contact ... not surprising when it was technically a criminal offence even to disclose what was on the departmental lunch menu. This paranoia flowed from the top, and very few ministers – Michael Heseltine apart - would expose even their most senior civil servants to us. But during the Thatcher years, the failure of several high-profile prosecutions left the "catch-all" Official Secrets Act a dead duck.

Whitehall's mandarins must have realised from what we wrote that we had no idea how government really worked, and took hesitant steps to lower the barriers. The doctrine of "open government" was first adumbrated in 1977 by the head of the Civil Service Sir Douglas Allen, but it was seven or eight years before it started to take hold. One step involved Denis Trevelyan, an amiable First Civil Service Commissioner who had dared to meet the *FT*'s Elinor Goodman and myself for lunch, taking a group of us down to the Civil Service College just off the A3. We sat in on a course for high flyers from Whitehall and the private sector; their problem-solving was impressive, then we were pitched into an exercise in which their finely-honed brains reduced us to pulp. On the way home, the reason for the timing of this apparent exercise in *glasnost* became evident, when a slightly shamefaced Trevelyan told us that the Cabinet Secretary had unveiled proposals for more open government - with the people most likely to ask informed questions safely out of the way.

The activities of MI5 and MI6 were then strictly off limits. Occasionally, as with the unmasking of Antony Blunt, stories broke, but if you ventured into that territory you were liable to be summoned to Number 10 and told that "certain people are not pleased". This made me doubly proud when at the *Independent on Sunday* I broke the story that the security services were paying informants through the Ernie premium bond computer.

Stories about honours were also a minefield - apart from the twice-yearly Lists on which we were briefed in advance, on pain of death if we contacted anyone. At one such briefing a senior civil servant wrily observed: "There's an OBE for the Fashion Editor of *Vogue;* I imagine some of you will know her." But the risks came from speculation, and this landed me in hot water with Sir Geoffrey Howe.

One of my Tory sources was the historian/MP Robert Rhodes James, who was close to the former Foreign Secretary. As an official at the UN, Robert had sat next at a dinner to a Polish bishop who showed on the back of his menu how, under the Nazis, they distilled vodka from potatoes. That bishop was the future Pope John Paul II. A few months after Mrs Thatcher's removal, Robert called me for a furtive drink and told me she wanted to nominate Howe for a peerage. Given his seismic part in her overthrow this seemed implausible, but Robert was adamant, telling me the recommendation had gone to the Political Honours Scrutiny Committee. I could have got the possibility of Sir Geoffrey receiving a peerage from the woman whose career he had terminated into print at no risk to myself by crafting a speculative diary paragraph. But I felt that in the *European* this would not be noticed, so I wrote it as a straight news story. Sir Geoffrey summoned me, and the dressing-down he gave me, though brief, was severe. When next I interviewed him, for the BBC, he was his usual agreeable self.

My time in the Lobby spanned 21 years, from late August 1978 to February 2000. My work was most intensive - and most influential, though I only realised this later – up to 1987 for the *Telegraph*, before going off to write leaders (and occasionally the Commons sketch). I returned late in 1989 with the *Independent on Sunday*, experiencing the very different rhythm of Sunday Lobby work. I stayed on, with the *European* and *Daily Record*, until 1996 when, after a brief period freelancing, I went into lobbying. I came back as a freelance shortly before the 1997 election, for the *Scottish Sun* and subsequently *Scotland on Sunday* and the *People*. I finally left when I joined the DTI, and my spell as a special adviser effectively ruled out a return.

During those years televising of the Commons came in, against Mrs Thatcher's wishes. All-night sittings almost disappeared, because every government after 1979 (save for John Major's toward the end) had a working majority, because of New Labour's more "family-friendly" hours, and because rule changes made it harder for awkward backbenchers or the Opposition to obstruct business. Security was largely taken away from the "men in tights", not that it seems to have improved much. The public can no longer simply walk into the building, but must queue to be searched. Even more symbolically, it has been impossible since the early '80s simply to walk into Downing Street; anyone allowed through the gates erected then has now to negotiate further checks.

The way the media covers Parliament has also changed. No national daily now carries comprehensive reports of the main debates, though the sketches survive. Many worthy topics are no longer covered, and there is less detail. The mystique surrounding the Lobby has broken down, and the Prime Minister's official spokesman is now on the record. Microphones and even cameras have penetrated the lobbies and corridors, from which previously they were barred. The presence and influence of the regional media has declined, but Sky has established itself and bloggers now jostle with the serious weeklies. The broadcasters have moved out to Millbank studios over the road, reducing the critical mass of media in the Palace. The turnover of Lobby reporters has accelerated, mirroring the way politicians rise and burn ever more quickly. And the Lobby has outgrown the front room at Number 10, moving in Alastair Campbell's time to the basement and no longer entering through that iconic front door. Yet for all these changes, Parliament on its day can still speak for the nation; its vote in 2013 not to get involved in Syria had global implications, and its bellow of impotent rage after the Taliban's recapture of Kabul in 2021 caught a national mood. And the Lobby can still generate unparalleled political reporting.

11: Thatcher's Children

For over half my time covering national politics, the Conservative Party meant Margaret Thatcher. Love her or hate her, she made a greater impact than any other prime minister in the last half-century. She made Britain punch above her weight, and imposed profound changes on our society and economy. Herds of sacred cows were slaughtered and cartloads of family silver sold off under a prime minister who realised things could not go on as they were, but left a governing ethos that knew the price of everything and the value of far too little; no wonder John Major's priority was to create a Britain "at ease with itself". But life under Mrs Thatcher was never dull ... and it was fascinating to watch her at close quarters.

Covering a Tory government for a Conservative newspaper might not have seemed the right job for me. I suspect Peter Eastwood sent me to Westminster to get close to Labour – he must have guessed where my sympathies lay – but inevitably I also covered the Tories. I had already got to know and respect quite a few people in the party, though my hackles still rose when they celebrated on election nights. And with the odds on a Conservative government as I arrived, I set out to cultivate as many as I could before an election was called. Just as well, as they would be in power for 18 years.

My image of Mrs Thatcher – acquired not least from Tories of my acquaintance - was of a shrill, heartless Cold Warrior with simplistic and wrong-headed opinions. So I was apprehensive when early in September 1978 I faced a first encounter with her during the Berwick and East Lothian by-election. I confessed this to the veteran *Times* man David Wood; he knew her well and offered to break the ice. We eventually met in the foyer of a North Berwick hotel, whose management had tactlessly left Ted Heath's latest book on display. I need not have worried: I found her businesslike but courteous – and in our encounters over the next decade she was never anything but, and sometimes actively kind.

It was impossible to see much of Mrs Thatcher without experiencing her at full throttle. At that year's Press Gallery children's party she berated the organisers for serving sausages, instead of chipolatas which were easier to cut up. At our embassy in Brussels, she chided the ambassador for keeping the curtains drawn, and flung them open. And when, early in her government, I confessed that I hadn't yet read an article by Leon Brittan in that day's *Telegraph*, she exclaimed: "What? Don't you even read your own paper?" Needless to say, she had. Worst of all, I once got her direct line at the Commons after misdialling; I hung up hoping she hadn't recognised me.

She made the same impact on everybody. A shellshocked but delighted Lord Carrington told me of the dressing-down she gave the Soviet Ambassador after the invasion of Aghanistan (she would subject Carrington to the same treatment after an unsuccessful European summit), and a director of the Midland Bank told me with a shudder how she threatened to move her account to Barclays if they didn't start opening on Saturdays.

Margaret Thatcher did not have a relationship with the House of Commons; she simply dominated it. Her performances in opposition led sketchwriters to liken her to a runaway typewriter, and while she delivered crushing put-downs she never related to Members as a whole. She showed what might have been in her remarkable final Question Time when she thrived on the interruptions from Labour. But usually she was in too much of a hurry to take in, then feed off, the atmosphere of the House as other great politicians have done.

Nor did she have a recognisable sense of humour. When the joke began circulating about a meal with the Cabinet when she had ordered a steak and, when asked about the vegetables, replied: "They'll have steaks, too", explaining it to her proved impossible. And when the entire Commons collapsed with laughter after Geoffrey Dickens' most celebrated gaffe, she sat there stonily.

Most of us in the Lobby found it impossible not to respect – and often like – Margaret Thatcher. Some went further: one tirade from her in the Lobby Room was punctuated by an aside of "Not bad, is she?" from the *Mail*'s Gordon Greig, for even at full throttle she could be engagingly feminine – the only aspect, apart from the dullness of her eyes, that Meryl Streep's uncanny portrayal of her in *The Iron Lady* did not capture. Moreover she not only possessed the good politician's ability never to forget a name or a face (recognising resident British correspondents in foreign capitals without the need for a prompt); she was genuinely interested in people, and had a kindly side she did her best to keep private.

At a party just after Conrad Black took over the *Telegraph*, Mrs Thatcher sought me out and asked how Lord Hartwell was taking it. David Harris told me how she invited political hacks down to her flat at Scotney Castle for lunch, only for her assistant to drop the casserole and rush out in tears. Maggie calmed her down, then rustled up a second lunch herself. Norris McWhirter recalled how when he fought Orpington Margaret and Denis, who were big noises in the constituency, hosted a drinks party for him. Norris's pregnant wife felt poorly, and Maggie insisted on leaving the guests and taking her upstairs to rest. And when, at a Downing Street reception for severely disabled children, a mother needed to take her daughter to the loo, Maggie offered to take the little girl herself. You don't get that from an ogre.

Her devotion to her son Mark, whom no-one else could stand, was legendary; one Boxing Day I made my check call to Number 10 and was told: "It's the usual Chequers Christmas: family, friends and Mark." Her daughter Carol was totally different, and fun to work with long before she became Queen of the Jungle.

She was still far from being my cup of tea, nor were most of her policies. I was with her all the way on the Falklands, and with a heavy heart took her side against Arthur Scargill, who should never be forgiven for the suffering he brought upon the miners. But large sections of British industry were laid waste early in her premiership to no obvious purpose, and her policy on Europe deteriorated from a genuine championing of Britain's interests to the downright toxic; it was also crazy for her to try to halt the reunification of Germany after the Berlin Wall came down.

Disconcertingly, I came to realise that how I did my job could impact directly on her. Early in her government I ran a story, from sources inside Central Office, that she planned to replace Lord Thorneycroft as party chairman. Each accused the other of leaking it. It was also alarmingly easy to plant ideas in her mind. One Friday, lunching with one of her policy unit, I asked if anyone had thought of privatising the railways, with the infrastructure in the hands of a track authority (you may blame me for the current set-up if you wish, though John Major went one step further and privatised Railtrack). On the Monday Norman Lamont complained to me that all she had done that morning was bang on about some new wheeze for privatising the railways. I held my tongue.

I heard that Mrs Thatcher was resigning over the PA system at Earl's Court station, and of John Major's triumph as I did some punditry for Radio 4. My snap verdict was: "John Major is the new Prime Minister and Michael Heseltine will have an important role in his government." When the mike went dead, Jim Naughtie told me I hadn't needed to be that brief, but in truth there was no more to say.

John Major I rated from the start. I met him soon after his election for Huntingdon in 1979, and within a year was predicting that he would lead the party; in the same article I also forecast that Paddy Ashdown, then not even an MP, would lead the Liberals, which with hindsight looks pretty impressive. John has a wonderfully engaging yet slightly diffident manner, but it didn't take long to realise there were no flies on him. Within months, the 1979 intake were rating him "the man most likely to". And as he moved quietly up the ministerial ladder, chats with him were always of value, even if he learned far more than you did.

The idea of John as a grey man is light years from the truth. He was never, as some detractors claimed, the boy who ran away from the circus to become an accountant. For anyone who has been rejected as a London bus conductor to become Foreign Secretary, Chancellor and Prime Minister, there had to be something there. For a start, he has a wicked sense of humour. When the last Conservative seat in Glasgow fell vacant Teddy Taylor, who had decamped to Southend, was boasting in the tea room of receiving letters urging him to go back to Scotland and fight it. Then John interjected: "How many were from Southend, Teddy?"

I identified with John's 1950s schoolboy side, his sheer normality and his slightly unnerving ability to bring things down to basics. Just before his first Budget, the *Sunday Telegraph* mischievously reported that no-one had been able to find his birth certificate; the reason, it turned out, was that his surname was actually Major-Ball. When I bumped into John in the Lobby, he lamented: "I spent the weekend in my attic looking for proof that my parents were married." And when, over tea at the Treasury as the shine came off Nigel Lawson's boom, Elinor Goodman and I asked him if there was going to be a hard or a soft landing, John told us: "I'm worried there may not be a landing at all."

I was delighted when John became Prime Minister (it seemed strange but refreshing to greet him as such at an impromptu victory celebration), and I had faith in his ability to do the job. Had it not been for the Tory split over Europe, he would be remembered as a more than competent premier; as it is, the contemporary verdict of "nice bloke, shame about the party" was right. It was ironic that for most of his premiership I would work for a paper – the *Daily Record* – where it was my duty to point out where he was missing the plot. It was all the more generous of him to write the foreword for my *Brewer's Politics*, and it must have seemed poor reward when months later, on the morning of his party conference speech, I compared him on our front page with Forrest Gump – but that was what Cabinet colleagues were calling him.

The animus against John came from the Eurosceptic, Thatcherite Right after his conclusion of the Maastricht Treaty. Many could not forgive him for having won the 1992 election when they had hoped to get into opposition and do to their party what Tony Benn had done to Labour. They were backed by the *Telegraph, Sun* and *Mail*, but the perpetual sniping affected John's relationship with the media as a whole, and increasingly weighed him down.

The closing months of his government bordered on farce, the plethora of resignations over sleaze having created a situation where lacklustre ministers could not be sacked as there was no-one capable of replacing them. Having started in 1979 with a host of promising front-benchers, all the seed-corn had been used up – just as Labour's would be under Gordon Brown.

In eventual defeat, John handled himself with dignity. I put in to see him for a chat, and an invitation came back to interview him about the dangers of devolution. As by now I was freelancing for the *Scottish Sun* who would welcome an opportunity to give him a kicking on the issue, I went into protective mode and didn't take up the offer. But I should have.

I was as staggered as anyone when the news broke years later of his affair with Edwina Currie, not so much because it was John who was involved – female Tories had told me he was highly tactile – but because I couldn't believe Edwina could keep anything quiet. I also knew how proud he was of his wife Norma's fundraising for good causes – and how determined to keep the staggering amount she raised out of the papers. I admire a politician who doesn't want to talk about money.

Ted Heath's government coincided with my time in Sheffield, where the miners' disputes and his Housing Finance Act entrenched the class attitudes he was trying to erase. I have discussed Heath with his colleagues, former staff and parliamentary supporters, and the saddest thing was to hear Peter Walker, his closest ally, confess that Ted had never opened up with him. Heath's tragedy was to be born the wrong side of the Channel; his bulldozing approach would have been fine for a French president. Like de Gaulle or Mitterrand, he was a man for the *grand projet* – Concorde, Maplin Airport, the Channel Tunnel – and we British prefer to delay, hold endless inquiries and muddle through.

In their desire to denigrate Heath (who admittedly conducted a guerrilla campaign against his successor) Mrs Thatcher's intimates cast her as a champion of conviction politics – yet Ted was just as intransigent. He also never stopped to ask whether a course of action was sensible as well as desirable; had he done so, he would not have lost control during the 1974 miners' strike. Jock Bruce-Gardyne had a telling story about that February's election, which Ted called after a fortnight's fatal hesitation. When Jock told a meeting up in Angus: "The question before you is who governs Britain", a voice at the back responded: "If you don't know the answer to that, you don't deserve to." From that moment, Jock knew the game was up.

At the 1983 party conference, a group of us were invited to dine with Ted at the hotel outside Blackpool where he was holding court. There were six or seven at table, including Ted's assistant Wilf Weekes, who went on to co-found the lobbying firm GJW (I once lunched Wilf at BHS in Blackpool, the only eatery we could find).

The conversation, as usual with Ted, combined reminiscences, Puckish asides and barely-concealed contempt for his successor, all delivered in his unique and slightly strangulated vowels, his shoulders heaving when he laughed. When Ted spied John Moore, his former acolyte being groomed for stardom by Mrs Thatcher, setting off to collect his dessert, he raised his voice to observe: "There goes the biggest shit in Christendom." Moore returned to his table, plate still empty.

The Conservative Party is more sociable than Labour, though inter-Tory civilities were abandoned during the Eurosceptic frenzy of the mid-1990s and again over Brexit. I first met Tory MPs in strength at the 1978 party conference, and once Parliament reassembled I got to know many more. A few of the older, seedier ones I didn't take to, but the younger ones were mostly congenial.

I already knew John Osborn, Sheffield's only Conservative MP. I had covered the campaigns of Colin Shepherd from Hereford and Leominster's Peter Temple-Morris. Jim Lester I knew from Notts County Council, and Leon Brittan from Trinity (and my contempt of court case); one of my first Westminster lunches was with him. A few heavyweights I had met when they spoke in Sheffield – Reggie Maudling for one, though his career was almost over. (The very first Tory grandee I met was Rab Butler, after he become Master of Trinity; I was surprised to discover he had a withered right hand, which a gentlemanly media had never mentioned). And finally there was John Biggs-Davison, MP for Epping Forest - *bête noire* for a past member of the Buckhurst Hill and Loughton Young Socialists, yet now immensely courteous to me; he had a very unsettling gaze, deploying it to great effect during gaps he would engineer in a conversation.

The 1979 election brought in a Trinity contemporary, Jos Cadbury, representing what had briefly been my home constituency of Birmingham Northfield, and my schoolmate Robert Atkins – who got me onto the sacred First XI square at Highgate when he invited me to turn out for the Lords & Commons. Our best players that day were the Conservative MPs Den Dover and Michael Morris, with the future Cabinet minister Peter Brooke providing the style. Making up our XI was Jonathan Orders, a recent Oxford Blue. The boy who lent me a pair of whites had been darning the crutch and had left the needle in; I found out the first time I bent to pick up the ball.

The school made around 250, then our batsmen found the Highgate attack a handful. Before long we were 94 for eight, and I was on my way to the crease. At the other end was Orders, on 60-odd including a couple of massive sixes. I didn't expect to stay long, but for the first time ever I could see the ball coming onto the bat. A long boundary on one side brought Orders several all-run fours while I picked up the odd single, and in an hour we put on 100 of which my share was 16, coincidentally my highest score at school. Then I was out, and ten minutes later we had lost by 50-odd runs, with Orders undefeated on 140. When we set off for the pub, I was almost too stiff to move.

Working for the *Telegraph* opened many doors, and the Members' Lobby and Annie's Bar brought me a good stable of contacts. I also became close to a vivacious and talented Conservative agent, going on to share her life for a time; through her I came to appreciate that Tory professionals were just as devoted and realistic as their Labour counterparts – though more numerous – and that the average Tory is as sincere as a supporter of any other party.

One of the first backbenchers I met was Ken Warren, the only one of the team who engineered Mrs Thatcher's overthrow of Ted Heath not to become a minister. An aeronautical engineer severely injured in a crash when he performed heroically, Ken represented Hastings. Ken – later Sir Ken – had an indiarubber face, an ability to look intoxicated even when stone cold sober, and a stupendous line in anecdotes. It was Ken who, canvassing a nursing home named Kybo House, asked the matron if the name had African connections and was told: "No, it stands for 'Keep Your Bowels Open". And only Ken could have mistaken the National Council for the Single Woman and Her Dependant for a group of unmarried mothers and realised just too late during his speech that the steely-haired spinsters he was speaking to had sacrificed all to care for their elderly mothers. For me, Ken's finest moment was in the bar of Blackpool's Imperial Hotel when, arriving broke from Brussels, he tried to tap Alistair McAlpine for a fiver. Spurned, he came back muttering: "Well, he is the bloody treasurer ..."

Three younger Tories stick in my mind. Barry Porter, who represented a Scouse Protestant enclave on the Wirral, set fire to a sex shop when in Paris for a rugby match by jamming 10p into a slot machine intended for a franc. Delwyn Williams, an irreverent solicitor from Welshpool, who when the veteran Nationalist Gwynfor Evans went on hunger strike for a Welsh language TV channel told him: "You realise you can only do this once." And Warren Hawksley, a Black Countryman and the nicest Powellite you could meet. Staying with him when he represented the Wrekin, I visited a gipsy site whose occupants were complaining about the criminality and filth of New Age Travellers camped nearby. I learned an important lesson speaking at Warren's constituency dinner: never launch into a disability joke when the chairman is in a wheelchair, even if he sees the funny side of it.

These MPs, and many others, weren't just good company; they were shrewd observers of the political game. The same went for the Commons secretaries I got to know – most of them Conservative – who had as unerring a nose for what would happen next as the Government drivers who were routinely able to inform their charges when they were about to be sacked. One of the secretaries worked for a senior minister, and after each party conference had to write to the hotel insisting that the charge levied for adult movies had been a mistake. Another, an aristocratic lady with a voice that could shatter glass, divided her working hours between two elderly and deeply unprepossessing MPs who each insisted on exercising their *droit de seigneur*.

From the secretaries, I learned that John Nott would be resigning as Defence Secretary to go into the City - sadly in a way that left me feeling I could not break a confidence. I also discovered that a Tory in the twilight of his career was summoning a young lady to his office to thrash the living daylights out of him; the noise led neighbouring secretaries to complain, appropriately, to the Chief

190

Whip. Chris Moncrieff also had the story, but it was not the sort the Press Association would break and I suspected the *Telegraph* would not be keen, either. As this concerned the inner embarrassment of the Tory party I rang Bill Deedes, who was both a shrewd judge of how far we should go and completely unshockable. I suggested this wasn't a story we would wish to break, but that if a tabloid ran it we would enthusiastically follow suit. Bill concurred. I could have tipped off the *News of the World* and earned myself a packet, but Moncrieff and I let the matter drop.

There was a tragic side to that story – of an elderly man with deeply unfulfilled needs - and many political careers lapse into depression. This was cruelly brought home in 1982 when Jos Cadbury turned his gun on himself; he could not live with the hardship caused to his constituents by the government he had been elected to support. From then on, the Tory whips kept an eye on their flock, and twice, through the secretaries' channel (the whips always knew who was talking to whom) I was asked to have a quiet word with a backbencher they were worried about. The first came through his bad patch, but the other saw his marriage break up shortly after throwing a memorable 40th birthday party for his wife at the Mirabelle, then hit financial problems. I engineered a chat with him, and was relieved when he seemed to get a second wind. Then I moved away from the Commons; he remarried but his finances worsened and he, too, committed suicide.

I was well aware that senior politicians dealt with me because of the paper I represented (though I would have forfeited their trust personally had I got things wrong or broken their confidences). In the process I got to know ministers: over lunch; calling them at home on Sundays; in broadcasting studios where tongues always loosen; and interviewing them in their Whitehall offices. There were chance meetings in the Lobby and the corridors of the House, waiting for taxis, on station platforms. Usually even the grandest were happy to talk unless they had work to catch up with or were obviously shattered, situations you came to recognise. Some would greet you at times and ignore you at others; Peter Walker and

Michael Heseltine shared this trait. Even Willie Whitelaw, the bluffest of men, was not immune. His daughter told a mutual friend that Willie wouldn't recognise her on the campaign trail and, for a bet, infiltrated herself into the receiving line at a party function; Willie came down the line, shook his daughter's hand, muttered the usual platitude and passed on.

Many ministers gave me the benefit of their time and judgment. George Younger, when Scottish Secretary, was happy to run through on a Sunday afternoon the issues confronting the Cabinet. Humphrey Atkins went out of his way to be helpful, as did Francis Pym, who would guide you without ever crossing the line and leaking. Francis had his feet firmly on the ground, confiding to me when Foreign Secretary that he was perfectly happy to know where the rest of the world was without feeling obliged to visit it. He also earned me my first appearance in *Pseud's Corner* when I quoted his rapturous comment about a new celery-cutting machine he had seen in the Fens. Norman Lamont, on his way up, gave me plenty of help. But the streak of insecurity that consumed him as Chancellor was evident from the start, when he told me how disappointed he was only to have been made a junior energy minister.

To my surprise, I struck up a rewarding acquaintanceship with Nicholas Ridley. I knew of him as an arch-free marketer who would have let the Falklands go, but when we first lunched I found him unnervingly familiar – until I realised how much he resembled my father. Ridley was no fan of the media, but I grew accustomed to calls from Jean Caines, his head of information, to come over because he felt it was time he spoke to a journalist. He once spent half an hour fulminating over how British Airways' chairman Lord King had stitched him up by handing over dud routes to British Caledonian, the effect of which was to force BA's competitor out of business.

Ridley despaired of the hold on public opinion exercised by the RSPB and other conservation bodies, and made the point in spectacular fashion when Environment Secretary. Obliged by local nimbyism to block some harmless development because it was in the Green Belt, he also rejected plans to landscape an industrial eyesore in North Kent, pointing out sweetly to those outraged by an apparently perverse decision that the site was, after all, in the Green Belt.

When as Trade and Industry Secretary Ridley went too far and denounced the EC as a "German racket", Jean Caines rang me to ask if I could see a way for him to get off the hook. I couldn't, and he went. Shortly before he died, I sent him my *Daily Record* column blaming a number of disasters, including the war in Bosnia, on German foreign policy – and got a warm note back.

Peter Walker I admired as a skilful politician and a great survivor; no-one when Mrs Thatcher came to power would have imagined he could survive in her Cabinet for over a decade. I wrote countless stories about his "coded messages" on the need to change course, but she recognised his ability and knew that having him on board reduced any threat from the left of the party.

Having covered local government when he was Environment Secretary - and especially his reorganisation which I felt was necessary - and had quite a lot to do with Walker's department and ministerial team, he was one of the first senior Tories I sought out. He gave me a copy of his book, *The Ascent of Britain,* which set out how he would have run the country before the economy went to pot in the mid-1970s; by 1978 its arguments strained credibility, especially his advocacy of a massive increase in steel production when the trend was sharply the other way.

Walker and Heseltine had in common lower middle-class backgrounds and success in business. But there the similarity ended. Heseltine was less restrained, and more of a showman. Walker would never have conducted a crusade within the Cabinet as Heseltine did over Westland, and only Heseltine could have resigned from it in mid-meeting - doing it, needless to say, on my day off.

You couldn't help enjoying Heseltine's bravado in the House – such as his "Save the prawns!" speech at the height of John Smith's "prawn cocktail offensive" in the City – even if you knew he was on thin ice. Nor could you doubt his ability to rally a Conservative conference, as when he declared: "I hear the sound of the Trades Union Congress on the march: 'Left; Left; Left, Left, Left ...'" But he could be shameless. When he launched the Conservatives' 1992 manifesto I spotted that it lifted from the Alliance's programme of five years before a commitment the Tories had rubbished at the time; when I asked Heseltine what had changed, he replied: "The Alliance has gone out of business."

It would be wrong to regard Heseltine as totally cynical. His passion for the arboretum he created around his Thenford home is genuine; indeed he invited me to see it. His concern for the planet transcended what he could achieve as Environment Secretary; he also unnerved me over lunch by detailing a recent holiday spent swimming with sharks.

I had found the younger Heseltine hard to stomach; his seizing of the mace in protest at Labour's nationalisation plans disquieted even some on his own side. But while there was no doubt after his resignation that he coveted the leadership, he would be totally loyal to John Major. By then he knew his moment had passed – maybe also that you can only throw the toys out of your pram so many times in your career.

It was a joy getting to know Willie Whitelaw, Mrs Thatcher's much put-upon deputy. It was easy to see him as a caricature, arriving from Cabinet in a shirt going through at the collar or peppering beaters on a weekend shoot. But he was all that is best about the Tory party: humane, decent and public-spirited. These instincts I saw at play as he fulminated at West Yorkshire police's inability to catch the Yorkshire Ripper; worked to prevent Lord Young – whose abilities he rightly questioned – becoming chairman of the party; and reproached Mrs Thatcher for applauding his critics on law and order, telling her: "I have been loyal to you through thick and thin, and I expect no less from you."

I saw most of Willie after he became leader of the Lords. His Friday morning briefings were a treat, and not just because he reverted to Lord Soames's assumption that the sun was over the yardarm after the grudging hospitality offered by his immediate predecessor Lady

Young. Willie's doctor had told him to give up red wine, so he turned to white, reckoning it little different to water. We put Willie's choleric mood one Friday down to trouble in Cabinet until he disclosed that he had been to the Portuguese Embassy the night before and been obliged to drink Mateus Rosé.

Willie possessed the easy camaraderie and sense of fun that are instinctive to a knight of the shires. While Mrs Thatcher sat stony-faced as the entire House creased itself over some unfortunate backbencher's faux pas, Willie, next to her, would be slapping his thigh, tears of mirth streaming down his face. It was his understanding of the way other Tories' minds worked – an attribute she never fully acquired – that made him so essential to Mrs Thatcher. He could also be surprisingly quick on his feet. Once he started a speech with a duplicate page left in. The Opposition spotted – I suspect before Willie did – that he was reading it out for a second time. A clamour began, only for him to look up and say: "Of course I'm saying this twice – it's important." My abiding memory of Willie is of him arriving at the Commons in the passenger seat of a government Mini, looking considerably larger than the car.

Nor was he a bad Home Secretary. But it would be left to Leon Brittan to challenge the Home Office's preference for Olympian thought over executive competence (though action was only taken two decades later after John Reid concluded that much of the department was "not fit for purpose", and even now things are not right). Willie was also hamstrung by having to defend the nonsense of being himself the police authority for London, because it was politically impossible to put the Met under local control while the "loony Left" ran the capital. But he deserves credit for sticking to his liberal guns despite demands from the conference claque for measures that only began with hanging and flogging.

Willie was happier, if less pressured, leading the Lords, but while he remained Mrs Thatcher's deputy until he suffered a stroke during the 1987 parliamentary carol service, his influence on her waned. She once remarked in a classic double-entendre that "every prime minister needs a Willie", and in the final stages of her premiership the lack of an avuncular figure who could tell her she was wrong was evident. By then, though, I doubt she would have listened to anybody.

Mrs Thatcher apart, the one leading Conservative I was nervous about meeting was Jeffrey Archer, and when Mrs Thatcher made him party vice-chairman I confided this to the *Glasgow Herald*'s Geoffrey Parkhouse, who moved in senior Tory circles; he told me to forget my worries and take Jeffrey out to lunch. I am glad I did. Jeffrey became a mine of information and a much appreciated tipster – giving me two hours' start on Lord Havers' resignation as Lord Chancellor. He flatteringly sought my opinion on how the government was doing, and at times seemed to act on it. It was fun, too, to go to the shepherd's pie-and-champagne parties in his penthouse across the river from the Houses of Parliament, always with interesting guests. (Before the 1992 election I invited Jeffrey and his highly accomplished wife Mary to our home in Highgate; while Jeffrey shone, Mary gave the impression that she would rather have been anywhere else.)

Usually when a politician resigns they go to ground, though Cecil Parkinson earned brownie points for taking drinks out to the reporters doorstepping his home after his resignation over Sara Keays. But Jeffrey insisted, the evening he resigned as vice-chairman when the allegations against him first took shape, on answering the phone himself. That takes courage. I said as much to Ken Baker, and was surprised how fast my comment went round the party.

Jeffrey is a truly interesting man, genuinely committed and happy to put in more than he takes out. In the late '80s I got to know Rupert Langham, an Ulster baronet's son left paralysed after a diving accident in the Australian outback. Rupert, supported by his mother and his nurse at Stoke Mandeville whom he went on to marry, lived the fullest possible life and with family and friends set up a spinal injury charity. Twice we put on a ball at the Grosvenor House, and when I approached Jeffrey for a donation he sent round signed copies of all his novels. When I thanked him Jeffrey replied:

"It's simple: I'm worth £20 million and you're never likely to be" – and it wasn't said with malice.

Frederick Forsyth in one of his thrillers had two spies meet at a service area on the M11 at a time when there wasn't one; Jeffrey pulled Forsyth's leg about it, but decided he needed a gopher to check every fact in his own books. I found him the son of a friend of a friend who was just down from Oxford, and he performed his task to Jeffrey's total satisfaction. I was disappointed the young man never thanked me – but remembered that I had never properly thanked Kenneth Fleet for my entrée to the *Daily Telegraph*.

When Jeffrey was given four years for perjury for having lied over his involvement with a prostitute, I felt the Establishment was getting its own back. His offence was serious, but the sentence out of all proportion. I wanted to tell Jeffrey as much, but if a letter from the special adviser to a Labour Cabinet minister telling a recently-convicted Tory peer he had been hard done by saw the light, there would be trouble. However once Jeffrey was released, I took him to lunch and told him myself. I am glad he has picked up the pieces – he may be a fantasist, but he is a force for good.

12: Labour and its leaders

Labour's leaders detested the *Telegraph's* opinions, but they read the paper to find out what was going on in their own party, and joining the Lobby I had the advantage that I knew how Labour worked. Getting to know every Labour MP with an election imminent was never an option, as many were retiring or facing defeat, so I began with those I had already met: Tam Dalyell, former candidates for Chigwell, MPs I had dealt with in Sheffield and Birmingham, and a few who had passed through Washington. Jack Straw came in at the 1979 election.

Through Tam I met Guy Barnett, an Old Cholmeleian Quaker who had sensationally won the 1962 South Dorset by-election and now represented Greenwich; he became a wise mentor until his tragically early death. Guy introduced me to John Silkin – who forgave my dirt-digging in the fervid days of 1974 – and the Tribunite Left, notably Russ Kerr, an Aussie who had flown with Bomber Command, and the underrated Oonagh McDonald. I played the Sheffield and Birmingham cards to secure a lunch with Roy Hattersley, then Prices Secretary; he confided as the "Winter of Discontent" began that NUPE, the most militant public sector union, was about to fall under Right-wing control (it didn't, and the rest is history).

After Labour's defeat, Jim Callaghan and Michael Foot were surprisingly accessible. The Leader of the Opposition then met the Lobby every Thursday, a practice that ended when Neil Kinnock boycotted briefings with the *Sun* present after Rupert Murdoch's union-busting move to Wapping. Joining a lunch group with established Lobby members brought early contact with Denis Healey, then in his fifth bruising year as Chancellor, the Industry Secretary Eric Varley - who described the "tranche warfare" he was engaged in with Chrysler's American owners - and Tony Benn, previously encountered at the Meriden co-operative.

I arrived just as Callaghan's government seemed in with a chance of re-election, with the economy in a less horrendous state than in 1974-76. He let the opportunity slip, and after the "Winter of Discontent" lost to Margaret Thatcher. This galvanised the Bennite Left, who implausibly blamed Wilson and Callaghan's failure to embrace full-blooded Socialism. The party began to tear itself apart after Labour MPs elected Foot over Healey to succeed Callaghan late in 1980. Benn and his allies pressed for the leader to be elected by an electoral college where they would have a better chance, and insisted that Labour MPs face reselection by their constituency parties. In the event few were ousted, but fear of the "bed-sit brigade" replacing them with hard-liners caused sleepless nights and contributed to the decision of a number to leave for the SDP. (Ironically, careless abolition of the electoral college three decades later would let in Jeremy Corbyn and revive the same scenario).

There was no shortage of Right-wing and "soft Left" MPs ready to criticise the Bennites' tactics, and the weekly meeting of the PLP often produced a bust-up. But the main focus for Labour's travails was its National Executive Committee (NEC), which decided what rule changes to recommend to conference and who should be disciplined. First at Transport House, and then in a Victorian terrace on Walworth Road, the NEC met monthly; we hung around waiting for the losing side in any crucial vote to come out, and the party chairman and general secretary to follow. (When McDonald's opened close by, its festive muzak included *O Christmas Tree!* – the same tune as *The Red Flag.)*

Early on I discovered that Labour's song book was to be updated, with *Jerusalem* replaced by *Glad to be Gay.* I broke the story the morning of an NEC meeting; Eric Heffer, an ally of Benn but also a High Churchman, got up to say he and his wife had had *Jerusalem* at their wedding, and he was buggered if some party hack was going to kill it off. The entire executive linked arms for a chorus of *Jerusalem* - the last thing they would agree on for a good five years. Early in 1981 Benn stunned – and polarised - the party by challenging Healey for the deputy leadership. He launched his bid at 3.15am; I had left the Commons minutes before and woke to his announcement, wondering how on earth I had missed it. Healey, when informed, grunted: "Yes, and tomorrow he will parachute into Scotland to negotiate peace with the Duke of Hamilton" – a comparison with Rudolf Hess. The bitterest of campaigns followed before Benn lost by a whisker, amid recriminations over the refusal of "soft Left" MPs to back him.

That September's vote could have destroyed the party by triggering a mass exodus to the SDP, but in fact the fightback, led by the likes of Roy Hattersley and John Smith, was already beginning. The Falklands put Mrs Thatcher well ahead in the polls, concentrating Labour minds. Michael Foot started condemning extremism, but the Labour Right felt more was needed. One evening as the PLP broke up, Foot and Hattersley burst out of the door having clearly just traded insults; it didn't long to establish that Foot had responded to criticism from Hattersley by saying: "I'll have you!", with Hattersley replying: "You couldn't knock the skin off a rice pudding." Foot's own supporters began telling me they despaired of his ability to turn things round.

Labour's leaders had not only had to deal with the constitutional Left but with Militant, which had gained influence in several constituencies and some unions as it organised a Trotskyist "party within a party". Reg Underhill had warned of this several years before, but even in the early '80s, with Militant filling the Wembley Arena and the Royal Albert Hall (I couldn't help labelling its rally there "the last night of the Trots"), half the NEC still insisted they were harmless. From my conversations in the pub with Bob Edwards after YS meetings I knew what made Militant tick and I built up good contacts, enabling me to cover authoritatively its rise and eventual fall. I had no doubt Militant was immensely damaging to Labour, but you knew where it stood and it was invariably good copy.

It took several decisions by the NEC and the party conference – and a series of court cases – to force Militant onto the back foot. Liverpool council's Derek Hatton-influenced confrontation with the Thatcher government strengthened Neil Kinnock's determination to get them out of the party; I spent two days waiting in a Liverpool street under a giant advert for gravy granules as an inquiry under Margaret Beckett tried to deal with them. But only when Militant suicidally challenged Labour candidates on Merseyside was its goose cooked. Even then, it would resurface north of the Border as the Scottish Socialist Party under the colourful Tommy Sheridan.

The disastrous 1983 election – Labour's worst since the 1930s – ended Foot's leadership. But the Liberal/SDP Alliance failed to break through and Labour seized the chance to renew itself, with Kinnock elected leader in a "dream ticket" with Hattersley, and young newcomers Gordon Brown and Tony Blair running rings round slovenly Tory ministers. The eclipse of the hard Left was assisted by Benn's defeat at Bristol East after his seat disappeared in boundary changes.

Somehow Labour got through the trauma of the miners' strike. Its leaders felt deeply for the miners and their families, but most believed – like me – that Arthur Scargill was wrecking the union.

After the miners' defeat Kinnock stepped up the momentum for change, bringing in Peter Mandelson – a regular contact for me – to change Labour's image, starting by shifting the politburo of the NEC to the side of the party conference platform.

Labour went into the 1987 election much more confident, but fared little better despite rave reviews for Hugh Hudson's Kinnock video. I left the Lobby that August, and by my return late in 1989 Kinnock was moving Labour toward the middle ground. Victory in 1992 looked achievable as unilateralism and the commitment to pull out of Europe were scrapped, but continuing distrust of Labour's tax and spending policies kept it in opposition for a fourth term. John Smith modernised the party further and gave it authority, before his sudden death in 1994 opened the door for Blair.

From my sixth-form years until my departure for Washington, Harold Wilson was Labour's dominant figure. He went from embodying the "white heat of technology" to a byword for Macchiavellianism categorised by his dictum that "a week is a long time in politics", and by my arrival in the Lobby his contribution to history had been fogged by his post-retirement "Lavender List" of dubious honours. Though Wilson was still an MP, he kept his head down as civil war engulfed the party.

Ray Gledhill, the *Yorkshire Post*'s local government reporter whom I worked alongside occasionally in Sheffield, had been a classmate of Wilson's in Huddersfield in the 1930s. Ray remembered him as a mathematical genius; they walked to school beside a railway, and when trains passed young Harold would add up the six-figure numbers on the side of each truck and give the total. The other boys never caught him out.

With Wilson long retired, an ex-member of MI6 told me over dinner that he had been a Soviet agent, with Peter Shore flying to Moscow every weekend to pick up his instructions. It was common knowledge that elements in the security services hated Wilson, but I was staggered by these claims. The clincher was the sheer improbability of Shore, whom I knew to be highly patriotic, selling out his country. There was also the matter of how he could have commuted to Moscow without anyone outside MI6 noticing.

The fact that ex-spooks were making such allegations was excellent material for my *Daily Record* column, but as Wilson was still alive and Shore still in the Commons I needed a response. I caught up with Shore in the Members' Lobby, and with exasperated melancholy he told me: "I suppose this is yet another attempt to undermine Harold." Despite having his own patriotism impugned, what incensed him was the lengths people would go to, after all those years, to get at Wilson, the target of more innuendo than any other premier.

Wilson's years in power coincided with a national readjustment that looked very like failure, and in some ways was; but to me his great achievement was keeping us out of Vietnam despite intense pressure from Washington. Nor did he ever quite lose sight of the people he was elected to help.

Jim Callaghan was far more successful as prime minister than in any of the three great offices of state – Chancellor, Foreign Secretary and Home Secretary – which uniquely he had held. As Chancellor he was forced belatedly to devalue the pound, having gone along with Wilson's insistence that $2.80, the value fixed in 1949, was set in stone. As Foreign Secretary he stood by as the Turks invaded northern Cyprus, despite Britain being one of the island's guarantors. And as Home Secretary - and a pretty illiberal one – he compelled Labour MPs to vote down boundary changes he feared would cost them the 1970 election ... which was lost anyway. His one success as a minister was in killing Barbara Castle's *In Place of Strife* union reforms.

Mrs Thatcher's determination on change made Callaghan's premiership look unadventurous. Yet he not only kept Labour in power for three years without a working majority but, with Healey as Chancellor, pulled the economy back from the abyss, got inflation down to bearable levels and got devolution for Scotland and Wales onto the Statute Book – though not into force. Had he gone to the country in October 1978 Labour might just have pulled it off; but he hesitated, and was swept away by the Winter of Discontent.

I arrived at Westminster just as Callaghan was deciding not to hold that autumn election, and covered the final eight months of his premiership, culminating in the no-confidence vote after the Scottish referendum that triggered the 1979 election. He led his government with skill; he may have observed: "A lot of people were cleverer than me, but I became prime minister and they didn't", but he showed a greater surefootedness, and awareness of what a Labour government is for, than Gordon Brown in a less embattled situation. Up to the moment when the *Sun* paraphrased his take on the Winter of Discontent as "Crisis, what crisis?" he remained a credible leader, even if Labour's compact with the unions was falling apart.

Callaghan didn't like the press, but though gruff was never disagreeable, and sometimes ready to talk. He had, after all, resumed contact with the Lobby after the relationship completely broke down under Wilson. After Labour's defeat, he let Michael Foot do most of the talking at the Opposition's weekly Lobby but he did usually turn up – difficult for a man who had just been prime minister. Under Foot's leadership, with the party divided, he said little. But he was deeply concerned at cuts to the Royal Navy, and with John Silkin, another wartime naval officer, came pretty close to predicting that Argentina would invade the Falklands. The party did not thank him when, on the margins of the 1983 election, he made plain his disdain for Labour's "non-nuclear" defence policy.

Late in his Commons career, a group of us took Callaghan to lunch. He spilt no beans, settled no scores, but gave us an insight into how the Labour Party had operated, argued and changed since Attlee's government was elected to build the post-war Britain. My lasting memory is of the fondness with which he spoke of his wife, Audrey. He devoted his last years to caring for her; it was poignant, but probably his wish, that he outlived her by just eleven days.

I was brought up to regard Michael Foot as a secular saint. He inherited Nye Bevan's seat at Ebbw Vale, and embraced unilateralism when Bevan eschewed it. He and Dad spoke together on anti-nuclear platforms, and I stood in Trafalgar Square in driving rain as Foot tried to energise the bedraggled Aldermaston marchers. When I reminded him of this decades later, he characteristically apologised for having gone on so long.

When first I met him, in 1974 at an election rally in Kidderminster, he seemed old and tired. Nor did he then, or later, show any recognition of my being my father's son ... which surprised me knowing how closely they had worked on *Tribune*. Yet my first impression must have been due to the rigours of the campaign trail, for even as the Callaghan government went down to defeat he showed vigour, political skill and humanity (being ready to lose that no-confidence vote rather than inflict further suffering on Doc Broughton).

I saw Foot regularly at those Thursday Lobbies as, in turn, Leader of the House, Shadow Leader and Leader of the Opposition. There were also enjoyable conversations over lunch, at his favourite haunt the Gay Hussar and at the Red Fort, nearby in Soho - which he found after nearly disappearing into a porno house by mistake (we observed his progress through the window). He was always courteous, never vain, and practical in his attitude to politics; unlike Jeremy Corbyn, who would also to the leadership after decades as a rebel, he had learned that ideology for its own sake was a luxury.

After one late-night sitting my cab home arrived before I could get down from the Press Gallery. Over to it went Michael Foot, only for my driver, with great presence of mind, to tell him: "I'm sorry, I'm waiting for Lord Comfort." With a chuckle, Foot told him: "In that case I couldn't possibly", and walked off into the night.

Norman Mailer compared Foot to an elderly professor of ornithology, and he certainly would not have been the choice of the PR men and image-makers who swarmed around Conservative Central Office. His election as leader surprised us all; I had a profile of Healey ready, and when Foot narrowly beat him I was stuck. Yet as was often the case, my piece wired to Fleet Street 30 minutes later was far better than the one I had written at leisure; I described

Foot coming to the helm "after 30 years goading the party leftward from the back benches".

Callaghan had waited 18 months before retiring to "take the shine off the ball" for Healey, but the fervid state of the party grassroots alarmed many Labour MPs, who hoped Foot could tame the Bennite tiger. It didn't happen. Foot was tolerant, and revered party conference decisions – having in 1960 secured the vote for nuclear disarmament that provoked Gaitskell into making his historic "fight, fight and fight again" speech. He was comfortable with the Left's desire to recommit Labour to unilateralism, knew enough about the laziness of some Right-wing MPs not to mind them being deselected, and knew the party wanted its leader to be chosen more widely.

Under Labour's constitution Foot, like his predecessors, was leader only of the Parliamentary party. When you rang party HQ to ask what was going on, you were told about committee meetings and events, never what the leader was doing. Just as Healey, when Chancellor, was only able to speak at the party conference during the IMF crisis by claiming his three minutes as a Leeds constituency delegate, so Foot appeared as an ex-officio member of the NEC, and delivered what was technically not the leader's speech but a parliamentary report.

Foot could not have become leader at a worse time. A special party conference was about to make constitutional changes that would trigger the formation of the SDP and drive nearly 30 Labour MPs out of the party, weakening the moderates' ability to fight back (and leaving them open to charges that they too were about to defect). Then came Benn's deputy leadership challenge, pitched so as to force Foot to side with Healey and create the impression that Benn alone supported the policies set by conference.

Though Healey won narrowly, Foot's authority was further weakened. And as he realised the true extent of the damage being done to the party by Militant, he struggled to carry a still Left-dominated NEC with him. More damaging was his U-turn over the selection of the gay Australian Marxist Peter Tatchell to fight a by-election in deeply working-class Bermondsey; Foot endorsed

Tatchell, then repudiated him when challenged by a Labour MP in the House. It was hardly surprising that the 1983 election, when it came, was a catastrophe.

Denis Healey's defeat for the leadership was the moment he realised how many colleagues he had upset over the years. His intellect was undoubted; who else on either front bench could have passed at La Scala for a native Milanese? But the clowning and calling a spade a spade that made him a star turn on television as he struggled to rescue the economy didn't play well with his peers. Mike Yarwood might raise a laugh with his impressions of Healey dismissing his critics as "silly Billies" or "out of their tiny Chinese minds", but potential allies in the party and the unions took offence – one reason why he had the fight of his life to stop Benn.

I knew about Healey's rumbustious side – and his desire to shock – long before I joined the Lobby. His son was at Highgate and Healey, then Gaitskell's defence spokesman, came to speak. Questioning NATO's reliance on nuclear missiles, he spoke of "generals in their palaces regarding their phalluses" – which played well with his audience, if not with the headmaster. I would become familiar with Healey's penchant for letting slip a four-letter word when the conversation lulled in an expensive restaurant, or justifying his manner by saying: "I get a lot of slaps, but I get a lot of fucks". And I relished his comment to a Kremlin welcoming party: "Same old Mafia again, I see!" Had he become prime minister, life would never have been dull.

The comic turn was, of course, a cover. Healey was a shrewd and combative politician who, from the day he addressed Labour's 1945 conference in battledress, fresh from the Italian campaign, seemed destined for the very top. He was an outstanding Defence Secretary forced by economic circumstances to end Britain's presence East of Suez and cancel cherished projects, yet held the respect of service chiefs whom he could argue to a standstill. And he was Chancellor during a very difficult five years for the British economy, managing to pull it out of free-fall.

That he did not become prime minister was due mainly to the Leftward shift in the party that rendered Labour unelectable just when he could have expected to lead it. That shift put Labour into opposition with union militants blaming the "Winter of Discontent" on Healey's persistence with an unrealistically tight incomes policy. This breakdown in trust, coupled with resentment among MPs Healey had upset, denied him the leadership when Callaghan retired.

Healey's subsequent victory over Benn was Pyrrhic. While the threat from the "hard Left" subsided, he was sufficiently out of step with the dominant mood in the party – especially on defence – not to be a credible successor to Foot; moreover he was in his late 60s. Instead he became an elder statesman with, as ever, the ability to rock the boat. Healey broadly supported Labour's leaders as they steered the party back to power, but he was wary of the first Gulf War and hostile when Tony Blair sent the troops into Iraq, characteristically dismissing Blair's claim that Saddam Hussein could target weapons of mass destruction on Britain in 45 minutes as "shit". But my lasting memories of Denis Healey will be of his courage in taking on hostile party conferences, his clowning on Debden Broadway with Jack Straw's mother during the Epping Forest by-election, and his insistence on leaving a Lobby reception early because he wasn't going to miss Placido Domingo.

Tony Benn's influence on Britain has been immense. As a young man he took on the Establishment single-handed, winning the right to disclaim the peerage he inherited. Had he failed, Rab Butler, not Lord Home, would have become prime minister. As Minister of Technology he made a reality of Concorde at the expense of projects that would have brought greater long-term benefits (he had thousands of aircraft workers in his constituency) and forced through the merger of Leyland Motors and the basket-case British Motor Corporation to create one gigantic lame duck. After the Upper Clyde Shipbuilders work-in of 1971 Benn, enthralled by militant trade unionism, set Labour on course to nationalise key industries and encourage workers' co-operatives. Foiled by Wilson who gave him charge of North Sea oil instead, Benn had by 1979 put himself at the head of the far Left's drive for "party democracy" which, combined with unilateralism and a commitment to pull out of Europe, rendered Labour unelectable for over a decade. (Many of the same people tried again with Jeremy Corbyn.)

At the launch of his excellently-written (and totally honest) Diaries, I couldn't resist telling Benn I had found him frustrating to report because of the contradictions he embodied. Personally unassuming and considerate, he wrought some valuable changes but aligned himself increasingly with intolerant forces that did immense damage not just to the Labour Party but to Britain's social and industrial fabric – and gave Margaret Thatcher an excuse to cut a swathe through British industry, with Labour too weakened by internal strife to defend it.

I first encountered Benn in Birmingham, working as Industry Secretary with shop stewards to rescue failing automotive businesses. By the time I reached Westminster he was nearing the end of a successful tenure as Energy Secretary, and increasingly involved in the drive by constituency activists to capture the party. I was there in Brighton the night Healey defeated him, in Bristol the day he was forced into fighting a marginal seat which he lost, but sadly not in Chesterfield for the surreal 1985 by-election that brought him back to the Commons with the tide having turned against him.

He was always courteous to me and ready to explain how things stood. Yet contacts with the grassroots mattered far more to him than the Tory press. The *Telegraph* never harassed him as had the *Mail* and the *Express*. Yet after he shortened his name from Anthony Wedgwood Benn in the early 1970s, Peter Eastwood insisted on using it in full, hoping it would annoy him.

Benn and his acolytes did have a case. The leadership, whenever the mood in the party was against it, would carry on regardless, relying on trade union block votes to defeat hostile conference resolutions. This worked in government, when decisions had to be taken without waiting for the next jamboree at Blackpool or Brighton, but not in opposition. Moreover many older Labour MPs seldom visited their constituencies and engaged only with a handful of trusted retainers. If the party was to be democratic, its leadership and MPs had to be more accountable.

Sadly the Bennites went further, arguing that the party should be run by whoever felt most strongly. This legitimised the right of a small, dedicated faction to choose their MP, then tell them how to vote. Floating just above this campaign was Benn himself, puffing serenely on his pipe and justifying propositions that appeared logical to the casual listener, but collapsed under examination. Over two years of frenetic campaigning before his challenge to Healey, he fine-tuned a series of statements to justify the extreme in terms of logic and moderation, slipping in the magic words: "What people really want to know is ..." before firing off the most contentious point of all. A favourite Benn dictum was to justify wholesale nationalisation with the assertion that this was nothing more than Henry VIII had done when he "turned the Church into the British National Ecclesiastical Corporation." Religious imagery figured strongly in his campaigning; from a Congregationalist family that opposed uniting with the Presbyterians, Benn became the heir of the radical Puritans whose insistence that theirs was the only way made Oliver Cromwell's life a misery.

Benn (like Corbyn a generation later) was in a minority at Westminster; hence his supporters' commitment to "extra-parliamentary action". He campaigned for fellow Labour MPs to lose their job security, belatedly joined their Tribune Group, then after his defeat for the deputy leadership - to which many Tribunites had contributed - he led out its more extreme members to form the Socialist Campaign Group.

It's easy to view Tony Benn's influence on British politics as wholly destructive, but at times he personified Parliament at its best. For me his finest moment came in 1987 when he persuaded a heavily Conservative House that its liberties were threatened by a motion backed by the Chair to prevent not only a banned BBC documentary on the Zircon spy satellite being shown there, but any such programme in future. The debate opened with near-unanimity; then Benn persuaded the massed Tory ranks, who had no love for him, that their liberties were being eroded. To me, this and his campaign to renounce his peerage are his fitting memorials, not his damaging dalliance with the "Loony Left".

When Neil Kinnock was elected in 1983 to succeed his mentor Michael Foot, I knew him only as a promising if garrulous Left-winger who drank with the *Guardian,* and a hilarious turn at party conferences (I loved his proposal to present Harold Wilson with a video on Rhodesia played backwards to ensure a happy ending). But over his nine years as leader I developed a great respect for him. I have no doubt that had Labour won in 1992, Neil would have been a better-than-adequate prime minister, even if his team and its policies were not yet quite ready for power - whose are?.

The real Neil is genuine, vigorous, enthusiastic, firm when he reckons it necessary and a fine orator who sometimes can't resist a *bon mot* that lands him in trouble. He can also be extremely funny, describing Tory policy on Europe as "like Brighton Pier – all right as far as it goes, but not much use for getting to France" or teasing Nigel Lawson with "Come to me, my melancholy Blaby" – a pun on his constituency. But there is much more to him than that. Most important is the strength of his marriage: not only is Glenys Kinnock formidable in her own right (and as friendly and personable as Neil), they make a tremendous team. He also has deep loyalties to the Valleys, strained to the limit when Arthur Scargill brought the miners out early in his leadership. Neil identified totally with the miners, knew the strike was disastrous, but could not bring himself to split the movement by attacking Scargill. This was not cowardice; he was not well enough established as leader to commit what many of his people would reckon an act of betrayal.

Neil's other great strengths are his patriotism, his sense of the proper and his fearlessness. Though the media pilloried him for his unilateralism, Neil's remark that "I am ready to die for my country, but I do not expect my country to die for me" reflected great credit on him. If his challenges to Margaret Thatcher at PMQs were halting, it was because he felt he could not insult a woman, even one pursuing policies he deeply resented. It is no accident that John Major, a couple of years into Tony Blair's government, said he would rather have lost to Kinnock.

Politically, Neil showed his fearlessness in refusing to back Benn for the deputy leadership and taking on Militant. I witnessed his physical courage when he hung out of the back of a Hercules flying over famine-devastated Ethiopia. He also persuaded an RAF pilot who took him up over the Irish Sea to execute a crash dive, despite orders to the contrary. Glenys knew she couldn't change him, and fondly nicknamed him Biggles. He also had a passion for rock'n'roll that made him the UK president of the Gene Vincent Fan Club and led him to tell a startled American reporter that the three greatest Americans were Eddie Cochran, Gene Vincent and Little Richard. Neil was totally relaxed with the press, because what you saw was what you got, and his confidences were usually respected.

When Neil was elected I wrote that the big question was: "Is there anything there?" I realised there was when he felt the need to give me a rocket. Patricia Hewitt, his press secretary, had told me Neil was trying to open communications with the Ulster Unionists, and had entrusted the task to Gerald Kaufman. The morning we ran the story, hard-line Loyalists struck in protest at some initiative to ease discrimination against Catholics; Neil reckoned the juxtaposition put him in a bad light and asked an embarrassed Patricia to call me in.

He started by telling me, in a measured way, that the story was a great embarrassment to him and there was no truth in it; naturally, I didn't betray my source. Then he slipped into a soliloquy on the difficulties of being leader of the Opposition and the frustrations of leading his party. I can't recall his exact words – I was in his office over half an hour – but I came out realising that I now understood Neil Kinnock, and liked what I saw.

The Wapping dispute led Neil to cancel meetings with the Lobby where the Murdoch papers would be present, and my travels with him ended when I left to write leaders – though I did spend a day electioneering with him in Ayr in 1992, and our paths crossed in Johannesburg as Nelson Mandela led South Africa to democracy.

When he had his best chance of leading Labour back to power I was at the *Daily Record*; had he won the 1992 election I would have had good access to Number 10 as I knew most of his staff. As it was, Neil went to Brussels where he became a successful Commissioner, but hard to see. Soon after Eurostar started, I went over with a photographer to do a double profile of Neil and Glenys, recently elected an MEP. Glenys, as ever, was approachable, organised, charming and articulate; Neil's office, despite prior arrangements, insisted there was nothing in the diary and the ensuing profile was somewhat lopsided.

Roy Hattersley, Kinnock's deputy on the 1987 and 1992 "dream tickets", I already knew; but I knew his parents better. I arrived in Sheffield after Roy, youngest ever chairman of the city's Housing Committee, had left to become MP for Birmingham Sparkbrook, but I got to know his formidable mother Enid, chairman of the Libraries and Arts Committee – and his quieter father, Roy senior, who chaired the Health Committee. Enid was a fighter – seeing off Derek Hatton when he arrived from Merseyside to stir up trouble among Sheffield's social workers – and loquacious in the extreme: I mentioned in her *Telegraph* obituary when she died at 96 that anyone ringing her could count on not getting a word in for the best part of an hour. But she was very helpful to me, as was Roy senior; I have mentioned our conversation the night his son was agonising over whether to rebel over Europe. I could never understand why a man of obvious gifts had a lowly administrative job in the NHS. It was years later before even Roy found out: his father had been the Catholic priest who married Enid to her first husband, then ran off with her.

Enid was very protective of her son; when he was minister of state at the Foreign Office I erroneously described him as a junior minister and my ears burned for days. But arriving in Birmingham, I could introduce myself knowing his mother had recommended me.

Roy – as anyone reading his books will know – is devoted to a womb-like Labour Party out of the Hovis commercials, with Co-Op ladies stuffing envelopes and making tea in old-fashioned committee rooms. He was most radical on education, totally committed to comprehensives and abolishing the public schools. It was ironic that having benefited from a grammar school education he, like other Labour figures of the time, should have pulled up the ladder and destroyed the system from which he had benefited.

Most of my dealings with Roy were in the context of Labour's internal strife. He was better placed than Denis Healey to fight back against the hard Left, and his contribution to the recovery that began under Kinnock and continued under John Smith was substantial. Had Labour returned to power earlier, I think he would have been a better Home Secretary (his portfolio in 1992) than Chancellor. It was Roy who for years kept Labour from committing itself to a Human Rights Act, fearing, rightly, that it would transfer power from Parliament to the judges.

John Smith was my favourite Labour leader: a great conversationalist with an excellent mind and a burning sense of what was right. Moreover, it was said of John at his funeral that he could "start a party in an empty room". With the *Daily Record* I saw a lot of him, both as Labour leader and as a highly influential Scot whose friendships transcended party. During one conversation when he was Shadow Chancellor, I mentioned that next morning I was off up Ben Lomond (a walk, not a climb, but still strenuous). John's reaction was: "Can I come too?", and the disappointment when he found he had a constituency surgery was genuine. After his first heart attack John made a real effort to keep fit, and set out with his chief of staff Murray Elder to bag as many Munros as he could (Murray eventually conquered them all, plus Kilimanjaro, despite himself having had a heart transplant). John had already tackled Ben Lomond, but was up for doing it again with a journalist he did not then know that well. And he would have been great company.

John blenched when I told him of a Labour supporter who was voting Liberal after seeing Glenda Jackson starkers in *The Music Lovers*. But he was no prude. He told in the party conference bar –

he hadn't given up whisky – of arriving at the Scottish football writers' dinner with a script neatly balancing politics with humour, only to be blown out of the water by the governor of Barlinnie prison. The governor told of a woman in a Glasgow tenement waiting for her husband to return after finishing his stretch. She confides to a neighbour: "He'll come up the stairs with a bunch of flowers, I'll be waiting on the bed with my legs apart ..." to be interrupted with: "Have you no' got a vase?" John tore up his speech, knowing the night wouldn't be his.

Like Neil Kinnock before him and Tony Blair subsequently, John knew the party had to change to be fit for power. But his pace was more measured than Tony's would be and he would not have gone as far; no-one could ever have accused John of throwing out the baby with the bath-water. He showed courage in getting "one member, one vote" on party matters through conference in the teeth of trade union opposition; it may not have been as politically sexy a change as Tony's abolition of Clause Four, but then John, unlike Tony, would never have ignored "OMOV" the moment it didn't suit him. He realised all too well that if you tore the heart out of the Party it would be an empty vessel no matter how many elections it won. As he said in his very last speech: "The opportunity to serve our country: that is all we ask."

John's courtroom style did not adapt to PMQs, but in debate he was formidable. No-one who was there will forget his dismissal of John Major as "the man with a non-Midas touch, in a country where the Grand National doesn't start and the hotels fall into the sea." No matter that it was written by David Hill; it's how you tell 'em.

He did have a flank to watch. The council in John's Monklands East constituency gained a reputation – not fully justified when the facts came out – for graft and nepotism, and this was a godsend for the Tories, who could find no other line of attack. John could hardly have denounced his own councillors, so Monklands-related attacks in the House left him looking embarrassed. Had he lived, the sniping could have undermined his image as a man of integrity. But as the Tories, for partisan reasons, had just reorganised local government with Monklands council abolished, the steam would have gone out of the issue before he faced the voters.

In one of our set-piece interviews, just before he became leader, John had the good manners not to alert me that I had sat on a piece of gum on the Tube and was leaving a trail on his furniture. And when he came to lunch at Anderston Quay, we maintained amused eye contact as Mirror Group executives expressed some pretty weird views.

My last conversation with John was in March 1994, at the House before Labour's Scottish conference in Dundee. Usually such interviews were formulaic: the leader setting the political scene, explaining how Labour was rising to the challenges, supporting whatever campaign the *Record* was running and setting some personal goals. We got through all that - then John erupted over a new compensation tariff for criminal injuries in England that put a cash value on the loss of an eye, molestation when a child and so on. As a criminal lawyer he believed this grossly unfair, and told me: "Can't you go back and get one of the papers to take this seriously? We simply can't see our people let down." I banged on doors and tried to get John's passion across to my colleagues and competitors, but none responded; I went home feeling I had let *him* down.

I tell elsewhere of the universal sense of shock when on 12 May 1994 news of John's death broke during the Scottish Conservative conference. The way the Tories reacted was a tribute to his ability to transcend tribal boundaries. John's government would have been Labour to its toenails, but it would have been a government for all the people. When he died, British politics lost part of its moral compass, as well as a man who would have combined humour, integrity and a streak of caution and achieved at least as much as did Tony Blair. Had he lived to form a government, I suspect I would have played a greater part in its success than the walk-on role his old friend Helen Liddell secured for me in the Blair administration, much as I valued that.

Tony Blair rose from being a promising newcomer to a political force in the two years I was away writing leaders. He first registered with me while I was at the *European,* with a barnstorming conference speech as Shadow Employment Secretary; it was one of the best campaigning speeches I'd heard – as I told him – but I was struck by its lack of substance.

It is easy to criticise Blair for having used his superb political skills primarily to get New Labour into power and keep it there. There is evidence for his ideological rootlessness – a mutual friend from his Islington set recalls that over dinner in the late 1980s he mused aloud whether he would do better to join the Tories. But I don't think any prime minister who brought peace to Northern Ireland, devolution to Scotland and Wales, an elected mayor to London and an element of reform to the House of Lords – and introduced the minimum wage - can be accused of achieving nothing.

But – with the huge exception of Iraq - he was over-cautious. He would shape up to take some truly radical step, then go looking for objectors rather than exercising the overwhelming mandate he'd been given.. From curbing the car to banning smoking in pubs, there were a host of issues where he was pushing at an open door, and I still wonder what he was afraid of. (With adopting the euro it was obvious: Gordon Brown and Rupert Murdoch). New Labour also believed you could eradicate social ills simply by legislating, and after 18 years out of office there were only a handful of ministers who knew better (the likes of Margaret Beckett and Michael Meacher). It was immensely disillusioning for Tony and the rest to get into power committed to be "tough on crime, tough on the causes of crime" and find that whatever laws they initiated to combat youth crime and anti-social behaviour, the courts would do their level best not to enforce them.

It was impossible to spend time with Tony without his enthusiasm rubbing off on you. Whether it was in his office before a flight up to Scotland (I came out once to find my tape recorder was blank; thank goodness I have shorthand), in his hotel suite as he worked on a speech, in the Cabinet room - where he told me I was sitting in Peter Mandelson's chair - or in the car driving him to Glasgow Airport, he made you feel part of his project. Yet while even as prime minister he expected you to call him Tony, it was a mistake to get too familiar. At the height of the 1994 leadership contest, when he and John Prescott were nicknamed "Bambi and Thumper", I went to his Islington home. During a long and informal chat, I noticed a pile of videos topped by *Bambi*. I couldn't resist asking if it was there for his kids or the research staff, and the temperature dropped. By contrast, Prescott bubbled with pride at the "Thumper" rabbit on his desk, a present from his campaign manager Ian McCartney.

For a Scottish newspaper umbilically linked to Labour, Tony's emergence as leader posed problems. The fact that Gordon Brown was one of our columnists wasn't one of them; Gordon had reluctantly accepted that Tony had overtaken him, and Tony had promised that toward the end of a second Labour term the baton would pass to him. The problem went deeper: how to project a Scot not seen by Scots as one of them.

Tony's mother was Scottish-born, his father grew up in a Govan shipyard family and he himself was born in Scotland. But his parents moved away when he was small, to Australia then to Durham, and while Tony went to school in Scotland it was to Fettes, which many Scots reckon as alien as Eton. Tony knew he would not be seen as a Scot, but I had to make our readers feel he understood them without overplaying the Scottish card.

By the time Tony led Labour to that astounding victory in 1997 I was freelancing for the *Sun*, whose support he had worked hard to secure (through Murdoch) after its crucifixion of Neil Kinnock. But the *Scottish Sun* didn't feel obliged to give him space, and in government he would only give us anything new if Alastair Campbell felt we were the best vehicle for it – which usually we weren't.

Days after the death of Princess Diana, at the height of the devolution referendum campaign, I turned up at Edinburgh's Caledonian Hotel to interview Tony. The *Sun* was backing devolution and words from the PM would help, so I got the same ten minutes as Scotland's other main media. But I made a serious mistake: I felt I had to tell him how much I – and most people I knew – appreciated how he had articulated the public's grief and influenced the Palace to show some humanity.

This was the moment I got closest to the private Tony Blair: he told me how his children had been affected, having met and liked Diana and her boys. When we moved on to the interview, he couldn't focus on a campaign that was clearly not at the front of his mind and the words I emerged with were less than brilliant; I should have done things the other way round. Furthermore, I unprofessionally left a copy of the *Scotsman* on the table and our photographer didn't think to move it when he took our picture. Not surprisingly, the *Sun* didn't carry a word.

Tony was a good parliamentary performer, but he spent as little time in the House as possible – noticeably less than other prime ministers. He squeezed two sessions of PMQs into one of twice the length, resigned his seat the day he left Number 10 while other former premiers have served out their time on the back benches, and when he decided to bring Helen into the Cabinet, the one place his office didn't think of looking for her was the Commons, where she was speaking.

Tony Blair today is judged through the prism of the war in Iraq. He got closer to George W Bush than he needed to, but it's hard to see how he could have prevented Donald Rumsfeld and Dick Cheney tearing up carefully-prepared plans for post-war Iraq, opening the way for anarchy. Yet Harold Wilson managed to keep Britain out of Vietnam without sacrificing the "special relationship" with Washington; and it may well be Tony's epitaph that he gave in too easily to Bush in the emotional climate after 9/11.

Politically I was closer to Gordon Brown, so it was painful to see his performance as prime minister. He has great gifts – as he showed when he rescued the "No" campaign during the 2014 Scottish independence referendum - but in Number 10 remained firmly stuck in second gear. To Gordon politics is an obsession, always with the aim of making life better for Labour's people. But his sincerity and commitment fell victim to a two-dimensional personality, a determination to pay off old scores and a propensity for getting bogged down in detail. When officials asked John Major for a decision, he would call for the file and give an answer the next morning, Tony Blair would ask for a sheet of A4 and get back the same evening, but Gordon would ask for all the files and come back in the morning asking for more files. Though he deserves credit for the way he helped guide not just Britain but the West through the global banking crisis, his reaction to other challenges, such as the furore over MPs' expenses, showed him consistently slow on his feet.

Gordon would have been on stronger ground over the banking crisis had he not spent a decade as Chancellor declaring that he had ended boom and bust by establishing a sound economy based on a financial services sector governed by a world-class system of regulation. It's hard to live that one down, even though the meltdown was triggered by improvident lending on the other side of the Atlantic. His achievements were, in fact, considerable, but after a few years of prudence he yielded to the temptation to throw money at the NHS, in particular; when I was in Whitehall it was pretty evident we could be spending less and still improving it. When the good times ended, the cupboard was bare.

Gordon has read pretty well everything about not just British but world politics; it was said – until he started playing tennis with Ed Balls – that his ideal afternoon off would be spent in the Library of Congress. He also understood where true power lay; he was determined to become Chancellor because he realised that from the Treasury he dictate the government's priorities, and keep colleagues in line. One reason there was a shortage of prison space during Gordon's premiership is that he had starved the prison building programme to prevent David Blunkett claiming the credit.

At the *Record*, Gordon was a star columnist, his contact with the paper being managed by Tom Brown, an avuncular fellow product of Kirkcaldy who is still a good friend. When I started writing *Brewer's Politics*, Gordon was a mine of information, and it was Gordon who sponsored its launch at the Commons. Though he wrote a well regarded biography of John Maxton, he never did himself justice as an author, possibly because there was just too much in his head, but he was generous in his encouragement to me. At Westminster Gordon rose because of his zeal in discovering awkward facts about the impact of Tory policies, and despite his lack of organisation. When as a student he reported a break-in, it was because he found his flat looking tidier than usual; his Westminster office was chaotic until Henry McLeish's first wife Margaret took it in hand, separating the policy papers from the unwashed shirts. Later Gordon was organised by Sue Nye, whom I had first known as one of Jim Callaghan's secretaries. He also made a superb choice of wife in Sarah Macaulay, whose sheer niceness is exceeded only by her ability.

Gordon and Tony both arrived at Westminster in 1983 and shared an office. Gordon was far more experienced; he knew his way around the party and the media, and was interested in policy. When John Smith became leader, there was no doubt that while Tony would be one of the stars of a Labour government, Gordon was the senior partner. But Tony was catching up, and Gordon, maybe because of their closeness, didn't realise it.

Late in 1992 Gordon asked me over to his (by now solo) Commons office on a matter of some delicacy. Tony, as Shadow Home Secretary, was off to Scotland and Gordon, acutely aware that Scots hadn't taken to him, asked me: "Can't you do something for Tony?" Eighteen months later, Tony was leader of the Labour Party and Gordon was trying to come to terms with an astounding reversal.

In the wake of Tony's election, I wrote that it might suit Gordon to move on from the Treasury portfolio and become New Labour's world affairs supremo. This was meant as a compliment, but Gordon, sensing the power he could exercise from the Treasury, thought I wanted Robin Cook as Chancellor. I liked Robin, but the job he was best suited for was Leader of the House, a role he would fulfil with reluctance – Tony having moved him from the Foreign Office - until his resignation over Iraq.

Gordon threw his full support behind Tony, but - understandably – he remained out of sorts and began to find criticism hard to take (not that he had ever welcomed it). And in September 1994 I wrote a column that did lasting damage to our relationship. I had been due to interview Robin, but when I got to his office, an embarrassed Gaynor Regan – his assistant and later his second wife – told me he had gone to chair a major economic speech by Gordon. In it, Gordon spoke of "post neo-classical endogenous growth theory" and much more besides. I sensed that the Tories would have a field day, particularly as the young Ed Balls had written the speech; indeed at the Conservative conference Michael Heseltine recited a slab of the impenetrable text and remarked: "It's not Brown's – it's balls." I was right to warn in my column that speeches like this would not help win Labour the election, but if I had thought – and certainly if I had consulted Tom Brown – I would have been more restrained. The last thing Gordon expected in his own paper was an accusation that he had delivered a speech full of "waffle and blether", and he was deeply hurt. I sought him out and apologised, but for my remaining year on the *Record* there was a distance between us. Even a panegyric when he managed to defeat Ken Clarke's plan to impose the full rate of VAT on fuel bills did not fully restore the balance – though Gordon was still ready to share his thoughts with me, notably on the folly of offering to buy back shares in the privatised railways.

During my time with the *Sun,* and after, I saw plenty of Tony but little of Gordon. He was not interested in controlling the media as Tony was, I was not a central player in the political game, and he reckoned I was not on his side. By the time I went to work for Helen, Gordon had established his fortress at the Treasury while still trying to call the shots in the Scottish party, and at all levels there was a desperation not to cross him. Yet I remained closer to Gordon's world view than to Tony's.

I was outside the political village by the time Gordon became prime minister. It should have happened three or four years earlier, as I knew what Tony had promised him. And the first decisions Gordon took - cancelling the "super-casino" and renouncing cluster bombs - were what you expect from a Labour government; under Tony there had been few moments when you could say that.

Whenever I'd been asked what sort of prime minister Gordon would make I had talked him up, out of a mixture of conviction and hope. But the mess he made in October 2007, three months after taking office, of deciding not to call an election brought me down to earth. Even from Sri Lanka, where I caught his press conference on CNN, it was plain the issue had been clumsily handled.

The prime minister Gordon became had his heart in the right place, but believed he could turn things round through hard work and the occasional piece of opportunism. The one time – the banking crisis apart – that he acted decisively was to shore up his own position when, in June 2009, resignations from the Cabinet briefly looked like forcing him out.

13: Liberals and Democrats

My mother – like her mother before her - was a Liberal. She reckoned them the only party serious about saving the planet, and one of my favourite photos of her shows her presenting a cake to Clement Freud. When I was 15 Eric Lubbock's stunning by-election victory at Orpington set my pulse racing, and I canvassed with the Young Liberals a couple of times before finding myself more at home in the Young Socialists.

When I arrived in Sheffield, the Liberals were unrepresented on the city council until two Tories defected. Both lost their seats in 1970, then weeks later Francis Butler, a local Methodist preacher and community activist, fought a passionate by-election campaign in inner-city Burngreave that caught Labour on the hop. His opponent was well-intentioned but not over-bright; sighting Butler while out loudspeakering, he announced: "This is Reggie Ellis, your Labour candidate ... don't vote for him, he's a bloody liar!" Butler swept home to become the first Liberal councillor elected in Sheffield since the 1920s. A generation later the Liberal Democrats would take power in the city; Francis was still on the council, sadly in too poor health to become Lord Mayor, an honour he richly deserved.

Some Liberals in Sheffield were uncomfortable with the possibility of success, but Francis was different. He worked his ward hard, allied with the Methodist minister John Vincent who would become a byword for radical activism. Yet even he would never have dared imagine that within four decades his party would be running the city, let alone that its leader would represent a Sheffield constituency (and be Deputy Prime Minister). Such advances locally were due both to the eclipse of the Tories, who despite having a few good people became about as relevant as whites in post-colonial Africa, and to dissatisfaction in working-class communities at what seemed an unresponsive Labour establishment.

Joining the *Daily Telegraph,* I interviewed David Steel on my very first day. I was at Jeremy Thorpe's press conferences during the referendum on Europe, and in Washington was presented with evidence that the Liberals were being targeted by a South African dirty tricks operation. I started work at the Commons with Thorpe close to going on trial for conspiracy to murder his former boyfriend Norman Scott and Steel leading the party; he had pulled it out of the Lib-Lab Pact, but it still seemed set for near-annihilation at the polls. Covering the Berwick & East Lothian by-election in the autumn of 1978, several of us drove over to Steel's office in the next constituency for a response to developments in the Thorpe case. We emerged from a chat with his agent with the news that the Liberals would be "quarantining" their former leader in his North Devon constituency until after the campaign. The fact that the Liberals held 11 of their 13 seats in 1979 despite the Thorpe case (he was acquitted) and a national swing to the Tories was an achievement Steel never received full credit for.

I had no trouble striking up friendships with Labour or Conservative MPs, but the Liberals seemed different. Their party officers and staff I always got on well with, and in Roy Hastings-Comfort, who ran the Liberal Action Group for Electoral Reform (LAGER) I met a possible Aberdeenshire relative. But with their MPs, maybe each was stretched by trying to represent a small party right across the country; maybe most were individualists who had won their seats at by-elections. Whatever it was, I found most of them, throughout my time at Westminster, hard to get on with.

I had long admired Stephen Ross, MP for the Isle of Wight, as a beacon of common sense, and on the air he had a very easy manner. But when I took him for lunch, as I had with dozens of other politicians, he had nothing to say, and I returned to the office wondering whether Ross was unexpectedly shy (astonishingly, some MPs are) or a Potemkin village.

Ross figured in a bizarre episode which told us Lobby reporters that we were being bugged. The *Daily Mail's* John Harrison was on his way to see Ross about some problem at Parkhurst prison when a retired copper attached to the House came up and said: "He won't be able to tell you much." John was flabbergasted, and when next I bumped into one of Mrs Thatcher's Special Branch men I suggested someone ought to be a little more discreet. In any event, the most any eavesdropper would have learned from my phone calls was the odd piece of personal trivia.

It was Stephen Ross who fed Mrs Thatcher her most crushing put-down. It was just after Bobby Sands' death by hunger strike in the Maze prison, and Sands' supporter Owen Carron had won the by-election for his seat at Fermanagh. Ross told Mrs Thatcher this embarrassment could have been avoided if Northern Ireland had proportional representation (he meant as a way of preventing politics becoming polarised). Back she came: "As there were only two candidates, I don't see what difference it would have made."

David Steel had the air of a perpetual schoolboy (an impression reinforced by his white-collared striped shirts). But you had to respect his persistence in the face of formidable odds, and I was lucky that when I arrived at Westminster his spokesman was Paul Medlicott, who had edited *Varsity* in my time. I became a regular at Steel's press conferences, small affairs in the grand but gloomy National Liberal Club – and grew accustomed to his post-election depressions, a concomitant to his upbeat (if never over-optimistic) performances during the campaign. Richard Holme, right-hand man to both Steel and Paddy Ashdown, told me how as polling day neared, Steel would be so shattered that the only way to brief him was to hold him up by the neck of his pyjama jacket and bellow in his ear.

Richard (later Lord Holme of Cheltenham, after the seat he tried so hard to win) had a raffish manner which concealed a very shrewd political brain. It was Richard who told me prior to the "Ettrick Bridge summit" at Steel's home midway through the 1983 campaign that Roy Jenkins' position as the Liberal/SDP Alliance's "Prime Minister designate" was untenable, and Steel would be taking the lead. That happened, in good measure because Holme made it happen.

Unlike some journalists who saw themselves as mould-breakers, I wasn't politically involved with David Owen, Shirley Williams and Bill Rodgers as they broke with the Labour Party. Some vociferous "social democrats" who cosied up to the *Telegraph* were motivated largely by a hatred of communism (with which they associated the most unlikely Labour figures) rather than the humane philosophies that drove the Gang of Four. Moreover, while I liked and respected some of the Labour MPs whose ties to the party were fraying in the winter of 1980-81, I was close to more who would stay and fight. Yet when the break finally came, I shared the emotional turmoil suffered by honourable men and women on both sides.

For me, the most traumatic moment came at Woolwich when John Cartwright told his local party he was breaking with Labour. John is one of the most decent of politicians: mild-mannered, thoughtful, tolerant, sincere, yet committed. He had also had an unusual sideline as match-day announcer at The Valley. Once, the club secretary hired an elephant and a camel to parade round the touchline at half-time, leaving John lost for words. Soon afterwards, Charlton's erratic striker Harry Gregory missed a penalty, only for a lone voice in the crowd to shout: "Bring on the f***ing camel!"

John knew the meeting would be tough, not just because he was breaking with old friends but because seven years previously he had led the attack when his predecessor, Christopher Mayhew, had quit for the Liberals. Now the guns were trained on John, and he and his wife came out close to tears.

As individual MPs were severing their ties with Labour, the "Gang of Four" prepared to launch a new party. I was doing the Sunday turn at Fleet Street the day they issued the "Limehouse Declaration" from David Owen's house, and in April 1981 I trooped along to the Connaught Rooms for the launch of the SDP, each defector from Labour standing behind a rostrum bearing the new party's initials, like a 1940s big band. I was there when Christopher Brocklebank-Fowler theatrically crossed the Chamber to become the only Tory to join the SDP, and watched the committee rooms upstairs where a few others were agonising over whether to follow him. I covered exhaustively the SDP's efforts to establish itself, and the tensions with the Liberals as the Alliance was hammered out and local egos bruised over which party should fight which seat. I got to one SDP conference, was pulled from the Liberals' historic 1981 assembly at Llandudno at the last minute and to my regret did not cover the pivotal by-elections at Warrington, Crosby, Hillhead, Bermondsey or Greenwich – this last caused by the death of my friend Guy Barnett on Christmas Eve, 1986.

Roy Jenkins' victory at Hillhead on the eve of the Falklands war was a stunning achievement for a politician attuned to the refinements of Brussels. When I received an indirect approach to go and work for him I was flattered, but couldn't see a career path opening up. Yet I regret not having got to know better the author of *Asquith* (one of my favourite books) and *Gladstone* ... who emerges not only as an awful bore, but wrong about pretty well everything.

Jenkins' autobiography was written too soon after Brussels, using the word "ratiocination" when "thought" would have done. While he would have been an imposing figure heading a government, Steel was right in reckoning that a general election campaign required a blunter instrument.

Everyone remembers David Steel and David Owen's joint leadership of the Alliance for *Spitting Image*'s wicked depiction of Steel as a dummy in the pocket of the Doctor's pyjama jacket. The image stuck, and for Liberals it hurt. Owen – whom I first met leading a disability demonstration in 1967 - was never easy to get on with; he was still suffering pain from a motorcycle accident while up at Cambridge. I shared his frustration with the beard-and-sandals brigade who turned up at Liberal conferences determined to make the party – and the Alliance – unelectable. There was also no doubt that David Owen in full, arrogant flight was a match for Mrs Thatcher; all he needed was a parliamentary party behind him, and that the voters would not provide.

After the 1983 election, when high hopes brought votes but few seats, Steel developed the mother of all depressions, Owen saying when they met for a post-mortem: "I can tell you as a doctor that you should be in bed." When I characterised Steel's post-election moods as "40 days in the wilderness eating locusts", Paddy Ashdown told me I was right. When 1987 produced much the same outcome, Steel demanded an instant merger. Strategically he was right, but his tactics were appalling: Owen said: "Over my dead body!", and meant it. A more delicate approach might not have achieved a merger, but there would have been a better chance of isolating Owen.

The stage was set for splits in both parties and difficult negotiations on merger, plus the notorious "dead parrot" policy paper which had to be hurriedly withdrawn. And my final *Telegraph* story before leaving the Commons told of hostilities breaking out within the SDP.

By the time I returned for the *Independent on Sunday*, the Liberal Democrats were a reality (initially with a poll rating even lower

227

than Nick Clegg's during the Coalition) and Ashdown was leading them. I had tipped Paddy for the Liberal leadership before he won Yeovil in 1983, alerted by party insiders. The hardness in his eyes showed he meant business, and I admired his candour in calling a press conference before the 1992 election to own up to an affair with his former secretary, the *Sun* making the nation smile by christening him "Paddy Pantsdown". I also chuckled at the introduction he received at a Chamber of Commerce lunch in Edinburgh: "Paddy Ashdown is the first leader of a British political party to be a trained killer ... Margaret Thatcher being self-taught". When during the merger this attribute of Paddy's first attracted notice, one SDPer ventured: "We could always say the Doctor finished off a few when he was in the NHS."

Paddy was quietly authoritative, and totally straight to deal with. He created a coherent single party out of two, and transformed it from some twenty oddball MPs, mainly winners of freak by-elections, into a respectable 60-odd with a credible front bench team.

Had I been interested then in being a spin doctor, an approach I had from Archy Kirkwood (one of their easiest MPs to get on with) might have tempted me. Paddy is the only leader of the party I could have worked for, but I wasn't comfortable with the merger he was tempted to negotiate with Labour either side of the 1997 election; if it had come off, where would opponents of the Iraq War have gone?

Even as political editor of Scotland's best-selling paper, I didn't have much contact with Charles Kennedy; he was embedded in the *Guardian* set. But he was unique: an MP at 23 while still studying in the States – George Younger told me how Kennedy sat in awe as the visiting Roy Jenkins expatiated on the paintings in Dover House - and the one elected Social Democrat to survive into the merged party. When Ashdown's nuptials with Blair were thwarted by Jack Straw and John Prescott, Kennedy skilfully repositioned the Lib Dems to the left of Labour and, for one week prior to the Iraq War, looked as if he might find himself leading a government.

It didn't happen, but Kennedy's anti-war stance (which I didn't share) took seats from Labour in 2005 when the scope to squeeze the Tories had run its course. I finally left the Lobby six months after he was elected leader, and at the Scotland Office my assessment of him was for a Labour secretary of state, not for publication. But I was sad to see the party slip away from him, and mourned his early death.

Ming Campbell I have always liked. David Steel told me Ming would win North-East Fife two elections before he did, and he had the ability to lead his party. Sadly he came to it too late, but his performance as LibDem leader showed what might have been. The Scottish political establishment reckon Ming one of their own; he and John Smith got on famously, and when Helen and I flew down from Edinburgh, we always hoped to find him in the departure lounge.

Nick Clegg came after my time, though *Today's Railways'* Peter Fox, a former LibDem councillor in his constituency, rated him. In opposition I disliked his obsession not just with the potential abuses of the "surveillance state" but any kind of technology to protect people's identities; perversely, this was one of the few things the coalition parties would agree on. Even more ironic that he should end up working for Facebook.

He owed his place in government, ironically, to Rupert Murdoch. It was Sky's insistence on televised debates between the three leaders that gave Clegg his opportunity to shine; it may not have won him that many votes, but it gave him the credibility for David Cameron to bring him into government almost as an equal. It was quite a shock for some Lib Dem MPs to wake up as ministers, but I was pleased for my old *Independent on Sunday* colleague Chris Huhne, and even more for Danny Alexander, first encountered 18 years before as the Scottish Lib Dem press officer. No-one can deny they had earned it, but they knew the public might not thank them.

I was uncomfortable over Labour's attacks on the Lib Dems for doing a deal the with Tories; the country had to have a government at a time of economic crisis and a Labour-led coalition would have lacked a majority. Moreover a Cameron government unrestrained by the Lib-Dems would have been under immense backbench pressure not just to pull out of Europe but to run amok. The coalition made mistakes, Clegg paying a heavy price for going back on his pledge to abolish tuition fees – not that he was in a position to deliver it. But the experiment had to happen ... and up to a point it worked. The Lib Dems' rout in 2015 owed almost as much to a last-minute rebellion against polls predicting another hung Parliament as to their limitations in office. Historians will probably be kinder.

14: Electioneering

The 1951 general election was the first I remember. In the playground in my first term, one of the big girls accosted me with: "Li'l boy, is your mum Labour or Conservative?" Nonplussed, I replied: "She's Mrs. Comfort." By 1955 we had moved to Loughton, until that election in Churchill's constituency; I remember huge Labour posters on the old bus garage, bought by the Co-Op for conversion into a bakery. When Harold Macmillan called the "Never had it so good" election of 1959 I had just started at Highgate. Much of the press coverage was of the young Margaret Thatcher, fighting Finchley, just down the road.

Then I discovered by-elections. There were far more then, as MPs were appointed judges, colonial governors and the like. I read the papers avidly as dull contests were fanned into mini-dramas, learning how to calculate swings. Dozens of servicemen began applying for nomination papers after realising it was cheaper to be kicked out of the forces for going into politics and lose your deposit than to buy yourself out; this inspired a brilliant squaddies' party political broadcast on *That Was The Week That Was*.

Most exciting was Orpington, where in March 1962 the Liberal Eric Lubbock overturned a massive Tory majority. Then there was the by-election at Kinross and West Perthshire fought by Sir Alec Douglas-Home, already Prime Minister, after disclaiming his peerage. When I went for my interview at Trinity soon after, I expatiated on "psephology" – the study of elections.

In the spring of 1964 I helped out at two by-elections. At Faversham, which Labour's Terry Boston won from the Conservatives, four of us spent the day canvassing; on the way home my friend Brian Smith's car broke down, with us discovering someone had draped a used condom over the bumper. For safe Tory Bury St Edmunds, the Labour agent for Edmonton and I were despatched to tiny Withersfield, to get our voters out and help the tellers at the polling station. It was fascinating to hear about the makeup of the village: one family with "rich" and "poor" branches, and the deference shown to "The Major". I wish I'd known then that Withersfield was the ancestral home of Don Bradman; I would have looked for Bradman graves in the churchyard.

For the general election I worked in our Chigwell constituency, where Labour's Eric Moonman had distant hopes of ousting John Biggs-Davison. Eric was Harold Wilson's ideal candidate: classless, technocratic (and an Evertonian), and someone you wanted to make an effort for: appreciative, and a hard worker with campaigning flair. His posters showed a crescent moon with spectacles and a rosette, a theme carried over into his election literature and quite a novelty for those days. I saw George Brown for the first time when he spoke for Eric in a packed school hall at Hainault.

After starting at university, I managed to get a request played for Eric on Radio Caroline. On polling day I knocked up at Cherry Hinton, on the edge of Cambridge, and that night watched the results in the Union. A landslide seemed on, but Wilson's eventual majority was tiny. Biggs-Davison held on comfortably; Eric Moonman would later be MP for Billericay.

I was also in Cambridge when the 1966 election was called – putting together constituency profiles for *Varsity* – but home for the campaign. We needed a new candidate, and the choice was alarmingly second-rate; I and some others used the fact that not everyone had been properly notified to halt the selection meeting, and we eventually found an excellent candidate in Eric Deakins, who had fought Mrs Thatcher in 1959, earning a mention in *The Iron Lady*. Eric was an international meat trader and passionately anti-Market, dashingly handsome and always with an attractive girl on his arm. On the doorstep, some older women confused him disapprovingly with the long-dead trade union leader Arthur Deakin.

One Saturday, my Congo friend Patrick Leathem and I were out with the loudspeaker car in affluent Chigwell. A bridal car pulled in front of us, and Patrick could not resist announcing: "The Labour Party congratulates the happy couple, and hopes they'll be back from their honeymoon to vote on March 28th." Their chauffeur nearly drove into a hedge.

On election night I went to the count in a Loughton school, where Biggs-Davison was again re-elected (as he would be six more times). I have always found election-night celebrations – especially by Tories – off-putting, but when the victors called for "three cheers for Biggs", we joined in; the Tories were non-plussed until we explained that Labour's agent was Harry Biggs. We retired to watch the Labour gains roll in; it was the last election night televised in black and white and the presentation, though less wooden, was still light years away from today's high-tech coverage.

That summer I worked in the electoral registration department at Waltham Forest town hall, thanks to my mother who was with social services. It was a small unit: Don Armer, his deputy John Thraves, and myself as a temp. Our task was the first, primitive move toward computerising the register: inputting 50,000 names onto spools of punched tape, from which the register could be printed out; each elector gained a card, bearing the same punched code for re-use in following years. The register contained the likes of Samson Hannibal and Ulrich von Nesselrode, but the most problematic name was Jessie Spinks: every time we fed it in, it came out a mix of letters and numbers, or backwards.

Don was still there 20 years later when I bought at flat at Snaresbrook which straddled the Waltham Forest-Redbridge boundary; he told me I should be registered in Redbridge. Labour Waltham Forest had declared itself nuclear-free while Tory Redbridge hadn't; so we residents decided that if war broke out we would occupy the Waltham Forest side of the block.

Waltham Forest gave me a first insight into the workings of local government which would prove handy in Sheffield. I also gained a valuable grasp of electoral law. Sadly councils don't always take it seriously nowadays; some make no serious effort to compile a 100% reliable register, and electioneering in Battersea in 2005, I was staggered at the official disinterest when an elector reported that someone had voted in their place.

The register I helped compile in 1966 was in force the next year when Eric Deakins fought the Walthamstow West by-election. The seat was solid Labour, but Wilson was unpopular and Eric, under pressure from headquarters, trimmed on Europe for the only time in his career. An anti-Market independent intervened, and Eric lost by 88 votes. He regained the seat in 1970 and held it to serve as junior trade minister under Wilson, a job he loved. Then Jim Callaghan told him: "You've had your fun. Now you can go to the DHSS, and after the next election (1979) I'll give you a decent job." But Labour was defeated, and eight years later Eric lost his seat.

In Sheffield, because I was reporting local politics I stuck to backroom work; from the 1970 council elections onward I helped out on the small, modern Batemoor estate. By now I was familiar with committee room routine: collecting the numbers of those who had voted from the tellers, crossing them off the lists of known supporters on the alternating sheets of paper and carbon known as "Reading" pads to Labour activists, "NCRs" to Conservatives and "Shuttleworths" to Liberals, and the increasingly energetic "knocking up" of those who had yet to vote.

Those 1970 elections in Sheffield were a dress rehearsal for a general election in more ways than one: Labour fielded a Mr Wilson, the Tories a Mr Heath and the Liberals a Mr Thorpe, a story I ran which for once the nationals picked up ... and Mr Wilson won. Labour's gains nationally led Wilson to call an election, for which I covered two constituencies: Hillsborough and Hallam. Hillsborough's MP was George Darling, an old-timer and Minister of State for Trade; he spent little time there between elections, when he installed himself in a city centre hotel, but he knew everybody. Hallam – recently represented by Nick Clegg – was the fief of John Osborn, Sheffield's last forgemaster politician. Of all the candidates, I liked most Hallam's Liberal Preetam Singh, a gentlemanly Sikh barrister devastated by the racist mail he received from clearly educated old ladies. Across the city, in Attercliffe and Brightside, the Tories were blooding young prospects: Tony Newton and Tim Renton, who would serve in the Thatcher/Major Cabinet. One was holding a meeting outside Ambrose Shardlow's crankshaft works – a Communist hotbed – when a shop steward challenged an obscure Tory manifesto commitment. "I'm certain we never promised that", said the young candidate ... only for the questioner to pull the Conservative Campaign Guide from his mac and say: "It says here on page 537..."

Ten days out, Labour led by 13 per cent. George Darling's meetings turned into teach-ins on how VAT would work once we joined the Common Market. George Brown, no longer in the Cabinet but still Labour's deputy leader, delivered a fiery speech from the City Hall steps, the desperation in his voice a sign of personal eclipse rather than a harbinger of defeat.

The final weekend, a Liberal meeting addressed by the future MP Michael Meadowcroft clashed with England's World Cup match with West Germany; astoundingly it was packed. England lost 3-2 after having the game in the bag ... and the same fate now befell Labour. On the eve of poll we sang *The Red Flag* lustily at an open-air meeting in Attercliffe, confident despite poor trade figures blamed by Wilson on an order for jumbo jets. On the day, Batemoor (in the Heeley constituency) seemed sluggish ... then at lunchtime an *Evening Standard* poll put the Tories 0.5 per cent ahead. We worked like Trojans, but the votes just were not there for our sitting MP, the almost eponymous Frank Hooley.

It would be wrong to say no-one expected Ted Heath to win. Sheffield Newspapers' Graham Cawthorne, in the Lobby since before the war, came up for the campaign and, while speculating in print that a defeated Heath would be ousted as leader, reflected a late change of mood in his final story. I was greatly impressed by Graham's having broken with the pack to call the election right, putting it down to a good political "nose" and excellent Tory contacts.

In 1973 the new South Yorkshire County Council was elected, plus a Sheffield City Council expanded geographically but shorn of many responsibilities. We had headaches putting together a supplement with biographies and mugshots of every candidate in an area stretching almost to Wakefield and Scunthorpe. Labour won both elections comfortably; I again spent a busy day on Batemoor, then a hectic late night pulling together the results.

The February 1974 election – called disastrously by Heath at the height of the miners' strike to determine "Who governs Britain?" - came with me about to leave Sheffield. This time I covered Hallam and Attercliffe. John Osborn comfortably saw off David Blunkett, fighting his first seat; I spent quite a bit of the campaign with David and his dog. Attercliffe was equally safe for the future Navy Minister and centenarian Pat Duffy. Little was seen of Tariq Ali, who polled just 424 votes as an International Marxist; he would have done better in Hallam, with its student vote.

By that October's further election I was in Birmingham with the *Daily Telegraph*. I mainly contributed constituency profiles, the most fascinating covering Hereford and Leominster, largely rural constituencies afflicted, as I wrote, by "an outbreak of politics as virulent as foot and mouth disease". The Liberals had always targeted Hereford – Robin Day had once been their candidate - but Leominster, to the north, was Tory territory. The veteran Sir Clive Bossom had stood down in February, leaving a majority of 11,167 to the silver-haired barrister Peter Temple-Morris. Bossom had not worked the seat, but the Liberal Roger Pincham, a substantial figure in the City, had, and Temple-Morris scraped home by 1,619 votes. Pincham reminded me of an 18th-century rector, while Temple-Morris was engaging and surprisingly frank with me, a total stranger, on how Bossom, PPS to Reggie Maudling, lost heart after his boss "crashed" over the Poulson affair. Peter and his wife invited me to lunch at the height of a frantic campaign; under Mrs Thatcher he would resign as a PPS to spirit her family out of Iran at considerable cost and personal risk.

In Hereford David Gibson-Watt, whose son Julian had been at Trinity with me, held on by 3,348 votes in the February, then decided to retire. His successor was Colin Shepherd, whose mother Dame Peggy had been a pillar of the Conservative Party; he was hard-working and charming, with a hint of reticence. The Liberal challenger, Colin Tannat Nash, by contrast, did not seem everyone's cup of tea.

The Liberals fell just short in both constituencies: Shepherd held Hereford by 1,112 votes and Temple-Morris hung on by just 579. Peter's majority would grow steadily until in 1998 he crossed the floor to Labour; Colin would survive many close contests, finally losing to the Lib Dems in 1997 after a productive career on the back benches. I kept in touch with him, partly because I became close to his agent; I lunched at his home at Ganarew, and he once joined me on the terraces at Edgar Street. In the 1983 election one of Colin's supporters found a novel vehicle for his posters: a goat tethered by the roadside. I couldn't help writing that if the Liberals won him over he would become a turngoat.

On the day of the second 1974 election, 10 October, I was in Wiltshire interviewing jockeys. Returning to Birmingham I put together a piece on resistance in Herefordshire to its shotgun merger with Worcestershire – which had harmed Tory chances there – to fill a hole in the paper until the results came in. As I was telephoning my copy, Dave Robinson shouted to me to come through; I was just too late to see a hot air balloon plunge to the ground, killing both people on board. I filed a report on that tragedy, then that night watched the results with British Leyland workers in a pub near Longbridge.

Fewer people vote in American elections, and – particularly post-Donald Trump - it can be difficult to register. Billions are spent by pressure groups as well as parties, and - since the Reagan administration removed the few constraints – there is no requirement for fairness from the media. Republican states are the red ones and Democratic states blue – and the successful Presidential candidate is the one who carries the Electoral College (George W Bush or Trump), not the winner of the popular vote (Gore or Hillary Clinton).

I arrived in Washington during the 1976 Presidential primaries. Jimmy Carter was ahead for the Democratic nomination but had not yet seen off Hubert Humphrey, while the Republican incumbent Gerald Ford - not helped by his campaign manager saying it was too late to "rearrange the chairs on the deck of the *Titanic*" - still had to defeat a Right-wing challenge from Ronald Reagan. Steve Barber broadened my education by sending me to work in a suburban Maryland committee room for his friend Frank Mankiewicz, who was running in a Democratic congressional primary. Contact with voters was entirely over the phone, instead of on the doorstep as in Britain then.

As Carter and Ford secured their nominations, I began to grasp the essentials of American electioneering. The economy and law and order came first, then defence, and only three foreign countries were ever mentioned: the Soviet Union, Israel and (for black audiences) South Africa. Northern Ireland, fortunately, was only an issue in a few Irish-dominated Congressional districts.

With a couple of weeks to polling, Steve sent me out to experience the campaign. I flew to Chicago – which I loved, having more chance to savour it as Ford cancelled at the last minute. I called at the parties' campaign offices, then headed for suburban Skokie for a rally of Jews for Carter; his jerky, Southern style wasn't right for his audience of rabbis, but his patent sincerity held it. In a bar afterwards, a man introduced himself proudly - to my horror - as a "speculator".

I flew on from O'Hare Airport (named after the fighter ace son of one of Al Capone's henchmen) to join Ford in St Louis, only for the polls to dictate another change in his schedule. Instead I drove deep into Missouri past field after field of Halloween pumpkins, absorbing local colour and following the campaign on the radio.

Reporting American election results for a British newspaper is a challenge; with a minimum five-hour time difference they don't start coming in till the first editions have been printed, and it can take hours more to get a result – and people can see the outcome on television. Steve tried to convince London there was no point in us writing a results-based story until very late on. He then popped out for a drink, and another demand came in for copy. I put together a short holding piece based on the latest projections (fragmentary results put Ford slightly ahead), held it till the last possible moment hoping Steve would return and bin it, then – reluctantly - filed. Only when Steve came back did he finally persuade London that comment at that stage was pointless.

The most important election for me was the one Jim Callaghan didn't call, as it led to my premature recall from Washington. By contrast with Gordon Brown's botched effort 29 years later, Callaghan did not set the party machine in motion; he kept everyone guessing (even Reg Underhill) so he could withdraw without losing face. When September 1978 opened with the polls favouring Labour, an election looked likely. Callaghan teased the TUC by reciting the Marie Lloyd song "There was I, waiting at the church ...", and the party conferences approached with a decision imminent.

It came as I was on the road with Mrs Thatcher. When word reached us at Cinderford, in the Forest of Dean, that Callaghan was to broadcast that night, she said: "He wouldn't be going on television if he wasn't going to call an election." With anticipation rising we toured a Rank Xerox plant - one of many factories she visited that would close during her premiership – then headed for

Lichfield, where she planned to open her campaign. For Callaghan's broadcast, we paused at an old city-centre coaching inn. Mrs Thatcher and her entourage retired to watch it, and the rest of us crowded round the television in the bar. Callaghan came on, kept us guessing for a moment, then said he saw no reason to put the country through an election at this point.

We were stunned. Mrs Thatcher came down with a face like thunder, blasted a TV crew who got in her way ... then gave a brief, professional reaction. When she faced her audience at a local school, she was ready to assure them of victory whenever the election came.

I discovered two things that influenced Callaghan to delay. One was an impassioned recollection to a party meeting from the veteran MP Arthur Blenkinsop of how in 1951 Attlee had gone to the country and lost when if he had hung on six months the economy would have revived. The other was a dinner where Callaghan's fellow guests included that master of theatre Harold Macmillan. As they were leaving, Macmillan sidled up, said: "You must be wondering whether to call an election soon .... That's a nice car you've got" – and walked off into the night. I wonder if Mrs Thatcher appreciated the debt she owed him.

The 1979 election was the first I covered from London, and I quickly got into the routine: the parties' daily press conferences, campaign developments from around the country, advance texts of evening speeches, politicians' utterances on television and radio ... then the moulding of all this into two or three coherent stories. Jim Wightman, my new boss, wrote the main one; I put together one or more secondary pieces and Tony Conyers hoovered up the rest. There was a steady stream of calls from people wanting to influence our coverage. Somebody who had an "in" with the *Telegraph* confided that the widow of Labour's Herbert Morrison was going to vote Conservative; I upset them by pointing out that she always had. I also got out on the road. Chris Potter of the *Sun* and I followed Callaghan round the Midlands in my yellow Avenger, and we had the field almost to ourselves. Today a media throng accompanies any party leader, screened beforehand and amid heavy security. But in 1979 things were different. Driving through Ashby de la Zouch, we spotted Jim's Rover driven by his chauffeur Joe Hazard and simply fell in behind it; the police escort was a single car. [Twenty years later, I found that Rover on display in the company's heritage centre at Gaydon].

There were few journalists - and just one television crew - following Callaghan that day, and not many more travelled to Cardiff with him when he spoke in his constituency (British Rail laid on steaks for all, served by a steward who had known Callaghan since Great Western days). The one policy line that lifted his audience that – and every - night was the claim that the Tories wanted to denationalise North Sea oil. In Manchester the PM had us in for an off-the-record drink, and next morning I bumped into him with his entourage in the hotel lobby: just three or four people including his son. It was all very intimate, very low-key.

One afternoon Callaghan called at the Labour Hall in marginal Ilford South. I arrived to find elderly Co-Op ladies making tea ... and a baffled French reporter asking where the workers were. I did my best to put him straight before Jim appeared, with a slightly larger police escort but still a model of understated power.

Election night was what I was used to in Sheffield writ large, with 640-plus MPs to be elected instead of 108 councillors and far more at stake. There was the same need for early-edition stories on the weather, the turnout, mishaps at polling stations and anything else that didn't prejudge the result. We killed a couple of hours over a drink or an uninviting sandwich, then the first results came in, with us trying to identify a national trend ... followed by a tidal wave as we raced to pick out seats changing hands, ministers defeated, or wins and – more often – frustrations for the minor parties. As the national picture became clear, we took in reactions from key players, Jim Wightman wrote the definitive final edition piece, and we unwound as the last results of the night trickled in.

Next morning, as Jim concentrated on Mrs Thatcher's arrival at Downing Street and the hopes for her new government, I called on Percy Clark, Labour's communications director, at a sombre

Transport House. When the defeat at Paddington of the recalcitrant Left-winger Arthur Latham came through, Percy half-smilingly said: "That's the last time he'll vote against a Labour government." The rest of the day I concentrated on Shirley Williams' unexpected defeat – as new town tenants voted for the "Right to Buy" – and the problems in store for Callaghan from the resurgent Left.

For the 1983 election I was at the heart of the *Telegraph*'s coverage. Mrs Thatcher, buoyed by the Falklands Factor, went to the country that June, gambling on the Liberal/SDP Alliance and a Labour Party whose manifesto Gerald Kaufman christened "the longest suicide note in history" cancelling each other out. Soon after the election was called, I rang the Conservative chairman Cecil Parkinson. "Can you call back in twenty minutes?" Cecil asked me. "I must just say goodbye to my wife." My reply came out as: "Are you sure twenty minutes will be enough?" When I mentioned the conversation to Jeffrey Archer after Parkinson's resignation over his affair with Sara Keays, Jeffrey said: "He must have thought you knew." Needless to say, I didn't.

For the first half of the campaign, I was on the road with Mrs Thatcher. Taking a chartered jet from Gatwick (what a contrast with four years before!) after her morning press conference, we landed at RAF stations from Norfolk to Cornwall and hurtled round the countryside in a coach behind the Iron Lady's battlebus. With us was Carol Thatcher, who - to our relief – turned out to be great company. Carol was writing a book on the campaign; Chris Potter waited to submit his expenses until it came out, using her text as a lucrative *aide-memoire*.

After a rally at Newbury racecourse, Mrs Thatcher invited a few of us onto her bus for a wide-ranging monologue on how the campaign was going. She was brisk and to the point, but solicitous as to how we were coping. I wrote my story, leading on her prediction of an "unusually large" majority, on our own bus, filing from a callbox on Reading station.

Up in Yorkshire, Mrs Thatcher paid a lunchtime visit to Harry Ramsden's at Guiseley (we went hungry as she ploughed in, shaking hands). Harry's may be the best chippie in the world, but its small rooms were quite unsuited to a media event; frustrated that his crew couldn't get a clear shot, ITN's Mike Brunson tore down placards waved by Tory activists. On the way into Leeds, I got to a phone box – the only means of communication then - to be told: "Thank God you've called in. You're needed back here."

At Labour's news conference Jim Mortimer, the party's Maoist general secretary, had solemnly - and incredibly - announced that the National Executive had confirmed Michael Foot as leader of the party. This followed campaign committee meetings attended by over 30 people, including Foot's Special Branch escort, admitted because no-one knew who they were. From the moment Mortimer dropped his clanger (no-one had previously raised the leadership issue), I was overseeing a slow-motion train wreck.

For a time, it looked as if Mrs Thatcher's majority would be even greater than the eventual 144, with Labour a poor third. Speculation erupted about the Labour succession, and Neil Kinnock played into Tory hands by talking of British soldiers having "left their guts at Goose Green" so Mrs Thatcher could demonstrate hers. So worried were the Conservatives of an Alliance upsurge that late on Mrs Thatcher declared: "The Labour Party will never die." Labour's vote did slump, but by less than predicted, and the Alliance was denied a breakthrough, two of the "Gang of Four" losing their seats.

The 1987 election, for me, was an anti-climax. Having immersed myself in Labour's attempts to rebuild itself and got to know Neil, I expected to be on the road with him. But Max Hastings was smitten by the feature writer Martyn Harris, often opening the morning conference with: "Well, what shall we find for Martyn today?" Max reckoned that Martyn with his South Welsh background would be the ideal person to send out with Neil. But Martyn was not up with the nuances of Labour policy, so when Neil said anything significant, he missed it.

So I spent the campaign in London, covering with my new boss, George Jones, the press conferences and the TV interviews on which the election was increasingly fought, as Labour regained some ground. The *Telegraph* was still – just – in Fleet Street, and on election night George did the main piece while I concentrated on Labour's revival and the far Left's efforts to break through, stories that didn't really develop. This was the last election where our stories were typed onto slips of paper, subbed, retyped by linotype operators and then set manually into the page; thereafter reporters could update their copy on their screen. Strangely, the new technology did not get the results onto the streets any quicker.

In 1988 John Biggs-Davison died, causing a by-election in my native Epping Forest. I persuaded the *Telegraph* to hold space for me, and set off for Loughton. Steve Norris was defending the seat, but the Conservatives were not over-popular and had there been a single third-party candidate they would have lost. In the event, strong support for the continuing SDP denied the newly formed Liberal Democrats a breakthrough.

It was strange reporting an election in a place I knew so well. The young - and even then formidable – Gordon Brown spoke on mortgages in the room where we Young Socialists had met twenty years before, and Denis Healey unforgettably clowned around on Debden Broadway with Jack Straw's mother. But when I got back to South Quay, I simply had too much to say. The words didn't flow and in the end the space went to something else. I was not helped by the *Guardian*'s Colin Brown, an old Sheffield colleague, having nicknamed the contest "The by-election that fell off the back of a lorry", given Essex's reputation as the home of spivs. But I was just too close to the story.

I most enjoyed the general election of 1992. Newly arrived at the *Daily Record* I was given a free hand, dividing my time between London, Scotland and the party leaders on the road. This time Labour looked set to win, and the *Record* pulled out all the stops.

There had been speculation that John Major, then ahead in the polls, would call an election the previous autumn. During the Conservative conference in Brighton, he asked John Wakeham, whose abilities as a fixer I always felt exaggerated, to get the word out that there would be no election. Wakeham did this by ringing several editors – only for Elinor Goodman to scoop them on Channel 4 News. This just left everyone except Elinor livid. Surprisingly for a former chief whip, Wakeham did not think of simply moving the writ for a pending by-election. Yet his clumsiness would be eclipsed by Gordon Brown's handling of the non-election of 2007.

A few days into the campaign, I flew up to Scotland with John Major. My editor Endell Laird expected me to interview him, and given our paper's sympathies, making this happen wouldn't be easy. Luckily his gatekeeper on the plane was Shirley Matthews, whom I knew from the agents' circuit. (Years later I would find her running the party conference from the office above QinetiQ's in Buckingham Gate.) Shirley told me I could have a few minutes with the PM on the plane before take-off from Teesside. Interviewing politicians you like but haven't seen for a while is difficult, as you have to discipline yourself not to talk about cricket, their family or the like, but I emerged with seven or eight paragraphs of quotes, rebutting the *Record*'s line that John had it in for Scotland. I expanded this into a double-page spread; Endell was delighted and I had no complaints from the Tories.

I carried on with Major to North-East Fife, where Ming Campbell was set to take a Tory seat. Jeffrey Archer was on hand to help John and a slightly worried Norma cope with the throng, and it was around now that John first produced his famous soapbox. In Cupar I was queueing for a sandwich when a blue van passed, emitting the unmistakable tones of Sean Connery talking up the SNP. The woman next to me was a picture of bafflement, exclaiming: "He's no' in there?"

After a couple of days in Glasgow with Tom Brown and Dave King monitoring the Scottish campaign, and one with Neil Kinnock in Ayr, I headed north to a sleety Inverness to join Paddy Ashdown, recently christened "Paddy Pantsdown" by the *Sun*. We were meant to fly to Aberdeen then on to Edinburgh, but a crash had closed Aberdeen Airport so we set out by coach on the tortuous A96.

Paddy spoke that evening in a school I would revisit in 2001 for a Labour rally with Helen, Henry McLeish and Richard Wilson (Victor Meldrew). Then we piled into the bus for a nocturnal drive to Edinburgh. Alan Leaman, Paddy's head of policy who was later unlucky not to make it into the Commons, now took his finest decision. He ordered a halt outside Aberdeen's celebrated Ash Vale chippie, and emerged with forty fish suppers.

As we hurtled south there were two subjects of conversation: Major's onslaught on Labour's devolution plans and, as reports came in, Labour's hubristic rally in Sheffield. Those two events turned the election, Major pulling out worried Scots Tories and striking a chord south of the Border, and the sight of Kinnock, described by one sketch writer as "like a tortoise having an orgasm", shouting: "Yeah, all right!" Sheffield was a mistake; as Derek Fullick of the train drivers' union ASLEF observed, "You don't belch till you've had the meal." But what turned it into a killer was a *Times* sketch by Matthew Parris, who nursed a visceral hatred of Peter Mandelson and blamed the fiasco on him.

Two days out, Labour were still bullish. But at the Lib Dems' final press conference Richard Holme took me aside and said: "There's something very strange going on with our private polls. I can't tell you what it is, because frankly I'm not sure myself." Was an upset on the cards? And if so, what?

On the BA flight up to Glasgow Helen and John Smith, then Shadow Chancellor, were next to me, and Gordon Brown and Robin Cook across the aisle. I asked John what he would do if the election produced a hung Parliament; to my astonishment he replied: "I'd do a deal with the Liberals on income tax." Gordon, hopefully less than 72 hours from becoming Trade and Industry Secretary, asked me how DTI officials would react to an interventionist in charge; I told him it was just what they were waiting for. Robin, though, was anxious; did I really believe the polls putting Labour ahead?

Around teatime on polling day I wandered over from my hotel to Anderston Quay, and with Tom and Dave began our preparations. There was news to mop up for the first edition: polling stations failing to open, people left off the register, and the turnout. But what could you write for an edition that would go to press with the exit polls available (just) but no results? The BBC's poll put Labour in, so despite my concern that readers in far-flung parts of Scotland would see the paper already knowing the outcome, we tentatively awarded the election to Labour.

The first results revealed a late swing to the Tories. We had posited a Labour near-whitewash for Scotland, but now a Conservative gained Aberdeen South. Labour was making gains in England, but not on the scale predicted, and we ate the last tired sandwiches with growing pessimism. Given the head of steam for devolution and Labour's apparent unelectability, would the Scottish party now haemorrhage support to the SNP?

I never sleep well on election nights; there is too much adrenaline flowing. So I woke after three hours to television coverage of Major's re-election. At Labour's Scottish HQ the mood was one of shell-shock until Anne McGuire, party chairman and later a capable junior minister, rallied the morning-after press conference with a chorus of "Always look on the bright side of life." I wrote my wrap-up piece including the final results and speculating on what lay ahead, then set off for home. At Glasgow Airport I bumped into Adam Ingram, Neil Kinnock's PPS; Neil had laid on a barbecue at his Ealing home to distract his entourage from their dashed expectations. Within weeks, John Smith would succeed him.

On the eve of the 1997 campaign Trevor Kavanagh recruited me to the *Sun*'s election team, working out of the Commons. With the outcome a foregone conclusion, I set to work on biographies of Labour heavyweights and took the odd call. But the campaign was so quiet that after ten days Trevor let me go; he had not enough work even for his own staff.

He did ask me into Wapping for election night ... and what a night it was. No-one had foreseen how comprehensively the voters would reject the Tories. Seven of Major's Cabinet – including, late on, Michael Portillo stunningly at Southgate – were unseated, swathes were cut through the Tory ranks, a host of new Labour MPs (in both senses) were elected and the Lib-Dems won seats they hadn't even targeted. My role was to monitor on the television and keep Trevor and editor Stuart Higgins up with events. The highlight, results apart, was when Rupert Murdoch, who had swung the paper behind New Labour except on Europe, called Stuart from Australia to see how things were going. He was well satisfied.

I covered the 1997 Scottish devolution referendum and the first Holyrood elections two years later as a journalist, but for the 2001 general election I was on the inside. As a special adviser, I ceased to be a temporary civil servant at the start of the campaign and became part of Labour's Scottish machine. Beforehand, STV came down to Millbank to discuss arrangements for election broadcasts north of the Border. Douglas Alexander led for Labour with me in support, while STV fielded their managing director and their corporate affairs director Rhoda Macdonald ... who 18 months later would succeed me as Helen's media SPAD.

There were about fifteen of us at John Smith House in Glasgow working under the direction of Lesley Quinn, Scottish Labour's unflappable general secretary. Lesley, a supremely efficient organiser with an encyclopaedic knowledge of electoral law, infused the team with her energy, and raised voices were a rarity. Behind her stern facade was genuine warmth, and I owe her a lot for rescuing my Filofax when I lost it at Heathrow.

My fellow SPAD George McGregor and I took turns to stay at base drafting speeches, setting up visits and liaising with the campaign team, or going out on the road with Helen in her "key campaigner" role. This was fun, if exhausting: covering long distances between meetings, bursts of canvassing and the odd television debate in a people carrier driven by a volunteer trade unionist, with Meta Ramsay, the charming yet steely former MI6 operative who had been John Smith's foreign policy adviser and was now a whip in the Lords, feeding us bananas and Red Bull.

We "blitzed" south Aberdeen with the effervescent Mo Mowlam, Labour's phone bank uncannily ringing voters just as Mo banged on their doors, and encountered the Tory front-bencher Andrew

Mackay in a car park at Nairn. There were "Helen and Henry Shows" in Aberdeen and Dundee, with First Minister Henry McLeish. For these, careful orchestration with Henry's SPADs – still wearing their civil service hats – was necessary. All the time I was fielding calls from reporters, and ringing ahead to make sure everything was in place for our next call.

Labour's Scottish campaign, as nationally, went unexcitingly. We were spared the embarrassment Malcolm Rifkind suffered when he unveiled a Tory advertising van, only to see it proclaim the virtues of a 24-hour Tesco in Stevenage. My private worry was that some photographer would snap Helen in front of Labour's poster showing William Hague morphing into Margaret Thatcher ... with a hairdo very like hers. I succeeded, but it was several years before I told her why I had sometimes steered her away from a photo opportunity.

Our anxious moment nationally came when John Prescott, grievously provoked, slugged an anti-hunting protester in Rhyl. Fearing the episode might force Prescott – due in Scotland next day - to quit, we had a nervous teleconference with our Welsh counterparts, then prepared to watch Labour's press conference. The Sky feed in the office was down, so we I begged a room off a local hotel. It was evident in seconds that the crisis was past – though Sky's Adam Boulton continued to report the rumble in Rhyl as an affront to national decency. Later the defence minister Lewis Moonie popped in after canvassing in Kirkcaldy; 40% of his voters thought Prescott had done the right thing - and 60% said he should have hit him harder.

Those teleconferences with Welsh ministers, party organisers and SPADS, moderated from Millbank by Douglas Alexander, were not the first activity of the day; Helen and I spoke before 7 am about the overnight media coverage. But they helped us learn from each other's experiences, gave us a feel for the wider mood and enabled Douglas to co-ordinate our campaigning. One call sticks in my mind: taken in my car on a boiling Sunday in Wiltshire. George Foulkes's contributions were punctuated by fervent cheering, and it was a let-down to discover he had been speaking to us not from an election rally but from the directors' box at Hearts.

Labour's key issue – public service reform - broke surface at the campaign launch in Birmingham. There had not been a whiff of this beforehand, and announcing it was a red rag to the unions – especially Unison – who were providing much of the finance and manpower for our campaign. No matter how hard Tony Blair and his outriders tried to depict reform as the natural concomitant to higher spending on public services, notably the NHS, the commitment made the rest of the campaign uneasy. My view that raising the issue was not worth the candle was reinforced when, the election won, we SPADs were summoned to Number 10 to try and work out what public service reform actually meant. I'm still not sure.

I spent polling day at John Smith House fielding reports from the constituencies, then went to Airdrie for Helen's count. After her comfortable re-election I put out her reaction to Labour's return by another huge majority – though on an embarrassingly low turnout - and after a brief unwind in the pub it was back to Glasgow.

The morning after began with Helen being interviewed at STV, then it was back to John Smith House for the victory press conference. In an anteroom, Helen and Henry chatted about the impending reshuffle, Henry delivering himself of the view that John Reid was a "sanctimonious bastard". Unfortunately there was a live mike in the room, and by lunchtime a transcript was doing the rounds of Scotland's finest. Word of the gaffe reached me as I handed in my campaign mobile at Millbank; after a round of embarrassing headlines the dust settled with little damage to Helen, but quite a bit to Henry.

I returned to John Smith House two years later for the second Holyrood elections. Helen was still Scottish Secretary, but every paper connected to Andrew Neil was dismissing her office as irrelevant. Jack McConnell was now First Minister, and reckoned he needed no help from a Secretary of State whose presence implied he was not totally master in his own house. There might have been a Helen and Henry Show, but there would be no Jack and Helen Show. I was now there as a volunteer, not a SPAD, and while I helped organise things for Helen – and ghost-write the odd article for Jack – my role was marginal.

A campaign visit to Clydesdale supporting Karen Gillon's campaign along with Jimmy Hood, the local MP, sticks in my mind. As we marched into Coalburn's new sports centre with a stock of balloons the caretaker asked what was in them. When Helen replied: "Methane" he told her: "The kids will love that".

On polling day in 2005 I went to Battersea to help my old Lobby colleague Martin Linton, defending an iffy-looking Labour majority of 5,053. Knocking up in Balham, one thing became clear: because of Iraq, some Labour voters were staying home or switching to the LibDems. One woman told me she had left the Party, and wouldn't come back until Gordon Brown replaced Tony Blair. Others were voting Labour but holding their noses. I didn't try to change their minds, but by dusk I must have persuaded about 80 supporters to turn out. Martin scraped back by 163 votes, so it seemed a day well spent.

By 2010 I had moved to a Labour constituency: Lewisham West. I put in an evening's canvassing off Honor Oak Road – the occupants of my childhood house were out – knocked up in Penge, then worked as a teller at Anerley Town Hall as late voters (many not registered) surged in. The Tories had gone in with a clear lead and Gordon had not had a good campaign, so the deadlocked outcome was a surprise.

Five years on, the voters defied the polls by turning against both Labour and hung Parliaments. After leafleting in Penge I knocked up in highly marginal Croydon Central. We had floods of volunteers and victory seemed assured, but it was an almost exact reversal of Battersea in 2005, the Tories hanging on by 165 votes. Two years later, after Theresa May counterproductively called another election, we won the seat handsomely.

I was 67 before I stood as a candidate, in Bromley council's Shortlands ward. I had no chance of getting in, which given a councillor's workload these days was just as well. I applied to go on

Labour's panel of candidates, and passed my interview at the party's since-demolished H G Wells Centre at Bromley South. I chose to try for two of the three wards which were rated winnable and didn't have sitting Labour councillors. There were nine good applicants for two slots at Crystal Palace, one of the winners I knew from when she worked for John Prescott. Next came my home ward of Clock House, where I made it to reserve on the shortlist. Shortlands – a rock-solid Tory ward – was my third choice, and after a front-room interview by a handful of members I was selected from four hopefuls.

My fellow candidate was Isabel Leslie, a Fifer like her husband Sandy who had lived locally for 43 years and was retired from a senior job at BT, and we worked closely between my selection in September 2013 and the election the following 22 May. Each of the ten weeks before polling day I spent one afternoon in Shortlands, canvassing and delivering leaflets, and one Saturday I joined a roadshow in West Wickham where my old Sheffield friend Richard Redden was standing. Usually I worked alone, although we supposedly had 24 members in the ward.

I don't usually enjoy canvassing, though I've done plenty of it. But this time I was asking people to vote for me, and those I caught in were almost all friendly. Most days only two or three of these – out of maybe 40 – were Labour; generally I would find several Tories, a couple of Lib Dems and the odd braying Ukip supporter. One day I canvassed the previous Green candidate, who conversed happily about plants. Another time I found a lady who was systematically recycling the Green Party's literature, having taken on board half their message. But the best moment came when a frail 102-year-old Glaswegian promised me his vote. He had bought his Victorian house in the early '60s, converted it into flats (keeping the coach house) and for many years driven round Beckenham in a pony and trap. He had given up golf at 100 – but proudly showed me the computerised driving range in his garage, thwacking a few balls straight down the middle.

A week before polling there was a hustings at the parish church – the only one held in the entire borough. Isabel and I found the two

Conservative candidates and the man from Ukip waiting, with the single Lib Dem and Green candidates unable to attend. It had become evident on the doorstep that there was only one local issue, a Michael Gove-inspired attempt to set up a primary free school on a confined site beside a dangerous road. Heavily Tory Bromley council, largely powerless in the matter, hadn't protested, and I argued that there was little point in electing Conservative councillors, no matter how sincere they were on the issue, if neither their council nor their minister was going to take any notice. Both the Tories – a long-serving councillor and a charming lady who had been fired from a senior job at London Transport by Ken Livingstone – were otherwise obviously going to do an excellent job. The Ukip candidate also impressed – and went the entire evening without mentioning Europe.

On the day, I knocked up in Clock House (which we won) until the polls closed. Next morning I went to Bromley Civic Centre for the count, in a rather cramped marquee. During the five hours before the Shortlands result – the second of 22 – was declared, the candidates sat across the bench from the counting team checking that they got it right. First the votes cast just for the two Conservative and two Labour candidates were bundled up, then all the votes split between two parties and for just one candidate were laboriously tallied. The Tories were winning easily, but it became clear Ukip had done well while I was picking up very few of those single and mixed votes – though the odd elector did pair me with every other candidate. Eventually the council chief executive called us together and told us the result, then we stood on a tiny rostrum for the declaration.

I finished fifth out of seven, with 484 votes – roughly what I had expected, though it would have been nice to do better. Ahead of me were the two Tories – with 1,959 and 1,752 – the Ukip'er with a creditable 655, and Isabel with 566. Behind me were the Green with 396, and the Lib-Dem – who had been in Brussels throughout – with 334.

I wasn't free to fight the next elections, in 2018, but would I do it again? Finding the time was difficult, but if I were less busy with other things and the party would have me, I might. I was relieved not to have been pressed about Labour's policies nationally, as I disagreed with many of them. But I did come away with my belief in the decency and commonsense of nearly all the voters reinforced – and a regret that 56% didn't bother to turn out.

15: The Conference Season

Every September the political circus leaves Westminster for a conference centre large enough for several thousand delegates, a big media presence, shoals of lobbyists and a host of commercial exhibitors. The season opens with the Trades Union Congress, continues after a short gap with the Lib Dems, the Greens and Plaid Cymru, and comes to a head with Labour and the Conservatives. The SNP winds up the season. The conferences offer compelling theatre, and the chance to meet ministers, MPs, party organisers and activists from all over the country as they argue and let their hair down. I have attended around 80, including the Conservatives' spring conference (formerly Central Council), special Labour conferences and those held by the Scottish parties ... mostly as a reporter, but also as a leader writer, special advisor and lobbyist.

For decades the two main parties alternated between Blackpool and Brighton. Blackpool's seafront with its trams and illuminations had more character than Brighton's semi-Mediterranean seediness (it has smartened up since). The weather (sometimes dreadful at both) seemed worse on the south coast, and from Blackpool on a clear day you could pick out individual houses far away in Cumbria.

Brighton had restaurants – if you had time to eat – and hotels where you could get a meal after 6.30pm. Blackpool still served the Northern high tea, and for decades you would be lucky to find a decent meal at all - one reason the parties now prefer Manchester. My favourite Brighton hotel was the Curzon, a Georgian survival up a cul-de-sac from the front, now sadly converted into flats; another devotee was Arthur Scargill. In Blackpool I started at the Carlton, which remained firmly stuck in the 1930s, then moved around. Blackpool's conference hotel, the Imperial, was more convenient for intercepting party contacts than the Grand or the Metropole in Brighton; its Oregon Bar became the epicentre of political gossip, while the downstairs disco, the Swamp, accommodated our baser instincts. Brighton had no equivalent, which was probably just as well.

The *Daily Record* put me in the Imperial – surreally watching an old Glenda Jackson film in my room having just seen her in the lobby - but I also experienced several versions of Fawlty Towers. At one in Fleetwood I was kept awake by dogs barking; when I asked why no-one called the police, I was told: "They're police dogs." Another by the Pleasure Beach was run by a Polish ex-fighter ace and largely housed Afghan migrant workers; my room overlooked the sealion pool and every morning at 5.30 the keeper brought a bucket of fish ...

I always looked forward to a meal in the dining car on the train up to Blackpool, usually to find no catering and space only in the guard's van; I first met Susan Crosland, widow and biographer of Tony, sitting on a suitcase in the corridor. You also had to change at Preston. However Blackpool's cavernous though ageing Winter Gardens are better suited to political theatre than the slabby and soulless 1970s Brighton Centre, designed for tennis and pop concerts and with inadequate anterooms for politicking.

My first party conference was in Blackpool: Labour's 1978 gathering after Jim Callaghan decided against an autumn election. In those days Labour's National Executive met in the conference hotel the previous Friday to decide its attitude to the resolutions, so we had a "dead" Saturday in Blackpool. That year a group of us went to watch Liverpool; another time the BBC's Brian Curtois and I saw Fylde playing Waterloo.

The mood was tetchy, with the Bennite Left organising to take over the party once safely out of power. I experienced for the first time the fringe meetings at which one idealist after another insisted the earth really was flat, and in the hall a particularly nasty debate over the Left's demand for MPs to submit themselves to reselection during each parliament. Michael Cocks, the chief whip, made a passionate – and poorly received - plea for the party to get behind MPs who were being nodded through the division lobbies in oxygen tents to keep Labour in power. I also saw Hugh Scanlon and Moss Evans wielding their unions' block votes like medieval barons. In the bar, I renewed acquaintance with party and union contacts from Sheffield days.

The next week I headed to Brighton, rather the worse for wear. The Tories were in optimistic mood; despite frustration at being denied an early election, they were sure they would win when it came. I met more familiar faces, including a former Sheffield colleague who was now a constituency chairman, and Richard Whiteley, still with Yorkshire Television; he was in his element at Tory conferences, and the ladies adored him. I also began to understand the workings of the Conservative Party, including the voluntary side known as the National Union, and started getting to know the party's agents, a tremendous bunch.

The Tories then were far more social than Labour. With a daily column to fill, my brief was to follow Mrs Thatcher round the receptions, dances, dinners and parties – coming back with stories (one year the agents' dinner was served gravy instead of chocolate sauce with the pudding). There were also exclusive parties upstairs in the conference hotel, hosted by the likes of Jeffrey Archer (whom I liked), Tim Bell (I didn't) and Lord King (downright obnoxious). The BBC's John Birt, later on, always looked over your shoulder in search of someone more interesting; Greg Dyke, by contrast, really listened. At Labour conferences, such parties – apart from the Mirror Group's – were a rarity until corporate Britain scented power.

Approaching the conference centre, you burrowed through a phalanx of activists forcing leaflets on you. Many wanted you to come to their fringe meeting on abortion, Europe or whatever, others (notably at Labour) pressed you to vote their way in an upcoming debate. Others simply wanted you to listen; in 1978 most were Iranian students protesting at abuses under the Shah; overwhelmingly middle-class and moderate, they would soon experience much worse.

The *Telegraph* in London was hit by a strike during that conference, but the paper still came out in Manchester. The only way of getting copy from Brighton to Withy Grove without provoking a walk-out there was to send it on the early afternoon train to Manchester. This made lunchtime our deadline.

That year's divisive issue was Rhodesia, with the Right trying to commit Mrs Thatcher to a settlement with Bishop Muzorewa that left Ian Smith with a foot in the door, rather than with Robert Mugabe. (History suggests they were right, but for all the wrong reasons). Reggie Maudling, under a cloud since the Poulson affair, led the charge, vocally supported from the floor. Replying was John Davies, the former CBI director-general Ted Heath had made Trade and Industry Secretary. Now Shadow Foreign Secretary, his floundering performance brought jeers from the Rhodesia lobby, and he sat down to mutterings of "pathetic". I wrote a piece reflecting this humiliation – used prominently the next morning - and preened myself as my copy was taken off to the station. Then Gerry Mulligan, head of the Tory newsroom, called us together and – to my mortification - asked us to go easy on Davies as he had just been diagnosed with a malignant brain tumour. Within ten months he was dead.

The 1979 conference season started on an embarrassing note. A Central Office source had told me Mrs Thatcher intended to replace Peter Thorneycroft as party chairman, and I ran the story the morning I was due in Brighton for the TUC. When the source was identified, he was given a rocket and it was the act of a gentleman that he subsequently took me to lunch. However for once in a blue moon – the BBC then usually pretended the *Telegraph* didn't exist – *The World At One* decided to interview me just as I realised the story didn't stand up. My solution, viable in the days before mobile phones, was to get to Victoria prontissimo, and take a very slow train to Brighton.

I missed Labour's 1979 conference – as nasty as the previous one - because I was covering the Papal visit to Ireland. But in Blackpool the Tories - except for Ted Heath - were celebrating. Late nights at the Imperial got me to meet more MPs and party workers and know others better. Having got up early with a hangover to see Peter Walker glad-handing on Fleetwood fish dock I found myself applauding, trance-like, as a minister finished his speech. Marcus Fox, a canny old Yorkshireman, caught my eye and said: "That's my job, not yours."

By 1980 Labour were close to breaking point. Conference decided that in future an electoral college, not the party's MPs, would elect the leader. But the decision was messily taken, with some union barons unconvincingly claiming their votes had been cast the wrong way and no agreement on the percentage split in the College between MPs, trade unions and constituency parties. I escaped for a drink in the Galleon Bar during the interval of the show next door, to find the Ulster comedian Frank Carson ("It's how you tell 'em") even funnier with us than he was on stage.

At Brighton, the Tories were edgy as the Heathites claimed the Thatcher revolution was failing. Mrs Thatcher scorned them, declaring: "U-turn if you want to. The lady's not for turning". I thought her over-shrill; I had yet to appreciate that a conference speech can be aimed at either the faithful in the hall or those watching at home, and this one was intended firmly for internal consumption. Only later did it come to be seen by a wider public as the kernel of her appeal.

Around this time the conferences acquired sign language interpreters. I didn't fancy their job: was there really a sign for "a new definition of Toryism"? But they were up to the challenge: one interpreter identified the Liberal gourmet-MP Clement Freud with frantic eating motions, and another, when Tony Benn was mentioned, simply tapped his forehead with his finger.

Early in 1981 I trooped out to Wembley for the special Labour conference that settled the makeup of the electoral college, triggering the foundation of the SDP. And when the next conference season came round, there was one extra to squeeze in. I had been due to go to the Liberals in Llandudno, where the alliance with the SDP was sealed with David Steel declaring: "Go back to your constituencies – and prepare for government." But our sketch writer Godfrey Barker was reckoned to be in control, so I headed for Bradford and the SDP. The new party held its "rolling conference" in three cities – Perth, Bradford and Norwich – with a "Train of Shame" ferrying MPs, hacks and party staff between them. The Bradford leg saw Shirley Williams throw her hat in the ring for the Crosby by-election – which she would sensationally win – committing herself to "climb every mountain". By contrast, David Owen's speech competed with a PA system blaring out *It's My Party and I'll Cry If I Want To*. In the evening, an excellent Bradford curry culminated in the *Mail*'s Tony Bevins emptying a glass of red wine over my head in protest at my loud nose blowing.

Labour's 1981 conference saw the culmination of its deputy leadership contest. Ever since Tony Benn's 3.15 am challenge to Denis Healey months before, the party had been riven by conflict between the Bennites, out to make Michael Foot's position as leader untenable, and the Right, outnumbered in the constituencies and desperately shoring up their trade union vote. My best MP friends were backing the moderate Left's John Silkin. The atmosphere at Brighton was tense and the outcome dramatic: with Silkin eliminated, Healey held off Benn by just 0.4 per cent, carried over the line by MPs who later defected to the SDP. The next day's papers carried an advertisement, placed before the vote, reading: "*Now* will you join the Social Democrats?", but this would - messily - prove the turning point for Labour.

Despite the Tory euphoria over recapturing the Falklands, 1982's conferences were forgettable. The next year's opened with the re-elected Conservatives apparently unassailable. Then, halfway through Labour's Brighton conference, the *Times* broke the story that Sara Keays, Cecil Parkinson's former Commons secretary, was expecting his child. Labour chiefs' private glee that the Tories were in trouble was overshadowed by fear that someone might land the party in it on live television. They need not have worried. A boiler-suited delegate strode to the rostrum, pulled a copy of the *Sun* from his pocket and said: "Comrades, is there nothing the Tories won't do to keep us out of the papers?"

It looked as though Parkinson would survive. The faithful at Blackpool celebrated electoral victory one last time with a turn from Ken Dodd, himself a Tory and as funny in the flesh as on the air. Parkinson delivered his speech to a more or less forgiving audience; the blue-rinse brigade had always loved him. Then Sara Keays' father fed further damaging information to the *Times*, splashed on the final morning as Mrs Thatcher prepared to speak. It was now clear Parkinson had to go, as Colonel Keays was not going to let him off the hook. Mrs Thatcher reworked her speech, and Denis Thatcher went down to Blackpool Airport to open its new terminal in place of Parkinson, the plaque being hurriedly changed. Abuzz with the drama of the day, we spent the journey back to Euston devising anagrams from Parkinson's name. My best effort, "Acorns in pickle", was trumped by the *Glasgow Herald's* Bill Russell with "Con in slick rape."

By the 1984 conferences, the miners were on strike – at least those who answered Arthur Scargill's call to come out without a ballot. One who didn't was Patrick McLoughlin, an agreeable Staffordshire NUM official who was vice-chairman of the Young Conservatives. Patrick – much later an excellent Transport Secretary - told me how he took a group of workmates to hear Scargill speak; though not agreeing with a word he said, they were mesmerised.

The strike dominated all but the final day of the conferences. The TUC, in Brighton, declared solidarity with the NUM short of actually doing anything. At night, we kept our doors bolted as coalfield women who had hit the bar roamed the hotel. Labour's Blackpool conference went through agonies; Neil Kinnock was not alone in having a heart attuned to the strikers, and a head telling him it would end in tears. And back in Brighton for the Conservatives, we found a massive security operation to make sure no pro-Scargill demonstrator got near Mrs Thatcher.

The police got things disastrously wrong. There was hardly any trouble from the miners ... but all through the conference a bomb planted weeks before by the IRA was ticking in Room 629 of the Grand Hotel, just above the Prime Minister and her husband. By the ball on the last night, security was lax; I walked into the Grand with a bag containing two bottles of wine I'd won in a raffle, and wasn't searched. I had a drink with Hugh O'Brien, an agent friend, then at about 2.30 am headed for the Curzon, and bed.

The bomb went off at 2.54. I slept through it despite being only 300 yards away, my hotel up a cul-de-sac being shielded from the noise. The night porter called to tell me the Grand had been bombed; I said: "Pull the other one" and turned over. To his credit he rang again, and I was downstairs in moments.

The front of the Grand had gone, and the emergency services were digging frantically in the rubble for survivors. The hotel guests had been moved to the opposite pavement, by the sea. Among them was Hugh, wrapped in a towel and in shock; he had stayed in the bar and told me later that after the explosion one shaken and bloodied drinker told the barman: "Christ, that was a strong one. Give me another."

I could just about have filed copy – our absolute latest deadline was 4 am – but only colleagues from the *Sun* and the *Mail* got anything in. I confess it didn't occur to me; I was struggling to take in what I saw, and my immediate thought was: "This is terrible. I've covered so many bombings that I know what to do, and I shouldn't." I returned to my room with Jim Wightman, who had been bombed out of the Grand, and we sat watching the television as rescuers tried to extricate Norman Tebbit, whose wife had been paralysed and who himself received serious injuries. Tebbit's courage that grim October morning was astonishing.

Five people were killed and 34 seriously injured ... though not Mrs Thatcher, who would cast the morning as "a day I was meant not to see." I walked to the hall with Jim Naughtie and John Biffen, Leader of the Commons; it would be the last time we could mingle en route, and Biffen put the night into context, saying: "I suppose this has been the greatest threat to our constitution since the Cato Street Conspiracy." [A plot to murder Lord Liverpool's entire Cabinet in 1820, in which one of my mother's ancestors was supposedly involved.]

The police – who would identify the bomber as Patrick Magee – interviewed everyone who had stayed in Room 629 beforehand, including several couples who preferred to stay anonymous, to ascertain when the bomb had been planted. The *Daily Mail's* John Edwards, there during the TUC, was asked to name all his visitors. One was his colleague Bob Porter. When they asked Bob, a hulking West Midlander, where he'd left his fingerprints so they could be eliminated, he replied: "On the bathroom floor, either side of the loo."

With hindsight, I'm astonished I didn't write a first-person piece next day for the *Telegraph* – indeed I only realised on the Saturday that none of our people in Brighton had been asked for one. All I produced was a straightforward account of what Douglas Hurd, the Home Secretary, said about the bombing and anti-terrorist policy when the conference reopened; as it didn't carry my by-line, there is nothing in the *Telegraph* archive to prove I was there. On any other paper there would have been a discussion at the morning conference about what was needed and who would write it. As it was, Jim (who was as shell-shocked as myself) and I went through the day on autopilot without any discussion between ourselves, yet alone with Fleet Street, about an atmospheric piece. We both assumed our sketch writer would do it.

With the Grand being rebuilt, Labour's 1985 conference relocated to Bournemouth, with a smaller hall but better hotels. The *Telegraph* team booked into a clifftop hotel with a view of the Needles, with the best suite taken by Alfred Sherman, an easy-to-dislike Thatcherite ideologue who tried to reclaim his sizeable bill from both the *Telegraph* and the National Bus Company, for whom he was lobbying. Outside the hall Frank Dobson, then Shadow Health Secretary, delivered a string of Rock Hudson jokes in the hearing of severe-looking female delegates in dungarees. And inside, Neil Kinnock put Militant to the sword.

Neil had been the star of my first Labour conference, with a hilarious speech telling how a Roy Jenkins supporter during a party election had been greeted by one trade unionist with: "Nay, lad, we're all Labour here". Then Neil was the darling of the Left, but by 1985 he was shifting his ground. Liverpool was in chaos as its Militant-controlled council resisted government spending curbs, and the party was suffering. Jim was covering Neil's speech and I had run out of shaving cream, so I went into town as Neil stood up, came back 25 minutes later and found him still in mid-speech. "He's going on too long again", I thought.

Then it happened. Neil suddenly let Militant have it with both barrels, and I realised I was listening to one of the great speeches. "I'll tell you what happens with impossible promises," Neil said. "You start with far-fetched resolutions. They are then pickled into a rigid dogma, a code, and you go through the years sticking to that, outdated, misplaced, irrelevant to the real needs. And you end with the grotesque chaos of a Labour council - a *Labour* council – hiring taxis to scuttle round a city handing out redundancy notices to its own workers. And then ... they talk of victory." Eric Heffer stormed out, and Derek Hatton shouted: "Lies!" But the reaction from the floor was ecstatic: Labour was back.

Security for the Tories at Blackpool was stifling after the previous year's foul-up. Manhole covers were sealed, the platform party commuted from the Imperial in an armoured bus, and every chicken for the hotel's kitchens underwent an internal search.

Entering the hall, everyone had a detector for explosives run over their hands - yet one Tory told me: "I work at ICI's high explosives division at Runcorn handling gelignite every day, and that machine gave me the all-clear."

By the next year, Peter Mandelson had started Labour's makeover. Traditionally the platform had been dominated by the National Executive, frowning in serried ranks behind the speaker. Coming from television, Peter made a highly symbolic change: shunting the NEC to the side so whoever was speaking had only the party's slogan and symbol behind them.

Early spring of 1987, with an election imminent, brought my first Scottish conference: Labour's in Perth. Caterpillar had just announced the closure of its plant in West Lothian, and a furious Tam Dalyell was orchestrating protests. Near the hall, I was amused to see a bar named "The Twa Tams". Looking for a meal, I chanced upon Helen Liddell and George Robertson at a table with a spare place. Though they were big Kinnock supporters, I couldn't resist telling them a story going round the Lobby, which thankfully they took the right way:

Neil comes home to find Glenys, widely reckoned the brains of the partnership, with a goldfish she has won at a CND bazaar. She has her fingers in the bowl, and is giving the fish instructions ("Swim round", "Back", "Through" and so forth) which it obeys. Neil asks if he can have a go. When she comes back, there is Neil, opening and shutting his mouth in time with the goldfish.

That autumn, after eight conference seasons with deadlines to meet and a column to fill, I was there less frantically as a leader writer. At the Conservatives' victory conference, Willie Whitelaw bent my ear to talk down the claims of Lord Young to be party chairman. Young - "other people bring me problems, David brings me solutions" - was Mrs Thatcher's new favourite; she credited him rather than the outgoing chairman Norman Tebbit with her re-election after mid-campaign jitters. Others - including Willie, who was still her deputy - were less impressed; Young's main achievement at the DTI had been to divert the cash previously needed to bail out nationalised industries to advertising agencies singing the department's praises.

1988 brought me my first Liberal conference. The smallest of the big three, it was traditionally a perk for the No. 3 in the *Telegraph's* Lobby team, who stayed at Westminster during the main conferences to cover the rest of the political news. Having a clear weekend between the Liberals and Labour – both in Blackpool - I arranged 48 hours at the Sellafield nuclear plant to get behind the official line that after earlier mishaps it was now entirely safe. The focus of my visit was the pending decision on whether to activate THORP, the £1.8 billion enrichment plant which it was claimed would deliver unlimited cheap electricity. (It never operated to capacity and closed in 2010, the last vestige of Britain's post-war dream of leading the world in nuclear power).

I stayed in British Nuclear Fuels' guesthouse, watching the Seoul Olympics in the Chairman's Suite. Over dinner a group of executives discussed issues facing the plant with me ... dipping nonchalantly beforehand into a bowl of shellfish caught close to the outfall pipe, to counter the belief – held strongly across the water – that Sellafield was contaminating the Irish Sea. When I chose porridge for breakfast, the waiter told me: "The tiles in the kitchen started coming off. We hadn't any glue, so we used Jack's porridge and it's stayed solid as a rock." I left Sellafield more worried about my inside than any threat from nuclear leakages. Later I was sounded out as a possible director of communications for BNFL ... the only time a headhunter approached me for a job I might have been interested in.

At that year's Conservative conference in Brighton, I landed Carol Thatcher in trouble. Carol, a *Telegraph* writer until Max Hastings risked damnation by sacking her, was looking for material. The anti-filth campaigner Mary Whitehouse had invited the press to a screening of pornographic films, and Carol jumped at my suggestion that she go. No sooner was the show under way than the police put a stop to it.

I only covered one conference while at the *Independent on Sunday*: Conservative Central Council in March 1990, held in Cheltenham as poll tax rioters rampaged through Trafalgar Square.

Joining the *European* that summer, I had to be on parade at the Mirror Group's big party at the Labour conference. Under Robert Maxwell this was a strange affair. Senior party figures put in a dutiful appearance - I remember congratulating Tony Blair on one of the most effective conference speeches I'd heard - but other guests came from Maxwell's personal diaspora. One elderly print trade unionist I met had apparently negotiated a deal with him that sold out his members. I also got talking with the glamorous ex-wife of Charlton Athletic's former chairman Michael Gliksten, blamed by the fans for their exile from The Valley. She lamented: "I have never understood why they hated Michael." So I told her.

As political editor of the *Daily Record* I covered all the 1992 Scottish party conferences – the Conservatives and Lib Dems for the first time. The most interesting was the Tories', with the Right, centred on Michael Forsyth, working to undermine Ian Lang, John Major's able and genial Scottish Secretary. It was held in Aberdeen's modernistic exhibition centre, the bleakest of venues. The demands of security and the need for commercial space have made it difficult to keep the Scottish conferences in cosy city centre locations: in Aberdeen they were banished from the stately Music Hall to Bridge of Don, in Perth from a charming little venue to a soulless sports centre before mercifully returning to a spanking new Concert Hall. In Dundee they still use the majestic Caird Hall, and in Inverness the Eden Court, an arts centre grafted onto a house of character; by night the east London Labour MP Jon Cruddas compared the city centre across the river to a "f***ing war zone." Edinburgh's new conference centre is a great improvement on the underwhelming Meadowbank, while Glasgow's SECC has space but no soul. And few of these new locations lend themselves to political drama.

In 1992 the Lib Dems were at Harrogate, and I hoped for strong national copy with plenty of input from Scots in the party. A Scot did provide me (and the world) with the story of the week, but he was 180 miles away, at the Treasury. On the Tuesday Britain's place in Europe's Exchange Rate Mechanism came under severe strain, presenting Major and his Shetland-born Chancellor Norman Lamont with a full-blown crisis. I did my best to cover both bases, but first thing on Wednesday went back to London. Lamont raised interest rates from 10% to 12%, then 15%, trying desperately to keep the pound within the range Major as Chancellor had signed up to. That evening he ran up the white flag and Britain quit the ERM. Interest rates fell back, but Black Wednesday would destroy the relationship between Lamont and Major, embolden the Eurosceptic Right, and prove a humiliation from which that government would never recover.

Despite yet another election defeat, Labour were thus in high spirits in Brighton for their first conference under John Smith, and I was now part of the team. I attended the *Mirror* lunch for John, hosted in the wake of Maxwell's death by the company's chairman, Sir Robert Clark. I also, for this and the next two Labour conferences, had to organise a dinner for my editor with senior party figures. There was usually only one evening *Record* executives could manage, it was hard to find front-benchers without commitments (though Gordon Brown would always do his best to be there) and finding a restaurant that could take us was a problem. In Bournemouth in 1994, we were reduced to taking a table in the hotel dining room, which did not impress my new editor, Terry Quinn.

My most memorable SNP conference was their 1993 gathering at Dunoon. At the opening briefing, colleagues passed round a *Private Eye* "True Story" about two gays in Colorado, a gerbil, a cardboard tube and a lighted match. Helpless laughter engulfed the room, and the SNP's agenda received less attention than it deserved. Outside on the pier, match-bound Celtic supporters were queueing for the ferry; I watched appalled as the IRA's paper *An Poblacht* did a brisk trade.

My own departure was hurried as I had a ticket for the Ryder Cup. (I stood within yards of Seve Ballesteros as he teed off, not that my swing improved). Just before, the receptionist in my small hotel handed me a letter with a Post-It note reading: "Give this to the ugly, bearded man in Room 3." (I then had a beard). I pointed out that I was in Room 4, and she offered it in turn to Andy Collier of the *Scottish Sun* and Andy Nicoll of the *Dundee Courier,* both of them bearded and hulking. It was duly claimed. The Post-it had been written by the other receptionist, and her replacement had not thought to detach it.

Labour's Brighton conference was dominated by the debate over John Smith's proposal for OMOV ("One Member, One Vote") for party decision-making. The outcome was touch and go, with several big unions – notably the T&G – determined to keep their block votes, and arms were twisted amid hints that Smith might quit. By the Mirror Group lunch I had the feeling the votes were in the bag, and congratulated John. His expression told me my confidence was premature, the crucial backroom deal being struck as we spoke. The hall crackled with tension as the OMOV debate swung to and fro. Margaret Beckett, Smith's deputy, fell short of backing him outright for fear of alienating the T&G, then John Prescott settled matters with a barnstorming if totally incoherent speech. Prescott, regarded till then as a loose cannon despite years on the front bench, tugged every possible heartstring with an appeal to "give him some trust", and sat down to a storming ovation. Reading back my shorthand, I could hardly find a single complete sentence; next day Matthew Parris wrote that Prescott had "gone fifteen rounds with the English language and left it slumped, bleeding, over the ropes". But what a speech!

For the *Record,* the keynote speech from the Labour leader – and a Scot, to boot – was an event for which all the stops were pulled out. I reported John's at length, stressing the point that here was a Prime Minister in waiting, made in an enthusiastic leader from Tom Brown at the terminal next to me. I was particularly pleased with my description of John's delivery as "like John Knox, with jokes." But I opened the paper next morning to see my piece rewritten out of all recognition, and my choice phrase replaced with "like a slick vicar". Sub-editors have saved me from myself often enough for me to forgive the occasional lapse, but this left me livid. I rang John McGurk, the deputy editor, and he told the sub in question that if he wanted my job he should apply for it, not sabotage my copy.

Nobody who was at the Scottish Conservatives' 1994 conference in Inverness will ever forget it. The session on 12 May had just begun when word shot round the press room that John Smith had suffered a second heart attack and, within minutes, that he was dead.

I was stunned. Weeks before, I had interviewed a vibrant and passionate Smith before Labour's Scottish conference, and I felt a personal loss. Most of the Tories felt it, too: they respected him in a way that applied to few other Labour figures. The conference broke up, and I flew back to Glasgow via Aberdeen in no less time than it took Tom Brown to tear down the A9. I left Ken Clarke – who had just flown in to speak – beached in the Inverness airport lounge.

The myth would be propagated that Tony Blair became leader because Peter Mandelson treacherously ditched Gordon Brown. But the die was already cast. Within minutes of John's death, the dozen or so hacks in the Eden Court press room agreed that the job was Tony's for the taking. Gordon had been the undisputed senior partner, and the previous autumn had urged me to help Tony raise his profile in Scotland. But we had all picked up signs in the party that Blair's popularity was surging; Smith, we later heard, had just three days before told his staff: "It's got to be Tony." This collective view we fed back to our offices, where tributes to Smith and pieces speculating about the succession were being put together.

By Labour's Blackpool conference that September, Blair was leader, and setting a cracking pace. His speech, near the end instead of halfway through as was customary, was upbeat and challenging, a pitch to Middle England that took with him most of a party desperate for power. But as he ended his prepared text, Labour's communications director David Hill appeared with extra sheets.

We could hardly believe our eyes. Blair was moving to kill off Clause IV, the commitment to common ownership that had been on Labour's membership card since the 1950s and was an article of faith, even for members who didn't believe in it. Elements in the unions and the constituencies were livid and a handful left the party, but John Prescott - despite doubts of his own - pulled out all the stops to get the change approved, at a special conference that replaced Clause IV with a less socialist "statement of aims and objectives."

At Bournemouth, the Conservatives were – as ever - split over Europe, with John Redwood's challenge to John Major only months ahead. They could see Labour moving into the centre, and were struggling to respond. For me the conference was made by Ian Lang's unguarded disclosure over dinner that Cabinet colleagues had nicknamed the prime minister Forrest Gump. I rang Terry Quinn, who recognised a really good tabloid story. I filed my copy, the art room at Anderston Quay got to work ... and next morning's front page bore the headline "Major Gump" and a picture of John sitting outside the White House with that famous box of chocolates. Luckily, I don't think he identified my source as one of his closest allies.

I had to pull out of the 1995 conferences, having just resigned from the *Record*, and when I went the next year, it was as a lobbyist with Politics International. I got round as many of my contacts as I could, bending their ears about London & Continental's plans for the Channel Tunnel Rail Link and Lockheed Martin's interest in the new air traffic control centre planned for Prestwick, and at receptions for other clients I welcomed guests and fielded questions. I was further from the political heart of the conferences than I had been as a newspaperman, but that was as it should be.

On the margin of Labour's conference, I happened upon the ultimate sensitive story, in terms of taste. A former Conservative MP told me over dinner how a doctor who had examined Tony Blair had mentioned that he was spectacularly well-endowed, and was known to his Oxford friends as "Dobbin". Tory circles feared that if the story emerged they could kiss the housewives' vote goodbye.

I was relieved to be officially out of journalism, as few papers would have touched such a story. I pondered, and eventually ran it past

Nigel Nelson, political editor of the *Sunday People*. Nigel counted ten, then put in a call to Alastair Campbell. Alastair, to Nigel's surprise, didn't explode and a few hours later the word came back: "Dobbin has no comment to make" ... which sounded like confirmation. Nigel led his column with the story, headlined "His Right Honourable Member." The *British Journalism Review* suggested Alastair had demeaned the future premier by not dismissing the story as "improper, trivial or facetious"; certainly I can think of no other leader whose staff would have colluded in a story so near the knuckle.

I had returned to the Lobby, as a freelance, by the time the parties met in the wake of Labour's 1997 landslide. The *Scottish Sun* asked me to cover Labour in Brighton, and a memorable week it turned out to be. It wasn't just the euphoria after 18 years in the wilderness; only a month had passed since Tony Blair's response to the death of Princess Diana had struck a chord with the nation. The public broke into applause as he walked through the streets; I am sure I shall never see that again. I was dining with the *Sun* team when Robin Cook came into the restaurant with Gaynor Regan, his secretary for whom he had just left his wife and who was understandably shy of a phalanx of hacks she didn't know. But I had got to know Gaynor, who was highly efficient and quietly charming, slightly through my dealings with Robin, and broke the ice.

Back at the conference hotel, one of my railway contacts came up in a state of excitement. Lord Stevens of Ludgate, chairman of Express Newspapers, had tried to board a Eurostar at Waterloo with a shotgun, and briefly been taken into custody. Knowing Stevens' reputation for short-temperedness, I admired the nerve of the security man who detained him. I contacted the *Sun*, found them strangely hesitant and received the same reaction from the *Mail*. For obvious reasons, I didn't try the *Express*. When no story appeared next morning, I went to the *Telegraph* diary, who ran a tongue-in-cheek piece making the point about Stevens' short fuse; honourably, the *Mail* paid me even though they didn't carry the story. The reason the tabloids wouldn't touch it was simple: press barons generally make sure their papers do not probe each others' peccadillos. But I was disappointed that supposedly self-confident papers like the *Sun* and the *Mail* should have killed a story they would have used had it involved a member of the public. You wonder what else doesn't appear.

By my next Labour conferences, in 2001, I was a special adviser. My role now was to keep my eyes and ears open for my minister, help draft her speech (if she was to make one), line up appearances at fringe meetings, and accompany her on the gruelling round of exhibitions, meetings and functions. At Scottish Labour in Inverness, Helen made her debut as Secretary of State weeks after succeeding John Reid. She was there not just to tell the Scottish party what their team at Westminster was doing and stress its importance even now Scotland had a Parliament of its own, but to underline the message – after stormy turf wars in the early days of Holyrood – that she and Henry McLeish were working together. I may have been over-frank in telling Henry: "Part of our job is to make you look good", but a strong and on-message First Minister was essential to Labour with a general election in the offing.

That September, Tony Blair arrived at the TUC in Brighton just as the planes hijacked by Al Qaeda hit the World Trade Center and the Pentagon; he took the platform to explain that tragic and world-shaping events were under way, then returned to London. Three weeks later in the same hall, he gave Labour delegates his assessment of the forces in play, the challenges they posed to Britain and how their government would respond. This was Tony at his very best, and for me, listening in an unusually quiet and thoughtful hall, one passage took the speech out of the ordinary: "This is a moment to seize. The kaleidoscope has been shaken. The pieces are in flux. Before they do, let us re-order this world around us." That re-ordering would founder on George W Bush's determination to get even with Saddam Hussein, but at that moment Tony not only spoke for the country, but lifted it.

Every Cabinet minister did a spin round the exhibition hall, with Helen needing to visit the stands where her support would mean most; we also had to steer her away from those that might cause her trouble back home ... notably those advocating planned parenthood. George McGregor and I both attended one reception as "witnesses" because Helen suspected someone who had asked to meet her might later misrepresent the conversation. In the event, it was harmless.

Some matters needed settling before Parliament resumed. One meeting was with Gordon Brown, who was resisting a post-devolution cut in the number of Scottish MPs. Gordon and Helen handled that on their own. Helen also met David Blunkett, who told me: "You turn up all over the place." The issue bothering David most as Home Secretary was illegal immigration. The Tories and the press were vocal about the upsurge in numbers claiming political asylum, but David told Helen: "It isn't the asylum-seekers that bother me most – it's the number here illegally who don't even claim asylum." He reckoned there were at least 400,000 in the London area alone ... and this before the numbers from eastern Europe really took off.

Scottish Labour in Perth late the following winter was my final conference as an insider. Helen was making a speech in the same session as Tony Blair, so it had to be good though it wouldn't get much press. George and I sat up late fine-tuning it, but the best line came from Helen herself. There was Tory criticism that Tony

was travelling too much, and Helen asked if they wanted him "kept under house arrest". Alastair Campbell turned round with a smile and said: "Well done!" I made sure he knew the line was Helen's.

This conference was dominated by Britain's curling team, all Scots, winning Olympic gold. The SPADs from Number 10, the Scotland Office and the Executive sat up late to watch the nail-biting final, as a sport few of us understood became riveting. In the morning, messages of congratulation winged their way from Perth. As the big names left, I went to see the police sniffer dogs unwind, chasing footballs in the old fire station they were using as a base.

Once I joined QinetiQ, the conferences took a back seat. Emerging from the MoD, the company was not ready to hold receptions and dinners and sponsor fringe meetings like an established business. But by 2005 it was felt worth my going to Labour in Brighton to mingle with delegates, report back on relevant debates and see what our competitors were doing. I heard a useful review of the challenges facing the government on science from Lord Sainsbury, and returned with a CND briefing paper on how to campaign against a successor to Trident (a project we were involved in), which had been thrust into my hand.

At that conference, party stewards ejected the octogenarian peace campaigner Walter Wolfgang for having the temerity to heckle Jack Straw. Jack thrives on heckling – he held street-corner meetings in Blackburn every weekend – and the stewards' clumsy attempt to stifle dissent did New Labour incalculable harm. It was all the more stupid as Wolfgang had been trying to get thrown out for years; I could also remember a time when removing hecklers would have almost emptied the hall.

The 2006 season was memorable for the over-complex accreditation procedure demanded by the security authorities. It was worst for Labour as the party of government, but the interminable queueing for passes by hundreds of visitors and exhibitors who had expected to receive them by post caused fury at each conference. Labour was staging its first Manchester conference for decades at the G-Mex, and arriving on the second morning, when the backlog should have been cleared, it took me an hour to reach the accreditation desk. Many people found no record of their applications, and some senior business figures due to speak on the Fringe turned round and went home. I was lucky: after 40 minutes more my pass was found.

It was a far cry from my first conferences 28 years before, which were free to attend, with no security beyond a perfunctory bag search. Moreover, you now have little chance of bumping into the party's heavy hitters. Security has given those reluctant to mingle the pretext to seal themselves off, and democracy is the loser. Furthermore the Labour conference - to the astonishment of just about everyone – turned for a time into a fan-fest for Jeremy Corbyn.

16: Out to Lunch

Lunching politicians has been an essential – and usually enjoyable - part of my work. The important thing is the conversation; good food and wine help to build confidence, but you mustn't drink too much or you won't remember what your guest has told you or – even worse – you'll get it wrong.

The conversation differs with how well you know your guest, but the essentials are much the same. You begin with how they are, how your proprietor is doing, how the government or their party is doing. There are pitfalls even here: I asked one Cabinet minister how his summer had gone, and he replied: "My father died." Not a good start; I should have known.

Then you move onto the substance. Your guest understands the unspoken ground rules and they may have a nugget of news ready. More often the discussion will flush out something they hadn't specifically come to tell you - and occasionally something they shouldn't. Yet there are rare occasions when you – and maybe they – leave the restaurant wondering why you bothered.

Pulling all the levers that might produce a story is a skill in itself, and sometimes you border on the black arts. Phil Webster of the *Times* and I lunched Kenneth Baker when he was Environment Secretary, when ministers were searching for anything they might be able to privatise. Off the cuff, we asked Ken if anyone had suggested selling shares in London Underground. When he hesitated, we told him: "If we run the story, everyone will think the idea comes from John Moore" [Mrs Thatcher's favourite of the moment, then Transport Minister and not overly popular with colleagues]. His eyes lighting up, Ken said: "Yes, I think this is an idea we might well give consideration to." Our stories appeared, unsourced as is the convention, and Moore indeed got the blame.

When a story generated shock-waves, Mrs Thatcher's press secretary Bernard Ingham (and later Alastair Campbell for Tony Blair) would go through ministers' diaries trying to identify its source. But not all stories originate over lunch, and sometimes we would hold one over to protect our source, or while we ferreted out supporting facts.

Lunches also help politicians find out what is going on, for while not as accurate a source as ministerial chauffeurs or Commons secretaries, we had our moments. Sometimes their questions spoke volumes; Peter Rees, under pressure as Chief Secretary of the Treasury, suddenly asked Elinor Goodman and myself: "What are they saying about me? - thinly-veiled code for "Am I about to be sacked?" We offered what solace we could, but Mrs Thatcher dumped him soon after.

Some guests are very hard work: one such was Peter Cropper, architect of the Conservatives' 1979 manifesto, yet four decades on

I can remember almost everything he told me. For me only one was an outright disaster ... and that was in Washington. London suggested the Swedish press attaché as a useful contact, so I took him to the Cantina D'Italia, which had become my haunt. He turned out to be as stiff as a Prussian and totally uninformative, but I think we both enjoyed the meal. Until, that is, the proprietor's bubbly 50-ish wife offered us a grappa and sat down to chat. Before marrying, she told us, she had sculpted on Ibiza, and had come to recognise the nationality of drunken revellers in the street outside. The Brits were noisy, the Italians thought they could sing, the Germans could be rude ... but the Swedes! "They were like pigs," she said as I tried to nudge her under the table. "I couldn't get out of my door without tripping over drunken Swedes lying on the sidewalk." My guest thanked me politely and left; I never saw him again.

I have lunched many politicians on my own. But the more senior they are, the fuller their diaries and unless you are especially favoured you stand a better chance in a small group. The disadvantage of the group approach is that if a story emerges you won't have it to yourself; the plus is that several heads are better than one when asking questions, and after your guest has gone you can work out between you what the best lines are.

Over my time at Westminster, I was in three lunch groups. On the first, I replaced my *Telegraph* predecessor Peter Gill. Its leader was John Harrison, a heavyweight with the *Express* and the *Mail* before joining the BBC; he became their South Africa correspondent and was sadly killed in a car crash just as apartheid was ending. Chris Hampson of ITN was the third member, and the fourth the *Sunday Express*'s (later *Sunday Telegraph's)* Alan Cochrane. An intelligent, bearded Dundonian, Alan went on to edit the *Scottish Daily Express* and be the *Telegraph*'s Scottish editor.

The second group I started as a defensive ploy. I became fed up with midnight calls about exclusives in the *Times* from Phil Webster, so I suggested we join forces. We made the team one of the strongest by recruiting Elinor Goodman, who left the *FT* soon after to become political editor of Channel Four News; she should have had the top job at the BBC, but they didn't persevere when she told them she needed time for her horse. Once the group was up and running, those late-night calls dried up.

I faded out of these groups after moving on to write leaders, but when I joined the *Daily Record* I needed to be in one again. This time my partners were Catherine Macleod, later political editor of the Glasgow *Herald* and Alistair Darling's special adviser at the Treasury, and the *Scotsman's* Ewen McAskill, subsequently diplomatic editor of the *Guardian*. While colleagues on London-based papers reckoned us in the second tier, the likes of Ken Clarke and Paddy Ashdown were just as happy to meet us.

Of all the politicians I have met, Clarke is the one who least liked talking about politics; when we lunched him as Chancellor he expatiated lovingly on the new bird table in the garden of Number 11. He also gave a marvellous insight into John Major's mind-set as the allegations of sleaze mounted against Tory ministers. Every so often Clarke and the PM would be talking in Number 10 – probably about cricket – when an official would tiptoe in and say: "Prime Minister, there's something you ought to know." Major and Clarke would catch each other's eye ... then burst into helpless laughter.

Westminster in the late 1970s was a gastronomic desert. It improved slightly with the arrival of the Atrium and the Curry Club, but even now you really need to go further afield, not least because you don't want other journalists at the next table. My favourite restaurant anywhere is Fouquet's on the Champs Elysées, gastronomic home of the French film industry and an unforgettable place to dine. But with politicians my favourite, and the staple of John Harrison's group, was Rules, close to Covent Garden: the ultimate "roast beef of Old England" restaurant. The helpings of steak and kidney pud were massive and the surroundings, panelled and adorned by stuffed game birds, traditional yet intimate. Tony Benn and Keith Joseph preferred a plate of raw vegetables, but Labour and Tory ministers alike tucked into two and often three courses of unashamed nursery food, washed down with a couple of bottles of red wine between the five of us. How we (and they) managed it every few days without getting coronaries is beyond me;

on the rare occasions I eat at Rules now, I skip the fine herbs omelette I always started with and often can't manage a pudding. Some guests had special requirements: Northern Ireland and defence ministers sat with their back to the wall, offering less of a target. We got to recognise their bodyguards and made sure they were offered a drink, even if they usually felt bound to refuse.

Rules revamped its menu in the late '80s, adding sauces to most dishes and downsizing portions to the merely large, and crammed in more tables, removing the spacious curved recesses where one could talk discreetly. When we took Jim Callaghan there just before he left the Commons, he told us we were sitting exactly where he had dined with his wife the evening they got engaged half a century before.

The guests who fitted most naturally into Rules were Christopher Soames, Denis Healey, Roy Jenkins and Roy Hattersley. Soames – truly larger than life - and Healey were not only great trenchermen and drinkers but relished waiting for a lull in the hubbub, then dropping a four-letter word. Healey was one of the best conversationalists in politics, mixing the serious with the ribald in just the right measure to prevent you grasping how exceptionally intelligent he was. Jenkins was the ultimate *bon vivant*, precise in his tastes: for him, the post-prandial cigar had to be Jamaican. We entertained Jenkins and Healey a couple of weeks apart, and when the bill arrived at the close of our lunch with Healey, I couldn't resist telling him: "Do you know, you're more expensive to entertain than Roy Jenkins!" The others told me off, but Healey went down the Shadow Cabinet corridor trumpeting: "I'm even more expensive than Jenkins!" Roy Hattersley built almost as great a reputation as a gastronome, but was pretty straightforward as a guest, requesting merely an outsize pepper mill. At one lunch Roy confided that "the Labour Party is going through a period of orgasmic change"; I think he meant "organic".

Healey, then Chancellor, was my first guest with John Harrison's group, but there was a last-minute wobble. Derek Scott, Healey's special adviser, told John that unless he sat in the lunch wouldn't happen, but John called his bluff. I got to know, and like, Derek as he joined then left the SDP, was married for a time to Elinor and advised Tony Blair on economics, but no other SPAD tried to make a lunch conditional on their presence. I would never have suggested I join one of Helen's lunches with a journalist: it would have been the ultimate vote of no confidence in my boss and their lunch partner. Had I mistrusted a reporter that much, I would have warned against accepting the invitation.

Some departmental press officers also tried to muscle in on lunches with a minister they feared might go off-message. The one time I readily agreed was when Robert Atkins, at the DTI, brought along Andrew Marre ... who had been at Highgate with us.

The joy of lunching ministers is that they may tell you things their officials don't want to come out, or don't even realise are afoot. Sometimes you come away with a dictum: Norman Tebbit told us ruefully: "As a minister you know 50% of the decisions you take are wrong. The trouble is, you don't know which 50% they are." And there's no better feeling than heading back to the office knowing you've been told something that will make your readers (and rivals) sit up. But there may be problems when your story appears. Sir Michael Havers, when Attorney-General, confided how the morning after a lunch with us that produced a highly topical story, Mrs Thatcher asked him how we had found out (we had offered no clue as to the source, beyond stressing it was authoritative).

Willie Whitelaw spent one lunch at Rules fuming at the West Yorkshire police's failure to catch the Yorkshire Ripper; if they didn't soon, he said, he would go up there and sort them out. We wrote the story pretty hard, with plenty of "understoods" to obscure the fact that our source was Willie himself. Next day I had an irate call from Donald Grant, head of news at the Home Office, accusing me of printing lies; I could not tell him I had been personally briefed by the Home Secretary.

As time went on, we cast our net wider. The launch of Channel Four in 1982 produced an avalanche of Tory criticism for promoting lesbianism and so forth. We invited Jeremy Isaacs, its chief executive, to Rules to hear his side of the story, and came away with a fascinating insight into how you launch a television channel. He agreed C4's early schedules had been skewed toward radical programmes, but said the reason was simple; the people making them were the only ones to deliver on time.

We also had a fascinating lunch with Bob Reid I, the first of two synonymous chairmen of British Rail, who was pushing through a reorganisation that became an immense commercial success. Rangy and impressive, he gave us a clear idea of where he was trying to take the railways. He listened to our own experiences; when I mentioned that track into the goods yard at Beckenham Junction had been relaid weeks before it closed he lamented: "I had hoped we weren't still doing that sort of thing". He also took away a few of our ideas; one was for a direct service between Dartford and Victoria ... which began a couple of years later. We didn't write much afterward, but the industrial correspondents felt their turf had been violated and fed into Reid's office the message that we couldn't be trusted. The door slammed shut.

Our most memorable lunch – and one I organised – was in November 1985, with the Prince of Wales. I contacted the Queen's press secretary, stressing the benefits the Prince might draw from an off-the-record chat with political journalists. I didn't mention that I'd been a contemporary of his at Trinity, as we had barely spoken. I was staggered when word came back that Prince Charles was up for it and had dates available. I expanded our group to make us more representative and booked a private room ... upstairs at Rules where his great-great-grandfather Edward VII had reputedly dallied with Lily Langtry.

It couldn't have gone better. The Prince was eager to know what we thought, and went out of his way to get a debate going. For our part we probed, but gently. He voiced reservations over the desirability of a Channel Tunnel, and I put the pluses to him. We all came away feeling the Prince was a good deal more serious and less flaky than the public imagines. He is intelligent and keen to be better informed, but did seem to be hearing from us for the first time views he should already have been exposed to.

The one story that emerged concerned his regret that the Household Cavalry was still all-white. This, he revealed, had worried his great-uncle Earl Mountbatten, who had suggested forming a new regiment, the "Blackguards". We let a little time elapse, then Alan Cochrane crafted a story that caused no repercussions.

Elinor, Phil and I initially entertained at the Boulestin, a discreet basement restaurant in Covent Garden which has long since relocated to St James's. The fare was *haute cuisine,* much lighter than at Rules. When we took Mrs Thatcher's Welsh Secretary Nick Edwards there, we tried a dish featuring young goat's meat. It tasted sharp, to put it mildly, and at the end our waiter told us: "The chef says he realises it wasn't such a good idea." When we lunched Michael Heseltine, the Boulestin's wine waiter confided: "It might help you to know that Mr Heseltine always has the Montrachet." We ordered it, and after two bottles at £38 each (1980s prices) Heseltine happened to mention that he was not fussy about wine. We made a mental note to change our venue. It was at that lunch that Heseltine, apropos the Toxteth riots, told us: "People say pimps and drug pushers are the problem, but when you get to a place like Toxteth the real leaders of the community are the pimps and drug pushers." Not a view he could have expressed in Liverpool.

We moved on to the less formal – and though I didn't realise it, trendier – Poule Au Pot, at the corner of Ebury Street and Pimlico Road. Its staple is excellent French country food; the cheese tart was a particular favourite of mine. Our choice caught on with the rest of the Lobby, and when last we lunched there, three or four other groups were entertaining politicians. Had I been a guest in that milieu, I would have clammed up. One lunch at the Poule au Pot ended with my almost colliding with Princess Diana on my way out without recognising her. As I sorted myself out, Elinor asked in disbelief: "Didn't you see who that was?"

Ted Heath, knowing total privacy gave him freedom to gossip, invited us to his London home, dominated by a magnificent model of his beloved *Morning Cloud;* John Harrison sought out a classical album the former premier would appreciate. Ted was in rollicking form – not always the case – and regaled us with tales of arriving in

Number 10 to find he couldn't get a cup of China tea, and discovering his first weekend in Chequers that the cellar was empty apart from "half a bottle of Wincarnis" left by Harold Wilson. Ted recruited a top mess steward from the RAF, and instructed him to raid the Government's hospitality cellars for the best wines he could find. When President Pompidou came to dine, he confided that they were a match for those served at the Elysée.

Elinor and I took Nick Ridley to L'Escargot in Greek Street, and the Red Fort and the Gay Hussar nearby were always popular with Michael Foot. Jeffrey Archer preferred the Caprice, which despite its location behind the Ritz was not an extravagance. Frank Dobson was at home in the curry houses of his St Pancras constituency, which I remembered from Dad's time at UCL. I was passing one when Frank, then running for Mayor of London, happened to emerge. I broke to him the news that Tony Blair's people were trying to stitch up Labour's selection for him by barring Ken Livingstone, and Frank retorted: "If they do that I'm pulling out." I rang the *Standard* and they splashed the story; Frank's New Labour minders were left trying to work out how someone had got to him.

My favourite Indian was the Jomuna in Victoria, known as the Standoori as Labour's Stan Orme was a regular. It served the hottest curries I'd encountered since my childhood stays at the Hotel Rhodesia in Folkestone, notably their phall, twice as hot as a Tandoori. Only one colleague could manage a whole one: the *FT*'s Margaret van Hattem, daughter of Dutch planters who relocated from Indonesia to Queensland; pint-size, stunning and charming, she became the soulmate of the writer Brian Inglis and died tragically young.

My haunt for lunching solo with politicians, until it made way for the St Martin's Hotel in the mid-1990s, was the Colosseo off St Martin's Lane. It faced the rehearsal rooms of the Coliseum, and in the summer you could hear the singers rehearsing. I first encountered it around 1980 when David Steel's birthday party moved on there from the National Liberal Club, and I fell for the menu, the ambiance and the staff, attentive but never intrusive.

The Liberal Party reckoned the Colosseo its own ... as did the South African Embassy, a bastion of *apartheid* loathed by Liberals even before South African intelligence framed Peter Hain for a bank robbery. Liberals and South Africans sat on opposite sides of the restaurant, with a demilitarised zone between which I and my guests occupied while the filthiest of looks passed overhead.

At the Colosseo one lunchtime I was deep in conversation when, suddenly, I heard my name spoken at another table. When I managed to sneak a glance at the diners, I did not recognise them. Nor would they have mentioned me so loudly had they known I was there. I wish I had caught the rest of what was said.

Another favourite was the Tent in Eccleston Street, since superseded by the successful Boisdale. Its walls were lined with canvas, but the name owed as much to the campness of its staff. I took Lynda Chalker there, and her eyes almost popped out of her head as the waiters fondled each other's buttocks. It was there that Lynda confided her wish to have a sign on her car reading "Don't do that. I'm the Minister of Transport." that lit up when she saw spectacularly bad driving. I ran the story, and Jonathan Dimbleby quoted it back at her on *Any Questions?*

Sometimes, when we were both tight for time, I lunched a politician on the premises. I've used the police canteen off Westminster Hall, known universally as "Plod's", more recently the foyer café of the new Portcullis House, and during recesses the Strangers' Cafeteria, MPs' own not-quite-greasy spoon. The Press Gallery then boasted its own restaurant, under-used but with good, cheap food and handy if you couldn't risk leaving the building. Early on I invited two MPs from different parties: Labour's Oonagh McDonald and the Tory Delwyn Williams. Though "paired" with each other, they were uneasy together and I never tried it again. Another memorable lunch in what our secretary Sally Hallam christened the Sanctum was with my bank manager. It was the final day of the 1981 Headingley Test, and we kept nipping out to the television as Bob Willis shot out the Australians to win a game we seemed so certain to have lost that Dennis Lillee and Rodney Marsh placed bets on England at 500-1. It was at the height of the controversy over Barclays' activities in South Africa; the bank maintained that its involvement benefited the Africans, but my manager had worked there and been shaken by the blatant racism he witnessed.

Occasionally you came out of a restaurant with a story even if you weren't lunching a politician. I was waiting in Simply Nico *circa* 2001 for the *Mail on* Sunday's Simon Walters when first Francis Maude and then Michael Portillo passed me en route to a table at the rear. It was at the height of intrigue over the Tory leadership, and the two were not thought to be close; I chatted with Michael – who would have been leader if the party had had any sense – and when Simon arrived I told him what was up. The episode made an intriguing piece for him.

Since joining the Athenaeum in 1988, I have lunched politicians there, among them Ken Baker, David Mellor and Norman Lamont. Just before devolution kicked in I invited Donald Dewar for a tour *d'horizon*. Though I had spent plenty of time with him one-on-one, it was only that day I grasped just what an erudite man he was. Sadly, he would not have long to live.

17: At the Beeb

I grew up with the radio on: my father listened to every talk programme, and my mother to piano music, plus *The Archers*. I did my homework listening to *Educating Archie* and the *Goon Show* on a crystal set with earphones. After Dad made our first TV set, I was glued to the hour-long morning trade sampler on how television was spreading north from London "over the cobbles of Macclesfield", including *London to Brighton in Four Minutes* and a French Scout parade transmitted via a "war-torn and disused casino". (You can tell there was only one channel then.)

When I was small, Dad often gave radio talks. One he particularly enjoyed was *Trains With Faces*, recalling the engines of his youth and their "personalities". Keen to capture a former Great Central locomotive whistle, he went to Neasden shed with his producer to record it, only to find the whistle had been changed. Once he stuck his neck out over Suez and the Bomb, radio used him less. But he did appear in the odd TV discussion, occasionally instigated a documentary and in 1966 devised a BBC "Play for Today", *The Devil's Eggshells,* starring Keith Barron and Leonard Rossiter.

I made my own television debut in 1963, in a barely visible role. The producer of a BBC charitable appeal for the Rainer Foundation - which helped young offenders – wanted a studio audience. A dozen Highgate boys, and girls from North London Collegiate, were bused to Lime Grove, and a few given questions to ask, the first (and most imaginative) being: "What is the Rainer Foundation?" It was all terribly wooden.

In my first year at Trinity the college competed in the second series of *University Challenge*, and I travelled to Manchester with the four-man team as reserve; we lost to Strathclyde. Three years later Granada approached Trinity again, and as the sole survivor I was made captain. We headed north with a coachload of supporters and our mascot, a cake bearing Trinity's motto *Semper Eadem* – "Always the same" – which Bamber Gascoigne took as a reference to the college food. Two episodes were recorded back-to-back. We sailed through the first, against Lancaster, then before the second, against Bedford College London, their captain hit the pub to stiffen his nerve. He returned in such a state that the producer, Douglas Terry, gave him half an hour to sober up or be replaced.

Maybe I should have had a drink as well. When we resumed, our opponents were a model of serenity and I was hyperactive. Several times I hit the buzzer before Bamber had finished the question, and while a couple of my answers were spot-on we went down to defeat despite tremendous efforts by my team-mates. I was downcast, knowing millions of people would be watching. The one consolation was that one of my answers ruled incorrect could have been right – about the location of the Iron Bridge in Shropshire – and Douglas Terry contemplated getting us back on a technicality. He told me I had been a star ... but I knew I had fouled up.

Terry's approach came after I had graduated. It was the more intriguing as 41 years later Corpus Christi, Cambridge would be stripped of the title because one of their team had started work with a firm of accountants. Feeling Corpus harshly treated, I wrote for the *Telegraph* about my own experience back in 1968 ... and received a charming, if incredulous, call from Bamber.

Not long after that call, in 2010, I plucked up the courage to enter Radio 4's *Brain of Britain*. I passed the telephone audition, and was invited to Broadcasting House for the heats. Again, two programmes were recorded back to back (during the interval, bizarrely, a drunken member of the audience was ejected). I didn't do well in the warm-up, but grew confident as the contestants in the first heat struggled, the victor emerging with 10 points which I was sure I could equal.

The presenter, Russell Davies, put us at ease and our heat began. The first question, like many others, was about atoms, and I hadn't the foggiest idea. The easy questions eluded me and after three rounds I was well behind. Then I began catching up, and by the end I had the 10 points that had won the first heat. Sadly, my fellow contestants had scored 16, 13 and 12. Nevertheless I enjoyed it, and it was intriguing to see how Broadcasting House had changed over the decades. And as I write this I've been accepted once again ...

Sheffield in my time was largely ignored by national broadcasters. The BBC in Manchester looked no further afield than Oldham, and Yorkshire Television was run from Leeds. Our sports editor David Jones, who doubled as one of YTV's football presenters, felt most at home at Don Revie's Leeds United.

We did have BBC Radio Sheffield, an infant but professional station with which we hacks had a friendly rivalry; one of its stars was Jeremy Thompson, later of Sky. I still have a pewter tankard from a broadcast quiz at Sheffield University between hacks and students; it was sponsored by Mars, so every answer had to contain some appalling pun about the company's products. Our star contestant was Paul Allen.

In Birmingham I saw little of the ATV crowd, but the BBC's Pebble Mill was both a source and a subject for stories. Allegations that the corporation was wasting money were rife in Parliament, and Phil Sidey, Pebble Mill's charismatic head, called me in for a briefing conducted across a mountain of chicken legs. "As you can see," Phil told me with a wink, "we have eliminated waste at the BBC." Duplication was also an issue long before director-general Mark Thompson, announcing budget cuts in 2007, received 56 interview bids from different programmes. At one Luxembourg EC summit we were having a late-night drink in Bernard Ingham's room when a call came in for the Beeb; each of its 12 staff present declined to take it.

Working with Pebble Mill taught me the art of puffing an upcoming documentary as an exclusive story, a practice today heavily overworked. My best concerned the explosion in 1944 at RAF Fauld, near Burton-on-Trent, where 3,670 tons of bombs had been stored in tunnels 90ft below ground. When some were moved with detonators in place, one went off; the blast – heard as far away as Weston-Super-Mare – killed 78 people, swallowed up an entire farm and left a crater three-quarters of a mile long and 400ft deep. Wartime censorship prevented much being reported, and many of the facts had only just been declassified. When the story appeared, a former officer at Fauld – whom I didn't even mention - complained that it impugned his conduct. He kept protesting until a BBC researcher handed over the report of the RAF Board of Inquiry ... which convicted him of incompetence.

American television when I was in Washington was dominated by the networks - CBS, NBC and ABC - based in New York and Los Angeles, with their programmes carried locally by "affiliates". The great television events for me were David Frost's interviews with Richard Nixon, and Alex Haley's *Roots*. The nation was still shell-shocked by Watergate, and when Frost got the previously reclusive Nixon in front of the cameras in 1977, the curiosity was immense. The interviews were broadcast not by one of the networks, but by independent stations – in Washington Metromedia's Channel 5, the forerunner of Fox. The ratings for the first, which Nixon ended with a tacit admission of guilt, were astronomical, then interest tailed off as Frost probed less controversial areas of his presidency. This pattern was reflected in our coverage: a strong scene-setter, a powerful story after the first programme then steadily shorter ones. Nixon emerged as an outstandingly gifted man brought down by his insecurity; as he plaintively put it, "I gave them the sword". Frost, through his restrained questioning, redefined the American public's view of Nixon, though there was still much to forgive. Twenty-five years later I met Frost when Helen Liddell appeared on his Sunday breakfast programme; when I mentioned I had covered those Nixon interviews, his eyes lit up and he started to reminisce.

Roots was even bigger. Haley's dramatised chronicle of his forebears' experiences in slavery, back to Kunta Kinte's abduction from the Gambia centuries before, changed many white Americans' perceptions, and gave black viewers a feeling first of pain and then of pride. Millions watched, riveted, each week as fresh indignities were heaped on each new generation. There was carping about some of Haley's facts, but the impact was explosive. Segregation may have ended in the early 1960s, but *Roots* won for black Americans dignity and respect.

In the late 1970s the *Telegraph* hardly existed where the BBC was concerned. Despite being by far the largest-selling broadsheet, it was rarely mentioned on *Today*'s review of the papers and our specialists were seldom interviewed. We would start getting noticed when Conrad Black took over - the *Telegraph* to my chagrin omitting me from a brochure promoting specialists available for interview, despite my broadcasting experience.

I acquired this mainly via the World Service. Its *People and Politics* programme had a three-minute mini-sketch in which a parliamentary journalist reviewed the week; around 1981 I was asked to do one, and became a fixture. The benign and chubby Norman Hunt (the Oxford don Lord Crowther-Hunt) put the programme together with the producer on Friday afternoons, my slot being recorded that morning. I wrote my script – reading it back to make sure there weren't any phrases to stumble over – at home, then recorded it at Bush House on my way to work. I would call at the programme's austere office to meet the producer – a BBC high-flyer on the way up – and make sure my script didn't clash with anything else in the programme (I had checked earlier, but things could change). Then we went down to record, with me at a table in the recording booth and the producer and studio manager on the other side of the glass. There might be a couple of "fluffs" requiring a retake, but generally I was out in twenty minutes.

My most memorable fluff came soon after the Falklands War. Referring to Tam Dalyell's campaign over its most controversial incident, I spoke of "the torpedoing of the Argentine crooner *General Belgrano.*" My producer Margaret Hill (future head of policy at the BBC and sister of Labour's press man David) got the giggles as inappropriate images forced their way into her mind. We broke up every time we looked at each other, and it was ten minutes before we managed a retake. My slip was in part Freudian; in *Evita* the future Eva Peron uses the crooner Magaldi as a stepping stone to fame. (By a remarkable coincidence Paul Keown, who stood in for Gary Bond the night Deborah and I saw the show around 1980, would as a priest marry me to Jeanette 34 years later).

When I couldn't do the programme, I found a substitute. One was the young Jim Naughtie, a Lobby colleague on first the *Scotsman* and then the *Guardian*; I had to be told by a *World At One* producer when we appeared together that it made bad radio for me to agree with him. Jim's easy broadcasting style made him a natural for *People and Politics* - and much more - and his wife Ellie produced the programme for a time.

People and Politics brought feedback. My childhood friend Giles Hollingworth heard me in Singapore. And from Pennsylvania Bob Gray, Professor of Government at Franklin and Marshall College and previously Under-Secretary for Defense in the Carter administration, called to ask if I would lecture to his students in London; we are still good friends.

A few times I was asked to do the World Service weekly talk, the mirror image of *Letter from America*. Holding your audience for 13 minutes took a lot of thought and skill, and you started with an empty canvas. One week I had a flying start as I had been to the RNLI's research base at Poole, but you needed three or four subjects to make the essay flow, plus a plausible way of linking them. Trying it made me realise just what a magician Alistair Cooke was, and I listened to his *Letters* with added reverence, right up to his death in harness in 2004, aged 95.

After a time I began to alternate with the *Guardian*'s Julia Langdon, and eventually I slipped out of *People and Politics*. Then Norman Hunt died; George Jones of LSE took over as presenter, and a couple of times in the 1990s I stood in for him. The highlight was interviewing Geoffrey Howe about his objections to legislation to counter Parliamentary sleaze.

Over time I was asked onto *Today, The World At One, PM, The World Tonight* and, on television, *Newsnight*. I even appeared on Radio 2's Jimmy Young Show to talk about positive vetting for civil servants; I knew nothing about it, but Jimmy's genial questioning got me through. Only working years later in Whitehall did I discover what it entailed. You had to list all your past activities and connections; you would not be penalised for anything you owned up to, but if you were caught concealing anything, you were out.

I loved the atmosphere in *Today*'s small suite of rooms spanning an upstairs corridor at Broadcasting House. My favourite presenter was Brian Redhead, the bounciest *Guardian* journalist when I worked there twenty years before. But the real treat was that politicians waiting to be interviewed, or just out of the studio, were at their most talkative. BBC studios and hospitality suites became a fruitful source of colour, and occasionally stories.

At Westminster I enjoyed working with the likes of John Simpson, Brian Curtois and John Sergeant from the BBC, ITN's David Rose, and Five Live's Peter Allen, who was then at Granada. Joining the *Daily Record* I was given the desk in the Press Gallery next to ITN's, which not only kept me close to the breaking news but brought new friendships. *News At Ten* had yet to fall victim to the scramble for ratings, and it was fascinating to watch a highly professional team putting their end of the show together. Leading them was Michael Brunson, as helpful to colleagues as he was authoritative on the air. His carefully impartial reporting concealed strong personal views; every so often during the epidemic of Tory "sleaze", Mike would burst in shouting: "He's gone!" as another minister bit the dust.

On my last day in the Lobby for the *Telegraph,* the SDP imploded and I had no fewer than 17 bids from different programmes (almost all BBC), from *The World At One* to *Newsnight.* Sadly you could not then be interviewed from Westminster, and there was no way I could keep going over to Broadcasting House and Television Centre if I was to write my story. But I did manage two or three of them.

I had also been noticed in the cerebral part of Broadcasting House, where Radio Four's weekly feature programmes were put together, by Anne Sloman, a formidable but charming lady who watched protectively over her brood of presenters. Around 1985 Anne asked me to join the rota for *The Week In Westminster*, the flagship Saturday morning political review. It was an honour, but the call came with the atmosphere in the office at its most difficult, and I knew that if I did the programme – which took up a lot of time at the busy end of the week – I would pay for it. Any other time I would have jumped at it - and with hindsight I probably should have. Anne was puzzled, telling Bill Deedes no-one had ever turned her down before.

She didn't give up, and later asked me to present *News Stand*, reviewing the weeklies in the adjoining Saturday slot. By then I was writing leaders in a very different environment and was delighted to accept. For a year or so I went into Broadcasting House every three weeks, trawled through a heap of magazines to develop a theme, then pulled a script together. I was again helped by having a highly professional producer; we also had the occasional studio guest, and actors to read excerpts from the weeklies. My favourite was Len Jackson, a long-serving newsreader with the ultimate "dark brown radio voice", a description not of ethnicity (Len was a Kiwi) but of vocal pitch. We had enormous fun the week I reviewed the sci-fi magazines, getting Len's voice distorted to create an echo chamber effect. I presented *News Stand* until I joined the *Independent on Sunday*, when it clashed with my working schedule. Regretfully I withdrew; had I known I would only be there six months I might have continued, but in any case the programme changed its format soon after.

When I left the *Sindy* I heard a rumour that Radio Four were seeking a presenter for PM, and went to see the station's controller Jenny Abramsky. She said they might be interested in me, but not for a programme as intensive and fast-moving. I was half-offered a job by the BBC at Westminster, but the gruelling hours and much lower pay discouraged me.

Radio is the purest form of communication: once the green light goes on you have every listener to yourself. I have never been as comfortable with television. It's easy to look in the wrong direction or become mesmerised by the autocue, and nothing is more intimidating than a remote studio where you stare into the void while answering questions from a presenter you can't see except through a monitor you mustn't look at.

During the 1987 election I did a Sunday panel programme in Lime Grove, 24 years after my first fleeting appearance there. I got a fan letter from a postman I'd worked with as a student, but BBC purists weren't happy when I suggested most people had switched on because *EastEnders* was next.

My first regular television slot came though Vidar Hjardeng, Central TV's current affairs producer whom I had got to know at conferences. Vidar - who made his mark in television despite near-blindness - asked me up to Birmingham (and later Nottingham) on Thursday nights from time to time for *Central Lobby*. There were a couple of MPs on the show and I was the tame pundit; our pre-studio tensions were eased by watching *Drop The Dead Donkey,* which was alarmingly true to life. I did the programme for a couple of years, including an election-night special when the party spokesmen in the studio received conflicting messages from headquarters on new-fangled pagers as to how things were going.

One night friends started ringing to say they had just seen me on *Boon* – a *Minder*-type series starring Michael Elphick. Vidar told me Central's drama department had requested a tape of a talking head and he had sent over one of me. In the episode, Boon is house-sitting; he opens a beer and sits down in front of the telly. There I am talking eruditely about Militant. Boon exclaims: "Sod that!" and switches off. I didn't blame him.

Years later, I was watching *Spooks*. Someone was looking in a bookcase, and stopped just as they reached *The Politics Book*, written by me. It was the only national publicity the book received.

My most regular television work came from 1990 on *The Channel Four Daily:* a serious breakfast show put together on a shoestring at ITN. The presenters were the young Dermot Murnaghan, even then a great professional, and Shahnaz Pakhravan. I learned from Shahnaz the great secret of women presenters in those pre-sofa days: she was immaculately turned out from the waist up, but wore ski pants as nothing below the desk top would appear in shot.

My role was to review Saturday's papers, delivering a brief script as cuttings flashed onto the screen. Once I had written the script – around 5.30 am - and made sure it was easy to deliver, it was put on the autocue … where my problems began. The words scroll onto a screen as you speak, and if you speed up, the autocue does as well. There's a natural urge to race it for fear it will leave you behind, and it took most of my 18 months on the programme to discipline myself to slow down.

The evening before one Channel 4 appearance in February 1991, the Brook Hospital, Woolwich, rang to tell me that my father, who had had a stroke a few days before, had now had a brain haemorrhage. The air ambulance had ferried him from Pembury Hospital, and he was to undergo surgery that night. The operation lasted 3½ hours, but when the surgeon came through he said Dad had such a constitution that he was only going into intensive care because there wasn't a bed on the surgical ward. I went straight from the hospital to ITN. Putting the script together helped keep my mind off things; I did my two slots, got a taxi home and went to bed.

I was just starting to enjoy the *Channel Four Daily* when it was terminated to make way for the populist *Big Breakfast*, with Johnny Vaughn and Denise van Outen. It's difficult to hold a wake at 9 am, but we had drinks in the studio and coffee in a nearby pub before dispersing into the early Saturday calm of Gray's Inn Road.

When I first appeared on CNN prior to Gordon Brown becoming prime minister, I was amazed to be told they don't pay journalists to appear because it violates their code of ethics. I forebore to mention that appearing gratis on commercial television to give the benefit of my experience violates mine. Nevertheless, when they asked me again during the 2010 election I went – and went back for the Scottish independence referendum. Nor, understandably, are you paid if you go on radio or TV to plug your book - but when *The Slow Death of British Industry* was launched I was delighted to go on *The Daily Politics,* fulfilling a long-held ambition to meet the incomparable Joan Bakewell.

My radio career took a new turn when I joined the *Daily Record*. I had already done a fair amount for *Good Morning Scotland*, which is every bit as good as *Today*, but now I was on more regularly, occasionally in the BBC's Glasgow studios but more often from London. This involved the "self-ops", studios from which contributors speak "down the line" to regional and local stations. Broadcasting House reception sends you along to the studio, you put on the headphones, then wait for the programme to be piped through to you. Several times someone forgot to switch on the "Glasgow feed", and I left without having made contact. After one interview the engineer in Glasgow asked if I had had a child in with me, and I had to confess I had brought John into the "self-op" because I couldn't get a babysitter. (Once when I was live on *Today* from home, Carrie, then about six, came into the bedroom and dropped the cat on me).

From the mid-1990s when the "self-ops" were concentrated in a suite at the heart of BH with their own studio manager, things worked better. One self-op still bears the scars of a Radio Scotland Christmas chat show with Rory Bremner; when we opened a bottle of champagne on air the cork punched a hole in the ceiling. Another memorable conversation "down the line" was with the one and only Tommy Docherty. Ruminating on the vagaries of fate, he recalled his mother saying: "Every time a door closes, a window will slam in your face."

I also appeared on Five Live chat shows. It's difficult to be on top form in a radio studio around midnight, particularly when the other panellists are 400 miles away. One night I was pitched against Roddy Forsyth, one of my favourite football journalists, on the issue of national identity: were we Scottish/English or British? Roddy had his answer crisp and clear: he was a Scot. I should have replied: "British when foreigners ask me, English when asked by a Scot", but instead I carelessly said "English". I wasn't asked back after I described Will Carling, in the spotlight over his friendship with Princess Diana, as "a great up and under merchant."

After I left the *Record* Mike Brunson told me there was room for a political contributor at Classic FM. Arriving at their Camden Town studios, I was alarmed to be asked to compere a selection of records. The harder I tried the worse I got, and I sincerely hope the demo tape was destroyed.

Talk Radio FM also invited me in; I had never seen such a shambolic operation and crept out with relief. I was supposed to line up the health guru Beechey Colclough for interview, but after I had been back to him six times with revised timings, he very sensibly went out. The one bright spot was encountering Jonathan King, who was on next. He had put on weight, but was still the introverted extrovert I'd known at Cambridge; I would be as stunned as anyone when he was convicted of offences against teenage boys.

My greatest concentration of radio work concerned the relaunch of *The Joy of Sex* in 2002: 46 interviews in a month. Most were for local stations, and after a dozen I had the formula off pat. The most challenging was for Five Live, with Gordon Brown's former spin doctor Charlie Whelan and Andrew Pierce, later a high-profile colleague at the *Telegraph*. I had learned to avoid the obvious bear traps, so when Charlie asked me: "How has *The Joy of Sex* improved your sex life?", I replied: "I hope it's improved everybody's." After the programme Charlie told me Gordon and his entourage years before had become convinced from my columns in the *Record* that I was agin him, then been staggered when I produced one of undiluted praise.

Joy has also involved me with several television documentaries, mainly for Channel 4 – and as I write, with ITN. Most have involved going to some empty backroom in Hoxton or Stockwell, to be interviewed for a piece on all-time best-selling books (or more often, sex); you give up a couple of hours and don't get paid. However when 20-20 Television produced a fuller documentary shortly after Dad's death, the production team spent days going through material I'd assembled for them, and then interviewing Corinne and myself. They weren't keen for me to see it before screening, but I managed to secure a preview tape from the *Telegraph*'s TV editor. They had developed the story well, with only the odd semi-embarrassing clip or soundbite, until the final quarter-hour when it all went a bit silly; apparently Channel 4's commissioning editor had decided there wasn't enough sex. The one shock was that they had named it *The Joy of Sex*; as Paramount held the movie rights I feared Channel 4 would hear from the studio's lawyers, but nothing happened.

18: Going to the Dogs

By the mid-1980s it was obvious that Fleet Street, with its flagrant overmanning and bloody-minded unions, could not survive much longer. Commercial printers had been using new technology for decades, and national newspapers' production methods had become downright embarrassing. I would write my story at the Commons on a typewriter, using two slips of paper with a carbon between. A messenger took the top copy to our teleprinter operator for transmission to Fleet Street. There another messenger took it to the subs, who would check it through, mark it up with instructions for the printers and add a headline. One more messenger took it to the back of the house, where the operator of a linotype machine – with a non-QWERTY keyboard (ETAOIN, to exclude non-members of the craft, and women) - retyped it again, pressing out lines of type (hence the name) from hot metal. Yet another messenger carried the type to the compositors, who assembled the page in a metal frame. Papier-maché was pressed against the frame to make a "flong", which was pressed against a roller in the foundry to produce a curved metal printing plate. These plates were inked, the presses rolled and the papers were loaded manually into the vans queueing in Shoe Lane.

Nowadays the reporter at the Commons (or anywhere else) types their story on a PC or laptop, knowing the length needed. They move it to the "edit" queue; the sub retrieves it, checks for grammar, spelling and clarity, trims it to fit, adds the headline and slots it into the page, already laid out. A simple command produces a photographic plate; these are curved around the rollers, then printing begins – no longer in Fleet Street but in business parks up and down the country. The process is cleaner, simpler, involves far fewer people ... but strangely seems to take as long, as there is less pressure today to get the latest news onto the streets. It is also simple nowadays to post your story on your paper's website - though reporters are also expected to blog and tweet when they could be out picking up stories.

Credit for the collapse of Fleet Street's archaisms must go first to Eddy Shah, who took on the unions at the *Stockport Messenger,* and next to Rupert Murdoch, who became so exasperated at their antics that he switched production of the *Times* and the *Sun* overnight to Wapping, where he had claimed to be starting a new evening paper. I have worked with several people who refused to move, out of solidarity with the hundreds who lost their jobs. I admire their integrity, but their loyalty was misplaced; the semi-skilled SOGAT union, in particular, had brought the industry to its knees trying to protect jobs that had been non-existent for half a century. Nor had they ever backed us when we were in dispute.

On the day in January 1986 when Wapping went live, I was doing the *Telegraph*'s Sunday political shift. As well as ringing politicians and spin doctors (we had just gone through Westland, and Peter Mandelson was coming into his own) and monitoring the day's broadcasts, I often compared notes with Phil Webster at the *Times*. We didn't disclose our exclusives, but made sure we hadn't missed anything in the public domain and discussed what weight to give it. This time my call was routed to Wapping ... where Phil eventually came on to tell me how they were getting the paper out surrounded by packing cases, with Murdoch in the thick of things. The unions had been wrong-footed, but within days violent picketing was forcing *Times* and *Sun* staff to run the gauntlet between Tower Hill station and the Pennington Street plant 600 yards away.

On the surface, Lord Hartwell's *Telegraph* was carrying on as if nothing had changed. One night Radio 4 broadcast a documentary on the paper straight after Mervyn Peake's *Gormenghast* – and it was hard to tell where *Gormenghast* ended and the *Telegraph* began. Each concerned an archaic fortress in which old men in cobwebbed turrets carried out elaborate rituals whose meaning had long since been forgotten.

Yet Hartwell knew things had to change. He was planning two state-of-the-art printing plants, at Trafford Park in Manchester and on the Isle of Dogs. Content would be sent there electronically, requiring new technology at all stages of production, with huge savings in labour. Our paper warehouse employed 160 people; the *Baltimore Sun*'s did the job with three.

The cost soared beyond Hartwell's reach - which is where Conrad Black came in. Black cannily negotiated a stake in the *Telegraph* in return for much-needed cash, and as the paper's finances deteriorated that stake became a controlling interest. Within weeks Hartwell was only a figurehead, though at the height of Black's commercial success with the paper, the Berry family's residual holdings would be worth more than when they owned it outright.

Things moved fast once Black arrived. Peter Eastwood, belatedly, retired. Andrew Knight arrived from the *Economist* as chief executive. Max Hastings succeeded Bill Deedes as editor, taking on Eastwood's job as well, and a legion of tired, eccentric and ageing men, symbols of the *Telegraph*'s stagnation though often its victims, left the building. Jim Wightman, my immediate boss, was not one of these; he had wanted for some time to rejoin his family in Scotland. His resignation on the eve of Black's takeover created an opening I was the obvious candidate to fill, having been deputy not only to Jim but to his predecessor. But Max, wanting new blood, appointed George Jones, who had taken the *Sunday Telegraph* political job when I turned it down, then pipped me to the *Sunday Times*. Fortunately we got on well.

New technology first impacted on me during the 1986 conference season, when I was issued with a Tandy – a primitive laptop – for writing my copy for transmission to a computer linked to the office. You could type your story anywhere ... which intrigued Militant supporters when I tried it at their Blackpool fringe meeting. With the Tandy came an acoustic coupler – two linked rubber-covered sockets – which you fitted over each end of a telephone receiver. There was an attachment to plug into a phone socket with the Tandy dialling the number, but as BT prohibited the use of jack plugs so only its engineers could install a phone, this was of little use. Moreover much of my conference output was written in hotel rooms, and the Tandy could not dial through a switchboard.

New technologies invaded the *Telegraph*'s Fleet Street building as the move of editorial and printing to separate sites in Docklands neared. Simultaneous adoption of new printing and composition methods was ambitious: a leader mistakenly set in the wrong typeface resulted in a proof 23 metres long, and with our printers being retrained, some casuals brought in were out of their depth. One Cypriot could only function because our Harrovian deputy editor, Andrew Hutchinson, still had some classical Greek. For me the critical point came when we abandoned our typewriters and switched totally to the Tandies, filing to a computer at the Foreign Correspondents' Association. Up to then the FCA had handled only a trickle of copy, and the *Telegraph* political team's output hit it like a tsunami.

Next I was trained on Atex, a comprehensive newspaper production system, by Lord Hartwell's son Adrian Berry, whose great interest was colonies in space and who stayed on under the new regime as science correspondent. The Tandies faded away, though the *Daily Record* used them until 1994. When a colleague covering that year's US Masters called at a Radio Shack in Augusta for a running repair; the entire staff were called out to see what for them was a museum piece.

During 1987 the *Telegraph* moved to South Quay Plaza, across the water from where Canary Wharf now stands. If anyone had told me when Carrie and I went there just six years before to see the replica of Drake's *Golden Hind* that the *Telegraph* would be based there, I would have laughed.

There was a pioneering atmosphere at South Quay. The Docklands Light Railway had yet to open when we arrived, so you had to catch a bus from Mile End. A motor launch was laid on for staff commuting into Charing Cross and London Bridge; the views were spectacular but it shipped a lot of water. Another boat - a former Orkney ferry moored behind the office - made a surprisingly good (and interesting to visitors) staff restaurant. The only alternatives were a couple of pubs and the café at Asda.

At first, I only went to South Quay for the morning conference – routine for any other newspaper, but an innovation for the *Telegraph* when Max arrived. George Jones and I took it in turns, as the journey from Westminster, even with the DLR, took a slice out of the day (now you can do it in minutes via the Jubilee Line). But it helped me get to know the new team who were giving the paper a younger, fresher feel.

Editorial moved in department by department, and the new printing plant at West Ferry, round the corner, came into use, production transferring from Fleet Street overnight without a hitch. A few weeks later Max – to my astonishment – suggested over lunch that I leave the Lobby and join the leader writers. Most

Telegraph leader writers in my experience were extreme Right-wingers who at party conferences needed a full-time helper to find the Gents. Nor were my politics a natural fit with the *Telegraph's*. But Max wanted to refresh the Lobby team – I had been there nine years – and there wasn't a suitable job for me on the news side as new arrivals poured in. I am very glad he asked me, as from my point of view the move worked.

A leading article represents the paper's policy, set out for its readers and those it seeks to influence. It usually picks up on some news item to draw conclusions about the way the country is going and what should be done about it. Rather like a pronouncement from the Vatican, it will refine and elaborate on a policy built up over the years. Occasionally, as when the *Express* briefly embraced Europe, there will be a radical shift; more often the leader column involves a restatement, encouraging readers to see things the paper's way. Leader writers (and the proprietors and editors who dictate the line to be followed) need the humility to realise that many, if not most, of a paper's readers pass the leader column by. Yet it does matter, not least because a heavyweight pronouncement – such as a declaration by the *Telegraph* or the *Times* that a Tory leader is not up to the job - can have profound repercussions.

There was a special irony in my writing leaders for the *Telegraph*. When Grandfather – a lifelong *Telegraph* reader - passed 90 in excellent shape, he confided that its editorials made him so hopping mad that they gave him the energy to get through the day. They had a well-deserved reputation not just for championing extreme (and frequently lost) causes, but for crankiness. So when the paper set out in its leader column from the mid-1970s the philosophy behind Thatcherism, few realised that a serious set of values was emerging that would dominate British politics for a generation. A further twist was that under the influence of T E ("Peter") Utley, the paper advanced a hard-line Unionist position on Northern Ireland; this was taken up again in Conrad Black's later years, and in the decade after the Good Friday Agreement the tone of some *Telegraph* leaders was almost one of regret that the

Troubles were over. The paper likewise adopted a robust but slightly cranky Euroscepticism.

Under Max the *Telegraph* remained committed to the Conservative Party, and to Mrs Thatcher, but the tone became more subtle as he sought to open up the opinion pages to a readership stretching beyond the idiosyncratic Right. He added some hobby-horses of his own, notably the iniquity of planting conifers in the Flow Country of Caithness to provide tax breaks for celebrities. But on many issues he was open-minded, and the leader-writing team he put together embodied a broad range of experience and opinions.

The genesis of a leader column is much the same on every paper. After the morning conference, the editor meets the leader writer(s) to consider which issues should be highlighted, what line should be taken and who should write each piece; he (or she) may well have had his ear bent by the proprietor over what to say.

Leader conference with Max was a joy, unless he was preoccupied by some disaster from the night before. When Muslims in Bradford protested against *The Satanic Verses,* Max, summoning up an author's heartfelt feelings toward the book trade, observed: "I never thought I'd see the day when someone would launch a jihad against W H Smith." His *bêtes noirs* were those conifers and the RAF, which he considered irredeemably middle-class, but he recognised the need to set a credible stance for the paper rather than reflect his own prejudices.

Even when Max was preoccupied, leader conference was bound to be stimulating, given the other participants. Chief among these was Bill Deedes, whom Max, with great wisdom, had invited to stay on as not just a bridge with the past but a source of common sense and boundless enthusiasm; Bill was already 74, but he had the energy of a man half his age, formidable contacts (starting with the Thatchers) and a reporter's eye for a story. His amused and thoughtful tone perfectly complemented Max's abrasiveness.

Jock Bruce-Gardyne was a loveable ideologue who as the *FT's* man in Paris had danced with Brigitte Bardot for a bet ("she was all woman") and was now waging war on BUPA over abysmal care after a brain operation. Jock had been a Treasury minister until he (unwisely but typically) criticised the Falklands War. He had lost his seat in Scotland, and when he found another in Cheshire his former chairman opined that the majority of 10,000 "Will no' be enough for Jock." I had always considered Jock's writings on the economy eccentric, but working alongside him I saw their logic. I was deeply saddened when his illness finally caught up with him, just after I left the paper.

Near-contemporaries were Simon Scott-Plummer, an authoritative writer on diplomatic affairs, and Robert Harvey, an equally agreeable economist and briefly a Conservative MP. Birds of passage included Martin Ivens, who went on to edit the *Sunday Times,* and Niall Ferguson, who was deciding between journalism and academia; he returned to Oxford to become an outstanding writer on the trends of history.

Finally there were the young Turks: Simon Heffer and Boris Johnson. Simon, a red-haired hive of industry, shared my love for English music – about which he writes beautifully - and Essex cricket; we even had John Major, when Chancellor, lined up to join us at Chelmsford until Simon's Enoch-influenced diatribes against him led John to withdraw. Boris, a joy to work with, arrived after being sacked by the *Times.* He came to a party at my home, and I dined with him and his first wife at their house near Olympia. We also saw a new production of *Henry VI* at the Old Vic; Boris had played Richard III at Eton, and was fascinated when, at the end of this preceding play, the director added the line: "Now, is the winter of our discontent made glorious summer by this Sun of York?"

Boris was clearly bound for greatness, but it was impossible to tell as what; when he won his seat at Henley, I e.mailed him saying: "In 30 years' time you will be a big beast. Your problem is what to do in between". There was then no Mayor of London, but it would be a job tailor-made for Boris until the Foreign Office fell vacant.

A leading article is a totally different art form to a news story. The reporter puts the key facts in the first paragraph, then backs them up with further information. With a leader you set out the situation, produce a few arguments, then deliver your conclusion. The *Telegraph* leader column usually comprises three items, with 4-

500 words to make each point. With a major issue it could be a struggle; I failed spectacularly over the report into the King's Cross fire, being rescued by my system crashing and Max rattling off an authoritative leader himself. There was some scope to be lyrical; I particularly enjoyed writing of New Age travellers and their "free-range children", and noting on the *New Statesman*'s birthday that it had been founded among the "dark, Satanic mills of Liphook".

We each had our special subjects. Bill took the Royal family and the Conservative Party, his dry touch enabling criticism to be applied lightly, but applied nevertheless. Jock or Robert dealt with the economy, Simon Scott-Plummer foreign affairs, and Simon Heffer, Boris and myself more general matters. If he was fired up or believed the subject required his authority, Max might turn out a leader himself. I was seldom asked to write anything I strongly disagreed with.

Writing two or three leaders a week each freed us all to make other contributions to the paper, though some produced more than others: Simon Heffer would have written the lot given the chance. I contributed quite a few news features, and the odd humorous "Sixth Column" for the leader page. I occasionally ventured a full-scale opinion piece, though Max's thermonuclear reaction (reflecting a rocket he had received from Conrad Black) to one about the kind of policies the Conservative Party might adopt post-Mrs Thatcher discouraged me. My next such piece was on a safer topic: how Cecil Parkinson would fare as Transport Secretary. I also turned in the occasional book review.

Perhaps a dozen times I went back to my old stamping ground to deliver the Commons sketch for the back page. I would sit in for Question Time and the start of the main debate, join the other sketch writers (the *Times'* Matthew Parris was my favourite) for a coffee before putting on my thinking cap, then turn out 6-700 words giving the flavour of the day. It was challenging to come up with a fluent sketch by deadline, but looking back at my cuttings I seem to have succeeded. One sketch of mine concerned Edwina Currie's appearance before the Agriculture Select Committee after her gaffe on eggs and salmonella; I couldn't resist comparing her with Mrs Tiggy Winkle. The most prescient concerned a debate about the struggle between Mohamed Al Fayed and Tiny Rowland for the ownership of Harrods; I described one MP's contribution as the "Chanson de Rowland" and asked why any Member would feel the need to speak on the subject unless paid to. Years later, it turned out that several had been. I had to be careful of literary allusions: when I confused *David Copperfield* with *Great Expectations,* I received more mail from readers than at any other time in my career.

We leader writers occupied a long table at the far end of the floor from Max's office and conference room. Increasingly, though, I spent my time at Max's end. He asked me to fill in for the leader page editor, Trevor Grove, when he was tied up with other projects, and by early 1989 I was doing this pretty much full-time. Trevor was a key player in Max's *Telegraph,* a first-class features man though by his own admission not so hot with news. His wife Valerie Grove (my former *Varsity* colleague Valerie Smith) carved out a merited niche as the *Times*'s star interviewer and biographer of the dramatist Dodie Smith. Trevor went on to edit the *Sunday Telegraph*, and when Corinne and I moved to Highgate in 1991 they became good neighbours. Climbing the greasy pole put Trevor under considerable strain; he told me he knew he wouldn't last long as an editor, and after the inevitable happened he re-emerged as an entertaining writer, notably about the family Dalmatian.

Editing the page, I sat opposite Veronica Wadley (now Baroness Fleet), Max's features supremo and later editor of the *Evening Standard.* Married to the investigative author Tom Bower, Veronica was very close to Max, and her excellent connections were matched by a commanding manner. Yet after two years at close quarters I still had no idea what made her tick.

Apart from making sure Max saw the leaders in good time, then working with the sub-editor of the day on the headlines, the leader page editor had the daily flagship article of 1,600 words to commission. Ferdinand Mount had the Thursday slot with a political piece that was always a joy to read, Max had quite a few ideas for the other days but I had to ensure there were always pieces of quality available – from academics, outside commentators or one of staff – lest we be left with a hole. The first of a series from Bryan Appleyard had been cleared for use by his publishers but fell foul of his contract with another paper, so I had to pull the second at a very late stage. During the 1989 Conservative conference, Max decided we should run a daily ideological piece; the first few worked well, but around lunchtime on the Thursday I realised the flagship article commissioned for the morning of Mrs Thatcher's speech was not going to arrive. There was a mild panic, then I spotted on my desk a pamphlet from the junior Treasury minister Peter Lilley on social and economic policy. I cleared publication with the think-tank he'd written it for, left a message for Lilley that he was about to see his name in lights and then, praying the pamphlet was worth reading, set about cutting it heavily to fit the hole in the page. Fortunately Max thought it worked, but it was a close run thing.

One innovation I made – though it did not survive me – was a Saturday leader-pager in which a writer from one of Britain's major cities expatiated on its glories. Michael Kennedy, doyen of music critics and our long-standing Northern editor, kicked off with a piece on what made Manchester tick. Next I persuaded the former Conservative MP Anna McCurley to do the same for Glasgow. I was just considering whether we could afford a piece on Sheffield from Roy Hattersley when the time came to move on.

I also oversaw the "Sixth Column" on the right of the page, provided most days by regular contributors. One was Perry Worsthorne, editor of the *Sunday Telegraph,* best known as the first man to say "fuck" on British television. I couldn't help liking Perry; we last met at a charity auction in his home village when Alex, then about eight, pushed up the price I was bidding for a cake. But he gave me one of my most difficult afternoons when he filed a column which, in passing, asserted that the Banque de France was "run by crooks". Andrew Hutchinson, editing that day, confirmed my opinion that Perry – whose copy was normally sacrosanct – would need to alter the offending phrase. Somewhat nervous, I rang Perry. He was not at all offended, and suggested I change it to "run by Jews"? When I told him this would cause even greater offence, he seemed genuinely surprised.

The urbane and witty Tory MP Julian Critchley uniquely had a deal under which he was paid for Sixth Columns he submitted whether they were used or not. There were half a dozen other contributors I could rely on, plus a few amateurs whose efforts I tried to burnish into usable English. I turned down some hopefuls who have gone on to be big names elsewhere, having vastly improved their writing style. Max would often suggest a subject and ask one of us to deliver, and I wrote some "Sixth Columns" myself. One was inspired by a drive with Carrie past the derelict Beckton Gasworks, daubed with slogans in Vietnamese; we had stumbled upon the set of *Full Metal Jacket*.

I also had to commission the political cartoon, or on some days a photo. The *Telegraph* had been struggling cartoon-wise since Nick Garland's departure for the *Independent* (he would come back), and none of the alternatives entirely satisfied Max. My preferred choice was (George) Gale, whose work I had admired in *Tribune* years before. George was good on caricature, but sometimes struggled to originate a topic. I also liked the work of Debbie Obeid, a cartoonist then getting started; some challenges I set her (such as illustrating a piece on Gorbachev's grasp of economics) were stiff, but her drawing was excellent. Very kindly, she came up with a special cartoon when I left.

A third option worked really well, but conflicted with broader policy. Matt Pritchett, the brilliant and always funny son of our columnist Oliver, had started doing the front-page pocket cartoons at which he has now excelled for a generation. He was also happy to contribute the odd big cartoon for the leader page, his Lowryesque tableaux filled with manic little figures fitting perfectly with the article beneath. But Max decided the "big Matts" were a distraction from what he did best; he was right, but I was sorry to lose him.

Choosing a photograph for that space could be a challenge, particularly with pieces about education and economics. It was embarrassing to fall back on yet another picture of pupils at their desks, or cranes and containers; you owe it to the readers to be imaginative.

Having pulled the copy and illustration together and run them past Max, I would head for the subs' desk to monitor their transformation into a page. Thanks to the new technology, I could H&J ("hyphenate and justify") the copy myself to make it fit - frequently after making drastic cuts that had to leave the reader unable to see the joins. But the task of checking everything, then putting in the headlines and captions, required a skilled sub, and we had the best - among them Jane Taylor, who 20 years later would help me graduate from Atex to the current DTI system, and Frank Peters, a moustachioed Cornishman from my *Northern Echo* days.

Devising a headline or caption is an art. It has to reflect accurately and concisely what the article says or the picture shows, and it must fit. Too long and it will "bust", too short and the page looks strange. Usually the headline over each of the leaders was easy, less so that for the "Sixth Column", which had to fit into short spaces on three or four decks. The main article frequently set a challenge, particularly if it dealt with the cerebral. Once in a while, though, inspiration struck. Ferdy Mount filed a piece asserting that the Chelsea Flower Show showed the crumbling Communist world benign capitalism at its best. Frank came up with the headline: "Let a hundred flowers bloom", echoing Chairman Mao. Then for the photo, a close-up of a woman in sunglasses scrutinising a plant which even I recognised, I suggested the caption: "I have seen the fuchsia, and it works" ... a play on the encomium for the infant Soviet Union from the American journalist Lincoln Steffens. In conference next morning, Max unusually asked who had come up with the headline and caption, and complimented us.

I also represented the *Telegraph* at award ceremonies – I have never won any – and was once left in charge of the paper. It was the day of Peter Eastwood's funeral in deepest Essex; Max and the top brass went, as was fitting, and for three hours I was the sole occupant of his end of the office ... apart from Max's secretary, who was doubtless under orders to call him if anything happened. Disappointingly, nothing did.

When we arrived at South Quay, Canary Wharf across the water was brownfield land. First the piledrivers arrived to sink foundations to bear a skyscraper – which at school we were told the London clay would not support – and then the great tower began to rise up. I suffer acutely from vertigo – having twice had to be helped off the Eiffel Tower – and wondered how I would handle working so close to such a massive structure. (Having later worked in it as high as the 26th floor, I am sure I would have managed.)

It was a problem I never had to face. Max told me he had hired Mary Dejevsky from the *Times* to take over the leader page (in the event, she stayed put), so my main task would revert to writing leaders which I knew wouldn't stretch me. Max had once asked me to become Industrial Correspondent, a job I hastily declined, and I wondered what else he might have up his sleeve. At this point Tony Bevins, political editor of the *Independent*, a loner whom I had always rated highly, told me they were starting a Sunday paper and asked me to come on board. I went over to City Road to meet its editor, Stephen Glover – one of the saner of the earlier *Telegraph* leader-writers - and his news editor Peter Wilby, who turned out to live round the corner from my mother. I decided to take the job even before Max's secretary told me she would have me sectioned if I didn't, and in mid-October 1989 (the day after being the only page editor to join a strike against redundancies) I handed in my notice. A tussle ensued over when I could leave to work on pre-launch dummy editions; Max observed that I seemed more frightened of Stephen than of him and that he could easily have made me redundant (it would have cost the *Telegraph* a packet). But after a marvellous lunch at Rules hosted by Bill Deedes, and a party in the pub, I cleared my desk. Months later the *Telegraph*'s transport correspondent John Petty died; had I still been there I would have gone for his job like a shot.

It was strange working for another paper after 15 years on the *Telegraph*, and I was new to the rhythm of Sunday newspaper work, which gives you just one chance a week to make your mark. But I worked enthusiastically on dummy editions, two Cabinet ministers – David Waddington and Peter Brooke - giving me interviews they knew would never see the light of day. I also gained a deputy in Stephen Castle; I had wanted Channel 4's Anne Perkins, but Stephen proved a first-rate political reporter, became a good friend and went on to be the *Independent*'s Brussels correspondent.

The "Sindy" launched at the end of January 1990, a strong story about a baby kidnapped from a hospital being reunited with its parents helping it sell over 700,000 copies. Before long, though, collective nerves and lack of organisation began sapping our morale. Our Tuesday conferences became an interminable picking-over of last Sunday's paper, with no-one daring to be critical and little talk of the edition to come. An observation of mine that most readers didn't study leading articles went down particularly badly (our leader writer was Chris Huhne). But I was most uneasy about the paper's news operation, which I was supposed to spearhead.

Peter Wilby, as he would prove editing the *New Statesman,* is a consummate intellectual, and an expert on the urban planner Lewis Mumford, but his reporting experience was confined to education and his team included seven former education correspondents. There was also an organisational problem: many stories got stuck at the news desk, staying unread as deadlines approached. On any other paper – apart from the drink-sodden *Sunday Telegraph* of the 1970s – the desk would have passed them on to the subs, unless they needed further work or clearly were not going to make the paper.

To get my stories used, I rejigged several for the business section. Peter confided that we were both under pressure because of a feeling on high that we weren't landing the heavy political stories. My view was that I was producing exclusives with one hand tied behind my back (having been ordered to operate outside the Lobby), and that they were not being used. The paper did, however, carry my disclosure that the security services were using the Ernie premium bond set-up at Lytham St Anne's to pay informants.

I also discovered that the Defence Secretary, Tom King, was livid with Michael Mates, chairman of the Defence Select Committee, for staying on after an official visit to Washington to drum up consultancy business in the Pentagon. King's PPS, plus a friend who was in and out of the Pentagon, confirmed the story, I wrote it and naïvely expected Stephen Glover to congratulate me. Mates complained, and Stephen made clear his disapproval. I left his office with the impression that when he said he wanted stories, he meant stories that didn't upset anybody - not quite the fearless ethos the paper was committed to. Within weeks, I was out.

Stephen praised my workrate and the way I had trained Stephen Castle, but said the news operation was not working; Wilby or I had to go, and he had decided it should be me. *Private Eye* reported that my job had already been offered to the *Sunday Correspondent*'s Don MacIntyre, who had honourably turned it down. Once I had cleared my desk, Don was asked again.

I left with six months' money, which was generous; the promised company Rover arrived on my final day and I never even saw it. Before leaving, I went to see Andreas Whittam Smith, the bishop-like figure who had launched the *Independent,* to tell him what was wrong with his Sunday baby. Tony Bevins couldn't understand why things hadn't worked out. But I had been foisted on Stephen, and was paying the price.

Out of self-respect I didn't ask Max if I could come back to the *Telegraph*. I did go to see Simon Jenkins, editor of the *Times,* in case there was anything doing (there wasn't), and Jenny Abramsky at the BBC. But the job that came up was as political editor of Robert Maxwell's *European* – and after the collapse of Maxwell's empire, of the *Daily Record.*

As the newspaper world's centre of gravity moved from Fleet Street to Wapping and Canary Wharf I saw little of either, being based first at Holborn and then dividing my time between the Commons and Glasgow. The call to the east first came in 1995, just before I left the *Record,* when Simon Heffer asked me to write Tony Benn's obituary for the *Telegraph* and a fascinating new seam of work opened up; I now worked occasionally in the tower I'd seen taking shape from South Quay, which had proved only a temporary home for the *Telegraph.*

Wapping also became part of my life. The *Sun*'s Trevor Kavanagh had through hard work, judgment and integrity became the most respected – and probably most liked - figure in the Lobby; just one reason why Trevor was David Cameron's first choice as his press secretary ahead of the ill-starred Andy Coulson. Trevor and Rupert Murdoch go back to their early days, but he has always been his own man. At Westminster Trevor had worked at the next desk to me – garnering exclusives over the phone without the rest of us catching onto them – and when I left the *Record* in September 1995 he suggested I stand in as leader writer at the *Sun* when Chris Roycroft-Davis, the assistant editor, was away or busy. So I went down to the Victorian warehouse which had become the headquarters of the Murdoch papers under such stormy circumstances, and met Trevor's editor Stuart Higgins, and Stuart's deputy Neil Wallis.

I had learned a lot about the *Sun* from Chris Potter; Chris had died nine years before in Kelvin McKenzie's heyday as editor, but not much had changed. Over the news desk a banner still hung reminding the staff that they worked for "the greatest newspaper in the world". The *Sun* under Stuart remained brash and self-confident, but was less frenetic. The secret of its success was total professionalism: experienced reporters, a news desk with a clear idea of what was too tasteless to print (purveyors of such stories were directed to the *Daily Star*), a team of executives with focus and commitment, and sub-editors who could not only turn out priceless headlines like "No-Knobby Bobby has Brand-New Jobby" (about a sex-change policeman) but were assiduous guardians of accuracy. I was eternally grateful to one – an Ulsterman – for spotting that I had got wrong in a leader the name of the Roman Catholic Primate of All Ireland.

Before long I was writing leaders on Sundays, and occasionally for entire weeks - the only person to have been the voice of both the *Sun* and the *Telegraph,* save for the *Sun* veteran Ronnie Spark who had contributed one guest leader for my old paper. In theory the challenge was the same: to spell out the situation and say what the paper thinks. But writing *Sun* leaders you have less than 500 words in toto, and three or sometimes four issues to address, so brevity is everything. This was particularly true of the short "And finally" leader. Compiling one was like writing a *haiku* – you had barely 20 words to state the situation, develop it and deliver a punchline. But I was particularly proud of:

> "Elephants swam the Atlantic, scientists have discovered.
>
> Then they died out.
>
> Couldn't they get their trunks off?"

I sat in at the morning conference, then saw the editor to discuss what subjects to tackle, conscious not only that the *Sun*'s leader column wielded influence, but that Rupert Murdoch would read it. Leaders on Europe needed to be hostile, and China avoided altogether lest we endanger Murdoch's chances of landing a TV franchise there.

In my two and a half years writing *Sun* leaders, I enjoyed dealing with important issues in simple language, or plugging into the national mood, as when we urged England on during Euro 96. I usually managed to avoid subjects where my own views differed from the paper's, but found it refreshing to let rip from time to time, even if the argument was not necessarily my own. When after the Strangeways riot an inmate was awarded £4,000 by the Home Office because his personality had been changed, I wrote: "Silly us. That's what we thought prison was supposed to do. Maybe he'll even go straight." And when the issue of gays in the military surfaced, I hazarded the view that "our squaddies should be able to concentrate on the enemy ahead of them without having to worry about the man in the row behind". Unfair, but liberating.

Though I was a semi-detached member of the *Sun* team, the paper had my full commitment. When Corinne and I moved to Swalcliffe Manor near Banbury, I suggested to Stuart that it was large and discreet enough to act as "Chateau Buyup": a place where the paper could shelter a celebrity while they told their story, instead of putting them up riskily in a hotel. I also helped trial a bandage strip supposed to stop snoring; mine blew straight off. I was also still writing obituaries for the *Telegraph*; there one day to fine-tune an obit, I realised with horror that I had the *Sun*'s news list in my briefcase. I left hurriedly.

The day Princess Diana died I was due to write the leaders, but Stuart decided as the story broke in the small hours that heavier guns were needed; efforts were made to contact me but I was already in London, staying at my father's now-empty flat, and arrived in the office ready to do my bit. National grief unfolded on television, Tony Blair setting the tone with his tribute to the "People's Princess". And around me highly professional colleagues were putting that mood into words and telling the story, not just of the traumatic events overnight in Paris, but of Diana's life and work and the impact of her death on the Royal family. As I was by then filing political copy to the *Scottish Sun*, I put together a special piece for them; like much else written at Wapping that day there was no room for it , but I was sad to be left off the collective byline.

Some time after, I learned that Diana's death had caught the Royal Household unprepared in one vital respect: there was no coffin ready. Thus, I was reliably told, she was buried in the one kept ready for the (much shorter) Queen Mother. None of the papers I was working for would touch the story.

I wrote *Sun* leaders for Stuart Higgins, his successor David Yelland and two deputy editors: Neil Wallis and Rebekah Wade (now Brooks). Under Rebekah the tone changed: freewheeling political incorrectness was out, though none of her predecessors would have mounted the reckless campaign against supposed paedophiles that would become her trademark. But the reason I stopped – with great regret – was mundane: I couldn't get a train up to London in time for the Sunday morning conference. I tried filing from home, but found myself dangerously out of touch and, at the end of 1998, I reluctantly quit.

As well as my occasional visits to the *Telegraph* at Canary Wharf until the paper moved on to Victoria in 2007, I worked higher up the tower – the 26th floor – until early 2000, helping with the *Sunday People*'s political coverage. (The Mirror Group had moved there from Holborn Circus after I left the *Record*). Usually I worked from Westminster alongside the political editor, Nigel Nelson, but when he was on holiday or away on a story I did a double Saturday shift at Canary Wharf. The atmosphere was very different from the *Telegraph* fifteen floors below, and not just because that paper boasted one of the best canteens in the business. We used totally different and, to me, less user-friendly technology: Mac, which fortunately I had experienced at the *European*. The *Mirror* library was more basic, staffing was very tight and there was a realisation that if you didn't deliver there would be a hole in the paper. But again, it was a highly professional team, led by Neil Wallis. As with any Sunday paper, there was a languor punctuated by frenetic activity if something important happened on a Saturday afternoon - as with the Omagh bombing, when I put together the day's main story and a leader against the clock. It was sobering that, as with most calamities, they virtually wrote themselves.

19: Into Africa

It's easy to write off Africa as a basket case of over-population, disease, famine, corruption and war, and undeniably most African countries have been ruled since independence by at least one megalomaniac. The greatest challenge after these is the lack of fuel in much of rural Africa that leaves families no choice but to strip the landscape for firewood. But I have met enough intelligent and motivated people across Africa to hope things can still be turned around.

To me as a child, Africa was where missionaries went to tell the people about Jesus – but also the home of apartheid. When we moved to Loughton, my father struck up a friendship with the "Coloured" South African author Peter Abrahams and we saw quite a lot of Peter, his wife Daphne and their children till they moved on to Jamaica. Dad was a passionate opponent of racialism, but his friendship with Peter made it personal. When I finally made it to South Africa as Nelson Mandela was elected president, I sent Peter my *Daily Record* column describing "a great country reinventing itself". Later, my host at a game lodge in Zambia turned out to be Andrew Sardanis, a remarkable Cypriot who had lived through colonialism and independence and rubbed shoulders with the mighty ... and was a great fan of Peter, whom he had never met. I was delighted to tell him more.

At Cambridge, my Rhodesian neighbour Trevor Derry's love of his country - if not its government - and its topicality as Ian Smith declared independence (defying the world for 14 years) made me look at Africa afresh. Kenya appealed to me most, and I and my then fiancée Lyn Blackwell (later Lyn Wong Colunga, of Edmonton, Canada) even considered going there for VSO. Nor could I resist taking Cambridge's then new course on African History.

Peter Eastwood hired me for the *Telegraph* in part because of this. He sent me first to Morocco, which hadn't been on my syllabus, when in the autumn of 1975 King Hassan capitalised on General Franco's failing health to claim the Spanish Sahara by staging a "Green March". Green is the sacred colour of Islam, and the King was invoking his special position as a direct descendant from the family of the Prophet. In a formidable feat of organisation, 300,000 Moroccans were bused into the desert and encamped on the border of the colony, awaiting a signal to march in; the southern portion was to be ceded to Mauritania.

On the flight out to Rabat, the idea seemed both romantic and alarming. And after an hour trying to file my scene-setter – all calls were routed manually via Paris – I realised it would be frustrating too. My initial goal was Marrakech, where the world's press was assembling, and three of us piled into a taxi, west to the outskirts of Casablanca – sprawling and overheated rather than romantic – then inland along a dead straight road, with the mountains looming ahead. I couldn't keep Crosby, Stills and Nash's *Marrakesh Express* out of my head.

While the marchers assembled hundreds of miles ahead, we explored the great *souk,* ate exquisite lamb in restaurants run by French stay-behinds, and tiptoed into the Mamounia, the great hotel from which Churchill painted the Atlas Mountains. At one briefing there from the information minister an American journo watched me taking shorthand, then exclaimed: "Gee, your Arabic is brilliant!"

Every day we took our copy to the central post office, laboriously punched out a "bande de telex" and handed it to the operator for transmission. Susan Morgan, there for both the *Guardian* and the *Express*, supplied one with liberal analysis and the other with more knee-jerk material. When we suddenly moved out, she handed the operator both tapes; *Guardian* readers were treated to a lively and politically incorrect assessment, while *Express* readers had their vocabulary (and outlook) broadened. Susan was great to work with; sadly she would be seriously wounded covering guerrilla warfare in Central America.

Our flight into the desert was my first experience of the C-130 Hercules, workhorse of most of the world's air forces and the plane in which Mrs Thatcher visited the liberated Falklands. The "Herc", in which you sit or squat hanging onto webbing along the sides of the fuselage, is noisy but almost uncrashable. This was just as well. We flew over the Atlas to Tan Tan, Morocco's farthest-south airport just where the coastal desert becomes really unforgiving. As we approached we were engulfed in a sandstorm and the pilot, after two attempts to land which had little to do with the runway, flew back to Marrakech.

To get to Agadir, where the King had taken up residence, I shared a car with Walter Meth, a veteran correspondent for Germany's DPA news agency. Walter had been sent to a punishment battalion in France for observing, as his bunker in Poland was bombed, that he would rather be up there in the plane. Captured by the French, he found farm work with plenteous food by giving his occupation as "journalist and peasant" - the next PoW declaring himself an "opera singer and peasant". Walter had a compulsion to drive at 100mph - and an urgent need for dialysis – so our journey over the mountains was hair-raising. When about to pass out he would stop, gulp down more water, then career off again, spurning my offers to drive. I was a gibbering wreck by the time we reached the Club Mediterranée at Agadir, where chalets had been commandeered for the media.

Club Med was idyllic. The guests, mostly French, were smart but bohemian and bent on relaxation. Drinks were paid for by plastic beads from a necklace given you on arrival. Sadly the groaning evening buffet usually clashed with the minister's briefing, which was the principal source of news.

I only made dinner there once, with a French Canadian TV crew, a glamorous reporter from Radio Monte Carlo and Walter (who had calmed me when I was woken by an electronically amplified muezzin, momentarily thinking we were under attack). My erratic French flowed with the alcohol, and as one of the crew disappeared with the girl from Monaco I observed: "Si vous n'êtes pas satisfait, vous pouvez toujours rentrer ici baiser Monsieur." What I intended to say was: "If you aren't satisfied, you can always come back and give Walter a kiss", but what my words encouraged him to do was far more drastic. Once my fellow diners had recovered their composure, they put me right.

At Club Med, we became prisoners of rumour. Algeria resented Morocco marching into its back yard, and tales circulated of anti-aircraft guns around the palace, which was disconcertingly close. It was also uncertain how Spain would react; Franco might be in a coma, but his Foreign Legion were dug in over the border. There was even a rumour that Idi Amin was sending a 'suicide battalion'; I facetiously wired to London that it was thought to have achieved its objective. I also filed – over an aged French language telex keyboard after a couple of Pernods – a rumour that UN general secretary Kurt Waldheim's plane had arrived, but with only the pilot aboard; fortuitously it crossed an urgent message asking if Waldheim was there. Yet as so often on foreign stories, the wait was the worst part. The only journalistic casualty was the *Sun*'s Jon Akass, who slipped in his bathroom and broke his leg.

We moved on at short notice, by Hercules to Tan Tan, then by bus 200 miles to the border settlement of Tarfaya, through swirling murk past stragglers from the march. As we passed Cape Bojador, reckoned by ancients the end of the earth, visibility eased to reveal the skeletons of ships that had cut the corner too fine. It was hard to believe the Canary Islands were just over the horizon.

Tarfaya truly was the end of the road: windblasted buildings, a mosque, a brothel and a post office in whose courtyard we were billeted in marquees and each issued with loaves, bottled water, sardines and a can opener; the French hack who broke mine got an earful. My tent and its occupants narrowly escaped incineration when Portuguese journalists involved in the revolution there showed their Spanish counterparts how to make a Molotov cocktail. One morning we were driven into the desert to meet the marchers. In those parts the Sahara isn't the undulating sea of sand you see in war films, but stony and almost flat with the occasional outcrop of scrub. We were delivered to a tent – one of thousands - where a housewife from Casablanca introduced her family and poured us sweet, minty tea which we accepted with the traditional thanks of "choukron".

Getting the marchers to the border and meeting their needs was a logistical triumph for the Moroccan army. The sandstorm had been an ordeal for those without adequate clothing or water, and the desert night was chilly. Troops in civvies were kept busy handing out blankets, and rations much the same as ours. One question was answered later when I hitched a lift back to civilisation with the march's civilian medical superintendent. Out of all the 300,000 people camped out in the desert, statistically there must have been some deaths, I suggested. "No", came the reply. "If anyone gets sick we fly them out. If they're malnourished, we take them in and give them a square meal." But he conceded there had been deaths ... from drowning. "Many of these people come from the interior and have never seen the sea. They just walk into the water and keep going. We have snatch squads along the shore, but on seven occasions they have been too late."

Roused from our tents, we were bused ten miles south to the border. Ahead lay undulating, stony nothingness, though we understood Spanish legionnaires were dug in a mile ahead and there was a fence of sorts in between. Then the marchers arrived, in huge squares like an ancient military formation. Unusually for the Islamic world, there were almost as many women as men; this was a community effort, not the testosterone-fuelled upheaval one so often sees. The signal was given to advance into "our Sahara"; the throng raised green flags on sticks and most brandished copies of the Koran, chanting as they surged forward. They passed us, row upon row, in an unforgettable spectacle, then we were taken back to Tarfaya to file. (We were totally dependent on the Moroccans for transport; the BBC's Bob Bufton uniquely managed to drive a hire car all the way down, but it became clogged with sand.)

It filtered back that the Legion hadn't opened fire, but only a symbolic truckload of marchers was continuing to the territory's capital of El Aaiun, 50 miles beyond. I realised matters were being decided elsewhere, so hitched that lift back from Tarfaya with the medical superintendent, who was bound for the hospital at Goulimine, a walled oasis where the desert gives way to the mountains. He kindly lent me his driver to get back to Marrakech.

There was apparently diplomatic deadlock, so I wrote a gloomy piece comparing the end of the March – whose participants were now being ferried home – with the Retreat from Moscow. Within hours, I heard that a deal with Spain to hand over the territory had been struck and King Hassan had pulled off a triumph. I started writing a fairer assessment, only for Ricky Marsh, my foreign editor, to call: nothing I wrote would get in the paper as Australia's governor-general had fired Gough Whitlam. I flew home.

Morocco has kept the Spanish Sahara – all of it since Mauritania pulled out - and its extensive phosphate deposits - but the territory remains disputed. Resistance by Algerian-backed Polisario Front guerrillas led Morocco to build fortifications protecting the mines and the road to El Aaiun, and there have been repeated UN efforts to stage a plebiscite. There are arguments over who the inhabitants actually are; in 1975 the indigenous population was put at 76,000, and while many of these fled to camps in Algeria Moroccan civilians moved in; El Aaiun alone now has a population of almost 200,000. It is not clear how many "Saharwis" were born there and how many are from Algeria; advocates of an independent Western Sahara have clammed up when I asked where they were born.

I was not long back from Washington – the removal van was outside – when Africa (or rather the Foreign Desk) called again. Jim Callaghan had flown to Kano, in northern Nigeria, for talks on Rhodesia with Zambia's president Kenneth Kaunda. He had taken only one reporter with him – from the Press Association - but the *Telegraph* would not be denied and I was leaving Gatwick in three hours. By then I had not only to make it from Shortlands to the airport, but get my jabs and a visa. I called a minicab, hurriedly packed and set off, first stop Nigeria's visa office in Fleet Street. Thanks to a crunch with a taxi on the way, I got there to find it had just closed ... at noon. More scared of my office than of the Nigerians, I got my jabs at Victoria, then jumped on a train to Gatwick. I hurtled through the terminal and reached the gate as the steps were being pulled away from the plane ... but was allowed on.
I had no idea how I would get into Nigeria, but the man in the next seat turned out to be Costain's fixer there. He took me to the head of the airport police, who told me – as an armed officer kept me covered – that he could give me transit papers for the duration of Callaghan's visit; I volunteered £150 (almost all the cash I had) and left the room with a warning that if I mentioned the conversation, those papers would turn out to be void.
I located David Healy, the PA reporter who had travelled out with Callaghan, and over a drink – the start of a long friendship – he told me he owed his presence to having worked in Zambia. David took me to the bungalow where Callaghan's press secretary Tom

McCaffrey was staying. Having joined the Lobby days before with Parliament in recess, I had never met Tom; moreover he had not wanted other reporters there. Nevertheless he greeted me courteously, and introduced me to Callaghan during a break in the talks.

Kano reminded me of Marrakech - a great Islamic city influenced by proximity to the Sahara - but its people were obviously African. The architecture, both of the old city and its colonial surrounds, was less grand, but there was that same strange mixture of bustle and slowness of life. Sadly no Western leader could go there today because of Boko Haram.

I headed for the British Council offices, where I chanced upon the High Commissioner. He alerted me that the Nigerian military had just announced a return to civilian government, enabling me to file a well-informed story. Then, all too soon, we moved on for Callaghan and Kaunda to meet President Obasanjo.

The hop to Lagos was my first experience of the ageing RAF VC10s in which prime ministers travelled for a generation. The VIP quarters were well-appointed, the stewardesses were charming but firm and offered a superior label of Johnnie Walker – but this was still a plane used more often for trooping flights to Hong Kong, Belize and the training grounds in Canada. There was even a route map in your seat pocket, with destinations few airlines fly to. Most of the seats faced backwards, giving a better chance of survival in a crash; civil airlines won't do this for fear of alarming the passengers. In Kano, the VC10's cockpit radio was the only secure link with Downing Street.

Lagos was teeming, steamy and hopelessly disorganised. A new airport terminal was tantalisingly close to completion, so we had to use its rickety predecessor. When I needed the Gents, I was directed to a row of squalid cubicles. Outside was a small boy; once I had paid him enough, he vaulted over the door and unlocked it from the inside. If you needed paper you had to pass another banknote under the door, and you tipped the boy again on leaving. I was relieved when the brief media statement was over and we were back on the plane for London. Tom McCaffrey came through to see David and myself; Callaghan and his Foreign Secretary David Owen stayed working up front.

In 1985 – the summer of Live Aid - I finally got to part of Africa that had been on my syllabus. Neil Kinnock was using his first visit there to see the devastation of famine in Ethiopia, and revive Labour's links with the parties that had won independence in Kenya and Tanzania. I went along, with Julia Langdon of the *Daily Mirror*, Martin Kettle from the *Guardian* and the photographer Andrew Wiard; Battersea-based Yusuf Hassan Abdi, representing the Islamic magazine *Africa Events*, joined us along the way. Yusuf, later a key UN official and a Kenyan MP, knew everybody, was related to most of them through his large and scattered Somali family, and had a nose for the big story. Accompanying Neil and Glenys were Patricia Hewitt and Neil's Africa expert Chris Child.

We stopped off in Rome to receive a soporific presentation from the UN's World Food Programme while a waiter with epaulettes took orders for tea or coffee; it was light years away from Ethiopians' battle for survival.

Arriving in Addis Ababa deprivation seemed far off; while you were expected to eat the chapati-like tablecloth after dining off it, this was not from desperation but local custom. Addis was tense under the grip of the Dergue – the unpleasant Marxist dictatorship that had overthrown Haile Selaisse – but the only sign of famine was the presence of aid workers in the capital for (restrained) R&R, and of British and Polish airmen to deliver emergency supplies. (A far larger Soviet garrison was there for other reasons).

Addis is 8,000ft up, and its atmosphere thin. The Embassy compound spans a long grassy slope, and the climb to the Residence required at least one pause for breath; I marvelled all the more at Ethiopia's great marathon runners. The Embassy was a useful meeting place with aid workers; the Kinnocks stayed there, and Glenys proved a consummate diplomat, not batting an eyelid when the Ambassador called her Gladys.

Neil flew out to the epicentre of the famine on an RAF Hercules which was dropping supplies - it would have taken days to drive there. Glenys's suspicion that he would find something dangerous to do was borne out when we reached the drop zone. Down went the ramp at the rear and in a trice Neil was hanging out, attached by the thinnest of safety lines, while the rest of us backed away. The zone was marked by a Polish helicopter, so a couple of pineapples were dropped for the Poles' lunch. Then out went the supplies on pallets, parachute-dropped with care as there were too many stories from disaster areas of people killed by high-velocity relief parcels. The drop was well away from the camps and there were no signs of privation on the ground, but we were assured that everything would go.

The Poles we dropped the pineapples for were not their country's original contingent. In a football tournament for the visiting forces the British had beaten the Poles, then lost to the Russians. The Poles rooted for us, and were sent home. Before they left, our RAF contingent invited them for a drink. They arrived with a drum of vodka, a gallon of orange juice and a plastic container. They poured in some juice, then began adding vodka, tapping the container with a fork. When it stopped going "thunk" and went "ping", they pronounced it ready to drink. Next morning the flight sergeant woke with a splitting headache to find all his men comatose; he carried them downstairs, tossed them into a truck and drove them back to base.

It was this visit to Africa that made Glenys a champion of the Third World - a role she would fill with distinction in the European Parliament. She began in a village outside Addis, meeting local women to hear about their lives - and telling me with a grin how the walls of one mud hut were papered with pages from the *Sunday Telegraph*. Weeks later, combing through Milton Obote's hastily abandoned residence in Kampala, I found drawers lined with that same newspaper.

Our next stop was Dar Es Salaam, for Neil to meet Tanzania's rulers and pay homage to ex-President Julius Nyerere, the father of African Socialism. Under his rule Tanzania, blessedly free of tribalism (apart from the red-clad Masai who were respectfully left alone), had developed reliable public services and a system under

324

which everyone had just enough. His government had also nationalised property, and driving north beside Dar's tempting but shark-infested beaches we passed magnificent 1930s houses, deserted because no-one in authority could work out what to do with them.

Nyerere was living in semi-retirement - with greater influence on government after leaving office than Nelson Mandela - in a large but unshowy bungalow a little back from the ocean. His garden was a riot of colour, with dazzling and gigantic butterflies. Neil took me in and introduced me; Nyerere came across as having a Gandhi-like moral force, but less of a smile.

The Kinnocks stayed at the former Government House, and the press at the 1970s Kilimanjaro Hotel. By the pool were a team of advisors from Sussex University; as the lights flickered and died for the umpteenth time a local told us: "They're the people who created this mess." Checking the hotel's news ticker one morning. I was greeted with "Rock Hudson reveals he has AIDS". The first signs of the HIV pandemic were a subtext for our visit but ... Rock Hudson! It seemed so improbable.

One evening the Kinnocks had us in for a drink. Neil was clearly enjoying Africa – far more than on his next visit when he was locked in a shed by over-zealous Zimbabwean security men - but inevitably the talk turned to home. Labour was licking the wounds left by the miners' strike and only just starting to ditch the far-Left policies that had brought electoral disaster two years before. Neil could see where he needed to get to, but was acutely aware of the obstacles. At one point he exclaimed: "We'd be all right if it wasn't for the f***ing party".

Next we went up country. Neil and Glenys minus the press were to visit a camp for ANC exiles; ostensibly they were meeting refugees and seeing a school, but there was almost certainly a military dimension the ANC did not want written about. While some colleagues went to see the animal wonders of the Olduvai I accompanied Neil and Glenys as far as Morogoro, buying a toy bicycle and rider made of coat hangers in its market, then overnighted at the "New Savoy Hotel". Patricia Hewitt and a police lieutenant were my companions; after my return to England the policeman wrote asking for a job.

We arrived back in Dar to find Yusuf with his tail up. There had been rumours of unrest in Uganda, and in the hotel Yusuf bumped into Obote's foreign minister, who had come to seek help from the government that five years earlier had sent troops to help oust Idi Amin. This time the answer was "Nothing doing".

We headed north for Nairobi with drama in the air. Nairobi was a culture shock after Dar: much larger, frantic, more Westernised but surrounded by fast-growing shanty towns to cope with the surge from the overpopulated rural areas and with a hint of menace; the wealthy were putting up razor wire. But it was then still Africa's nerve centre, and the city where Westerners working throughout the continent unwound (today they make for Cape Town).

Neil was there to meet leaders of KANU, the party through which Jomo Kenyatta had led Kenya to independence. Under his successor Daniel arap Moi, Kenyatta's one-party state was increasingly out of touch and, reputedly, corrupt. Desultory meetings were scheduled with party figures before Neil headed into the arid region bordering a then-peaceful Somalia to highlight the need for development. This couldn't compete with a military coup 300 miles away, and I peeled off to cover events in Uganda.

With no contacts there, the border closed and little chance of getting through on the phone, I was thrown back on the wire services (which London had already seen), rumour (always handy), the High Commission (the calibre of our diplomats in Nairobi was lower than in Dar), Yusuf (invaluable) and my secret weapon: the BBC's monitoring station outside Nairobi. Valuable to the Foreign Office and no doubt to MI6, this small anonymous building tracked broadcasts across the region, and had its antennae directed at Uganda. Helped by my World Service connection, I was allowed to listen in provided I didn't divulge my source.

For the week following the coup, led by a little-known army officer, Tito Okello, I got most of my information from crackly broadcasts from Radio Uganda. I was able on day one to piece together a reasonable account of what had happened, who was involved –

soldiers from the northern Achole tribe - and what it meant; from elsewhere I learned that they had driven through Kampala chanting the traditional Achole war cry of: "Balls yesterday, balls today, balls tomorrow". When the *Times* correspondent arrived hot-foot from London, he told me the quote had made his day.

Waiting to get into Uganda, I made the most of Nairobi. It wasn't tourist weather; a cold snap led to squadrons of locusts dropping dead outside the Press Club. I called Sam Kiarie, my Washington neighbour who was now with Kenya's immigration service (how senior he was I would soon discover), and caught up with his family over a Chinese. Another evening the Kinnock hacks went out for a curry, our ranks swelled by the larger–than-life Keith Graves, the BBC's Middle East correspondent.

Recently in Beirut, Keith had gone to see *Rambo* in a cinema full of mujaheddin. After watching the film in a battered auditorium surrounded by hyped-up foes of the West nonetheless turned on by Sly Stallone in full cry, Keith got talking to the manager, who told him that on the first night the militiamen had taken their weapons in. When Stallone got going, the cinema rocked to the sound of gunfire, shattering balconies, falling masonry and the groans of cinemagoers hit by flying stonework or ricochets. After that, they had to leave their Kalashnikovs outside. I filed the story to our diary column without naming my source; back in Fleet Street I found it pinned to the noticeboard as "the archetypal Peterborough".

Over a beer I got talking to a game warden who turned out to have previously been a Marine protecting the US Embassy in the Ivory Coast. He had been returning to Abidjan from leave by the ocean when, ahead of his train, a lorry broke down on a level crossing. Instead of removing it, the locals erected an impromptu grandstand and waited to see what happened. The packed train hit the lorry at speed; several passengers were killed and the Marine sustained multiple injuries, having to quit the service. He had always been fascinated by African wildlife, reckoned Kenya's game service the most professional and was coming to see the crash as a blessing in disguise.

After a few days, word came that a border crossing was being temporarily reopened to let foreigners leave Uganda. We flew up to a nearby airstrip, took a minibus to the border post and waited. Before long, two or three buses discharged a bewildered group of Europeans carrying suitcases, and citizens of other African countries with bags and bundles. The Anglophones ranged from florid salesmen in their fifties and their despairing but capable wives to a stunning Welsh nurse who had gone to windsurf on Lake Victoria; they told of shots late at night and the occasional body in the road. Some had been confined to the colonial Speke Hotel in Kampala, with plenty of heavy Belgian beer from Rwanda and – one enterprisingly discovered – cannabis plants in the garden; their memories were a little hazy. One expat from British American Tobacco had already had to quit Liberia twice with his family. When, dictating my story, I used the phrase "old coup hands", the copytaker interrupted: "You mean as in

    'I'm an old coup hand

    From the Rio Grande'?"

A week on, the border reopened. I drove up overnight with a group including Michael Buerk's cameraman the world-renowned photographer Mohammed Amin - later killed in an aircraft hijacking - for the lifting of the barrier. We saw nothing of the scenery or towns en route, and were at the mercy of "stingers" left by the police to puncture the tyres of fleeing criminals.

The Kenyan official who inspected my passport told me I could not leave the country as I didn't have permission. No-one had ever told me I needed it, and I suspected I was being shaken down. I went for broke, telling him: "I had dinner with Sam Kiarie the other night and he said I would have no problem leaving Kenya." My passport was returned with a smile, I rejoined my fretting colleagues, the barrier was raised and we set off for Kampala.

Apart from one corpse in the road, our drive was uneventful. The scenery was verdant, food growing almost unaided, and I grew used to the sight of women carrying plastic drums of water on their heads, stopped by a banana. You had to pinch yourself to realise Ethiopia's famine was not that far away.

Our first call, nearing Kampala, was at a club for expats – not a vast place with verandahs and lawns, more like a cricket pavilion. The half-dozen people there told us they had been left alone, and were surprisingly relaxed despite the gloomy honking of cranes outside, reckoning that anything unpleasant would already have happened.

Our priority was to find the leaders of the coup and persuade them to talk. We located a modern government complex, and the troops guarding it motioned us onto the lawn. With me was Brent Sadler of ITN (later CNN), fresh from the embarrassment of having jammed the network's switchboard after inadvertently saying "Oh, shit!" on air (he had recorded a retake, but the studio played the original). Brent set up his crew and nipped off for a pee, and within moments a burly, smiling middle-aged officer arrived with a fairly relaxed group of aides; clearly any resistance had been short-lived. I used the old photographer's trick of asking him to write down his name so we could confirm the spelling, and back it came: Bazilio Okello, Tito's brother. We had hit the jackpot. He wasn't going to hang around, so I did Brent's interview myself; it was broadcast with my questions edited out, which was fair enough.

A handful of British hacks joined us in Kampala, plus the highly professional Sheila Rule, from the *New York Times*. Sheila managed to organise a birthday festivity for me in the Speke when the only commodities available were chicken, Nile perch and beer. I felt deeply ashamed when, a couple of years later, she was posted to London only to be turned back by immigration officials for no other apparent reason than that she was black.

Gradually our number grew. Andrew Wiard was a welcome addition, less so Jasper, a tall South African in his late twenties who reminded me of Victorian pictures of Christ, and had an arrogant naïvety amounting to a death wish. Edgy soldiers were billeted at the Speke, and Jasper upset one so much that he took off his safety-catch; it took great courage and diplomacy by Andrew to avert bloodshed. One night I did awake to troops firing outward from my balcony; I stayed rigidly in bed.

The Speke soon palled, so a few of us decided to break out to the next hotel for dinner, despite an imminent curfew. We ate –

chicken or Nile perch again – to the accompaniment of Kenny Rogers' *Coward of the County*, then set out for the Speke, one block away across a broad avenue. We had got halfway when a machine gun opened up, apparently at me - the only time I've been shot at in my life. Adrenalin was pumping as we tumbled into the foyer, where my colleagues cursed me for having gone curfew-busting in a white T-shirt that made us all sitting ducks.

Unless there was something particular to see, like Obote's looted mansion, I worked from the Speke, filing over the phone. I nosed around the city centre, which must have looked impressive at independence two decades before; the fine public buildings were still there but the streets had cracked up. I called at the British High Commission for a briefing, and checked out the deserted station, with a machine from colonial days offering platform tickets for two old pence. I never went to the central post office to telex; only on my return did I learn that a heap of herograms from Peter Eastwood and Ricky Marsh were waiting there.

Britain had governed Uganda through what it took to be the local hierarchy: the predominant (near Kampala) Baganda tribe, the Kabaka (or King) and his first minister. The problem was that by recognising the Kabaka, we ossified a system that was changing, and disrespected the other tribes. Since independence the Baganda have hardly had a look-in, and I was warned that a visit to their royal compound would be viewed as tactless if not subversive.

There were rumours that some of Obote's forces were holding out in the north of the country, and a BBC crew and I decided to see for ourselves. We drove to Entebbe airport, once a refuelling post en route to South Africa but with its modern terminal almost deserted and still scarred from the Israeli commando raid a few years before. There a pilot – the double of Noel Edmonds – agreed to fly us.

Lira and Gulu, some 300 miles north of Kampala en route to the Sudan, have since suffered at the hands of the Lord's Resistance Army, which kidnapped children to train as soldiers. But as we circled over the airstrip at Lira we hoped to find a town newly liberated and at peace. Anti-aircraft guns were trained at us, but the pilot went in anyway and luckily the troops held their fire. In

Lira we found a bank looted by Obote's departing troops, with only a few coins (a rare sight in an inflation-ravaged country) left behind. Firing squads had left blood on walls, but life was returning to normal and people were happy to talk.

Gulu's lengthy runway had been a wartime staging post (the game show host Hughie Greene told me he had called there delivering bombers from Canada to the Soviet Union), but visitors were now rare. Nearby we found a game lodge from which wardens and tourists had fled, leaving the animals at risk from poachers and marauding guerrillas.

We got back to Entebbe at dusk, thanked a relieved Noel Edmonds and booked into what had been the airport's VIP suite. Barely had I hunkered down than Brent was banging on my door; his bed was alive with cockroaches, so he ended up sharing mine. Driving back to Kampala we called at the Lake Victoria Hotel. whose last guests had fled after finding bodies in the pool. We paused only for more Nile perch (tasty the first few times) washed down with beer.

The story ran out of steam, I went back to Nairobi - and before heading home, arranged a quick safari with colleagues in the Masai Mara. Beforehand we dined at the Carnivore, a restaurant fabled not for the quality of its menu but the quantity. Given a bottle of red wine, a baked potato and a salad, you start with a rasher of bacon, a sausage and a chop then work your way up through the animal kingdom. Steak, buffalo and antelope came next, and eventually you hit the Big Five - though the wine was so poor you wouldn't remember the last few. A few years later, that renowned trencherman Mike Gatting took an MCC touring team to the Carnivore. Next day the cricketers searched in vain for wildlife, until one exclaimed: "Gatt's eaten it."

We were nursing hangovers when our aged DC3 touched down at an airstrip in the Rift Valley and we scrambled into an open 4x4 with roll-bars. The scenery was magical, but my eyes were playing tricks; I thought I saw an elephant's head and tusks in the long grass, but it turned out to be an ostrich incubating her eggs. In a short equatorial day we saw elephants, giraffes, zebras, cheetahs, lions and the inevitable herd of wildebeest waiting to be eaten ...

everything bar rhinos which, given their ferocity, I didn't mind (buffalo are actually more dangerous). We got closest to a sleeping cheetah and surprisingly near to the lions, but my abiding memories were the grace of the giraffes, and the zebras standing around lacking the imagination to be a horse.

I have been on two safaris since: to Chaminuka during my 2000 visit to Zambia, and South Africa's Welgevonden eight years later. There we got to see white rhino at close quarters, had a lion stare us down with his rich yellow eyes from four yards as we sat in the lodge's shaded Land Rover, saw and heard lions stalking buffalo at night, and watched an angry young elephant trumpeting through the bush as his family scattered. We watched baby warthogs frolic by the lodge, sticking close to the zebras who would be first to hear a lion, and, when we disturbed an owl eating a cricket, watched transfixed as the three legs it left behind continued to move.

In 1992 I travelled with John Major to the 50th anniversary of El Alamein. Flying into Cairo late at night, we woke to the sounds of the most teeming city I have experienced. The Museum of Egyptian Antiquities opened early for the visiting PM, and we were shown Tutankhamen's spectacular golden sarcophagus and the mummified Rameses II, preserved for 33 centuries and looking uncannily like Gandhi.

I never saw the Pyramids, though our motorcade passed frustratingly close. Instead we were whisked to the palace at Heliopolis where Major met President Mubarak while we waited in a lavish tiled anteroom, then to the British Residence, a survival from a more graceful age. There, John gave the Lobby an informal half-hour on the verandah.

I imagined Alexandria as an Egyptian Nice with the odd classical survival on the seafront, and smart hotels like the one in *Ice Cold in Alex*. Instead our bus from the air base passed shanty towns humming with rubbish in the heat, and when we there it was clear Alexandria had seen much better days. Save for a charming British consulate where Major and Malcolm Rifkind met veterans of the battle and I interviewed heroic but modest Scots for the *Daily*

Record, I saw nothing to counter the aura of fading scruffiness - certainly not my hotel where the room rate of £8 seemed about right.

Next morning we drove west into the Sahara. Compared to Morocco, 17 years before and nearly 2,000 miles away, it was rockier, with patches of sand and much less scrub. The townscape soon ended, and we drove for about 90 minutes (a disconcertingly short time given Rommel's intentions) to the war cemetery not far from the sea, close to where Monty began the fightback.

Alamein was immensely moving. Veterans and serving soldiers were there from all over the Commonwealth, the Aussies in their slouch hats, and the lament *Flowers of the Forest* evoking the bravery of the pipers who had led the Scots into battle across minefields through withering fire.

Eighteen months later I persuaded my editor, Endell Laird, that Scotland's biggest-selling daily should cover South Africa's first multi-racial election. Toward the end of my time at the *Telegraph* Nigel Wade had offered me Johannesburg; I would love to have gone, but John's development was at a difficult stage. However I had a window on apartheid's disintegration through Bill Deedes, whose contacts in the National Party realised the game was up despite Mrs Thatcher holding out against meaningful sanctions.

It took statesmanship on both sides to create a new South Africa, and on Nelson Mandela's part – and those of the ANC colleagues imprisoned with him for so long – magnanimity from which came greatness. As the election loomed, there was no guarantee the path would be smooth. The racist extreme Right were threatening violence, and there were fears that passions might boil over in the townships. At the *Record*'s expense I acquired a flak jacket; it was hot and heavy and I never needed it. But as my taxi drove in from Johannesburg airport I feared I might; a bomb went off outside my hotel, leading David Steel to dive under a table.

I started in central Jo'burg, where the parties – predominantly the ANC – held their briefings. I saw key players in action: Tokyo Sexwale, who became the first premier of Gauteng ... and Mandela himself, across a crowded room. I got closer to his estranged wife Winnie, an icon for many despite the murder of the teenager Stompie Moeketsi at her home three years before. I sat in the front row as she gave a small press conference on housing, then gave one of her minders change for a payphone; I did not expect it back. Winnie was under strict orders to behave, and I did not detect any of the magnetism or passion that had kept her so close to the top.

Soweto was a magnet for me, but I struggled to find it on the map. For white South Africa this concentration of 800,000 people close to Johannesburg didn't exist, save as a source of cheap labour which had to be home by nightfall and as a looming threat. I took my flak jacket, but as I left the motorway and drove between rows of small, neat bungalows Soweto was decidedly calm. It was midday and most people were out; those I met were friendly, and happy to talk politics. They couldn't wait to vote, not just because most wanted the ANC in power but because they were finally being treated as equals in their own country. One directed me to Mandela's former home; it was neat, with one carefully tended tree in its tiny garden … as unassuming as the man himself.

In Johannesburg I caught up with Bronwen Jones, who seven years before had persuaded me to contribute to her Channel Tunnel book. Emigrating to South Africa, Bronwen had founded the charity Children of Fire to tackle one of the country's great ills: the terrible burns caused to children in tiny, crowded homes by overturned paraffin stoves. Through sheer persistence, she built up a network of experts and volunteers to care for the most severely-burned children, taking several into her home alongside her son Tristan, and eventually adopting two of them and bringing them to Britain. Bronwen - awarded a BEM on the recommendation of our High Commission in Pretoria - is difficult to say no to; when a special adviser, it took all my willpower to stop her hijacking me to drive her round schools where she was speaking.

By my return in 2008 she had helped dozens of young burns victims, including a refugee boy from Chad (local Islamists accused her of trying to convert him to Christianity) and an Estonian lap dancer abandoned by her boyfriend, and was educating the younger ones at her home. I invited Bronwen to dinner, but she suggested Jeanette and I go round for a pizza – then drove us at twilight in our glad rags to the Joe Slovo squatter camp, where 8,500 people live in a space 300 yards by 100 between an affluent suburb and an old gold mine tip, in tiny corrugated iron shacks. You go in past a row of communal toilets, down a narrow track with barbed wire either side. The "streets" are part rough and stony and part second-hand carpet, a few enterprising types even managing to drive in vans. The odd drunk, apart, the atmosphere was lively rather than threatening. There were card schools at several corners, but also thriving small shops, and from the tiny homes – one defying gravity with a second storey – came the sounds of televisions and computers.

Bronwen took a sack of toys and another of maize and, firing off backchat at the locals, headed for a rendezvous with Alice, the camp's matriarch. She handed out the toys as children mobbed her, then went deep into the camp to distribute the maize before she made for her car in the gloom, asking a young lad who had failed to show up to weed her garden to escort us. I left traumatised, but with some hope; in any other country conditions like that would spark riots. Many in the camp had ambition: I saw one smart young woman, probably a receptionist, return from work and dive into one of the camp's smallest hovels. Six years later most of it would burn to the ground – and be instantly rebuilt by its occupants.

By the time the polls opened on 26 April, 1994, I had rebased to the opulent, liberal suburb of Sandton. City centre muggings were a factor, but the count was at a trade centre out of town and the magnificent Sandton Sun was closer. Sandton boasts a fine shopping mall, with a cineplex where I saw *Schindler's List* with Mark Dowdney, the *Mirror*'s foreign editor. What heartstrings could Steven Spielberg have pulled had he tackled the grotesquery of apartheid?

At the Sun I found Bill Deedes – and Peter Hain, whom I'd never met despite having covered his acquittal on Pretoria-inspired bank robbery charges 18 years before. I emerged from our dinner a confirmed Hain fan, and seven years on, would work for him momentarily when he succeeded Helen Liddell at the DTI.

The Kinnocks, there as EU observers, invited me to join them touring polling stations. On the first day I drove out of Sandton past lines of designer-clad white housewives queueing to vote with maids and gardeners, then 100 miles northward to Warmbaths (a one-horse town now named Bela Bela). The town was easy to find, but not the Kinnocks. I missed them at several polling stations and returned with little to write, having acquired only some urgently-needed nail scissors.

Over three days, 19.7 million South Africans voted in an almost carnival atmosphere. I monitored events on television – something the apartheid regime resisted for years lest it corrupt or broaden Africans' minds. By 1994 SABC had two channels, and with several official languages this made election coverage complicated. Most was in English or Afrikaans, with modules in Zulu and the other main vernaculars; anyone wanting to follow the election in, say, Zulu, had to make frequent "channel shifts". SABC had done a tremendous job bringing forward vernacular broadcasters after years of all-white and predominantly Afrikaans presentation, and most of the coverage was excellent, but there was one bad moment. I was watching a Zulu reporter interviewing rural voters, some of whom had walked for miles. Their enthusiasm was so infectious I could guess what they were saying, but afterwards a white woman presenter declared: "I didn't understand a word of that, but some of our viewers must have found it really interesting," I cringed.

Then the count began. Elaborate preparations had been made at the trade centre to bring us the results, with booths provided for even the smallest parties to add their spin. But the votes weren't being counted. In Britain, huge constituencies declare in two hours because council cashiers who count money fast are brought in; South Africa used teachers, who can count but not rapidly, so a process expected to take a day at most was still unfolding ponderously after 48 hours. From the early trends, I filed a piece giving victory to the ANC and citing a joyous mood in the townships; 24 hours later I had little to add, and on day three the authorities, plainly embarrassed, took steps to speed things up.

I had booked my flight home confident that by then Mandela would have named his Cabinet; in the event I got back, switched on Ceefax ... and the full results were still not in. When they were, the ANC had 252 seats out of 400. But problems over the count could not take the gloss off a historic moment not only for South Africa, but for humanity. It was a privilege to be there.

When I returned in 2008 most of the forebodings of white South Africans had not come about, but the ANC had yet to deliver on its pledges of better housing, more jobs, and water and electricity for all. South Africa's problems were exacerbated by two million refugees from the chaos in Zimbabwe, which made all the more baffling president Thabo Mbeki's backing for the increasingly megalomaniac Robert Mugabe. The ANC lost more of its momentum and idealism under the self-enriching Jacob Zuma, but is hopefully now recovering under Cyril Ramaphosa.

In 1999 Democracy International, run by the former Conservative MP Geoff Lawler, commissioned me to fly to Lusaka, devise a programme for media-training Zambian government ministers for the British Council and then, if the programme was approved, go back and deliver it.

Since independence, Zambia had slipped back because of the falling price of copper, an exodus of white miners and the debilitating struggle next door between Ian Smith's army and guerrillas backed by Kenneth Kaunda. Yet Kaunda earned brownie points with the West when, in 1991, he submitted himself to the voters after a quarter of a century, and lost to Frederick Chiluba, members of whose government I was to train.

Lusaka had just gained its first shopping mall, complete with Subway and Game, but had otherwise moved forward little. Yet things worked, and the city had not, like so many African capitals, been swamped by shanty towns. I stayed in an agreeable hotel with endless cricket on satellite TV, and worked from the Zambian Institute of Mass Communications, based in a converted colonial house; Alastair Lack, who had produced me on the World Service 15 years before, was there advising on setting up an Archers-type radio soap. The Institute's director, Mike Daka, would have starred in any British newsroom. He had worked right across the Zambian media, knew every public figure in much of Africa (and had clashed with quite a few), had studied in Britain, the States and Russia, and was planning to set up his own radio station. Mike introduced me to the officials and politicians I needed to get on side, briefed me on the help they needed and the issues to cover and avoid - and filled me in on Zambia's situation.

Copper was in recession (it has since recovered), HIV was becoming a major problem, and some remote areas were experiencing near-famine. But above all, the balance with Zimbabwe had shifted. Traditionally Zambia was the poor relation, and visitors from Harare would patronisingly observe that Zimbabweans used coins as well as banknotes. But as Mugabe ran Zimbabwe into the ground the worm had turned, and Mike was sending food parcels to those same friends. From markets up country came tales of farmers newly arrived from Zimbabwe, and Mike's son reported from his boarding school an influx of white pupils. While many of the whites who left Zambia after independence were racists expecting privileges, those now arriving had a deep commitment to Africa. And in 2014, Zambia would be the first independent African country to have a white president, albeit briefly, in Livingstone-born Guy Scott.

The foreigners who had made the greatest impact since independence were the Chinese who constructed the Tan-Zam Railway from the Indian Ocean in just five years, opening up vast tracts of the interior and bypassing Rhodesia during UDI. Despite the temporary presence of thousands of Chinese workers, not a single local woman had given birth to a Chinese baby. (Years later I was told that Stranraer's maternity unit is routinely on alert nine months after a NATO exercise in the area).

I flew home after a fortnight, submitted my proposal and a year later returned to conduct the course. This proved harder: the dates I'd been given did not suit the politicians, and some got cold feet. It took intervention from the British High Commissioner, heavy lobbying by Mike and myself in the Parliament building, and the persistence of Samantha Chuula, my local British Council contact who turned out to come from Ilford, to get the show on the road. Meanwhile I located some human rights activists and started training them.

The training followed my usual format. There was a Q&A on what participants hoped to achieve, followed by modules when each delivered a speech, was interviewed on the radio in the Institute's studio, was "ambushed" and, finally, gave a press conference. Throughout, the trainees (we did about 15 politicians in groups of three or four, and rather fewer activists) could comment on how their peers were doing. They avoided pitfalls my British trainees had succumbed to, such as going on television with a pencil behind their ear, but came up with their own. The Minister for Mines, questioned on the shaky future of one of the remaining copper mines, merrily volunteered that another was under threat; his colleagues put him straight. But the greatest laughter came when the Trade Minister, a Gospel preacher, was in full flight and his mobile went off.

Apart from my safari weekend at Chaminuka, my main recollection from that second visit is a shade embarrassing. To thank the British Council, I gave a talk on handling the media. I arrived to find a poster identifying me as the author of *How to Make Friends and Influence People,* a couple of hundred locals turned up and I was mortified when several produced copies of the book – which I'd never even read – for me to sign.

Even though some of the politicians only joined my course after having their arms twisted and we lost nearly a week, by the end most were performing well. So were the activists, though their agenda and needs were very different. A number had had trouble with the authorities despite Zambia's relatively liberal atmosphere, but the British Council invited all the trainees to receive their diplomas together. The ministers didn't all know we'd been training their critics, and there was an awkward moment when a couple saw who else we were working with. But over drinks after the certificates were handed out, some struck up conversations.

Within a couple of years, Chiluba was out of office and the politicians I had trained were in opposition. But I retain a soft spot for Zambia, the most congenial country I've visited in Africa. My final recollection is of the magnificent sunset as I waited for my plane home – visible only from one of the cubicles of the airport Gents. Typical of how Africa hides its light under a bushel.

20: Eastern Approaches

When I was seven, my father went to Russia on a medical delegation, Britain's first in the thaw after the death of Stalin. He returned respecting the doctors and scientists he met, but unimpressed by the Soviet system. He brought me a game where you fished for wooden mushrooms, two tiny chocolate biscuits and some floppy postcards in washed-out colour - after my "show and tell" at school my teacher complained that I was preaching Communism.

The visit left Dad with a working knowledge of Russian, with which two years later he surprised the crew of a Soviet coaster at Sligo. He also gained correspondents including the dissident Zhores Medvedev; when the Kremlin crushed the "Prague Spring" of 1968 Medvedev wrote him that "our car has taken an unexpected turn". At conferences he met Czech and Hungarian scientists who were freer to travel and less scared of the State; but the Hungarian he liked most was the Swiss-based octogenarian Fritz Verzar, who had been a medic with Emperor Franz Josef's army.

Dad's reaction to Brezhnev's crushing of the Czechs was to protest in Trafalgar Square, starting a chant of "Dubcek – Svoboda!" after attempts to chant "Czechoslovakia" failed dismally. With several friends (including a couple from Militant who saw the Soviet action as Stalinism at its worst) I milled around outside the forbidding Czech Embassy in Notting Hill. In the pub we got talking to a baffled gay travel agent from Adelaide who came back with us for dinner, presenting a huge bunch of flowers to my mother.

My first experience of a Communist country was a Yugoslav holiday in 1973. The hotel at Rabac on the Croatian coast exuded uniformity rather than plenty, and nearby a (closed) coal mine bore the name "Tito" and the hammer and sickle over the gates. But Yugoslavia was unquestionably independent from Moscow, and I felt less oppression than on my only visit to Franco's Spain. Most Yugoslavs defined their nationhood by the heroic resistance of Tito's partisans to Nazi occupation, recalled by the charred entrance to the magnificent caves at Postojna, where the Wehrmacht stored their arsenal until the Partisans found a way in and blew it up.

Soon after, I discovered Fitzroy Maclean's *Eastern Approaches,* perhaps the best book ever written by a man of action. Maclean, then a Conservative MP, tells hilariously yet movingly of his experiences as a junior diplomat in Moscow during Stalin's show trials, a member of the Long Range Desert group, forerunner of the SAS, and Churchill's personal emissary to Tito, fighting alongside the Partisans. A friend met Maclean at his hotel in Argyll not long before he died, and asked if he felt his exploits had been in vain given the carnage when Yugoslavia fell apart. Maclean replied: "My time in Yugoslavia taught me two things: they are the warmest and most hospitable people in the world – and every fifty years they are seized with an overwhelming desire to kill each other."

My favourite tale of that troubled region came from the *Telegraph*'s Bob Oxby, who accompanied Brian Clough on his teams' travels in Europe. Before an away match they would wander round the city, Bob filling in Clough on great events that had happened there. In Sarajevo Cloughie spotted a pair of footprints in the pavement; Bob explained that this was where the First World War started, with the Bosnian Serb Gavril Princip shooting Austria's Archduke Franz Ferdinand. Clough pondered, then said: "Eee, if I'd just shot an archduke I wouldn't stand around with my feet in wet cement."

Months after Yugoslavia I had my first experience of the Soviet Union, accompanying Sheffield's civic delegation to its twin city of Donetsk, in ethnically Russian and then peaceful eastern Ukraine. The party consisted of the Conservative Lord Mayor Ken Arnold, the Labour Housing Committee chairman Harold Lambert and the town clerk Denis Harrison.

Nothing was too much trouble for our hosts, who were immensely proud of their city. We toured a steelworks – founded by a Welshman before the Revolution – and a coal mine; the pithead facilities were less basic than in Yorkshire but conditions below ground were worse. We were taken to a circus to see bears playing ice hockey, and visited a brewery after expressing the wish to during a boozy lunch punctuated by the toast: "Sovietsky-Britanski druzhba!" ("Soviet-British friendship!"). The dinners went that way too – one night we carried on without the interpreter, though none of us had a word of Russian and our hosts spoke no English. They didn't want to discuss politics, and when Ken Arnold tried to explain Northern Ireland they cut him short, saying it was none of their business. We were kept on a tight schedule, and at one point Arnold, not the easiest of men, rebuked me after I was bundled into a car ahead of him.

The broad streets and the powerful lighting – not doubt for security - impressed, as did the contrast between the professionalism of the doctors in a hospital we visited and the shabby parts we stumbled upon. But my sharpest memory of Donetsk registered after getting my photographs back: in a panoramic shot from my hotel window was a KGB man with a motorcycle combination, watching me through binoculars. I was told in Donetsk that I must be exceptionally politically reliable to be allowed abroad at 26; the only effort to compromise me was when our interpreter half-heartedly asked me to take an icon out of the country.

After three days in Donetsk, we flew to Moscow. We stayed in the Ukraina Hotel, one of the towering wedding-cake structures erected around the city under Stalin, whose grotesque majesty contrasted with the paucity of the cuisine. Every corridor had a *babushka* keeping watch on the guests while outside, beefy women swept the streets as the first frosts bit the Moscow air. We toured the Kremlin, its armoury, its churches and its collection of Fabergé eggs, and saw the Blue Period Picassos in the Pushkin Museum. We stood in wonderment in Red Square and were taken to see the giant tank traps marking the German front line, disconcertingly close to central Moscow. Today, those tank traps rub shoulders with a giant IKEA, founded by one of Hitler's Swedish supporters.

The town clerk and I pressed our hosts to get us into something musical, and they delivered in style. First came *Carmen* at the Bolshoi, with colour, verve and attack; the Bolshoi's trump card was to use its corps de ballet for the dancing and even our non-music lovers were thrilled. Next they took us to the Kremlin's massive Palace of Congresses, the 1960s glass and concrete edifice which is one of the Soviet Communist Party's happier legacies. We arrived without programmes, and it was well into the concert before we realised it was Khachaturian's 70th birthday tribute, with the great man conducting. There was music from his ballet *Spartacus* (the theme from *The Onedin Line),* and a piece played by dozens of voile-clad female harpists, each on a little rostrum projecting from the wall which normally sported a giant portrait of Lenin. At the end, the composer received a tumultuous ovation.

While we were in Moscow, the 1973 Yom Kippur War broke out. One of our Intourist guides told us the Zionists had launched an unprovoked attack on their neighbours, another more shrewdly and riskily that Moscow Radio was saying the Israelis had started it, but as the Egyptians were going flat out across Sinai this seemed unlikely.

Months later, Donetsk's civic leaders came to Sheffield. They were welcomed warmly, but less lavishly than we had been. Their visit coincided with the miners' strike and three-day week, with steelworks operating part-time, dimmed lights and less public entertainment than usual. There was no football in Sheffield that weekend, so they went to watch Leeds. Their visit did, however, lead to Sheffield United entertaining Dynamo Kiev; nowadays Shaktyor ("Miners") Donetsk is a force in Europe despite that city's beleaguered state.

There were awkward pauses when our visitors, accompanied by minders from the Soviet Embassy, met councillors who were striking miners, and when they were shown in the library at Rowlinson school – where Deborah taught - a montage of books on Russia including a photograph of Trotsky. Their leader tactfully observed: "Yes, we too are taught how he betrayed his country." While English was widely taught in Donetsk's schools (next to a shrine known as "Lenin's Room"), just one Sheffield comprehensive offered Russian. Our visitors weren't taken there; one of its old boys had recently been arrested by the KGB.

In 1975 I experienced the Iron Curtain itself, on a West German government press trip to West Berlin. We drove in through the communist East along a poorly surfaced autobahn, with hoardings bleakly advertising monolithic State-owned companies and road signs inferring that "Berlin-Hauptstadt der DDR" was the main destination rather than "Berlin-West", where almost all the traffic was heading. Once through the border checkpoints we could see the Curtain – a pair of high wire fences, separated by what we assumed was a minefield, watch towers, and a dynamited railway viaduct. We felt uneasy driving east, and relief arriving in West Berlin (although the city effectively contained two million hostages). We decided to take the U-Bahn to East Berlin and nose around. The journey was eerie, passing non-stop through stations with armed police on the platforms. At street level we came from a vibrant modern city (heavily subsidised from Bonn) to something limping, damaged and artificial. Partly because East Berlin's focus had moved away from the former city centre close to the Wall – which we could only get close to from the Western side - there was a spooky aura of dereliction, accentuated by the Communists having deliberately left several majestic buildings in ruins.

Next day the British Army were to drive us to a briefing at our embassy in the East, over an unglamorous shoe shop close to the Brandenburg Gate. But a horrified Army press officer told us they couldn't, as we had recognised East German sovereignty over East Berlin (technically still the Soviet Zone) by having our passports stamped. "Hang on", we told her. "You are taking us to the British Embassy in East Berlin. That means you recognise it yourselves". "No," she replied. "The Embassy is our Embassy *to* East Germany, not *in* East Germany." We gave up, and went under our own steam.

The Head of Chancery briefed us in a secure room, switching on a machine making a noise like an outboard motor to make it harder for anyone to eavesdrop. On the way back, having found no souvenirs, we paused at the last, unprepossessing, shop before Checkpoint Charlie when one of our party spotted miniatures in the window. Back at the hotel our West German host collapsed with laughter; the "schnapps" was anti-flatulence mixture.

From West Berlin, we took a train to Hamburg. Having bisected the Wall, we were passing through a historic but dingy Potsdam when two West German border guards began struggling in the corridor with a strange-looking woman. I wondered what sad human story was being interrupted.

It would be 20 years before I returned to a reunified Berlin for a conference in a restored and modernised Reichstag, still haunted by that 1945 photograph of a Soviet soldier hoisting the Red Flag over the ruins. There was a hilarious moment when the translator referred to a "joint Franco-German force of amphibians." As I passed through Checkpoint Charlie – now a tourist attraction – I had my wallet stolen.

At Westminster I covered the repercussions of the Soviet invasion of Afghanistan, and the Kremlin's efforts – abetted by some in the West – to stop America deploying cruise missiles after it had moved its own SS20s into the European theatre. My Washington landlord Nigel Wade, now in Moscow, gave me valuable insights – also playing Good Samaritan when my mother, returning from a tour of Central Asia, was stranded in a Leningrad hospital with back trouble. Her diary made a fascinating read in the *Sunday Telegraph*.

Nigel's guidance served me well when, in December 1984, Mikhail Gorbachev – then little known in the West – came to London. Gorbachev, Mrs Thatcher said, was "a man I could do business with"; I stuck my neck out in print and described him as the next leader of the Soviet Union – as he became when Andrei Chernenko died a few months later.

The "man I could do business with" phrase was first used by Attlee about Stalin – something I suspect Mrs Thatcher didn't realise – and around this time I was given a direct insight into the personality of "Uncle Joe". One evening in the Strangers' Bar I found John Parker, Labour MP for Dagenham for half a century, reminiscing about his experiences in Moscow on a parliamentary delegation early in 1945. They were briefed on Soviet war aims by Molotov, the foreign minister later famed for his repeated "Niet!" at the UN. Then they were summoned to the Kremlin, and to their astonishment ushered into Stalin's office. The Soviet strongman greeted them warmly, asked what they had been told and shot Molotov a filthy look when one of the MPs let slip that their briefing had been quite candid. Mellowing again, he told them: "I am delighted to welcome representatives of our gallant allies ... particularly as I was in London once myself. It was in 1908 for a conference of exiled Socialist revolutionaries at the Kingsland Hall ... and you'll never guess who the chairman was." Lenin and Litvinov were suggested; no-one dared mention Trotsky. Then Stalin broke into a smile and announced: "No, Mussolini!"

Mussolini had indeed been a socialist then, and I did my best to check out the story. Stalin had been in London for the conference, but Mussolini was schoolmastering in northern Italy. Uncle Joe's claim had added poignancy because, only weeks after that meeting in the Kremlin, Mussolini was strung up by Communist partisans.

Around 1985, Peter Eastwood asked if I would like to take over from Nigel in Moscow. It would have been a good career move, but again John needed a lot of support, and I had heard plenty from Steve Barber about young men posted there who hit had the vodka or been compromised by the KGB.

When Conrad Black acquired the *Telegraph*, Nigel became Foreign Editor before going off to edit the *Chicago Sun-Times*. One evening he and Chris invited me and a girlfriend to dinner. We were just finishing when their Persian cat's tail brushed against a candle on a bookcase and caught light. Unaware of its blazing extremity, it jumped down, extinguishing the fire. After about twenty seconds it felt a sensation in what was left of its tail and turned round to look. Meanwhile the pungent smell of singed fur reached Chris in the kitchen. When she called out: "What the hell's that?", Nigel replied: "The cat's burst into flames", and she was through in seconds. The cat made a full recovery.

The autumn of 1989 saw Hungary opening its border with Austria, the fall of the Berlin Wall, the "Velvet Revolution" in Prague, and the beginning of the end for Soviet Communism. That summer I took John, Carrie and her friend Lizzie to Portoroz, across the Adriatic from Venice in what is now Slovenia. There was talk of Yugoslavia's cuddliest region, with close ties to Austria, securing nationhood, yet nobody in their wildest nightmares conceived a chain reaction in which the rest of Yugoslavia would descend into carnage - even though, since Slobodan Milosevic's assumption of power, I had been writing worried leaders about the return of Pan-Serbism and the folks who brought you the First World War. Indeed my piece on Slovenia's ambitions appeared on the travel, not the news, pages.

I was in Washington when the Berlin Wall came down, and at the *Independent on Sunday* as events accelerated with massive demonstrations in Prague, and the fall and execution of the Ceausescus. But my insights on Russia came from a different direction; Corinne Reed, whom I would marry soon after, was head of PR at McDonald's and involved in launching their first restaurant in Moscow. That event, with thousands of Russians queueing for their first experience of guaranteed food, symbolised the collapse of the old order. (At Moscow airport that year, I saw a gargantuan cafeteria manageress plonk a plate of "nice beef" before a Hindu passenger and stand over him to make sure he ate it.)

My move to the *European* kept me close to the post-Communist story, given Robert Maxwell's roots in the region and his determination to cash in. I was sent to eastern Europe several times: firstly, in September 1990, on what turned out to be Mrs Thatcher's last overseas tour: to newly-free Czechoslovakia and Hungary. Our ageing VC10, nursed by a devoted RAF crew, touched down first in Prague where we stayed in a monstrous concrete Communist-era hotel, whose designers had had just enough taste not to inflict it on the city's glorious old town, where our meal of beer and sausage cost 70p. Next day at the medieval castle Mrs Thatcher met Vaclav Havel, recently freed from his toil as a janitor to become President of Czechoslovakia; Slovakia's breakaway was not yet in prospect.

Then to the modernistic Parliament building, and an unforgettable moment. Alexander Dubcek had been recalled from exile as a forestry worker when the crowds in Wenceslas Square took control. Now Speaker, he movingly praised the Prime Minister as "not the Iron Lady, but the Kind Lady." Afterwards they walked across the square to the memorial to Jan Palac, the student who burned himself to death in protest at the Soviet intervention. The Press Association's Chris Moncrieff rushed up and shook Dubcek's hand; I wish I had. Sadly, Dubcek was killed in a car crash not long after.

After a stop in Bratislava, another fine city marred by brutalist architecture, it was off to Budapest, ever since my favourite European city after Paris. Our minibus, escorted by police motorcyclists wearing capes with an enormous eagle on the back, hurtled into town at 70 mph, dodging trams coming the other way. Mrs Thatcher was to review a guard of honour outside Hungary's Parliament, a clone of the Palace of Westminster. I did a double-take at the blond, Aryan ranks in Wehrmacht-style uniforms; they must have often doubled as extras in war films. The officer drilling them did not bellow his orders, but spoke them through a lip mike; then the band broke movingly into the *Rakoczy March*.

The focus of the Budapest stop – apart from the stupendous food derived from all the goose that doesn't go into a duvet – was on Raoul Wallenberg, the Swedish diplomat who saved thousands of Hungarian Jews from death until shamefully seized by the advancing Russians. Eleven years before, I had spent a freezing week in Stockholm covering an international hearing into Wallenberg's fate, chaired by the then-unsullied Greville Janner. There had been sightings of a man who might have been Wallenberg in the gulag up to the early 1960s, and his family – including a devoted niece – clung to the hope that he might still be alive. If he were, it would have been humiliating for the Kremlin to produce Wallenberg, no doubt by then in pretty poor shape, after denying all knowledge since the end of the war. My own suspicion was that Wallenberg did not die in the notorious Lubiyanka prison *circa* 1948, but lingered on for years in prison camps, probably losing his mind before dying an unrecorded death. His heroism captured my imagination as Mrs Thatcher unveiled his statue in a country where he had been a non-person until months before.

Soon after I joined the *European*, Maxwell asked us to cover a conference in Budapest on Russia's ability to feed itself as Communism collapsed. amid fears of mass starvation. There I got talking with the middle-aged central European next to me ... discovering that Maxwell had sent him too. Tommy Lapid, who now lived in Israel and later became Minister of Justice. seemed unsure why he was there; but he had excellent contacts and told me a lot about the region since the Holocaust, which he had survived as a youngster. I came to realise Maxwell had many Tommy Lapids, several of them based on the upper floors of Maxwell House with the remit of wandering round eastern Europe handing out cash. The process worked both ways; one day Maxwell rang from Sofia to say he had sold the Bulgarians a printing press, and a minion from their embassy would be calling with a briefcase full of banknotes.

Shortly before Maxwell's demise, Ian Maxwell asked me to join him and his father for breakfast at the Meridien in Piccadilly with Anatoly Sobchak, Mayor of Leningrad (as it still was) and a coming man in post-Communist politics. I arrived to find Ian with a couple of suits from Maxwell Communications who were making a pitch to Sobchak for a Leningrad Yellow Pages (he wasn't interested). Maxwell didn't appear, but eventually Ian took a call from him and conveyed his apologies; back at the office someone suggested his much-vaunted Russian might be too rusty to be practiced in public.

My third visit to Budapest was made in style, on the inaugural run there of James Sherwood's Venice-Simplon-Orient Express. Rick Lidinsky, by then Sherwood's vice-president in Washington, had arranged for Corinne and me to travel out on the luxury train from Victoria. After the trundle to Folkestone in a classic Pullman train and a stormy crossing to Calais, we joined the beautifully restored Wagons-Lits (ours had served as a Wehrmacht field brothel) for Paris, Vienna and Budapest. The ambiance and company could not have been bettered (apart from the novelist Jeanette Winterson who was prickly throughout). Fine meals in opulent surroundings were preceded by drinks around the piano with Prince and Princess Michael of Kent – charming and nothing like the "Princess Pushy" of repute. The night aboard took us the length of Switzerland into Austria, and by the second evening we were nearing Budapest. We dined early and light, then emerged from the train in black tie and cocktail dresses ... to be faced with a huddled mass of Romanian gypsies hoping for a train west. We were swiftly ushered into the Emperor Franz Josef's waiting room for champagne and canapés.

Something dramatic – no-one quite knew what – was afoot in Yugoslavia, and I interviewed a worried Hungarian Foreign Minister, Dr Geza Jeszenszky. His concern was that the Serbs might start persecuting ethnic Hungarians in the Vojvodina, less than 100 miles to the south. In the event it would be the Bosnian Muslims who bore the brunt of Milosevic's genocidal urges.

I also reported on the opening of the first Jewish secondary school in Budapest since the war, funded by Albert Reichmann, one of the Canadian brothers who were making Canary Wharf happen. Over the phone from Toronto he gave me a moving account of why it was so important to help Hungary's Jews regain their identity and self-confidence after decades of alternating persecution and discouragement. Sadly, they are now under fire again.

That same year – 1991 – I got back to Russia, accompanying John Major on his first visit as Prime Minister. Moscow had changed little in the 18 years I'd been away, but the tectonic plates were shifting fast. Major's advisors reckoned that though Communism was on the way out, the Soviet Union would hold together and Gorbachev would complete the transformation to democracy and capitalism, so they advised him not to meet Boris Yeltsin, whom they didn't rate. Within months power passed to Yeltsin as Russia's first popularly-elected president, after he forced old-school plotters who put Gorbachev under house arrest to free him. With Yeltsin besieged by tanks in the White House parliament building, Major showed superlative political footwork in phoning to offer support, emerging from the crisis with memories of his earlier snub erased.

Major's priority on this visit was to patch up relations following the Gulf War, the Kremlin having reluctantly acquiesced in US
-led action to drive Saddam Hussein's forces out of Kuwait despite Russia's strong links with, and geopolitical interest in, Iraq. After the Falklands war a Soviet warship gave full honours to *HMS Hermes* as they passed in the Atlantic; this time the mood was different. When John returned from meeting the defence minister General Yazov, I asked him if Yazov had congratulated Britain on a job well done; his reply was a weary shake of the head.

This Moscow trip should have brought me a world exclusive. Gus O'Donnell, John's likeable press secretary who was later Cabinet secretary and head of the Civil Service, told me Major had invited Gorbachev to the next meeting of the G7 ... a breakthrough in east-west relations that had not been on anyone's radar screen. My story was blocked by my news editor, because I couldn't say whether Gorbachev had accepted; I suspected other forces at play. With hindsight I should have gone over his head, but that was something you only did once. Six months later the story – not from me - made the splash in the *Evening Standard*.

March is pretty icy in Moscow, so we travelled in thick suits and overcoats. But as we took off from there we were told we were flying to the Gulf ... by a circuitous route over Egypt because Iraq was still a war zone. Next morning we touched down at Riyadh, then were flown on to a Saudi airstrip close to Kuwait. A Royal Navy helicopter was waiting to fly the Prime Minister and a pool of hacks into Kuwait; the rest of us were to wait for them. An argument broke out on the tarmac between Sky News' Adam Boulton, who had been told there wasn't room for him, and the British commander Sir Peter de la Billière; Adam won.

We stay-behinds were ferried to a small tented camp housing a US Marines medical unit. In the Saudi heat we must have looked like aliens, but they made us most welcome. Suddenly shots rang out a hundred yards away as a Saudi sentry opened fire on a truck whose driver forgot to slow at a checkpoint. Everyone hit the deck, and we got to our feet covered in sand.

Something happened here that summed up the rapid changes then taking place in Russia, and in the superpower relationship. One of the Marines offered us haircuts – fortunately not as short as theirs – and I paid him with dollar bills I'd been given in change the day before ... by a Moscow taxi driver.

Three years later I was back in Moscow with Major. Yeltsin was now the only show in town, and the stampede to capitalism was leaving its mark. The city was more colourful, most of the giant exhortatory red banners had gone, new hotels were springing up and Western products were advertised on bus shelters (when I saw on Moscow TV the votes in a pensioners' ballot being collected in a giant Whiskas tin, I wondered about their diet). The place was full of Western businessmen out to make money in the new Russia; few would succeed. Russian politics had already gone through enough upheavals to suggest the Chinese had got it right allowing capitalism without first releasing the Party's grip; Gorbachev rashly did it the other way round.

This time I hoped to see a family friend: John Scarlett, a senior diplomat at the Embassy. I hadn't seen John since we were students, when I went to parties at his home and his sisters came to mine, but I told my mother I would look him up. I asked our embassy escort if I could see him, and got a noncommittal reply. Asking again, I received a definite brush-off. Back home, the reason for the evasions became clear. John was the MI6 station chief, and currently in a safe house because the Russians were accusing him of suborning an aircraft worker. He returned home soon after amid a diplomatic row that must have been brewing as Major met Yeltsin; the diplomats I asked if he was around must have thought I was onto the story. John, of course, went on to chair the Joint Intelligence Committee, take the heat over the "Dodgy Dossier" justifying the Iraq War, and become head of MI6.

Major went on to Nizhni-Novgorod, Russia's fourth largest city 300 miles east of Moscow where the dissident Andrei Sakharov had been kept under house arrest. Named Gorky under the Communists, it had been a closed city for 45 years, as had Sverdlovsk in the Urals which Carrie had visited on the first Western school party allowed in. When we ventured out from the city's Kremlin into the slushy streets, we found the people far less Westernised - and you needed roubles, not dollars, to buy lunch.

The flight back by chartered British Airways jet had a sting in the tail. We disembarked at Heathrow's VIP terminal, but were bused to Terminal Four for processing. Astoundingly, my luggage went missing between terminals; I went home without it, receiving an embarrassed call next day that it had turned up and would be sent over by taxi. I wondered what would have happened had a Downing Street bag suffered the same fate.

I returned to Russia in 2005, for a teach-in in Kaliningrad on relations between government and the media. Kaliningrad was formerly Konigsberg, the capital of German East Prussia, but after being flattened by the RAF and captured by the Red Army it became an enclave giving the Soviet fleet a year-round base on the Baltic. The 60-mile triangle bordered by Lithuania and Poland – which had annexed the rest of East Prussia – became part of the Russian Federation, but the Soviet workers lived in 1930s German tenements, the stately *Hauptbahnhof* with its tracks reworked to the Soviet broad gauge still dominated its square, and the cathedral, where Kant is buried, was left derelict. In the countryside, historic German churches and Teutonic castles rotted.

One participant in the seminar – in a new conference centre next to a decommissioned Soviet submarine – was the chairman of the local journalists' union. In the late 1960s, a decision had been taken to dynamite the remains of the city's medieval *Schloss* and replace it with a concrete "House of the Soviets". The young reporter got up a petition to the Supreme Soviet from local intellectuals urging the castle's restoration: he was sent to work on a refrigerator ship for ten years, and not allowed to write about politics until Communism collapsed. The House of the Soviets was half-built, then abandoned; the authorities were now hoping to clad it in less appalling materials and use it as flats or offices.

On the margins of the conference, Kaliningrad's future was under discussion. As Russia's most westerly point, the city and its hinterland – with Baltic resorts where Muscovites spend $1 million on holiday homes – could become a trading window to the West. The airport was being upgraded, an Orthodox cathedral was nearing completion and the old one had been restored, though not for worship. Some rural castles and churches were being patched up, and bids were in for EU funding to restore the medieval riverside quarter which had been bombed out of existence.

Russia was clearly committed to Kaliningrad, but not sure what to do with it. Representatives of German foundations combing the city for projects to support were telling us: "Psst! We want it back" - but that is not on, even if Russia were in less nationalistic hands than now. However a Russian Kaliningrad with European businesses allowed a foothold could benefit both sides.

The quickest way to Kaliningrad is to fly to Moscow, then catch a domestic flight halfway back again. Changing airports in Moscow, I marvelled at the colourful new cathedral built to replace one Stalin demolished to make way for a swimming pool. Exploring the back streets, I could now find things to buy. And flying out of Moscow's newest airport, I witnessed at first hand the security necessitated by continued strife in Chechnya.

Anyone flying from Moscow nowadays has to take off their belt and shoes to clear security. The process went smoothly for my BA flight to London until an extraordinary couple appeared: a man who could only have been a gangster, and his girlfriend, with legs 4ft long and laced-up boots stretching almost as far. When security staff told her to remove them, he gave them a life-endangering glare. Sadly I had to hurry for the plane; another human story whose ending I shall never know.

An e.mail from Kaliningrad soon after put the fear of God into me. My session had been a big success, so would I like to take part in a sequel in Grozny? Bearing in mind that the few Brits crazy enough to visit Chechnya had been kidnapped and murdered, I declined. Maybe my performance in Kaliningrad hadn't been that great after all.

Eleven years later, I returned to Kaliningrad, with Jeanette on one of the first cruise ships to call there. Kaliningrad was to be one of the 2018 World Cup host cities, and some new construction was under way, including rebuilding of the synagogue next to the cathedral. But otherwise very little had changed.

22: In and out of Europe

I always felt we should go into the EEC, and in 1975 and 2016 voted to stay in. I believed in a united Europe that traded freely within its borders and was a force for good in the world, but was never happy that a nucleus of bureaucrats and lawyers from the original member states kept searching for new things to regulate. I was devastated by the decision to come out - largely because I feared it would trigger Scottish independence and the end of our country as we knew it. But the way the EU has behaved towards us since we left makes me suspect Brexit was the right choice, despite the mess it has created in Northern Ireland.

During our 46 years of membership, Britain did have a voice in Europe, and in terms of sovereignty probably gained almost as much as we gave up. If we lost out, it is partly because British governments never committed themselves as wholeheartedly as the French and the Germans (not to mention the Irish) - and because Whitehall slavishly over-enforced the rules.

The politics of Europe first impacted on me in Sheffield one evening in April 1972 when I went over to the pub after a committee meeting with some councillors, among them Roy Hattersley senior. He wasn't a drinker, so something was clearly going on. That night the Commons were voting on Edward Heath's application to take Britain in; Harold Wilson had gone back on his earlier commitment to join, and Labour MPs were whipped to vote "No".

That day, Roy senior told me, he had had an agonised call from his son. Pro-Marketeers led by Roy Jenkins were going to rebel, and while Roy Hattersley shared their views, rebellion was not his style. Roy senior didn't tell me what advice he had given, but when the time came Roy joined Jenkins and 70-odd other Labour MPs in voting to go in. What happened next caused lasting rancour: Jenkins and the hard-core pro-Europeans resigned from the front bench; Hattersley didn't, and was promoted. Roy was accused of careerism and lack of principle ... but his call to his father suggested otherwise.

Wilson's volte-face on Europe was reflected in the constituencies. The Brightside party had been broadly pro, a stance arrived at in front of the cameras for a BBC documentary. But the Jenkins-led rebellion enraged the anti-Market Left just as Labour was gaining trade unionist recruits politicised by Heath's Industrial Relations Act. By 1974, the Brightside party was firmly anti-Market - one of the issues that led it to replace its MP Eddie Griffiths (who had also failed to move from North Wales) with the hard-line Marxist Joan Maynard.

Labour returned to power that year committed to renegotiating Britain's membership then holding a referendum, and staged the poll the following spring. Peter Eastwood appointed the experienced A J "Mac" McIlroy to cover the "Yes" campaign for the *Daily Telegraph,* and me to follow the "Noes".

The most memorable – and embarrassing – incident of the campaign came as it started. Returning from lunch, I found in my pigeonhole an envelope containing what seemed to be the manifestos for the two campaigns. Their release by the Government was a couple of days off, and while Mac and I reckoned we had a major leak, it was possible what we had was either not authentic or not the final version. We started gutting the manifestos for the next morning's paper and, as late in the afternoon as we felt we safely could, checked with Number 10 to ensure we had the genuine article. It turned out the manifestos were authentic, and ready for distribution: by 9 pm every paper had a set, and our story was only an exclusive in the sense that the television news said they had been released after a leak to the *Telegraph.* With hindsight we should have gone ahead, with only a late call for a government reaction.

The referendum campaign was strange. The Labour Cabinet was split down the middle. The Conservatives were officially for, but Mrs Thatcher was not over-keen – though she did launch the party's campaign - and some prominent Tories joined the "No" camp. Only the (pro-Market) Liberals were united. The "Noes" comprised the awkward squads of both main parties: Tony Benn, Arthur Scargill, Michael Foot and Peter Shore for Labour, Enoch Powell (by then an Ulster Unionist) and Neil Marten from the Tories. Foot would not appear with Powell after his "Rivers of Blood" speech, and Marten would never have shared a platform with Scargill, whose shock troops had brought down Heath's government. Most spoke solo, notably Enoch whom I heard make in one day one of the best and probably the worst political speeches I have heard, the first at a London press conference and the latter in a cavernous modern hotel suite in Birmingham.

The "Yes" camp paraded Heath, Jenkins and David Steel, while the "Noes" alternated between anti-Market Labour figures and Tories - except when Peter Shore and Marten, both old-fashioned Imperialists, formed a double act; Shore's appeal to the voters not

357

to turn their back on "British farms" in Australia and Canada was unforgettable.

Gauging the mood from old contacts in Birmingham and South Yorkshire it became clear the "Yes" side would win, not because of Europe but of Tony Benn, the radical Industry Secretary who had become a bogeyman for the Tory press; the none too subtle message from the "Yes" camp was: "Tony Benn is a loony. Tony Benn wants to come out. So we should stay in." And on 6 June 1975, Britain voted two to one to stay in the EEC.

Labour ended its boycott of the European Parliament, and I covered the first sessions at Strasbourg in which all of Britain's MEPs participated, getting used to the hemicyclical Chamber, the very different procedure and the racks of documents colour-coded by language – those in English edged in purple. There was also the culture shock of encountering Continental politicians with consensus and coalition-building in their DNA. The Parliament then had a minimal legislative role, yet enough members had issues they wanted to air or investigate for it to have a purpose. But they came from national parliaments, and the British MEPs could be pulled back at any moment for a close vote at Westminster ... a frequent occurrence as the Callaghan government lost its majority.

The first elections to the Parliament were held in June 1979, within weeks of Mrs Thatcher coming to power, with the parties even wearier than the voters. Callaghan launched Labour's campaign in what I couldn't resist calling a broken-down gym; the Tories, getting their government up and running, also had difficulty mustering enthusiasm – though they would do well - and the Liberals' commitment to Europe was offset by their exhaustion and the likelihood that they would not win a seat.

For me, the high point of a lacklustre campaign was a meeting in the St George's Hall, Bradford. Lord St Oswald, Conservative candidate for West Yorkshire, had persuaded Harold Macmillan, then 85, to come out of a long retirement to deliver one last election speech. The hall was packed and the atmosphere crackled as Macmillan, ancient but exquisitely tailored, walked slowly onstage. He had got out only one word - "Actors" – when a reporter accidentally emitted a burst of music from their tape recorder. "Supermac" paused a moment, observed: "Yes, and musicians!" - then went on.

The years rolled back as Macmillan delivered an astonishing *tour d'horizon* explaining out why he had tried to take Britain into Europe and what he hoped could be achieved. He began by recalling Queen Victoria's Diamond Jubilee – when he was two and a half – and the Great War, where he had lost many friends in the trenches. You could almost feel the tears welling up before he pressed on to recall how that war, supposed to end all wars, had been followed by a second. He recounted how France and Germany had resolved after 1945 never to fight each other again, and how first Churchill and, later, he had tried to tie Britain into that accord. Now we were in, Macmillan believed a great period of peace and common endeavour lay ahead. It would have been a formidable speech for any politician, but for a man of his age, years out of the limelight, it was staggering. Macmillan's timing, his phrasing and above all his historical sweep made it a privilege to be in Bradford that night.

Back in opposition, Labour again turned against Europe, and this time the pro-Market Right had somewhere to go: the SDP. Not all Labour's anti-Markeeters were on the Left, and not all its Europeans were tempted by a breakaway party, Roy Hattersley for one. But the defections delayed Labour's eventual reconciliation to Europe under the originally hostile Neil Kinnock and Robin Cook. As he left for the SDP Lord George-Brown, admittedly a spent force, told me he was fed up with the carping about "butter lakes and wine mountains".

Mrs Thatcher's arrival on the European scene was bound to create waves. At her very first summit Valéry Giscard d'Estaing barged past her when they reached a door; she might be a lady, but *he* was President of France. I also remember Lord Carrington telling of his return from gruelling and unproductive negotiations over Britain's share of the community budget. After a 15-minute tirade from

Maggie, Carrington interjected: "Prime Minister, could I at least have a drink?"

Although the European Parliament then rotated between Strasbourg, Brussels and Luxembourg (and still, absurdly, has two centres) it was usually Strasbourg I went to – with only two flights a day from London, at highly unsocial hours. Interest was keenest in late Spring, when the Mayor of Strasbourg laid on an open-air asparagus feast as part of his campaign to keep the Parliament from pulling out. I made new contacts, as well as meeting Westminster friends who had made the switch - among them David Harris, my old boss from the *Telegraph* - and got used to a minority of Barbara Castle's Labour group voting with the French Communists.

The MEP who made the greatest impact was Ian Paisley, even though his bull-like interruptions were boorish and counterproductive. Early on, he caused consternation by complaining that the Union Jack outside the Parliament was upside down. Having extracted the maximum amount of capital, he admitted privately that it had been the right way up, but no-one could spot the difference. It was amusing to see Paisley with his supporters in the airport lounge at Strasbourg, Paisley with an orange juice and the other Loyalists knocking it back as if there were no tomorrow.

Over 20 years, I covered European summits in Birmingham, Brussels (several), Copenhagen, Dublin, Edinburgh, Essen, the Hague, London and Rome. I also made it to G7 summits in Munich, London and Birmingham, and a security and co-operation summit in Helsinki. Months before the 1992 EC summit in Edinburgh, Foreign Office officials asked a group of us for organisational tips. We urged that as the media is cooped up for hours at such events, there should be a couple of outlets selling Scottish produce. We got there to find only a tiny newsagent's kiosk, and a great opportunity to promote Scotland – and keep the hacks happy - was lost when we were stuck all night in the Meadowbank Centre as Spain screwed more money out of the regional budget.

In Copenhagen, I upset non-British hacks by turning the media centre's televisions over to a Test match during one of the interminable periods of waiting. It was there that John Major entered his hotel to the strains of Fleetwood Mac's *Albatross*, something I couldn't resist feeding to a diary column. In Essen I spent dinner with colleagues discussing a vivid passage in *The Battle of the Bulge,* switched on in my room and was confronted with that very scene. In Munich I spent a congenial evening in a bierkeller with Alastair Campbell, still with the *Mirror* but already teetotal. And in Brussels I discovered that President Mitterrand was followed everywhere by his personal ambulance.

Shortly after leaving the *Independent on Sunday,* I had a call from David Burnside, British Airways' take-no-prisoners head of PR who would become an Ulster Unionist MP (I was one of the few hacks who had never asked him for a free flight). Robert Maxwell had just launched the *European,* and was I interested in becoming its political editor?

I was well aware of Maxwell's reputation. My father had edited *Experimental Gerontology* for him, and had tried to suggest ways of making his operation more businesslike; for years the Maxwells sent a Christmas card. I had also reviewed the ponderous autobiographies of Communist leaders Maxwell published in return for unspecified favours. A colleague, invited to at a bash at his Oxford home, found the bathroom shelves lined with bottle after bottle of salad cream: the mind boggled. And we had all heard of people in the *Mirror* building who Maxwell had fired on the spot ... discovering after paying them off that they didn't work there.

I went to see Ian Watson, editor of the new paper, whom I knew from the *Sunday Telegraph,* in Orbit House, across from the *Mirror.* The *European,* a weekly broadsheet, had already produced its launch edition and had alarming gaps in its staff, political coverage among them. He persuaded me the job would be professionally rewarding and told me the salary I should ask for, which was handsome. Ian then took me over to Maxwell House, the HQ of Maxwell Communications where Captain Bob had a top-floor suite; he was reputed to urinate on passers-by from the roof. Entering through the kitchen I couldn't help noticing the wine rack, each square holding not the usual bottle but a magnum and three bottles. In an ante-room, Betty Maxwell was awaiting her helicopter to Royal Ascot, and courtiers hovered for last-minute instructions.

Maxwell was not quite as bulky as I had expected, but still larger than life, doing his best to be amiable but with a trace of menace. He greeted me warmly, saying: "You will be our bureau chief." He wanted British political coverage with a European slant, but also for me to get the paper's coverage from Brussels up and running. Then he asked how much I wanted. When I repeated the figure Ian had mentioned, Maxwell shot back: "After what happened at the *Independent,* you should be paying us." But he agreed.

I found some familiar and reassuring faces at the *European,* but one or two key personnel manifestly over-promoted. I moved into the office of the paper's former PR lady, with numerous unreturned calls on the answering machine; equally worrying was a mountain of unread faxes in the newsroom. Providing political cover wasn't that difficult, and I was no longer hogtied by the *Independent's* boycott of official briefings. I did get over to Brussels and Strasbourg, to catch up with Leon Brittan, now a Commissioner, cover the European Parliament – filing its crucial vote on the Gulf War to the *Mirror* - and see who could be tempted to join the paper. Through no efforts of mine, we acquired one of the best EC-watchers in Rory Watson. Thereafter it was a sign of Maxwell's priorities that I spent more time in Budapest (admittedly no penance).

The gulf between Maxwell's ambitions for the *European* as a paper covering the entirety of Europe and reflecting its opinions and a London-based weekly with a small polyglot staff and a circulation struggling to exceed 200,000 was considerable. Even those figures were suspect; when in week three I bought a copy outside

Lancaster Gate station, the vendor punched the air with his fist and yelled: "I've sold one!"

Throughout my 18 months there, we had a credibility problem that an increasingly high standard of journalism did not entirely dispel. I got to value my colleagues: David Prescott, my highly competent deputy; Peter Millar, able to see anything from a Central European perspective; Askold Khruschelnycky, a chain-smoking Ukrainian traumatised by the atrocities he witnessed in disintegrating Yugoslavia; and Mike Maclay, who had arrived via the UN and *Weekend Word* and went on to be Carl Bild's spokesman in Bosnia and special adviser to Douglas Hurd. The paper was well designed and skilfully produced; here I learnt to write my story straight into the page on a Mac. But gaps remained, some filled when John Bryant, replacing Ian Watson, led an influx from the failed *Sunday Correspondent*.

Maxwell had proved with his short-lived *London Daily News* that he could come up with a brilliant idea, then implement it in a way that guaranteed disaster. At the *Mirror* he had, as one colleague put it, "stopped at alternate floors and lobbed out a hand grenade"; parts of the business were still rooted in the 1950s, others ran efficiently until he started interfering. Maxwell's newspapers were also a means to an end: the creation of a business empire spanning the Iron Curtain. And when he did take an interest in our journalism, it could be pretty unhelpful.

At the height of the Gulf crisis Maxwell appeared in the office, livid at our front page picture which showed a Saudi prince at the wheel of his Rolls, wearing a gas mask. He ranted that it demeaned war, and threatened the picture editor with the sack; we felt he was really angry because the photo demeaned Rolls-Royce ownership. Yet it's better to have a proprietor who turns up unexpected than one you never see, and Maxwell was certainly keen to be involved. He could also be quite engaging; he once formally introduced me to his press officer Andy McSmith, an old Lobby hand I had known for years.

Maxwell's habit of collecting people embraced the *European*. Notably he recruited Lionel Stoleru, economic advisor to French presidents, a Socialist deputy and, probably more significant, former head of the France-Israel Chamber of Commerce, to beef up our economic coverage. Stoleru's main contribution was huge claims for taxis from City Airport to Heathrow, but he did bring a talented young lieutenant in Fabrice Croppi – now a senior French banker - who was (understandably) baffled by Maxwell's world. At Fabrice's instigation I found myself in Paris interviewing the *Chef de Cabinet* to a senior politician, who turned out not to speak a word of English. It didn't produce much copy, but I did get to call at our magnificent Embassy, finding a Trinity contemporary, Dick Wilkinson, handling the media.

I had not been long at the *European* when Sir Geoffrey Howe sensationally resigned – making his speech 20 minutes before we went to press – and Mrs Thatcher was forced out. My bosses were surprised the Tory leadership contestants were not rushing to write for us; I tried to explain that we were well down their list of priorities. Covering John Major's "honeymoon" was a pleasure, and I earned the odd foreign trip with him, mainly to the EC summits (most memorably in Rome) that led to the conclusion of the Maastricht Treaty in December 1991.

I had arranged to join Rory Watson in Maastricht, and had even found out – exclusively – that the Community would be renamed the European Union. I was also invited to an Anglo-German Konigswinter conference beforehand; I gone to a junior Konigswinter in Cambridge years before, and saw this as a great chance to develop influential contacts. But it was not to be.

Weeks before, Maxwell had gone missing from his yacht the *Lady Ghislaine* off the Canary Islands, his body turning up in the sea. His papers carried sycophantic tributes – my own cautious piece about his brief career in the Commons was spiked - and at Westminster Alastair Campbell decked the *Guardian's* Mike White for disrespecting the great man's memory. Ian Maxwell, decent son of an impossible father, took over running the *Mirror* and began sitting in at the *European's* editorial conferences. And I, on the advice of the *Telegraph's* accountants, transferred my entitlements there into the *Mirror* pension fund.

Days before Maastricht, the house of cards collapsed. It turned out that Maxwell Communications was hopelessly in debt ... and that Maxwell had raided the pension fund to keep it going. Whether or not he killed himself, he knew on the *Lady Ghislaine* that the game was up. The Mirror Group was solvent, but Maxwell's other interests were not. When the administrators called at the White Hart – or "Stab in the Back" – next door to ask why no rent had been received, they were stunned to hear from the landlord that Maxwell had collected it personally, in cash. Upstairs, the cashiers asked me to return my advance expenses for Konigswinter and Maastricht. I cancelled but Rory went ahead, paying his own way; probably I should have too.

For two or three weeks we worked on unpaid. Ian Watson's successor John Bryant left for the *Times*. Charlie Garside, his deputy, bravely kept a team together until new proprietors could be found. But I had just taken on a hefty mortgage, and could not work for nothing: that Christmas, for the only time in my life, I drew the dole. So when Helen Liddell, who as a Mirror Group director had been called down from Glasgow to sort out the pension fund, told me the *Daily Record* needed a political editor, I jumped at the chance. She had actually rung for Askold on another matter; he was out and I took the call.

I have no regrets about leaving the *European* then. The paper's new owners would be Eurosceptics, and while Europe is about more than an organisation based in Brussels, you cannot produce a credible paper that actively opposes the institution binding together the countries in which it circulates. It survived for several years with some excellent journalism, but lost readers and eventually died of implausibility.

Several *Mirror* staff had been seconded to the *European*, and over a dozen including me had contracts with the Mirror Group; mine – signed personally by Maxwell - gave me a year's notice. Management declared our contracts void when he died; when they refused to negotiate we began legal proceedings which I stayed in after joining the *Record* – an irony that tickled my new editor, Endell Laird. Delaying tactics by the *Mirror* and the slowness of the legal process meant it was 1995 before a date for trial was set; I would eventually emerge with three months' money – but no job.

While at the *European*, I was invited to join the judges of the European Woman of The Year award, for the British female making the greatest contribution to Europe and people's understanding of it. We met a couple of times before making a decision, going through the CVs of eight or so nominees. Some were academics and businesswomen, others active in voluntary organisations – political or not – with a bearing on Europe. One year the choice made itself: Juliet Lodge, a professor at Hull University, had made so obvious and distinguished a contribution. Other times, there were several strongish contenders. And the final year, well into my time at the *Record,* the choice was made for us.

We received several promising CVs, but the sponsors of the award had decided it should go to the Labour peeress and lawyer Helena Kennedy. As far as I could tell she had done little, if anything, for Europe, but there was no room for argument; Helena's fan club had decided that as this was the only award she had never received, an injustice had to be remedied. There was never any suggestion that she knew what her friends were up to, but I left the panel feeling our other, genuine, awards had been cheapened … and suspecting I knew why Dame Sally Greengross, whose connection with Europe was also tenuous, had won just before I joined.

My time with the *Record* covered the period when John Major was struggling with his Eurosceptics. He became more and more frustrated as they brought him to the brink of defeat over the Maastricht Treaty, finally branding his Cabinet critics "bastards". In June 1995 he challenged them to take him on, and John Redwood responded … flanked by a group who looked like a caricature of Little England, with the Northampton MP Tony Marlow in a striped blazer. By contrast, Major unveiled in the garden of Number 10, hitherto out of bounds to us, a team headed by the witty, civilised Ian Lang. On the morning of the ballot, I wrote that he needed a majority of 120 to retain credibility … and that was almost exactly the outcome.

Early in 2000, I joined the Department of Trade and Industry as its consultant on European presentation. The initiative had come, again, from Helen, who having asked me to be her special adviser hours before she was reshuffled from Transport, felt on becoming Minister of State at the DTI for Europe and energy that the department needed help in highlighting the government's thinking. The post was not a political one, and its centre of gravity was not in the main building at the top of Victoria Street memorably described by Ian Lang as *"Magnifique, mais ce n'est pas la gare"*, but down the road with its European Policy Directorate in Kingsgate House. In charge of EP was John Alty, an amiable and highly intelligent Liverpudlian who could deputise for ministers with aplomb and later strove to save MG Rover. My boss was Rosa Wilkinson, an inspirational high-flyer who had started in the civil service handling benefits. A Doncaster girl with Asian origins, Rosa was the ideal guide to how the civil service works and how to operate within it; without that grounding I could never have coped as a special adviser. It was Rosa who taught me the imperative of locking your filing cabinet each night, to avoid being "breached" (disciplined). Also in Rosa's tiny section were James Dormer, an able young official who had converted to Islam to win the hand of a charming Indian girl, and Rosemary Howard, who having worked for Alan Clark had incurred lascivious comments in his *Diaries*. She showed true style by attending his memorial service in her best hat.

Two things struck me about the 180 staff at EP, and indeed the DTI as a whole: the sheer ability of most, and the staggering ethnic range. Anyone who expected a phalanx of 54-year-old white males (like me) was in for a surprise; traditional Whitehall types there certainly were, but in EP there must have been a good 20 nationalities. Notably, there were several exceptional Caribbean women who had come in a decade before at low grades; today they join higher up and progress further.

I arrived weeks before the Lisbon Summit, at which Tony Blair secured unexpected support across Europe for economic reform: encouragement of innovation and small business; less red tape, completion of the Single Market; and the opening of closed national markets, particularly in energy supply. Usually EU summits are attended by the Prime Minister, Foreign Secretary and Chancellor, though the Chancellor's role is limited. This time, unprecedentedly, the DTI was involved, with John Alty among the officials supporting Blair, Robin Cook and Gordon Brown.

I plugged myself into the preparations, and in the aftermath of Lisbon, where France and Germany momentarily failed to grasp the threat posed to their State monopolies, fed ministers, and the Department generally, with explanations of the agreement and its benefits for Britain. I provided material for speeches, and for events highlighting the Lisbon agenda, and drafted for Helen a pamphlet titled *Making Europe a World-Class Competitor*. Every fact for this had to be dug out and checked and great care taken to avoid crossing the line into politics, and the text had to be cleared exhaustively not only within the DTI but with the Foreign Office and (twice) Downing Street. The process took about four months – which I was told was quick - but the outcome was non-controversial. The same could not be said of an *FT* article I was asked to draft for our secretary of state, Stephen Byers; I cleared it all the way up the civil service ladder to Number 10, only to discover there was a parallel, political, clearance ladder. The political office in Number 10 killed the article; I never discovered whether they had problems with it, or whether Byers' special adviser Jo Moore saw it as a threat.

I had not realised how big a stake the DTI had in Europe; indeed most people didn't and that was one reason for appointing me. EP dealt among other things with the Single Market, enlargement of the EU, policing of State aids ... and the Euro. Whitehall was preparing to take Britain in once Gordon Brown's conditions for adopting the Single Currency – accepted by Blair against his own instinct to join regardless – were met. The Treasury laid down a very careful line which we stuck to slavishly, but the Government was preparing business for the practicalities of joining, and trying to defuse the visceral opposition of elements of that community in advance of the promised referendum.

Blair aimed to create a coalition for the Euro that transcended party, like the umbrella group that had campaigned for a "Yes" vote in 1975, so Britain in Europe was formed. I knew some of its staff: Kitty Ussher (later a DTI minister), who had impressed me when she was at the Centre for European Reform, and Danny Alexander, whom I knew from the Scottish Liberal Democrats and would be George Osborne's deputy in the Coalition. Helen's pamphlet was commissioned by BiE, and I sat in on Byers' launch of the organisation. In the campaign's back room, we discussed how the climate could be created for a "Yes" vote. I felt that just as the 1975 referendum had hinged on Tony Benn, one on the Euro could become a plebiscite on Peter Mandelson. As it turned out, Gordon made sure that referendum never happened. And when we finally had one, it was fought on the political class's refusal to take concerns over immigration seriously and a desire to give that same élite a kicking.

I was also involved with "3 e's" – a pitch to business emphasising the benefits of engaging not only with the Euro but with exports and e.commerce. With officials handling these specialities, I drafted Helen's speech for the launch, at Bolton Wanderers' Reebok Stadium. We had a nightmare journey up: our train was late, there were no seat reservations, almost no food and no staff apart from one harassed steward, and we were heckled obscenely in first class by a drunken and no doubt ticketless yob. We were met in Manchester by a government driver who kept her cool despite every minister arriving at points across the North-West several hours late. Next morning there was a good turnout at the Reebok, Helen spoke, and I uncovered new examples of smart business with Europe to highlight.

The next "3 e's" event was in Leicester, featuring Patricia Hewitt. As is usual when a minister speaks away from their speciality, the relevant policy officials (and I) contacted her private office to arrange to brief her. It became clear after several calls that

Patricia's staff were either unwilling to diary a meeting, or incapable of doing so. On the day, faced with this unfamiliar-looking speech, she asked them: "Why am I doing this?" In her position, I would have done the same.

Much of my work at the DTI involved ferreting out facts – learning the hard way that any "fact" cited in ministers' speeches may well be wrong. Tony Blair teased Jacques Chirac that while Électricité de France supplied Number 10, no British energy company could operate in France. His political point was justified, but when I checked, it turned out that Downing Street got its electricity from a combined heat and power scheme, with EdF purely as backup. Most of the factoids I was given to demonstrate how Britain's involvement in Europe was paying dividends survived the checking process, but I was uneasy about a claim that a Glasgow firm was exporting bratwurst to Germany. I tracked the "fact" back to Scottish Enterprise, and when I asked them for chapter and verse they admitted the firm didn't make bratwurst, let alone export it.

Presentation of government policy toward Europe was co-ordinated by a committee known as Minecor which met monthly under the chairmanship of the Foreign Office minister Keith Vaz, and I attended with an official from EP. Minecor's deliberations came under the heading of "public diplomacy": the New Labour term for projecting to the public how and why our foreign policy is being conducted. This is not merely spin conducted by diplomats; in the past, the FCO had taken the view that Britain's dealings with other countries were its own private property. Because Europe impacted right across Whitehall, every department was represented at Minecor; some sent a junior official, some a senior one and a few a junior minister. Some of its meetings were held on easy chairs in Keith Vaz' office; Alastair Campbell came along once to set out Number 10's agenda post-Lisbon. Others, at Defra and Maff, were more formal; had she stayed longer at the DTI, Helen would have hosted one.

I also sat in on EU ministerial councils in Brussels - not the most exciting of cities, which is one reason Britons never really took to a united Europe based there. Ministers covering each area of policy met four times a year, plus one or two "informals". Different DTI ministers attended each council – Industry, Competitiveness, Energy and so forth – and there was some overlap with other departments as Brussels' division of responsibilities did not match ours. Moreover senior officials from UKREP, the British mission to the EU, attended some councils instead of a minister. Nevertheless, four times during my stay Helen represented Britain at a Council and I went along, accompanying John Alty or one of his senior staff and a DTI press officer (one had been at school with David Beckham, which made me feel very old).

We went over by Eurostar the day before to meet at UKREP on how the council would go, which items to intervene on and issues we should know about. If there was time, Helen met the resident UK media, to explain the Government's line on the issues they were reporting and take their mind on the state of play in Europe. My role was to remind Helen of points worth making, note matters to follow up and have a word with individual reporters afterward. Inevitably, they wanted to know when the Government would make its mind up on the Euro; all we could do was play a straight bat. (Even so, there was room for misunderstanding. When Helen went to Berlin, one German reporter created a sensational story about the Euro even though she cleared every word with the senior DTI official present).

On the day, we headed for the Lipsius building, opposite the Commission. Having queued to get through security as a journalist – and mocked the besuited "pilot fish" who accompanied the political big noises - I felt smug as we were whisked through. (When I went back with QinetiQ I again had to queue, to the amusement of Charles Clarke, sweeping past with his entourage).

The proceedings went on most of the day, and I would sit in when Helen or one of her key officials needed a break, listening to the simultaneous translation. Though there were just 15 member states then against an eventual 28 (and nine when we first joined), things would get out of hand if everyone spoke; luckily only two or three items usually produced a debate. This consisted of half a dozen ministers reading out a prepared brief, with the quicker-footed responding to points made. This could, in turn, lead into a negotiation, and a solution all present could live with.

In my year and a bit at the DTI, some important decisions for Britain were taken at Ministerial Councils. One that caused us serious headaches was "droit de suite", a levy on art sales to pass to the artist's descendants. London's auction houses fought it tooth and nail, reckoning it would drive sellers to market their Picassos in Switzerland or New York where the levy did not apply. We delayed it and reduced its impact as much as we could, but in the end it went through.

I was there, however, when Helen saved the Jammie Dodger. The Council was discussing a Bakery Jams Directive, pressed for by the Belgians, to prevent bakers describing as "jam" the fillings in certain cakes and biscuits. I don't know what the Belgians put in their doughnuts, but it apparently isn't jam, and someone in Brussels was determined to impose uniformity. We argued that people buying a Jammie Dodger knew perfectly well what was inside, and it would be absurd not to call it jam ... or to have to rename the Dodger. Helen persuaded the Council, and we emerged to tell the media the Dodger had been reprieved . (We subsequently killed a move to prevent Cadbury's describing their products as chocolate). Soon after, a large box of Jammie Dodgers arrived from a grateful Burtons. Helen kept it in her office in Airdrie ... offering a Dodger to constituents who called in with a problem and stayed for a cup of tea.

I also sat in on diary meetings in her top-floor room overlooking Westminster Abbey. There were far more requests for meetings or visits than time available, and ruthless prioritising went on. Even with an event firmly in the diary, urgent Government business or a delayed flight could force a change; in my experience of Whitehall, 70% of ministerial engagements get rescheduled or never happen.

In her private office I also worked on upcoming events, or briefing to go into Helen's folder. The staff of eight was led with great professionalism by Richard Riley, a more senior official than would normally run matters for a Minister of State; Helen had inherited him from her predecessor John Battle, more a liberation theologian than a politician. The business of a minister's office swirled around me, as – especially on the energy side which I was not concerned with - heavy hitters from the industry came in to see her. I would love to have attended Helen's meeting with Arthur Scargill on miners' compensation for lung disease, which was one of the Blair government's successes - save for the huge sums skimmed off by some solicitors - as billions were distributed to sufferers and their families. It was, I think, the first time Arthur had set foot in the department since the 1970s. But I had no reason to be there.

I was there as the fuel crisis of September 2000 blew up. It was ironic to me that the blockade of oil refineries was led by farmers, who don't pay fuel duty anyway, but it was certainly effective. The oil companies had farmed out deliveries to contractors, and when their drivers refused to cross the picket lines Big Oil was powerless. For government, there was the problem of finding out who was actually running the refineries; the manager ultimately responsible for Stanlow on Merseyside, one of the hardest hit, was based in Milan. Helen attended a Privy Council at Balmoral as the crisis developed, then spent long hours on the phone trying to keep supplies moving. The dispute was ended by Gordon Brown abandoning Ken Clarke's escalating "green" duty on petrol and diesel; then the work began to make prevent a recurrence.

After a while, I was asked to give a lunchtime talk to DTI staff on what the department was doing on Europe and how it was presented to the world outside. I couldn't resist recalling a *Telegraph* feature I'd written just before joining on how the DTI's interpretation of EU directives had outlawed in Britain a dental whitening treatment performed by dentists worldwide, suggesting that "someone in the DTI had started digging and doesn't know how to stop." At the close, a rather determined spinster informed me that she was the "someone". As far as she was concerned, the treatment was unsafe and she had a duty to prevent it. I had read the literature myself and found nothing, apart from one Japanese scientific paper, to create any doubt; moreover I knew people who'd had the treatment with no ill effects, whose dentists faced six months in jail if they continued it. The DTI had banned the treatment under the EU's Cosmetics Directive, which outlawed in cosmetics chemicals widely used in dentistry, while other member states had allowed it under the Medicines Directive. "Gold-plating" of EU regulations, or a prudent precaution?

When Peter Mandelson resigned as Northern Ireland Secretary and John Reid replaced him, Helen was promoted to take his place as Scottish Secretary. I readied myself to work to her successor at the DTI, who to my delight was Peter Hain. Peter had a very different view of the portfolio, and most of my preparatory work for Helen went out of the window, notably a meticulously planned visit to Washington. His diary meetings reflected his different interests and strengths; at them I was very impressed by his PPS Caroline Flint, who would go on to be Gordon Brown's Minister of Housing.

Peter has a natural eye for presentational opportunities and didn't need any help from me. Three weeks into his tenure, Helen asked me to be her special advisor; I told Peter I'd like to accept, and left the DTI for the political end of the Civil Service.

That wasn't the end of my involvement with Europe. Helen in her new role not only had Scottish business in Brussels, but plenty to say about how Europe was benefiting Scotland. Those speeches drew heavily on my research at the DTI, and old colleagues found their phones ringing. Nor was it my final contact with the DTI, for from 2003 onwards I worked on developing QinetiQ's relationship with the department as it morphed from an agency of the MoD to a FTSE 250 company. At QinetiQ I encountered the 90% of the DTI with which I had previously had little or no contact ... though on a couple of occasions I was delighted to engage with John Alty, by then in charge of business relations. The remarkable thing about the DTI - now Business, Innovation and Skills - is that most business people say it is too large - but needs more resources to deal with their own particular interest.

23: North of the Border

Early in 1962 a Scottish CNDer wrote to my father saying he needed a song, but could only play hymn tunes on his accordion. Dad rustled up *What a Friend we have in Gaitskell*, and the man sang it with gusto behind the Labour leader in the Glasgow May Day procession. A furious Gaitskell denounced CND from the platform as "peanuts who are not worth a tinker's cuss". Years later I heard another story from that rally - from Maria Fyfe, by then MP for Maryhill, who had decked herself out as a fortune-teller, reading palms for Party funds. When Gaitskell called at her tent, Maria launched into why he should commit Labour to ban the bomb. Gaitskell told her: "The press are outside, so you'd better tell my fortune," and crossed her palm with silver. Maria studied his hand and told him: "You will be our next Prime Minister, and live a long and happy life." Within nine months, he was dead.

That summer I criss-crossed Scotland on a rail rover ticket, shortly before Beeching took a hatchet to many scenic routes. I saw my first midday drunks in Inverness, encountered my first midges chopping firewood at Carbisdale Castle youth hostel, had my first taste of Irn-Bru ... and crossed to Arran in weather so filthy I didn't see a thing. One fellow traveller enthused about Scottish folk music, but had never heard of Dad's favourite group the Glasgow Eskimoes (Scottish republican CNDers); he meant Andy Stewart.

The highlight for me was Last Tram Night in Glasgow. I had booked a place on the Omnibus Society's special which toured what was left of the system the weekend before. Punters kept trying to get on, so the conductor repelled them with the iron lever used to change the points. I got a chance to drive the tram a short distance up the Dumbarton Road; I notched-up too vigorously, there was a loud pop and it ground to a halt. Then, with my cousins Andrew and Elizabeth and their Grandma Doyle, I watched in torrential rain as the final cars rumbled into Dalmarnock depot, crushing our pennies under their wheels.

After I left school, we took a family holiday in Orkney. Dad had been there in 1938 with a friend, carrying out an archaeological dig on what turned out to be a farmer's potato clamp. We flew up to Kirkwall over tropically clear blue waters, landing on a grass strip where a caravan served as the terminal. We stayed first in a guest house at Birsay on the west coast – where I thought the landlady was talking Norwegian when she answered the phone – then in Stromness, whose narrow streets echoed with the Animals' first hits. In Stromness Museum we found the snail collection Dad had classified 26 years before. We stood atop the cliffs beneath which HMS *Hampshire*, carrying Lord Kitchener, sank during the First World War; you could imagine the wreck just below the surface. We crawled into the prehistoric Maes How, and explored the timeless village at Skara Brae, Pitchish brochs and stone circles; nowhere else in Britain confronts you with the distant past.

We looked across to the Old Man of Hoy, and were captivated by a mirage that made the mountains of Sutherland look unnervingly close. But the greatest experience was driving along the Churchill Barrier, constructed to link islands and keep U-boats out of Scapa Flow after one sank the *Royal Oak*, to visit the tiny Italian chapel on Lamb Holm, lovingly created by PoWs with ironwork crafted from scrap and devotional paintings on stucco. Flying home, our pilot considerately flew over Wembley during the Cup Final: still the closest I've been to one.

Soon after graduating in 1968, I drove up to Edinburgh in my newly-acquired Singer Chamois for the wedding of my ProngSoc friend Martin Lander and Evelyn Birkett, a bundle of energy from a patrician SNP family. The ceremony was in Cluny parish church, Morningside ... where I would attend John Smith's funeral 26 years later. The reception was a whirl of kilts and Lovat jackets; I had learnt the Gay Gordons and the Dashing White Sergeant in my teens, but could not remember quite enough.

My first reporting assignment in Scotland was the 1979 devolution referendum, meeting key players north of the Border – among them Helen, then Labour's Scottish general secretary - for the first time. Lined up behind the Callaghan government's proposals for an Assembly with specific powers devolved to it were most of the Labour Party, the SNP (with varying degrees of enthusiasm), the Liberals and some mainly Heathite Conservatives. Against the plan were as many Tories, Robin Cook and Tam Dalyell, a few Nats who thought it a sell-out and much of the business community. The bar for approval had been set high by an amendment from George Cunningham, a Scots-born London Labour MP, stipulating that devolution must secure not only a majority of votes cast but 40% of registered voters. Was there enough enthusiasm to pass that test?

Scots love debate, and with the referendum they got it. Apart from "Yes" and "No" set pieces. there was a nightly roadshow in which Tam set out the case against devolution and Jim Sillars – who had broken with Labour for not being devolutionist enough and would soon join the SNP – put the arguments for. Chris Potter and I caught up with them in Hamilton, only to find that the Labour whips at Westminster had refused to let Tam "pair" with Jim for a crucial vote and Tam's place had been taken by Archie Reid, an NUR official who lacked Sillars' pyrotechnic style. Over a dram the night before their final debate, Tam would suggest to Jim that each announce the other had persuaded him to change their mind.

In Edinburgh I met a group of young Nationalists: graduates, well off and highly articulate. One of their complaints – and a factor in their joining the SNP - was that they couldn't ski abroad without flying via London; at the Scotland Office a generation later I would set up an "aviation summit" to encourage more direct flights. Among the group was Roger Mullin, who four decades on, I suspect to his surprise, would become MP for Gordon Brown's old seat of Kirkcaldy. He had paid his way through college by donning a silver singlet to recite the works of Robert Burns at an Ayrshire hotel. Inevitably the odd American came up and told him: "Oh, Mr Burns, I do love your poems." And Roger would sign their menu: "My love is like a red, red rose. Robert Burns."

On the day – March 1 1979 – there was a 51.6% "Yes" vote, with more than 60% of Scots turning out. But the Cunningham threshold was missed and devolution shelved; the SNP tabled a no-confidence vote in the Callaghan government, the Conservatives took it up, it was carried by one vote and Mrs Thatcher won the ensuing election. Callaghan taunted the Nationalists as "turkeys voting for an early Christmas", and indeed they lost all but two of their 11 seats. One factor in the sizeable anti vote had been Tory – and some Nationalist – canvassers telling people voting "No" could trigger an election. They turned out to be right.

For several years at Westminster, my involvement with Scottish politics was limited to Scottish question time – generally a whinge about the evils of Thatcherism – and the odd lunch with politicians who happened to be Scots. My boss Jim Wightman, having his family up there, covered the Scottish conferences, and it was 1987 before I experienced my first: Scottish Labour in Perth.

On the evening of 21 December 1988, I was at the Commons secretaries' Christmas dinner along with John Prescott, then shadow Transport Secretary. Midway through the evening, Prescott got an urgent call and disappeared. It was rumoured that a NATO fighter had crashed onto a petrol station, then that two planes had collided. Only when I got home did I learn the full horror of Lockerbie, with a bomb exploding on a PanAm jumbo full of American students going home for Christmas; the airliner crashed in pieces onto a peaceful Scottish town, vaporising two houses and killing 11 people on the ground.

Next day I was writing the *Telegraph's* parliamentary sketch. The mood was sombre as MPs struggled with the enormity of the disaster, and I couldn't help comparing the carnage of Lockerbie as Christmas approached with the calm and hopefulness of Bethlehem. Andrew Hutchinson reckoned this "Sylvie Krin" journalism, akin to the mawkish parody column in *Private Eye,* and the reference was left out. The sketch still conveyed a forceful message.

In the Lobby I had operated in a different world from my Scottish counterparts, except on the biggest stories, and never imagined I would join them. Yet little more than two years after leaving the *Telegraph* I became political editor of Scotland's biggest-selling paper. When Helen mentioned casually that there was a vacancy, she hadn't expected me to show interest. But the job was one I could get my teeth into after time with papers with little feel for politics (or, at times, journalism), even though some doors that opened easily to me at the *Telegraph* now required a hefty shove. So after meeting the editor, Endell Laird, at a London hotel I started work in February 1992.

A well-written tabloid then selling 700,000 a day, the *Record* had a strong Labour heartbeat. Glasgow journalism was just as professional as Fleet Street's, but its reference points were different. The fact that the key decisions affecting Scotland were taken 400 miles away at Westminster and that day-to-day matters were run from Edinburgh left the Glasgow media much closer to the people. The competition was also very different. In London seven or eight papers fought for "scoops"; in Glasgow the race for mass circulation was a two-horse one. Traditionally it had been between the *Record* and the *Scottish Daily Express*: old hands recalled how the two had vied for the exclusive picture when a man was charged with being drunk in charge of his dog. The *Record's* photographer had the presence of mind to put a bag over the dog's head as the pair emerged from court.

The decline of the *Express* (with Tory fortunes in Scotland) had left a vacuum that was being filled by the *Scottish Sun*. When I joined the *Record* it outsold the *Sun* by nearly three to one, but the margin narrowed as the *Sun* went aggressively for our heartland, targeting Scots who pronounce their country with an "r" in the middle. It could not have captured them with the red-blooded Thatcherism it exuded south of the border, so Rupert Murdoch let the *Scottish Sun* develop a line of its own; the day the closure of Ravenscraig steelworks was announced, the *Sun's* Glasgow editions called for it to be nationalised ... while those printed at Wapping hailed the closure as overdue. The *Scottish Sun* took a gamble espousing the SNP during one of its less popular phases, but did not suffer. Where it scored was with razor-sharp journalism, on which the *Record* has long prided itself. The *Scottish Sun's* finest night was when Inverness Caledonian Thistle unexpectedly defeated Celtic, an inspired sub coming up with:

> Super Caley go ballistic
> Celtic are atrocious.

It was only matched when, just before the 1992 election campaign, the *Sun* – in London and Glasgow – broke the news of Paddy Ashdown's affair with his former secretary with two all-explaining words: "Paddy Pantsdown!" Our editorial conference that morning acknowledged true genius.

The *Record* was then based in a 1970s monolith on Anderston Quay, with a grandstand view of the perpetual roadworks on the Kingston Bridge. It wasn't a welcoming building, but the atmosphere made up for that. Endell presided over a staff of great professionalism, keen humour and a total lack of bull; you were as good as you were. I worked most closely with Tom Brown, an avuncular and vastly experienced former *Express* man who as a fellow son of Kirkcaldy was Gordon Brown's journalistic mentor, and Dave King, a highly accomplished political and industrial reporter. I must have seemed from another planet, but they welcomed me with a crash course not just in Scottish politics but in what made the paper's readers tick.

Anderston Quay's culture was a microcosm of Glasgow's, with humour in the face of adversity and gentle sectarian ribbing (it gets ugly in places, but not in the office). I was told how the skilled printers - Prods to a man at one time - would rush to the canteen on Fridays "to grab the fish before the Catholics". And when a noted (and Catholic) Glasgow PR man sent out a Christmas card of himself with Nelson Mandela, it appeared on the notice board captioned: "I'd rather be a darkie than a Tim". "Teuchters" (Highlanders) were also mocked; when Western Islands Council lost millions in the crash of the Bank of Credit and Commerce International, a Stornoway-born colleague observed: "That's what happens when you give crofters real money." The humour outside was as rich. A taxi driver told me of an American fare who, asked what he thought of Glasgow, had replied: "It'll be great when it's finished." Given the vast tracts near the city centre that lay vacant in the early '90s, it was fair comment.

One of the Scottish lobby who helped me a lot was Catherine Macleod, then with Grampian Television; she would become a *grande dame* of New Labour as political editor of the *Herald* and advisor at the Treasury to Alistair Darling. I also came to appreciate Geoffrey Parkhouse, whom the *Herald* paid to be a gent-about-town but had a great nose for a story. The subs dared not change Geoffrey's copy ... until he interrupted a convivial evening to file total gibberish on the constitutional implications of the Queen falling off her horse.

The *Record* shared a room at Westminster with, among others, ITN, the *Sun* and the *Evening Standard,* so if a story broke, I was one of the first to know. I returned to the Downing Street briefings, given by first Gus O'Donnell and then Jonathan Haslam, one of my information officer tutees a decade before. I sat in the Gallery for

Prime Minister's Questions and major announcements next to the ever-friendly Matthew Parris, and I never missed the monthly Scottish Questions, when the 72 MPs I was concerned with took centre stage. Scotland's parliamentarians were becoming livelier and more articulate; when I first arrived, the police in the Lobby had told me that any man in late middle age who I didn't recognise was probably a Glasgow MP.

There was also the Scottish Grand Committee, which was transplanted to Edinburgh by its Labour majority on the eve of the 1992 election as a Parliament in waiting. That day's proceedings in the old Royal High School – which would have housed a Scottish Assembly had the 1979 referendum succeeded – were highly emotional, as John Smith, Robin Cook, Donald Dewar and Gordon Brown looked to victory with devolution to follow (and probably Robin as First Minister). Subsequent sessions, at Westminster, came down to Henry McLeish battering the handful of Tories present with figures, an exasperated George Foulkes accusing him of "arid statistical ping-pong".

During my time with the *Record*, the main item of Scottish legislation was the Conservatives' reorganisation of local government, highly controversial as councils' boundaries were tightly drawn – the Bill even mentioning specific properties - with the apparent purpose of guaranteeing the Tories a handful of councils; when elections were held they failed to win a single one.

I was also bidden to meetings with Scottish ministers in the "large Ministerial room" or "small Ministerial room". It was a standing joke that the burly Peter Fraser usually briefed in the small room, and the flyweight Lord James Douglas-Hamilton in the large one. Occasionally the Secretary of State would meet us in his office on the Ministerial Corridor; this was just off the Press Gallery but a one-way door meant that while you could return from it quickly, getting there took ages. Working there with Helen eight or so years later, we had John Prescott in the next room; sometimes the DPM would sound off so loudly that we couldn't hear ourselves think.

I now had privileged access to the Labour leadership, but had to work harder with the Tories and the SNP as I was required to lambast them in print. Most Tories knew me from my *Telegraph* days and reckoned that if they were fair with me, at the very least I wouldn't kick them any harder. With the SNP it was harder, but they needed publicity and there were times when the *Record* gave them a fair hearing.

The SNP at Westminster meant Alex Salmond. Scottish Labour consistently underestimated Alec, to its cost, and in the 2007 Holyrood elections it finally paid the price; the fact that Alec went on lead a generally surefooted minority administration, win re-election outright and come unnervingly close to winning the 2014 independence referendum shows what a consummate politician he could be. While Salmond made his name interrupting Nigel Lawson's Budget speech – something no other MP had thought of doing – he was never just an opportunist. His course to power was a zig-zag, pulling out of Holyrood, then returning after John Swinney was found wanting as party leader and eventually heading south again, but more than justified by results. My friend Mike Maclay described him as "a cross between Yogi Bear and Macchiavelli", and I did encounter his dark side. But Alec had a good economic as well as a political brain, honed at the Royal Bank before it got delusions of grandeur, and his understanding of North Sea issues was consistently better than Gordon Brown's. Moreover, he proved a difficult man to oppose; Labour's attempts to attack him, and indeed the SNP, were seen deep within the Scottish psyche as unpatriotic.

I also got to know the SNP's "heid bummers", as its Scots-language literature describes them. Mike Russell, the party's general secretary and later Education Secretary, particularly impressed me: shrewd, with a strong grasp of the issues and always ready to talk. When the SNP – I suspect to its own surprise - came to power, most of its key players grew in office; I was particularly impressed at how Kenny Macaskill, days into being Justice Minister, responded to the attack on Glasgow Airport by doctor/terrorists. Of course, he later had to take the flak for the premature release of Abdel Baset Ali Al-Megrahi, jailed by a Scots court sitting in Holland for the Lockerbie bombing.

Travelling up for Friday's morning conference at Anderston Quay I became a regular on the Glasgow sleeper, though I never slept well. There were usually MPs on board – and Kirsty Wark until the train's departure was brought forward, preventing her getting to Euston after presenting *Newsnight*. Over late night drinks, the MPs would get things out of their system, including the occasional chunk of undiluted bile about absent colleagues. Sadly the sleeper became increasingly unreliable, and Donald Dewar, who had almost lived on it, finally gave up after missing a crucial meeting with Tony Blair.

Joining the *Record* didn't mean I saw more of Scotland – rather the same bits very often. Forget the majestic scenery, politicians stick to where the votes are. I spent most of my working time in Glasgow or Edinburgh, plus family visits to Aberdeen. Conferences took me to Dundee, Inverness – a spectacular train ride - and Perth for Labour, Conservatives and LibDems, and these plus Dunoon for the SNP; elections got me round Ayrshire, and made me all too familiar with the A96 between Inverness and Aberdeen.

I saw more of the country on trips organised by the Scottish Office: eight or ten Lobby hacks shown the best of Scotland's scenery and fed upbeat messages on the economy, culminating in dinner with the Secretary of State. We took in rural Perthshire, East Lothian and Arran (this time the fog and rain lifted). We stayed at the Dunkeld House – where for £12 you could try a dram salvaged from the *SS Politician* in *Whisky Galore* – tasted what became my favourite malt at the charming Aberfeldy distillery, and encountered Dolly the Sheep at the Roslin Institute. She oozed star quality, and one colleague from the *Herald* was so smitten, we nearly left him behind.

On these trips I got to know the Scottish Office press team, especially Jayne Colquhoun and Brian Simmons who would later be colleagues. By my last, a Scottish parliament was imminent and Donald received us as First Minister–in-waiting. Over dinner at Bute House he turned to Lockerbie, arguing that the continued investigation was futile as there could never be a successful prosecution. I persuaded the others that Donald's break with the Government's position was significant, and we should file a story – obviously not attributed to him – saying senior ministers were having a rethink. Unusually, Donald had this one wrong; soon a brief rapprochement with Libya led to Megrahi being handed over.

My first two years at the *Record* embraced Labour's optimistic march into the 1992 election, the trauma of defeat, and its regrouping under John Smith. Labour's Scots were vital to its prospects for office, and the *Record* was umbilically linked to them. Gordon Brown wrote for us and was keen to help, Donald spared a lunchtime for me to pick his brain on a legal matter and extol his favourite authors, and Robin Cook was generous with his time despite a frantic campaigning schedule. There were strains – when Tom Clarke was elected to the Shadow Cabinet, Robin refused me a comment – but they were buried in the interest of "one more heave" for victory.

John Smith was utterly genuine and, had he lived, would have kept a Labour government on the high ground. The shock of his sudden death to everyone in politics, especially north of the Border, showed just how respected he was. It was hardest (his family excepted) on his staff, who had to organise what was effectively a State funeral. On the day, Cluny parish church was packed by the great and the good of Scotland, many struggling to hold back tears; it was a tribute to John's infectious warmth that his old friend Jimmy Gordon could raise a laugh from such a devastated gathering by observing that he could "start a party in an empty room". An achingly moving Gaelic lament apart, my keenest memory is of Maureen Smith, Scottish Labour's press officer, remarking that she had never before set foot in a Protestant church. Given the party's strong Catholic base, I am sure she was not alone.

John's death not only necessitated a new leader but a by-election in Monklands East. Helen, locally-born, a good friend of John and an experienced campaigner with a national profile, was the obvious choice to fight his seat, but she had to weather a firestorm. The SNP – firing bullets shaped by the Tories - threw everything they had at alleged graft and nepotism at Labour-controlled Monklands council, in the hope of driving a wedge between Helen and her local backers. There was a tinge of sectarianism to the criticisms, as the councillors in the firing line were Catholics who supposedly favoured Coatbridge over Protestant Airdrie. The polls were worrying, and with days to go Helen voiced public disapproval of what the councillors were alleged to have done. This horrified Tom Clarke, the MP for next-door Monklands West and an equally good friend of mine; as a former provost of Coatbridge, he defended the council. Helen was elected with a majority cut from over 15,000 to 1,640; she blamed Tom for the narrowness of her victory, he insisted he had rescued her. For a time I was one of the very few people speaking to them both.

With Tony Blair as leader, things changed. Though he was born in Edinburgh of Scottish parents, Scots reckoned him English. The Scottish party and the *Record* rallied behind him to secure a return to government after 18 miserable years, but he had to work to keep them on side. I saw him whenever he came up, for an interview beforehand and again as he left. On the way out of Glasgow's City Chambers after a euphoric rally with Labour poised to sweep the local elections, I asked how he would handle such a visit if there were a backlash against his government; Tony said it was up to him to make sure there wasn't.

Despite our support for Labour, we were still a newspaper and a row was a story. Much of the Scottish party found it hard to swallow Tony's abolition of Clause Four, but he took his biggest gamble by announcing – unilaterally – that instead of simply legislating for devolution, New Labour would hold another referendum. He broke the news to George Robertson, his Shadow Scottish Secretary, at George's home in Dunblane immediately after the massacre; George found it hard to take. As it turned out, Tony was right: holding the referendum brought on board the Lib Dems and the SNP, and gave the scheme that resulted in the Holyrood Parliament greater authority.

John Prescott, rallying the party as an election neared, fronted with Robin the Rolling Rose Show: a farrago of music, alternative comedy and upbeat political messages taken to the faithful – and the recruits who were flocking to New Labour – up and down the country. The *Mirror* papers publicised the show in return for promotional opportunities; I was in Aberdeen when it came to town, and was roped in. Unusually for a party event it was worth going to; the music was up to date – with the theme tune M People's *Moving On Up* - the politics from Prescott and Cook inspirational, and the jokes edgy. When a Mickey Spillane-type private eye was asked: "Have you got a light, dick?" he replied: "I don't know – I've never had it weighed." At the end local celebs and party VIPs were called on stage, and I made my only ever theatrical appearance, waving as I walked down the stairs to join them.

Things were now changing at the *Record*. Terry Quinn, who succeeded Endell Laird at the start of 1995, realised the centre of gravity for Scottish politics was shifting, and redefined my job as 'Westminster editor'. Soon after, the lawsuit several of us from the *European* had launched against the Mirror Group four years before made the High Court calendar ... and group managing director Charlie Wilson let me know I must drop my claim or be fired. As the chance of ever getting to court had seemed remote and my relationship with Terry was still fragile, I had never burdened him by mentioning the case ... though Jim Cassidy, editor of the *Record*'s sister paper the *Sunday Mail,* had urged me to. So it was a bolt from the blue for Terry when I flew up to Glasgow that August – missing Alex' first birthday party – briefed him on the history of the case and told him I had no choice but to quit. Terry rightly felt I had left him in the lurch, but I suspect we were not that far from a parting of the ways. As things turned out, I would never again work full-time in journalism – a return made less likely by a house move from Highgate to Oxfordshire soon after.

I now went freelance, a solicitous Ming Campbell asking: "Have you consulted your bank manager?" *Scotland on Sunday* had lost their Westminster reporter and were happy for me to cover for several months, and through writing leaders for the *Sun* I picked up Lobby work for the *Scottish Sun*. This was never as intensive as it had been for the *Record*, and fizzled out when they moved to a new

IT system without telling me. But the paper's editor Bruce Waddell, who would move on to the *Record*, gave me two unforgettable assignments: the devolution referendum of 1997 and the first Holyrood elections two years later. Each time the paper went into the campaign without a political editor ... after the second, hiring the *Dundee Courier*'s Andy Nicoll at my suggestion.

Weeks after Labour's 1997 landslide, Donald Dewar launched his devolution White Paper – proposing that, this time, all powers be devolved except those specifically reserved to Westminster. Overseeing the process were Donald, Home Secretary Jack Straw and the new Lord Chancellor Derry Irvine, who a generation before had broken Donald's heart by going off with his wife. They had hardly spoken since until they shouldered the pall at John Smith's funeral, and one of the first things Tony Blair did on entering Downing Street was tell his Scottish Secretary and Lord Chancellor that their personal history must not impair the delivery of a Scottish Parliament. To their credit, it didn't.

A planeload of politicians and journalists flew up to Edinburgh for the launch; I sat between Alistair Darling, who still nursed doubts about devolution, and David Steel. Next morning we hacks trooped out to the new Scottish Office building on the quayside at Leith to study the White Paper and question Donald. The division between devolved and reserved powers looked almost surgical (and would hold up remarkably well) though one oddity struck me: why need the Home Office retain control over mass hypnotism in Scotland? None of us spotted the only grit in the oyster: the devolution of planning powers which would give Scotland a veto over the construction of nuclear power stations. John Reid spotted this on the eve of devolution, but was advised he could not block it.

The referendum of 11 September 1997 took place less than a fortnight after the death of Princess Diana, with the nation still in shock. The "Yes, Yes" campaign restarted with a media event at Rosyth featuring Gordon Brown and Sean Connery, briefly together in a common cause. I caught up with them in a tiny office at the Dockyard, and after statements from them and umpteen photos we boarded boats across the Firth of Forth, the campaigners with their banners tossed around beneath the Bridge for the photographers and us in something more robust. Connery was there again when the campaigners rallied in Edinburgh's old Royal High School. I could never understand why Donald blocked a knighthood for him; if ever an actor deserved one, he did, and the episode left a sour taste.

Scots voted for their Parliament by almost three to one, and empowered it to vary income tax by up to 3p in the £. We monitored the results from Edinburgh's plateglass convention centre, and apart from the glee of Alex Salmond and the Scottish Lib-Dem leader Jim Wallace, my main recollection of that night relates to Diana. I got talking with Dan Balz of the *Washington Post,* who had been sent over - he was told almost for a holiday - to give its London correspondent a break, only to be hit by the global story of the year. An outstanding reporter, he took it in his stride.

A year later came the Scotland Bill, implementing the White Paper. Donald launched it in Glasgow, in shambolic circumstances: the sleeper expired, hours late, at Carlisle and the key players shared taxis up the M74, arriving late and out of breath. I kept a watching brief for the *Scottish Sun* on the Bill's progress through Parliament, but it had been so tightly drafted and had such a clear mandate that it produced little copy.

Scottish Labour at Westminster became bogged down in painstaking efforts to disown Tommy Graham, the corpulent MP for Renfrewshire West. Gordon McMaster, his parliamentary neighbour, had committed suicide and from the grave accused Graham of hounding him to his death by peddling false allegations that he had had a homosexual affair with a party worker.

Tommy was not the sharpest tool in the box. One day as Scottish MPs picked up their air tickets at Westminster, he rang his wife at their home near Glasgow Airport to ask if it was foggy there; when a colleague asked what conditions were like in Edinburgh, Tommy asked her: "Would you mind running upstairs?" But he had a wicked tongue, and on the sleeper tried to poison me against another fellow MP. Eventually he was deprived of the whip, but the process wore down everyone involved ... not least David Hill, the most respected member of the Number 10 press team, who told the Lobby when leaving for the private sector: "And I don't give a monkey's about Tommy Graham."

For the first Holyrood elections in May 1999, I again installed myself in the *Sun's* offices at Kinning Park, across the Clyde from the *Record*. It became clear to me that David, Tony Blair's emissary to the Scottish campaign, was there not simply to ensure a Labour victory after some early and unpleasant infighting, but to ascertain whether Jack McConnell, Scottish Labour's general secretary who had secured a clean sweep of the Tories at the 1997 election, was up to the job - and a key position in Donald's first Cabinet. The *Sun* broke my story in its early editions on election night, David having persuaded me not to run it until the campaign was over. So when Tony returned to Edinburgh to celebrate Labour's near-outright victory to a deafening display from a group nicknamed "Dykes with Drums", the only discordant note was my report that he doubted Jack's ability. Jack, who became Finance Minister and later, of course, First Minister, took it in his stride.

Scottish Labour had expected the Parliament to start with the backing of a grateful media. Far from it; even the *Record* accused Donald's administration of having "hit the ground crawling". MSPs did not help by voting themselves hefty allowances, then adjourning for a long summer break. Labour was handicapped because fewer heavy hitters had switched from Westminster than expected, and bright newcomers like Sarah Boyack and Susan Deacon became ministers straight away instead of serving a deputy's apprenticeship. There were also "turf wars" with Westminster, culminating in a stand-up row between Donald and John Reid, who had pipped Helen to become the first post-devolution Secretary of State after sniping from Gordon's camp at her handling of the election campaign. Labour did raise its game and push through sorely-needed Scottish legislation that Westminster had never had time to consider. But the jury was still out when Donald died in November 2000, after just 18 months as First Minister.

Three months after that, I returned to Scottish politics, this time on the inside, when Helen became Scottish Secretary. With devolution, the Secretary of State had become the embodiment north of the Border of powers reserved to Westminster: the economy, defence, foreign affairs, social security and so on. By my arrival at the Scotland Office the "turf wars" were over – indeed some Whitehall departments were unlawfully trying to transfer outposts north of the Border to the Scottish Executive - and Donald's successor Henry McLeish was a constructive partner. I had always liked Henry, despite Don Revie having signed him for Leeds United, and shared his fascination with American politics; he was a technocrat in the best sense of the word, and far more in touch with ordinary Scots than his critics made out. Helen was keen to support him with initiatives such as "Helen and Henry Shows" during the general election, highlighting the partnership between a successful Westminster government and a Labour-led team at Holyrood.

The infant Scottish Executive inevitably developed different priorities, because of Scotland's particular needs and the Scottish party's very different ideology. Other divergences stemmed from poor co-ordination; an important part of my role was telling my Holyrood counterparts of central government initiatives they had not been brought in on, and alerting Whitehall departments when they took Scotland for granted.

The issue that exercised me most – which thankfully only broke after the 2001 election - was free personal care for the elderly, which Henry delivered in Scotland but was not applied by Labour south of the Border. It was not simply a matter of diverging priorities: there were implications for the UK social security budget as the structure Henry came up with conflicted with the way attendance allowance for the infirm elderly was paid. Alistair Darling, as Work and Pensions Secretary, was determined to defend the uniform system of benefits, reckoning that under Henry's plan Scots would have their cake and eat it. Both Henry and Alistair were adamant, yet anxious to avoid a damaging row. I spent much of a short holiday near Perth standing on the hotel's lawn – the only place I could get a signal - fielding calls from

Henry's people refusing to give ground, and from Alistair's saying much the same. The crisis passed without irreparable damage, though I'm not sure my good offices achieved anything.

George McGregor and I divided up the SPAD tasks to make the best use of our experience and contacts; my focus was on Westminster and the media and his on the Scottish party. Having nearly joined Helen when she was Transport Minister, I now organised meetings for her with Network Rail's John Armitt as it emerged from the shambles of Railtrack, and a session between Gorge Foulkes and the Strategic Rail Authority where we pressed issues our Holyrood partners felt were being ignored. I also encouraged Helen to call that "summit" to press for more direct flights from Scotland; despite the meeting coming shortly after the 9/11 attacks fourteen airlines attended, and the Scottish Government took the issue forward with its Route Development Fund.

After Alistair Darling moved to Transport, we were involved with his airports White Paper. By mid-2002 a rail link to Edinburgh Airport was national policy; the business case for one to Glasgow Airport was weaker, but politically Labour had to promote one. Ironically both the Glasgow link and the increasingly gold-plated Edinburgh Airport Rail Link (EARL) would be casualties of the SNP administration. Edinburgh Airport also gave us some fun at the expense of the Liberal Democrats. A second runway was considered for the White Paper, bringing protests from the Lib Dem stronghold of Edinburgh West. Then the Home Office proposed using former RAF quarters there to house asylum seekers; this produced even greater outrage, so we challenged the Lib Dems to say which offended them most: the second runway or the asylum-seekers. In the event, they got neither.

Working for the Secretary of State was not a passport to tour Scotland ... though it did bring an invitation to a Royal garden party at Holyrood, a tremendous experience despite the bitter cold of an Edinburgh July. Helen went where the people were, and engagements in the Highlands were hard to justify. She did visit the set of *Monarch of the Glen*, but there was no call for a SPAD to be there and in any case George McGregor, brought up in Fort William, had a better claim than me.

The 2001 election was scarcely over when Henry ran into trouble over the disorganised state of his office finances when MP for Central Fife. Continuing innuendo loosened his grip and that November he resigned, insisting there had been "a muddle, not a fiddle". Jack McConnell, the obvious successor, brought a greater confidence and assertiveness, particularly in pressing – more than Henry - for the transfer of further powers from Westminster, and a readiness to take risks. Henry tried to be a safe pair of hands, but Jack liked nothing better than punting the ball over the stand.

Reckoning the SNP had to be beaten at its own game, Jack distanced himself from Westminster and New Labour, and showed a different attitude toward the Secretary of State. Henry had treated Helen as almost the senior partner; to Jack the idea of even a "Jack and Helen show" was unthinkable; her existence cramped his style. Whereas Helen and Henry had talked regularly, Jack met Helen formally at St Andrew's House; the meetings were candid and generally friendly, but we were once kept waiting in a room that had obviously just been used for someone's lunch. My contacts with Jack's special advisers were almost as productive as with Henry's, but they too left no doubt where the initiative lay.

I left the Scotland Office in September 2002 when press coverage of the new edition of *The Joy of Sex* made my situation difficult and caused embarrassment for Helen. By then, pressure was building within the Edinburgh political and media village - orchestrated by Andrew Neil but with a suspicion of backing at Holyrood - for the abolition of the stand-alone post of Secretary of State. An early sign had been a leak to the *Daily Telegraph* of Helen's draft diary, giving the impression that she had little to do. Neil's papers trumpeted that devolution had made Helen's post redundant, and her marginalisation in the 2003 Holyrood elections gave them further ammunition. (Her antennae were as acute as ever. When a visit was planned to a subsidiary of Halliburton soon after the invasion of Iraq from which the US conglomerate profited greatly, she had it pulled from the schedule).

Had Clare Short not resigned over Iraq when she did but stayed until an imminent reshuffle, Helen might have replaced her as Secretary for International Development. But by going before the Holyrood elections, Clare forced Tony Blair to pick someone who could start at once, and the job went to Baroness Amos. In that June's reshuffle, Alistair Darling became Scottish as well as Transport Secretary, slimming down the Scotland Office. Helen left days before she was to host the customary Dover House reception for Trooping the Colour, but she played her part: the new Secretary of State greeted guests at the top of the stairs, then Helen shook their hands as they passed into the room.

With the SNP in power, the Secretary of State became Westminster's principal voice in Scotland, prompting Gordon's decision in 2008 to make the holder once again a stand-alone Cabinet minister.

Helen became High Commissioner to Australia in July 2005. She boarded the plane amid jubilation at London securing the 2012 Olympics, and left it to learn of the 7/7 bombings and having to organise a memorial service. When I went to Australia in 2005 for Carrie's wedding Helen had VIP guests, but when I went back with Jeanette for another wedding the next year she invited us to stay.

Canberra is a city of 300,000-odd inhabitants devoted to government, and so carefully planned that you're bound to get lost; I later met a Brit who claimed to have designed much of its road network, and held my tongue. Compared with Washington, first and greatest of the political company towns, the climate is less extreme, but the absence of traffic, the slow pace of life and the wide open spaces hinted at what America's capital must have been like in the 1930s before it attracted armies of bureaucrats, lobbyists and car dealers.

We arrived at the Residence, Westminster House, before Helen and her husband Alistair who had been to the Melbourne Cup with official guests. When they got back, the Union Jack was hoisted (and lowered when she set off to work the next morning). Helen took us out to see the sights in her 4x4, then we had drinks in the garden – with a tree planted by every recent Australian Prime

Minister - and a beautifully-served dinner. There was plenty to catch up on: politics at home, family news and the latest on Helen's former staff, about whom she cares greatly. Alistair, a keen golfer who was enjoying the odd round at Royal Canberra, showed us his screensaver with kangaroos standing round him as he putted.

At QinetiQ I kept in touch with Scottish MPs, organised politicians' visits to Rosyth and the West Freugh range near Stranraer – driving down from Glasgow through stunning if eerie coastal scenery – and on August Bank Holiday 2005 nearly fulfilled a lifetime ambition to visit St Kilda. The remote outcrop beyond the Outer Hebrides whose inhabitants lived on seabirds – avoiding fish because they had seen so many fishing boats sink – was evacuated in 1930. To mark the 75th anniversary Patricia Ferguson, Scotland's Tourism Minister, flew out to St Kilda to unveil a plaque, making the final hop from the QinetiQ-operated MoD range on Benbecula. I persuaded the necessary people that I should escort her, and joined the chopper at Cumbernauld airfield for the flight up.

We skimmed the summit of Ben Lomond, which John Smith had nearly climbed with me fifteen years before, overflew the MoD's bomb storage bunkers at Glen Douglas and the Loch Fyne Oyster House where Gordon Brown and John Prescott supposedly plotted the Labour succession, and refuelled at North Connel. Then we flew low over Rum, Eigg, Muck and Canna as deer raced away from us, across the Minch and over the lochan-strewn boilerplate of Benbecula.

The weather report from St Kilda was poor, so I took our guests to the officers' mess, and with the staff off for the day did my best to provide refreshments with most of the cupboards locked. We visited a St Kilda exhibition in the local school, and were touring South Uist amid surprisingly heavy traffic when word came back that (1) the cloud had cleared and (2) there wasn't room on the chopper for everyone. I volunteered to stay behind, rejoining the party for the return flight to Cumbernauld, with the highlight swerving to avoid a golden eagle. Maybe I will get to St Kilda another day.

19: Editors

A national newspaper editor needs powers of leadership, a nose for news, loyalty to their staff and an understanding of the readers' interests and prejudices. I have worked under some twenty editors; the best have possessed all these qualities, a few hardly any. And the finest were Max Hastings and Bill Deedes of the *Daily Telegraph,* and the *Daily Record's* Endell Laird.

Appointing Max to edit the *Telegraph* when Conrad Black acquired it from Lord Hartwell was a gamble. His physical presence is commanding, but while he was a courageous war reporter and an acclaimed military historian, he had never run anything. Yet the choice was inspired; under Max the old *Telegraph* was left behind at Fleet Street, the paper gaining a more vibrant feel based at the Isle of Dogs.

In some ways Max simply brought standard newspaper practice to a 19th-century organisation; until he arrived there was no morning conference of departmental heads and the paper just happened, through the professionalism of a production team headed by a succession of fine night editors: Harry Winslade, Andrew Hutchinson and David Ruddock.

New printing capacity allowed Max to inaugurate a range of Saturday supplements, given a distinctive feel by his design guru Don Berry. Most of his appointments were inspired – though not all were intentional. Wanting to recruit the highly-rated Nigel Horne to edit the op-ed page, Max did not make his intentions clear to his secretary or read the resulting letter properly, and found he had offered the post to Alistair Horne, a distinguished man of letters. After a reaction that would have done Basil Fawlty proud, Max took Alistair Horne out for an expensive lunch to persuade him he didn't want the job. Another gamble was making my Cambridge contemporary Richard Chartres, later Bishop of London, religious affairs correspondent. Meeting Richard at a function years later Max asked him: "Haven't we met before?" Without missing a beat, Chartres replied: "Yes, when you sacked me." Max also had the courage to fire Carol Thatcher (though I was sorry to see her go), knowing full well how her mother would react.

Though Black – visionary proprietor first, trickster much later - was supportive, he pressed Max to take a more Right-wing line than was sensible at a time when Mrs Thatcher's government was under heavy fire. I contributed to his problems in this respect. One day when I was editing the leader page, the main comment piece fell through and I ran one I had written myself on what a Tory government might do in the post-Thatcher era. I had run it past Bill Deedes and others who reckoned it fair comment, but when Conrad read it he went ballistic with Max. He, in turn, sent me a note describing it as "not your finest hour", largely because I could have shown it to him first - as I would had he been around. Reading it now, it wasn't as good as I thought.

Black's other constraint on Max was financial. My last action before handing in my notice was to join a one-day strike against a dozen redundancies, including Jim O'Brien, my successor in Birmingham. I was the only page editor to walk out, telling Max I felt honour bound. Had I stayed, that could have marked the end of my career as a newspaper executive - not that that side of the business appealed to me. Only when I read Max's book *Editor* did I realise he had absolutely no room for manoeuvre.

Max and I have nothing in common. His main interest is shooting (influential people are categorised by "He shoots with X"), his snobbery can be breathtaking, and he has the attention span of a gnat. Yet he is the only editor for whom I would have cheerfully gone over the top.

My four years under Max did not start auspiciously. My boss Jim Wightman had quit and I had applied for his job after six years as his deputy. Almost the first thing Max did was call me in and tell me the paper's specialists needed freshening up and he was bringing in George Jones from the *Sunday Times* as a "story-getting" political editor. I was poor company when I got home to the flat I was sharing with Norval Lyon and his new American wife Lynn - who had laid on a surprise "Noche Mexicana".

Max came to appreciate my efforts, save for one Budget day when, in the heat of the moment and with the MoD – as often - unhelpful, I got the name of the Chief of Defence Staff wrong. He sent me a pained note that I "of all people" should make a mistake that made him a laughing stock in every officers' mess. Nowadays, I could just have Googled it.

On the days I edited the leader page – increasingly often as Trevor Grove, officially in charge, moved up the editorial ladder – I operated a stone's throw from Max's office. I quickly got to how his bêtes noires. One was the Church of England, which he regarded as feebly led and lacking in conviction. (Max, as far as I know, possesses no strong religious convictions, but quite reasonably he expected the Church to have them.) Eventually he was invited to Lambeth Palace for lunch with Archbishop Runcie, and asked me to go with him. After a solecism at the outset when I inadvertently took the Primate's drink, I found the surroundings and the conversation fascinating, but could tell Runcie was not impressing Max. He might have won an MC as a tank commander, but he came across as kindly but defensive. Runcie stressed the antiquity of his office, "predating the united monarchy", but bemoaned the fact that many expected him to exert the same authority over the Anglican Communion as the Pope did over Roman Catholics. Max's view, which he just about managed to suppress, was that at least Runcie could have a damn good try. Nor were we impressed when Runcie, in the ultimate oath-from-the-pulpit moment, described a prominent public figure as an "arsehole". From then on, for Max the moral leadership of the nation rested with Cardinal Hume.

Days after the King's Cross fire, with passengers in revolt at the unreliability of the Tube and management threatening protesters with prosecution, I wrote my most outspoken *Telegraph* leader, beginning: "Is anybody actually running the London Underground?" The reaction was instantaneous, though not hostile: a call from LU's head of communications, Neil Garrie – who became a friend – suggesting I meet his chairman, Tony Ridley. Ridley, who had previously launched Hong Kong's rapid transit system, left me with the impression that he had about as much control over the Tube as Runcie had over the Church. An invitation followed for Max to lunch at 55 Broadway: not a meeting of minds. I have seen Max (despite his height) on the Tube and he knows what commuters expect; he came away convinced they were being let down.

The afternoon the report on King's Cross was published, I sat down to write the definitive leader; it got overlong and flabby, then my computer froze. With the deadline approaching Max, en route to a dinner, sat down and thumped out 450 words saying everything I'd been trying to say. It was one of many reminders – including his threat one election night to take over a struggling reporter's story and write it himself - that he could do the job of almost any of his staff, better than they could.

Despite his preoccupations, Max could be deeply human. When Carrie, then 13, was savaged by the school caretaker's Alsatian, he sent flowers almost before she had arrived at hospital. The wounds turned out to be superficial, but the shock was tremendous and I could not understand how the police allowed the dog to live.

Max stood by his leader writers if the great and the good objected to what appeared; it was the *Telegraph*'s opinion, and he personified the paper. When I wrote a trenchant leader about coal the NCB chairman Robert Haslam accused Max of letting David Hart, the sinister defence consultant who claimed to have orchestrated the defeat of the miners, dictate our policy. Max told him: "I wouldn't allow Hart in the building." Another time we commented parochially on breakdowns on the Docklands Light Railway. When Sir Arnold Weinstock, head of the now sorely-missed GEC, accused Max of denigrating world-beating British technology, he replied: "I can see the bloody thing out of my window and it's been stuck for 40 minutes."

My next editor, Stephen Glover of the *Independent on Sunday,* was a total contrast. He had been one of the *Telegraph*'s more sensible leader writers, and one of the three pioneers who left to launch the *Independent*. But even as we worked on pre-publication dummy editions of the *IoS,* I began to sense that I would not have been his personal choice. It also became clear that the new paper's staff was dysfunctional. Despite Stephen having recruited a talented group – Sebastian Faulks, Ian Jack, Chris Huhne, Peter Wilby, Cal McCrystal, Lynne Barber (plus Allison Pearson, then an impressive young features sub) - the team lacked critical mass, and balance.

The *IoS* enjoyed a triumphal launch, selling some 700,000 copies, but the shortcomings soon showed. At the start of each week, a post-mortem picked over every detail of Sunday's paper, and as sales fell back, the discussion became sterile and the atmosphere tense. Stephen lacked the confidence to handle pressure, and it communicated itself to the staff - above all to Peter Wilby and myself. Stephen is intense, Peter a shade lugubrious, and while I start off enthusiastic the moodiness of others brings me down.

Quality Sunday papers are news- and politics-driven, but while we had a good news team and I considered myself a competent political reporter things didn't work out. Matters were not helped by Stephen expecting exclusives while failing to back his staff when they delivered them; *pace* our contretemps over Michael Mates. My task was further hampered by his insistence that I follow the *Independent's* policy of boycotting Lobby briefings, yet still try to persuade Bernard Ingham to let us interview Mrs Thatcher; I was peeved to discover that while I was barred from obtaining political steers from Bernard, Chris Huhne had carte blanche from Stephen to make precisely such calls – and any insights gained weren't passed on to me .

Stephen – though now an often insightful columnist on the press – did not seem to have the instincts an editor needs. Some time after I left, he accused Max Hastings in the *Spectator* of being a poor editor, and I fired off a comparative assessment. It never appeared, but I know the *Spectator's* editor Frank Johnson, an old colleague of us both, enjoyed it.

After Max, my favourite editor was unquestionably Bill Deedes. I would have put him first, but he was not an editor in the conventional sense, nominally being responsible only for the comment pages and not for news, sport, features, City and so forth. These lay with the *Telegraph's* overly maligned managing editor Peter Eastwood, but Bill's influence was nonetheless immense.

Bill is such a legendary figure that I can keep my description brief. Forced to leave Harrow at 16 when his father faced ruin after the Wall Street crash, he joined the *Morning Post* in 1931, moving to the *Telegraph* when the papers merged. He covered every prime minister from Ramsay MacDonald to Gordon Brown, the war in Abyssinia with Evelyn Waugh – who modelled William Boot, the hero of *Scoop,* on him – and Princess Diana's campaign against landmines in Africa. In between he won an MC in Holland, served in Harold Macmillan's Cabinet and became a bosom pal of Denis Thatcher. He was modest, entertaining, determined to squeeze the maximum out of life ... and unfailingly helpful to me.

When first I worked for the *Telegraph,* Bill – still an MP - edited the Peterborough column, to which I would become a frequent contributor. Soon after I joined the staff in 1974, he succeeded the distant Maurice Green as editor, and for a decade not only positioned the paper as the intellectual bedrock of Thatcherism, but exerted an influence way beyond his office round the corner from the newsroom. Though I was not strictly his responsibility, there were times we had to talk. When I reported from Birmingham that an Asian father of twelve was drawing £156 a week in benefits, The Race Relations Board accused the *Telegraph* of racism; Bill called me and I pointed out that anyone with 12 children in Brum was assumed to be Irish, and that in the wake of the pub bombings that community had enough on its plate. Bill sagely passed my view on to the race relations people as his own. They made clear, publicly, that they were not happy, but let the matter rest.

Bill was philosophical when I inadvertently landed him with a prosecution for contempt by naming a ward of court. He could have gone to jail but was supportive throughout, though he blenched when I equated the girl's father having misled me about the wardship being over with John Profumo having lied to Bill over his affair with Christine Keeler.

Home from Washington on leave, Bill got out the whisky for me and I was not at my sharpest as I left after a shrewd three-hour grilling about American politics. During it he betrayed more commonsense and less hidebound attitudes than his comment columns; I could also sense that he wished he could get back to reporting ... as eventually he would.

Everyone in the building respected Bill - including the printers, who had little time for the paper's Victorian and rudimentary management. When trouble hit the back of the house, Bill would seek out the cause; if this involved a visit to the pub, so be it. Quite a few times his charm and diplomacy prevented a costly stoppage, though some disputes were so intractable – or illogical – that not even he could resolve them.

I came to know Bill as a colleague after Max succeeded him as editor: a highly experienced predecessor working for a novice. With anyone else this would not have worked, but Bill in his courtly way never gave Max advice unless asked, and Max knew that Bill was a priceless journalistic asset whose retention through radical changes would reassure the readers. He could not have expected the arrangement to last for twenty years, under three further editors.

Bill was an amusing, authoritative but never overbearing foil to Max at leader conference, a compiler of excellent leaders who insisted on researching everything, and a fount of wisdom for the rest of us. In the office, mastering the new technology or chuckling over the day's events, he was a reassuring presence, in the pub at lunchtime a sheer delight. Always the youngest at heart, each of his stories – always solicited, never inflicted – was told with a twinkle. Once we got him onto the Abdication, which he reluctantly admitted having covered for the *Morning Post*. His most vivid memory was that when Stanley Baldwin told the Commons he had responded to Edward VIII's decision to renounce the throne by saying "Sire, this is grievous news.", the entire Press Gallery froze, trying to work out the shorthand outline for "Sire".

When I asked Bill if he had covered the 1935 Spithead Review marking George V's Silver Jubilee, I hit the jackpot. The event achieved notoriety through the alcohol-fuelled radio contribution of Lieutenant-Commander Tommy Woodrooffe, which caught the spirit of the moment and propelled the phrase "The Fleet's lit up" into the national vocabulary. Bill recalled how the press were ferried out to a cruiser and installed in the wardroom. "We each bought a book of chits, a penny for a gin and twopence for a double, and it was only when I got a postal order from the Navy for the chits I hadn't used that I realised how much I'd drunk. We all went on deck for the fly-past, and as the planes flew over we fell over one by one [Bill accompanied this with dramatic hand movements]. Woodrooffe started off with us, but the trouble came when they put him on his old ship. After his broadcast, the general view was that he'd just about got away with it, but when we got back to London we realised he hadn't."

Bill was invited to lunch with local directors of Barclays Bank, at a steak house in Bethnal Green close to the mission where he had lived in the 1930s, and took me along. He was delighted to find that some East End landmarks had survived the Blitz and subsequent council vandalism, and the reminiscences flowed. On the way from South Quay, we passed the Blind Beggar, where Ronnie Kray shot George Cornell in 1966; our driver chipped in to reveal that he had driven for the Krays.

When I left the *Telegraph* late in 1989, Bill chaired a lunch for me, at Rules. We next worked together a decade later when, freelancing as an obituary writer, I shared the leader writers' terminals at Canary Wharf. I was horrified when I found Bill in the Gents with his shirt off having returned from a scorching-hot Australia, and saw the damage done to his skin. He was often away from the office, globetrotting with notebook in hand. Then one day when I'd been told Bill wouldn't be in and logged onto his machine, I heard a familiar voice behind me and there he was, well over 90 but with the twinkle as great as ever. As I started to move, Bill told me: "No, you stay put. You're working."

A year before he died, I bought a signed copy of *Dear Bill,* his book of recollections. Bill recalled a debate at the Oxford Union in the 1980s with Jack Lynch, the former Taoiseach. Lynch had been provided with a bottle of the Irish whiskey Paddy, a choice Bill thought possibly tactless. I wrote to tell him he could rest easy, as when I met Lynch I had been advised that Paddy was his favourite tipple. Bill thanked me ... and hoped I had bought the second edition of his book, not the first which he considered poor value.

Endell Laird was living proof that to produce a successful newspaper, you must understand its readers. Under his editorship the *Daily Record* sold 750,000 copies a day in Scotland, remarkable for a country with just 5 million inhabitants. I don't blame the subsequent fall-off entirely on his successors; the challenge of the *Scottish Sun,* the emergence of the internet, Labour's loss of support to the SNP and a declining interest in print all contributed. But Endell knew exactly how to pitch the paper: bold but not brash, proudly Scottish but never xenophobic, pro-Labour but seldom implausibly so, and speaking to an educated working class as its equal. A popular tabloid, yes, but never dumbed-down.

If you met Endell in his golf club you would have reckoned him a retired bank manager, and probably a Tory. Birdlike but stocky, he was authoritative but never overbearing, with the quiet confidence that comes from being on top of the job. Hailing from Forfar, he had, like so many fine journalists, begun his career at D C Thomson in Dundee. His time there, before editing the *Sunday Mail* in Glasgow and then its sister paper the *Record,* included a spell on the *Dandy* - not mentioned in his *Who's Who* entry.

Endell got the paper out without histrionics, helped by a having a highly experienced and sure-footed team. Blunders – such as leading the paper with a story about faulty breast implants on the night Ravenscraig was doomed to closure – occurred on the rare occasions he was away from the office. And every so often he would take up a cause that cemented the paper to its readers – notably the appeal for Scotland's first children's hospice that raised over £5 million.

There were other non-Scots than me on Endell's staff, and other graduates, but I was the only one with no tabloid experience. He knew I would need help adjusting to house style and to Scotland's political and media culture, and I learned from him (and Tom Brown and Dave King) how far I could credibly go in reflecting these. The 1992 election gave him a chance to see me under pressure, and for the next two years he gave me his total confidence.

Though Endell was not young, it was a shock when he announced his (enforced) retirement. I was honoured to be one of the small group at his farewell dinner – and the only one not based in Glasgow – and left it conscious of the passing of an era.

His successor, Terry Quinn, had a background in local evenings and magazines, and a different approach for the paper: more colour, a less conservative layout, a somewhat brasher tone. Some changes he introduced were improvements, some were inevitable, but the feel of the *Record* became lighter, more like a free sheet than a national. Terry did have a feel for politics, aborting a trip to London virtually in mid-flight when he heard John Major had quit as Conservative leader to challenge his Cabinet "bastards". But he didn't do subtlety; when the Tories selected a banker to fight the Perth by-election, he was only interested in stories making a play on the word.

In one respect, and to my cost, Terry was ahead of his time. Two years out from what seemed even then an inevitable victory for Tony Blair, he realised ahead of other editors that once devolution kicked in, politics in Scottish papers would need to be covered mainly from Scotland. To that end he renamed me "Westminster editor" instead of "Political editor", that title going to Tom Brown. I had no problem over that – at the *Telegraph* I had never had a title – but it also became apparent that except for major UK political stories (on which we sometimes used *Daily Mirror* copy anyway) I would get less in the paper. The issue never came to a head, as I resigned when my long-running lawsuit against the Mirror Group for not honouring the contract Robert Maxwell had given me with the *European* reached the crunch. Terry was understandably peeved, but we parted on reasonable terms - though he did observe that I would "never make a tabloid journalist". Weeks later, I was writing leaders for the *Sun*.

My very first editor, at the *Guardian,* was Alistair Hetherington. Though I was there only as a messenger, I was keenly aware of the civilised authority with which he ran the paper as it continued its relocation from Manchester. He came across a man of firm convictions, ready to listen but conscious there was a time when the talking had to stop and a newspaper got out.

Positioning the *Guardian* somewhere between the Liberals and Labour – rather than further to the left as has been tried at times since – Hetherington was a shrewd judge of readers' instincts in the run-up to the 1964 election.

I was fortunate to have Harold Evans as my next editor, on the *Northern Echo* in 1965. Harry had made his name on the *Manchester Evening News* and would go on to greatness at the *Sunday Times,* then superstardom in the States. The *Echo* under Harry was a vibrant place, with an enthusiastic staff responding to his dynamism. What made it different – and the people of the

North-East sit up – was the crispness of layout, the imaginative headlines, the feeling that the paper was going somewhere. While he would become a legend for sponsoring investigative reporting – encouraging my mentor Mike Corner to undertake it at the *Echo* - Harry was at his finest on the production side. I can see him now on the back bench, slight, dark-haired and bespectacled, locked in creative discussion with his night editor and chief sub.

At the *Echo* I wrote what I thought was a brilliant feature about how a family – the Charges - had turned a disused chapel outside Darlington into their home. Having gone there to interview them, I took the Charges' cuttings from the library to check a few points, and spotting some discrepancies with names, unwisely went with those in the cuttings rather than those in my notebook, mixing up two branches of the family. Their complaints left me feeling very small. Harry called me in, catalogued my mistakes and how I should have avoided them ... then added as he saw my shoulders drop: "Don't worry, you'll walk onto a national." I'm glad I proved him right.

Michael Finley was my first editor as a career newspaperman. He inherited a *Sheffield Telegraph* famed for investigative reporting, but with its circulation slipping. His solution was to rename it *Morning Telegraph* (it was heresy to preface this with ("*The*"), replace the Gothic masthead with something lighter and add the rubric "Serving Four Counties" with more effort going into covering outlying towns and villages. I don't blame Finley for its eventual demise in 1985 and the paper he inherited did look a touch old-fashioned, but his concept had too narrow an appeal given the *Telegraph*'s roots in industrial Sheffield. What he did right, however, was hire a talented young staff, led outstandingly on the news side by Mike Corner.

Finley suffered the frustration of editing a paper in a city almost ignored by the national media; to the BBC Yorkshire meant Leeds, and the dailies were not much better. Stories we broke seldom gained a wider circulation, let alone any kudos for our paper. Sheffield was then, as now, an exciting city to live in, bursting with creativity; but all the outside world heard about was the slow decline of its staple industries. Finley – sensibly – set out to offset this by getting on television, and I would switch on late at night to see the familiar heavy glasses and bow tie ... though my landlady did once say: "I saw your editor on the box last night, talking about Biafra. He was still talking when I woke up."

Finley moved on to the *Kent Messenger,* to be succeeded by Michael Hides, a humane, bearded production man I remembered as chief sub on the *Guardian.* He had a reputation for being able to throw a telephone further – with cord attached – than anyone else in the business, but I never saw him erupt. Mike Hides was a kindly soul, very close with his disabled but ever cheerful wife Margaret, but his great love was the Peak District National Park, where the scope for building readership or advertising was limited. He also recruited older, less sparky recruits than Finley. But his instincts were sound; he resolved one argument in conference by saying: "I don't know much about football, but I do know that if there's a cup tie between Preston and Derby and the winners are playing Sheffield United we ought to cover it."

I already knew Ian Watson, the *European*'s launch editor, as a successful City editor and assistant editor of the *Sunday Telegraph.* No Mirror Group executive wanted the job, and when Robert Maxwell summoned him Ian, despite widespread scepticism over the viability of the project, put together a credible and cosmopolitan - if overstretched - staff.

Ian's roots were in Fleet Street, and urging the staff out for yet another bonding evening in the pub, he declared: "My aim is to create a pissy-arsed newspaper". (It also became quite a good one.) His style was relaxed and tolerant. Halfway home from British Airways' Christmas party, I realised that I had Ian's raincoat, with his season ticket to Gidea Park in the pocket. He just accepted my mistake as one of those things.

Ian was open to ideas, but editing a pan-European newspaper made what his City sources could tell him largely irrelevant. He also, inevitably, had his run-ins with Maxwell. Increasingly Ian's conversation became dominated by the mini-castle he was building outside Aberdeen, and as circulation proved sluggish – mainly because of the flaws inherent in any Maxwell project – Maxwell replaced him with John Bryant.

John came from the short-lived but imaginative *Sunday Correspondent,* and brought several of its key players with him, notably James McManus as news editor, and as economic commentator David Blake, perhaps the brightest person intellectually I've ever worked with, and with whom, possibly to my cost, I lost touch when he moved on to Goldman Sachs. John was slim and energetic; it was easy to imagine him as the *Daily Mail* athletics writer who championed the South African runner Zola Budd to the point where Leon Brittan unwisely enabled her to represent Britain in the Olympics. Under him the *European* developed a greater sense of direction, but he was smart enough to sense things would not last. John put the *Correspondent* behind him but Maxwell did not, paying a six-figure sum for the title in case it should come in handy. One morning we were speculating on the future of the Warsaw Pact, the Communist counterpart of NATO, and I could not resist suggesting Maxwell might bid for the title. John chuckled, but some of his acolytes blenched.

Some weeks after Maxwell's mysterious demise at sea the fact, and then the enormity, of his financial difficulties and his looting of the pension fund came to light and the money ran out. John Bryant left for the *Times* - taking most of his team with him - and Charlie Garside, his deputy, took over, leading a staff who worked without pay until a new proprietor was found – by when I had left for the *Daily Record*. John later edited the *Telegraph* in the interim as the Barclay Brothers steadied the ship after acquiring the paper from Conrad Black; he always looked too preoccupied to approach.

I never worked with the most colourful editor of my time, Kelvin MacKenzie - a genius at the *Sun,* though legendarily rude to his staff. I did have dealings with his mother Mary MacKenzie, pint-sized and bubbly press officer to the eccentric GLC leader Horace Cutler. But my only memory of Kelvin in the flesh is, improbably, of him speaking from the pulpit of St Margaret's, Westminster, at Chris Potter's memorial service; he had been supremely supportive to Chris during his bouts with cancer.

Kelvin stories are legion and most, I am sure, are true. There was the time a reporter found his story wasn't going into the paper and told him: "We have to use it. It's true." Kelvin grabbed a motor horn, honked it and bellowed: "True story alert! We've got one at last." But my favourite concerns his sacking of the *Sun*'s astrologer. He called in his secretary and dictated a letter beginning: "As you will already know ..."

Kelvin had gone by the time Trevor Kavanagh recruited me as the *Sun*'s stand-in leader writer, but his successor Stuart Higgins was formidable in his own way. He may have inherited a superbly professional team, but under him the paper retained its freshness. He kept the *Sun* firmly in line with Rupert Murdoch's views, and prevented it drifting tackily down market. Stuart's authority was based on his excellent record as a Royal reporter, and when he left I couldn't resist asking why the press had taken so long to latch onto Prince Charles' relationship with Camilla. His reaction left me in no doubt that the problem hadn't been finding the facts, but getting them printed.

David Yelland came next. He conveyed an impression of energy and firmness where Stuart had exuded solidity, but his approach was not that different. Increasingly, though, my Sundays writing leaders left me answerable to his deputy, Rebekah Wade, later a controversial editor of the *News of the World* and the *Sun* itself, and News International's chief executive until forced out for a time over the phone-hacking scandal. I found Rebekah, who had yet to target supposed paedophiles, surprisingly politically correct; after my first day on her watch, I could see quite a few topics that would not feature in *Sun* leaders while she was in the chair.

Neil Wallis I first worked with when he was Stuart Higgins' deputy, then again when he edited the *People*. Short and energetic, Neil is the most entertaining editor I have worked for; nor did he mind his staff calling him a wassock if the situation merited it. His spontaneous humour could reduce an editorial conference to stitches. When the *Sun's* Scouse Whitehall correspondent Dave Wooding mentioned the London Eye, Neil told him: "I thought you lot had stolen the hub caps." At the *People* I happened to mention that from our Westminster office you could see the Eye creeping round, only for Neil to retort: "Now I know what we're paying you to do." Yet if Neil told you to jump, you jumped.

Neil gave me the best example of the choices an editor faces. We had an exclusive story that Tiggy Legge-Bourke, long-time supernanny to Princes William and Harry, had allowed one of them to abseil down a dam in Wales. The story was strong – every other paper splashed it - but we had also found that the woman who had tipped us off had a shady past. Neil's hunch was to lead the paper with this, featuring Tiggy's misjudgement slightly less prominently. He asked me if he was doing the right thing, and I concurred. But the moment I saw the paper I realised we had fallen into the classic trap of following up our own story without first giving it the full treatment. We were left with a tacky front page, enabling every other paper to give what began as our exclusive a better show.

One editor I never worked under has impacted on my career: Andrew Neil. I had been wary of him, despite his facility as a broadcaster, ever since David Steel, a near-contemporary of his at Edinburgh University, described him to me as "meretricious". But I admired what he was doing at the *Sunday Times*, and when late in 1984 Mike Jones, its political editor, asked if I would like to come over from the *Telegraph*, I was tempted.

My first sight coming out of the lift was a young and staggeringly glamorous Nigella Lawson, with legs up to her armpits. I think the interview went well; I elaborated on how I could feed into the work of the paper's specialists and *Insight* team. By the end I was joining the *Sunday Times*, and told Mike I was looking forward to it. A few days later a rather sheepish Mike told me Neil had instead hired the *Sunday Telegraph*'s George Jones, apparently as he was being paid less than me. Just over a year later, Max preferred George to me as political editor of the *Daily,* citing George's "story-getting" at the *Sunday Times* as the clincher.

While I was working for Helen, Neil conducted an increasingly personal campaign against her through the *Scotsman* and *Scotland on Sunday,* culminating just as I left in an edition of *SoS* crammed with falsehoods, half-truths and misinterpretations about her tenure. I had always kept Helen – who shared my misgivings – away from Neil unless he was interviewing her, but soon afterward she was persuaded to invite him in to clear the air. The meeting was a disaster, as Neil grabbed her prompt-sheet on his papers' transgressions, then published it with a slant of his own. When the stand-alone office of Secretary of State was temporarily abolished months later, the *Scotsman* claimed the nation had been saved £1.9 million a year simply because Helen was no longer in post. David Steel was right.

24: Spin

I may well be the only person who has been asked to be a spin doctor by all the major parties. The SDP came for me first. Roy Jenkins, then party leader, was looking for an assistant, but I didn't want to leave newspapers and doubted the job had prospects. And while I was with the *Daily Record,* Archy Kirkwood, one of my favourite Lib Dem MPs, asked who I would suggest to handle the parliamentary media. I suspect he would have bitten my arm off had I shown interest; instead I floated a few names.

In the run-up to the 1983 election Tony Shrimsley, a respected Lobby man who had gone to Conservative Central Office as head of communications only to become terminally ill, invited me to join him with a view to taking over, and later, when I was at the *European,* the party chairman Kenneth Baker obliquely sounded me out over lunch about a job. Working for the Tories in the late Thatcher days would certainly have put me at the centre of things, but handling the media had never appealed to me as much as working for it; and above all I could not have worked for a party I didn't believe in. The same applied when, later, I was headhunted about becoming head of policy for the Institute of Directors. This could have opened a lucrative career path, but I wasn't comfortable with the IoD's policy line under the arch-Thatcherite John Hoskyns.

Labour didn't approach me until the summer of 1999 when I was freelancing for the *Sunday People* and *Scotland on Sunday* and trying to get my media training off the ground. I was visiting my mother in her nursing home (she would live nine months more) when my mobile rang and it was Helen, then Transport Minister and deputy to John Prescott. Having been left by Prescott to make a statement on privatising air traffic control which was bound to go down badly, and been pilloried by the *Evening Standard* for being a Scot in charge of London's transport, she needed help ... and as a minister entitled to attend Cabinet she was allowed a special adviser. I promised to think it over quickly and get back to her.

It was a dream job given my interests, but I'd heard about the atmosphere in Prescott's department and wanted to run some checks. The second call I made produced a shock: "Haven't you heard? Helen's been reshuffled to the DTI." And she had - to a post where she didn't qualify for a SPAD. It was probably for the best; at Transport I would have been caught up in the ructions weeks later over Prescott being driven the 200 yards from the conference hotel to the hall to protect his wife's hairdo. I personally was a fan of Prescott's transport policies, sabotaged by Number 10 who thought them too anti-motorist. But when he circled the wagons, Helen and I would have been on the outside.

Months later I did join Helen at the DTI, in her capacity as the department's Minister for Europe, as a non-partisan consultant on European presentation. Stephen Byers was Secretary of State, with one of his two SPADs the legendary Jo Moore. She saw me as a threat, and did her best to keep me on the margin. But I knew the limits of what I was there to do and got on with my job, with Jo throwing the occasional spanner in the works. Dan Corry, Byers' other SPAD, was unfailingly helpful.

Weeks after Helen's promotion to Scottish Secretary, she called me again. She had spent the weekend fielding press calls after a row over a visit to the shrine at Carfin Grotto by the Irish prime minister Bertie Ahern, and asked me to handle the media for her full-time. I said yes straight away.

Until then – over twenty years in the Lobby - I had been a recipient of spin. I had taken no great exception to it; nor do I today. It is naïve to imagine any person, organisation or party will want to be seen in a needlessly negative light, or let their merits be concealed. Excesses of spin – including downright untruths – are deplorable, and an insult to the average recipient's intelligence. But in my experience, spin doctors who lie or mislead usually come unstuck.

In the Lobby I had dealt with Whitehall press officers, for most of whom I developed a high regard (indeed I helped train a few of them) and special advisors (SPADs). These were much closer to ministers, the Government's political agenda (and problems), and the ultimate political game. Moreover, during the Thatcher years they met weekly in parallel with the Cabinet.

Several Conservative SPADs were particularly helpful to me: Katherine Ramsay (now a fellow *Telegraph* obituarist) for Nick Ridley, Keith Simpson (later an MP) for Tom King, and Elizabeth Buchanan for Cecil Parkinson; she went on to the Palace. I usually called them to test the water rather than for anything new and dramatic; on rare stories such as how the Cabinet felt about the timing of an election, I might even ring most of them. Yet while some were media-savvy, I would not have called them spin doctors; spin emanated from Central Office.

With the proliferation of the media, efforts by governments and parties to set the agenda intensified. The written press, in particular, was kept further from the story; carefully crafted and distributed soundbites, and photo opportunities with no questions asked, were deemed safer or more productive.

Equally, the complete lack of media-savviness once shown by some parties and Whitehall departments has largely given way to co-ordination and professionalism, which can benefit the working journalist. It certainly helped us when departments finally had a press officer available outside office hours ... the Foreign Office only falling into line when a diplomatic rupture with Saudi Arabia was threatened over the television drama-documentary *Death of A Princess* and the *Sun's* David Kemp had to get Douglas Hurd out of bed to find out what the line was. But you always had to ask yourself why you were being told something.

Spin goes back to the Pharaohs, at least, and there was plenty in ancient Rome: just read Caesar. Disraeli was a master of presentation, having Queen Victoria crowned Empress of India. Lloyd George and Churchill were past masters; Asquith was not, witness his clumsy handling of the suffragettes, with whom most of his Cabinet sympathised. Attlee was not interested in publicity, though definitely in results, while Harold Macmillan, a consummate showman, brought Bill Deedes into his Cabinet to co-ordinate Government information. (Extraordinarily Bill was given no part, after helping frame the very first Commons statement, in damage limitation over the Profumo affair). Harold Wilson became paranoid and tried to manage the news, notably once the *Mirror's* Joe Haines became his press secretary. When relations with the Lobby broke down in the final months of Wilson's premiership, Haines blamed the hacks ... but in truth he had been rumbled.

Jim Callaghan's press secretary Tom McCaffrey, though a career civil servant, was no stranger to spin; he had briefed to deadly effect from the Home Office against Barbara Castle's *In Place of Strife*. But Number 10 in Callaghan's day was pretty open; you could talk to anybody in his office without arousing suspicion. Of course, Downing Street wasn't gated off then.

Margaret Thatcher brought in another civil servant (indeed a former Labour candidate) to handle the media: Bernard Ingham, now seen as a professional Yorkshireman rather than the class act he was. He gave you instant access to what the Prime Minister was thinking; when he erupted, you knew she had. And the two things he did that aroused greatest suspicion were, to a tidy administrator, entirely logical.

Bernard felt the Government Information Service was underperforming, so he took control of it and picked from the departmental press offices an accomplished cadre of communicators. If that was empire-building, give me more of it. His other sin, to some, was to make sure every department told Number 10 what it was doing. Astonishingly the first Downing Street often knew then about embarrassing departmental announcements was when they surfaced on the news agency wires or in parliamentary answers. Bernard believed it only right for the Prime Minister to know what her government was up to, so PR disasters could be averted. The issue was not a new one; Richard Crossman never recovered from insouciantly increasing NHS charges on local election day. But since Bernard got a grip, shambolic departures from any government's central message have been rare.

The one time I saw Bernard completely thrown was during a routine briefing in his front room at Number 10. After he had gone through the Prime Minister's day, one of the hacks asked why she was seeing Maurice Saatchi. "What makes you think she's seeing Maurice Saatchi?" retorted Bernard, plainly unaware of any such arrangement. "I've just seen him going through the front door," came the reply.

The most devastating example of spin during the Thatcher years was Michael Heseltine's handling of Westland – the helicopter maker he wanted to partner a European firm rather than be taken over by America's Sikorsky. Shock waves reverberated across

Whitehall from the MoD, culminating in Heseltine's dramatic resignation in mid-Cabinet and Leon Brittan's enforced departure as Trade and Industry Secretary. Old-timers had told me how Jim Callaghan unprecedentedly briefed against *In Place of Strife;* now Heseltine was doing the same.

One Sunday John Ledlie, the MoD's head of information, called me to say the Secretary of State wanted a word; Heseltine then ran through in detail the arguments for rejecting an American takeover, with criticism of colleagues thinly concealed. Meanwhile Colette Bowe, head of information at the DTI - a highly intelligent Scouser who went on to do deservedly well in the City - kept me posted on the merits of the American option and the shortcomings of Heseltine's solution. She herself hit the headlines over the leak of a letter from the Solicitor-General, Attorney-General, Sir Patrick Mayhew, to Heseltine citing "material inaccuracies" in his claim that a link with Sikorsky would lose Westland European orders. Colette had fed the letter to the Press Association, and Leon walked the plank for having told her to, but many of us detected the hand of Number 10, though Bernard robustly denied involvement. Colette later told me she had personally agreed with Heseltine; Westland, with further irony, is today part of the Italian defence conglomerate Finmeccanica.

Meanwhile Peter Mandelson, lured from television by Neil Kinnock to make Labour electable, ruthlessly changed the way a party widely perceived to be in thrall to "loonies" presented itself. Up to then, the candour of Labour's press operation about the party's shortcomings and divisions had contributed to its disastrous electoral performance. Many damaging leaks had come from Percy Clark, Labour's head of communications in the Callaghan years, who saw exposing the craziest plans of NEC Left-wingers as the only way to save the party. When Percy retired, the once and future MP Max Madden took over. A capable former journalist, Max was ideologically in step with the NEC's Bennite majority and we had to look elsewhere for destructive inside stories.

Mandelson's subsequent sidelining of the NEC's elderly "politburo" on the conference platform and adoption of the red rose as the party emblem were only a start. Neil appointed a campaign co-ordinator who was not a member of the NEC - Robin Cook- and in due course Tony Blair would achieve what would have been unthinkable in the 1980s by sidelining the party chairman, elected annually by the NEC on the "Buggins turn" principle, and appointing a "Party Chair" in Cabinet responsible directly to him.

Party headquarters began to project Neil rather than treating the leader as just another member of the party. And working from Fleet Street on a Sunday, Peter became the obvious contact for me to ring. Just as a call from Heseltine meant copy during Westland, Peter would always give the day's Labour story a whiff of Kinnock's reforming drive ... and let you in just a little on his long-term strategy.

During the Thatcher years, a view grew up among liberal journalists that the Lobby was a tool of news management, because we received unattributable briefings from Bernard twice daily and the Leaders of both houses once a week (and the Leader of the Opposition, until Wapping). I disagreed, though some of the circumlocutions to disguise who had briefed us bordered on the farcical. Much of what Bernard told us was purely operational: the Prime Minister's day, and what was coming up in the House. And if what you were told was implausible, there was nothing to stop you asking questions, checking elsewhere, or simply disbelieving it. After all, we were not geese being force-fed to produce *pâté de foie gras*. Hence my riposte to Bernard when he said Mrs Thatcher opposed sanctions because black South Africans would lose their jobs: it was the first time she had shown concern over anyone losing their job, anywhere.

Dissatisfaction with the system began with *Panorama*'s Michael Cockerell, who had spent a frustrating time in the Lobby before blossoming in current affairs. Robert Harris, now acclaimed as a novelist (*Fatherland* must be the best "what if?" thriller ever written) but not at home as a political reporter, followed suit, then the *Guardian,* the *Scotsman* and the newly-founded *Independent* decided to boycott the briefings. As I found at the *Independent on Sunday*, there was a touch of hypocrisy as other links with Number 10 were kept open, but it enabled those papers to claim the moral high ground, while making their reporters' job fractionally harder. Eventually, under New Labour, the briefings became more open – having outgrown that tiny front room in Number 10 – and the dissenters went back in. Nowadays the briefings are on the record; the spin continues in private.

Interlocked with arguments about news management was the debate over Freedom of Information. I had worked in Washington under a Freedom of Information Act and found it useful - provided you knew exactly what to look for. But most of America's big political stories continued to come from leaks, and I expected the same here if Britain followed suit.

It took years to bring in Freedom of Information. Clement Freud had a Bill on its way through when the Callaghan government – which was far from keen - fell. Mrs Thatcher made cautious steps toward "open government", but only repealed the notorious "catch-all" section of the Official Secrets Act (which made it an offence to communicate *any* official information) because juries would no longer convict under it. And while Labour returned in 1997 committed to freedom of information, its legislation was modest. It has helped uncover some murky practices – yet the *Telegraph*'s seismic exposé of the stratospheric level of MPs' expenses was the result of a leak, albeit paid for. Freedom of Information is only of use if you already know what questions to ask ... or are supremely lucky.

It's hard to imagine that John Major's ill-starred government could ever have benefited from spin, given the internecine warfare over Maastricht, and the tidal wave of "sleaze" (most of it predating his premiership). Yet Major and his colleagues owed their survival until 1997 to two brazen examples.

While John Redwood's leadership challenge was unsuccessful, the outcome was not decisive: 218 MPs for Major, 89 for Redwood, eight abstentions, 12 spoiled papers and two non-voters. I estimated in print that Major would still be in trouble if his majority was 120; in the event it was 129. Yet the media reported a knockout, for one simple reason: Michael Ancram and Ian Lang announced the result as such, and by the time anyone questioned this, Major was home and dry.

Months later came the Scott Report on ministers' connivance at breaches in the arms embargo against Saddam Hussein. If one thing could terminally damage any government, it was this ... even though the roots of the scandal lay in the Thatcher years. The trial of businessmen accused of violating the embargo had collapsed after Alan Clark, one of the ministers responsible, confessed to having been "economical with the *actualité*" about how much Whitehall knew. And by the time Sir Richard Scott reported, there was little doubt in the Lobby that Attorney-General Nicholas Lyell and Chief Secretary William Waldegrave (a Foreign Office minister at the time) faced an early bath.

Robin Cook, who was to lead Labour's attack, was allowed only five hours to digest the report, while ministers implicated saw relevant sections well in advance and had the opportunity to comment. And when the debate took place, Lang, in a display of sheer brass neck, announced that the whole episode had been got up by Labour, and that the real villain was not the ministers who had misled the House but Robin. It was shameless, but in the short term it worked: Lyell and Waldegrave survived by a single vote.

Under New Labour, the art of spin reached its height. Strategic decisions on presentation were taken at the "centre", and the detail fed out to the professionals who ran the departmental press offices, and the special advisers who dealt with the partisan aspects. At the heart of the operation was Alastair Campbell, who had arrived in the Lobby for the *Daily Mirror* as I left to write leaders.

Alastair, a man of fierce loyalties, joined Blair with Labour preparing for government, and moved into Number 10 determined to control the news agenda and keep everyone in government "on message". Events were choreographed to present a daily theme:

education, jobs, health, Europe or whatever. Ministerial visits, photo opportunities and soundbites were matched to it, and other issues kicked into touch. Departmental activity followed suit, catalogued in a daily "grid". It worked well for a time, and helped ensure Blair a "honeymoon" that lasted a couple of years.

With more tolerance from the "centre", that honeymoon could have continued. Most government information professionals I knew privately welcomed a Labour government after years of drift, or were content to work for it. But early on, some of the more paranoid SPADs decided that their departments' heads of information were lacking in commitment, and undermined them. A few of the longest-serving could not cope with a change of tack, and their departure was inevitable. But some heads rolled without reason, and the atmosphere created was not good.

While New Labour was elected pledging to be different from the Tories and purer than pure, some excesses of news management (and acts of braggadocio by individuals) raised concerns both over breaches of ethics and whether ministers were briefing against each other. Careless comments by Derek Draper – an assistant to Peter Mandelson in opposition but never a SPAD – gave the (erroneous) impression that advisers to Labour ministers were soliciting "cash for access". Mandelson, having played an immense part in Labour's return to power through his stewardship of the Millbank "war room", turned out to be far better at spinning for the party than on his own account. While his officials adored him, his botched handling of his personal difficulties forced him out of office not once, but twice. In addition, the pre-existing tensions between Gordon Brown and Mandelson – and increasingly between Brown and Blair – put Gordon's loyal but rumbustious SPAD Charlie Whelan on a tightrope of diplomacy he was not equipped to negotiate; Blairites were convinced he was briefing against them from the Red Lion in Parliament Street.

Campbell's attempts at controlling the news inevitably put him at loggerheads with experienced operators who reported what was going on, only to have their stories branded "garbagic". It never happened to me: in the Sunday lobby for the first two years of the

Blair government, I was treated fairly. I attended Alastair's briefings (moved to the roomier basement of Number 10), was called in when Blair met the Scottish Lobby – and was once rung with copious briefing on Blair's reaction to an England cricket victory, hardly a resonant issue north of the Border. But I would rather have too much information than too little.

Some colleagues had stand-up rows with Alastair or, more frequently, vituperative calls from him, when they printed stories conflicting with New Labour's view of itself. When Number 10 and the Palace disagreed about the role Blair should play in the Queen Mother's lying-in-state the colleague who broke the story got the sharp end of Alastair's tongue, and things got worse for him once it emerged that Downing Street's denials did not match the facts.

The Labour spokesman I trusted most was David Hill, a Brummie whose sister had produced me at Bush House. David, who contrived to resemble all the Marx Brothers, was invaluable to his party and to the media. I first got to know him as Roy Hattersley's research assistant, correctly calling the 1983 election in Birmingham seat by seat. It took time for Labour to realise what an asset they had, but in the early days of Blair's government his straightforward communication of what was happening in the party was invaluable. When it became clear even to Tony that Campbell's relationship with the media had become too adversarial, David was recalled from lobbying to re-establish trust.

Halfway through 1996 I joined Politics International, a small lobbying firm based in Horseferry Road which was headed by Andrew Dunlop, previously of Mrs Thatcher's policy unit (and later as Lord Dunlop a Scotland Office minister). Andrew was at the top of his league, able to talk authoritatively but never patronisingly with heavy-hitting clients, and it is a nice piece of symmetry that George McGregor, my fellow SPAD at Dover House, now leads PI's much larger successor. I was there less than a year, before Andrew realised they needed more Indians rather than another chief, but my experience with PI has proved invaluable.

Our highest-profile client was Sir Richard Branson. We represented Virgin Atlantic, driving forward his campaign to prevent British Airways merging with American Airlines. Once when Branson was due on television, I gave him a hurried last-minute briefing in a taxi from his Holland Park home (travelling solo, the informal Branson preferred chauffeured motorbikes). We were also close to his successful bids for the West Coast and Cross-Country rail franchises. I alerted Will Whitehorn, Branson's presentational guru, to the risks of applying Virgin's branding to a clapped-out service; Virgin went ahead and endured several years of stick before acquiring the trains and infrastructure to offer a credible product.

Another client was Andersen Consulting, now Accenture ... they of the planet-sized brains. They wanted a promotional video about what Andersen could deliver for its clients - outsourced because anyone inside who took it on risked their career if it was not liked at the highest level. After meeting my Andersen partner, Ian Williams, I worked up the project, for which a princely £170,000 had been budgeted. As director I suggested John Deery, who had just made a highly-acclaimed Labour Party video for John Prescott. Ian agreed and John got to work, suppressing his opinions about a truly terrible script I had put together.

As the project took shape, we had an early afternoon meeting in the Andersen building near the Temple. There were four of us in the room, and halfway through I realised one of us was snoring ... and then that it was me.

What a production the video was! John shot the first section (in 35mm) in a futuristic office building: a board of directors are about to take a singularly crass decision when commandos abseil into the room, truss up the stick-in-the muds and the chairman says: "That's one way. Now let's see what Andersen would have done." The film ran pacily through Andersen's way of doing things, with case studies, before returning to that boardroom. When John showed it to the Andersen team in a Soho post-production suite, they loved it. Then came a viewing back at Andersen, for the all-powerful senior managing partner. He watched it stonily, then said:

"You're taking the mickey, aren't you?" As far as I am aware, that £170,000 video has stayed unplayed ever since.

I set up and attended meetings with civil servants, ministers and the Opposition on behalf of PI's clients, prepared briefing on how clients should conduct themselves during a general election and what a Labour government would do with the privatised railways, kept clients abreast of developments, helped them face the media and put their case to politicians. One failure – through no fault of our own – was when a combative client in the cement industry was appearing before a Select Committee. We coached him by setting up a hearing, with former MPs, and feeding him just the sort of questions we knew would test his short fuse; I did warn him that the simplest are sometimes the hardest to answer. On the day my old Sheffield chum Irvine Patnick asked him: "How much is a bag of cement?" and took umbrage when he didn't get a straight reply. Events moved rapidly downhill, the chairman eventually threatening to cite our client for contempt of the House if he didn't answer the question.

I most enjoyed working with London & Continental Railways, who had just won the franchise to run Eurostar and construct the Channel Tunnel Rail Link. I also promoted Lockheed Martin's bid for a New Scottish Air Traffic Control Centre at Prestwick with ministers and Opposition alike; Lockheed was indeed named preferred bidder on the eve of the 1997 election, only for the project to be shelved as air traffic control was privatised.

I left PI as three friends - Jane Bowles and Simon Storer from Eurotunnel, and Peter Kendall from British Rail - were launching a PR firm, and while it never got off the ground it did provide the basis for a media training team. Rob Lawrence, a video producer with links to the three, was asked by his friend Andrew Jeacock at Royal Ordnance to find someone to media train his managers. We did several courses with them over two or three years, mainly equipping managers to say the right things when their factories suffered job cuts or were closed.

Almost all the trainees were able, after a bit of training, to give a coherent radio or television interview. One thought so slowly you could almost hear the cogwheels in his brain. A Val Doonican lookalike, down to the pullover, was so relaxed that we suggested him for lifestyle programmes, not the news. Another manager went through an entire television interview with a pencil behind his ear. One head of HR showed how it shouldn't be done by suggesting redundant engineers could be retrained in flower arranging. And we anticipated events uncannily by ambushing one RO executive with the question: "Why did you invite General Pinochet to the Farnborough Air Show?" Six months later Pinochet was arrested in London, and our trainee faced just that question. We did a session in Warrington for English Partnerships and came close to winning a contract from BAE Systems, but when I next did media training it was on my own, in Zambia for the British Council.

In February 2000 I arrived at Dover House in Whitehall to be Helen's special adviser, working alongside the able and agreeable George McGregor, who had come from Unison. We advised on policy, sat in on Helen's meetings, checked facts from officials for questions in the House (after she was supplied with month-old unemployment figures), wrote speeches, and accompanied her to party events. Occasionally we joined her meetings with other ministers, always held in the office of the most senior. At one shortly before he pulled the plug on Railtrack, Stephen Byers told Helen he reckoned the company had 18 months to prove itself – evidence to me that his forcing Railtrack into administration was a counsel of desperation and not – as his critics claimed – premeditated.

Jo Moore had moved with Byers to Environment and Transport. There, she suggested as the 9/11 attacks happened that it might be opportune to slip out mildly embarrassing data about councillors' allowances. That caught me in two minds. You naturally release good news when there is nothing else around, and this was the corollary. But her e.mail suggesting it was a good time to "bury bad news" as thousands were dying on live television was crass, to say the least - and Jo was not helped by having made plenty of enemies. My own mind that afternoon, sitting a stone's throw from Number

10 amid rumours that one of the hijacked planes was heading for us, was on other things.

Jo was missing from our next fortnightly SPADs' meeting as the storm broke over her. Byers stood by her and at the meeting after, the member of Tony Blair's team chairing the meeting welcomed her back; we applauded dutifully, but our misgivings over the damage done must have been evident. After one further misjudgement, Jo went.

While the SPADs conducted serious business together under the Tories, our meetings, in 10 or 12 Downing Street, were usually to be briefed on some promotional initiative. There were exceptions: we became exasperated that the First Division Association, the senior civil servants' trade union, kept publicly rubbishing us SPADs, so we decided to counter this by joining the FDA en bloc. First we held a straw poll of which unions we belonged to; astonishingly for a group of so-called spin doctors, only two of the 30 or so round the table belonged to the National Union of Journalists: myself and Steve Bates, an ex-BBC man working for John Reid. We joined the FDA ... and its leaders kept on rubbishing us.

I enthusiastically supported one initiative from Blair and Charles Clarke: for ministers to hold party Q&A sessions around the country. Helen was keen but dates were hard to find, and we ended up doing just two, in Enfield Southgate and Gosport. At Southgate, where Stephen Twigg's astonishing defeat of Michael Portillo was still being savoured, the meeting turned into a debate between NHS workers on the state of Chase Farm Hospital (where Dad had been a houseman nearly 60 years before). Some complained that money pumped in wasn't getting through to patient care, others about poor management. I reported this to Charles; maybe it was a coincidence but six weeks later the hospital's chief executive was fired.

Most questions in Gosport were about pension reform, something Helen was well up with from her time at the Treasury. I left puzzled that such a heavily working-class town was still represented by a Tory after Labour's double landslide. I knew from my Lobby days that Peter Viggers, Gosport's long-serving Tory MP, had built up a strong personal vote; later I would see the interest he took in QinetiQ's site there. It was cruel that so committed a backbencher should be brought down by his expenses claim for a duckhouse.

Dover House in Whitehall is an elegant mansion once home to Lady Caroline Lamb, with a sweeping staircase from a circular hall, massive reception rooms – for the ministers - and more modest servants' quarters, not designed as offices, for their staff. The SPADs' small first-floor room overlooked Horse Guards Parade, with a side view of the rear of Number 10; our Lib-Dem successors had a marvellous view of the Olympic beach volleyball.

The greatest occasion in my time there was the Queen Mother's funeral. I shall never forget the sailors' slow march across Horse Guards behind the coffin, or standing in Whitehall as all her titles were read out, knowing that with the passing of the last Empress of India they would never be heard again. Out there I bumped into Alistair Darling with Gordon and Sarah Brown. It was not long after the death of their first child; I felt desperately sad for them, and struggled for words.

The ground floor of Dover House, normally the fiefdom of the Scottish Executive (now Government), for a time housed John Prescott. He christened his rooms the "Barnett Suite", a friendly dig at the Barnett Formula determining the share of spending for each part of the UK, which he was trying to end and Helen was fighting to preserve. "Prezza"'s SPADs, Ruth Hamill and Ian McKenzie, gave me valuable advice and occasional help.

As much of Helen's work was in Scotland and most of the Scotland Office's 130-odd staff were up there, George and I often spent Mondays and Fridays in Meridian Court, the Executive's modern building in Glasgow, or our small Edinburgh foothold in Melville Crescent (there was a bigger office in Leith full of lawyers). I came to realise the impact of a phone call from the Secretary of State's office when I secured a speedy police response after rogue tarmackers resurfaced our drive very badly while we were out and demanded thousands of pounds. They never got a penny.

My appointment as a special adviser had to be approved by the Cabinet Secretary. I underwent security clearance, but was not, surprisingly, positively vetted. Nor did I have to register my interests, as MPs do; most SPADs, being around 30, have little to declare, but I had fingers in commercial pies. Fortunately no conflict of interest arose, save over my involvement with *The Joy of Sex,* which in due course became too hot a potato for me to continue; Helen approved my involvement in the relaunch of the book, but when the coverage became an embarrassment I had to go. A special adviser's first loyalty is to their minister. You go in to bat for them with their colleagues' SPADs, difficult MPs and the media. Although Helen and Alan Milburn are good friends, I remonstrated when he gave an interview to the *Scotsman* rubbishing the Barnett Formula; Prescott and Byers, though equally critical, largely put their arguments in private. Any media SPAD is regularly instructed to convey displeasure to an editor over a negative or spiteful story, complain about an interview not used or turned into a knocking piece, or try to stop the production team of *Question Time* packing the audience with their minister's opponents.

To me, supporting my minister meant fighting her corner, not undermining her colleagues. I never briefed against other ministers, though I was sorely tempted. But I did – once - break my self-imposed rule of "no personalities." Helen was going to Wales to campaign in a by-election, and the *Herald* asked why. I explained that Scottish and Welsh Labour worked closely together, as did Helen with Paul Murphy, the Welsh Secretary. But the MP whose seat was now vacant had been universally detested, and I couldn't resist telling the reporter that Helen wanted to make quite sure he was dead.

Helen's ministerial team comprised George (now Lord) Foulkes, his successor Anne McGuire, and Lynda Clarke, Advocate-General and now a Scottish judge; they all sparkled at our Thursday morning meetings. After DfID, George found the Scotland Office's rigidity and formal pace frustrating. Sincere as the day is long, he could be a loose cannon: it was George who revealed to the Commons that, thanks to sloppiness at the time of devolution which John Reid had spotted but been unable to stop, Holyrood had a veto on the building of nuclear power stations in Scotland, with planning policy (devolved) overriding energy policy (reserved). We had hoped this would stay undetected while we tried to rescue the situation; once George had spoken, there was no chance.

Two unsolicited favours I did for George and Anne show the breadth of a special adviser's work. "Big George" - to distinguish him from George McGregor - had a meeting request from the head of the Taiwanese mission to the UK. Given our lack of diplomatic relations with "Nationalist China" the Scotland Office official who handled foreign affairs recommended refusal, but the one covering trade and industry, mindful of our trading links, proposed acceptance: I suggested they formulate a single, agreed, response.

Another time, Anne McGuire was due to meet the US consul in Edinburgh. A junior official submitted a briefing note beginning: "The United States of America is a very big country. Its president is George W. Bush and its capital is Washington, DC." I suggested to Anne's private secretary that it would be best if the minister did not see this; either the official should be asked to do it properly, or the job handed to someone who knew what our current issues with Washington actually were. Maybe I was exceeding my powers: SPADs aren't supposed to give orders to civil servants. But I had no wish to see one humiliated.

Escorting Helen or George to broadcasting studios, I had to find out who else was on the programme (if a Conservative, were they senior enough?), clarify the subjects to be covered and not covered, and for television, make sure there was nothing compromising in shot. During an interview I noted points to be followed up, and looked out for ways my minister could do better; however Helen is a complete professional. Radio was less challenging, though I was bemused when the BBC in Glasgow whipped big George into make-up before a late-night radio interview.

When Helen appeared on a Budget night *Question Time* from Leeds, I spotted just before the show went live that her name was captioned wrong, and got it changed. (She was on with Michael Howard, whom I hadn't seen for ages and is far nicer than he likes people to think). For any Cabinet minister, and particularly a territorial one, the hours after the Budget are taxing; there is a heavy TV and radio schedule putting across the Chancellor's messages to media he cannot personally reach. Each has to keep rigidly in step not just with what the Chancellor has said but with the barrage of statistics put out. One year Helen became nervous that figures I'd given her for increased NHS spending over-egged the pudding; only next morning, after I had managed to catch one of Gordon's SPADs, could I assure her we were OK.

The Scotland Office was headed by Ian Gordon, a shy and slightly academic civil servant. His relations with Helen and George were correct rather than close, though he supported them totally. My contacts with him were limited, though his door was always open; I did however have a bizarre conversation with him over some potential crisis one Saturday, while I was helping a farmer friend herd his sheep.

Jayne Colquhoun, my old Scottish Office contact who had become Helen's private secretary, oversaw the now much smaller press office. A supremely competent civil servant, Jayne understood the media, was on top of goings-on in the department and was quite prepared to tell me if I was overstepping the mark. I worked closely with her and the press team, particularly Brian Simmons, nicknamed "Adolf" for his firm stewardship of one Lobby trip to Scotland, whose sideline is blending excellent whiskies. It wasn't my job to brief about the day-to-day activities of the department, but I could flag up to the press team points ministers wanted to get across; I also alerted them when reporters rang me about matters in their purview, to avoid wires getting crossed.

Briefing the (mainly) Scottish press during the 2001 election and at Westminster, I discovered which of my former colleagues would report fairly and who would twist facts, who had a grasp of what we were trying to do and who lived in a parallel ideological universe; Fraser Nelson, then of the *Scotsman* and now of the *Spectator,* fell into this category despite his obvious brilliance. Douglas Fraser of the *Sunday Herald*, Kenny Farquharson of *Scotland on Sunday* and David Scott of the *Scotsman* took pains to be fair. And the *Herald's* Catherine Macleod, who was becoming something of a

Labour institution, expected the best stories to herself ... a problem as they were in short supply.

The Scotland Office handled Whitehall's ongoing responsibilities after devolution, did a lot of liaison work behind the scenes but had strictly limited executive powers. So we did not have much for the media, beyond supplying them with speeches, keeping them posted about ministerial activity, and giving them a broader political view. The *Telegraph* rubbed these limitations in when it got hold of Helen's diary for a particularly quiet week (just after a gruelling trade promotion trip to the Far East), and inferred that she had nothing to do. This was difficult to rebut, but I did explain to the *Telegraph*'s reporter that the Alistair McGowan Helen was diaried to meet was not the impressionist, as he imagined, but Tony Blair's Scottish political secretary. Moreover the diary – an early draft – was misleading; ministers, even in small departments, are always extremely busy. A leak inquiry, as is customary, did not unveil the source of the story, but it was pretty clear it came from Holyrood. Andrew Neil seized on it to fuel his unpleasant campaign to oust Helen and abolish the stand-alone office of Secretary of State.

Something I *had* been involved in led to another leak inquiry. Helen had offered to assist Jack McConnell by giving the media an advance steer on GERS, the annual report on the state of Scotland's economy. I was tasked with briefing Catherine, and was unwisely precise. Ministers at Holyrood assumed a leak and raised it with Jack; he said nothing about having agreed to it but ordered an inquiry. I first heard what was afoot in a phone call on the early morning Edinburgh-London train; I was used to getting bad news on that train, but this was the worst. Luckily the inquiry never came near me, and the matter ran into the sand - I suspect as much to Jack's relief as Helen's.

The one constant in a SPAD's day – except in departments like the Home Office where they are simply too busy – is the large brown envelope that thuds onto your desk first thing, full of correspondence between ministers. Its contents give an invaluable update on the formulation of policy - and warned us when something was afoot that would impact on Scotland. We then alerted our counterparts at Holyrood, and warned the department in question that there were implications they hadn't thought of.

Most of the correspondence was addressed to the Leader of the House (Margaret Beckett, then Robin Cook) as ministers promoting legislation jostled for places in the Queen's Speech or worked with others to get their Bills into shape. The process was painstaking as 'i's were dotted and 't's crossed; the danger of haste was illustrated when Robin hurried through an Export Control Act to crack down on unscrupulous arms dealers, only for colleagues to discover after his resignation and tragic death that the wings of legitimate defence contractors had been severely clipped, several exhibits having to be pulled from the Farnborough Air Show.

The daily envelope alerted us to departments at loggerheads with each other, and flagged up imminent decisions. The process of policy formulation could take years, especially where European directives were involved – but there was no guarantee it would reach its conclusion, no matter how close that seemed. There was always the chance that some enthusiast with access to Tony Blair like Charlie Falconer or Frank Field would persuade him to do something else. These sudden rejections of a policy worked up in enormous detail greatly irritated the ministers and officials involved ... though Tony was within his rights.

Occasionally human feelings leapt from this desiccated correspondence. An exchange between the Home Office and the MoD over which ex-servicemen were entitled to a wartime medal burst into life when an exasperated David Blunkett told Adam Ingram exactly what he thought of chairborne officials who tried to deny valiant men the fruits of their bravery. I wasn't the only SPAD to be moved; someone leaked the letter to the *Guardian*.

The few actual stories the Scotland Office had custody of, we wanted to get out on our own terms. One concerned the Chester Street affair. When the remnants of British Shipbuilders were privatised, the pension and insurance sides were passed to owners who put the assets in one company and the liabilities in another, which they called Chester Street. When asbestosis claims from former shipyard workers began to roll in, Chester Street announced there was nothing in the kitty. The Treasury and DTI saw little wrong with this, but the sufferers did - and so did Helen. She lobbied colleagues hard, and got Andrew Smith, Gordon Brown's deputy, on side. Just before the 2001 election, Smith called in leaders of the insurance industry and showed them two press releases, one announcing that they were getting together to help the victims and the other that he was setting up an inquiry. Prudently, they chose the former.

One story I tried in vain to keep control over concerned the number of Scottish MPs. A reduction had been built into the devolution project, as before Scotland had its own parliament it had more MPs per head than England or Wales. But implementing the legislation proved a headache, as Gordon was dead against. There was a fair bit of traffic between Helen and Gordon – and one meeting from which SPADs were excluded – before we could proceed.

Infighting ensued over which MPs would end up with which seats, and I was at a poisonous meeting of Scottish Labour MPs where Charles Clarke, then party chair, announced that Labour was reworking its evidence to the Boundary Commission. When Charles asked me how Helen would react I told him: "It all depends whether this has been cleared with her" ... and it hadn't.

When the dust settled, Helen and John Reid were ranged against each other for Airdrie and Shotts - Helen, who by now had left the government, doing the honourable thing. At Helen's handover to John, in the executive suite at Airdrie United, John delighted the locals with wisecracks about sectarianism they wouldn't have taken from anybody else - and I, for the only time in my life, ran down the tunnel and onto the pitch.

Getting the reduction in Scottish seats through for the 2005 general election was only half the problem. The Scottish Parliament contained one member for every Westminster constituency, as well as regional "list" members, so fewer MPs would mean fewer Holyrood seats, which politically was impossible (though a few MPs who didn't rate the new parliament were praying for it). Breaking the link involved amending the Scotland Act, which required scarce legislative time and raised the prospect of others trying to tamper with the devolution settlement.

Resolving the issue was Helen's responsibility, but any solution had to satisfy Holyrood. Eventually Helen and Jack McConnell agreed that membership of the Scottish Parliament should remain at 129 when the number of MPs was cut from 72 to 59, subject to a consultation (suggested by Jack to ease party misgivings) over the practicality of having two parallel sets of constituencies. Some MSPs queried the need for the consultation - whereupon Jack told them Helen had insisted on it.

To the media, the story that mattered was the decision to stick at 129. Old colleagues pressed me for months, but as the matter was not settled and we were anxious for Helen to announce it first to the House, I stood my ground - only to be outflanked by an exceptionally well-informed story in the *Herald*, which Helen initially thought must have come from me. From where I sat, the leak could only have come from a minister.

The size of the Parliament was one of many issues where George McGregor and I kept in close touch with the Holyrood SPADs, first for Henry McLeish and then for Jack. They were able and friendly and a few times I sat in on their meetings, but when push came to shove they were answerable to the First Minister, as we were to the Secretary of State.

25: Books – including that one

When my grandmother saw the long through lounge at Havengore, she announced: "What this room needs is books". Many of them are still with me, and recently I struggled through her copy of Proust's *À La Recherche du Temps Perdu:* by halfway through, I couldn't care if the irritating Swann asked the girl out or not.

The stimulus for my father to write came at 15, on that tramp steamer to Buenos Aires; on his return he wrote *The Silver River,* recounting his adventures. He also began writing poems; some made a schoolboy anthology you can still find on Amazon but many early verses stayed in his notebook. When we discussed producing his "Collected Poems" – I'm still seeking a publisher - he was adamant I should not include them.

He arrived at Cambridge a published author, and throughout the war produced a torrent of verse, polemics, fiction and even a play, and edited *Poetry Folios,* his particular pride. Paper rationing meant his books won acclaim rather than sales; the one potential bestseller was *The Power House,* a novel published late in the war which did well in America.

Some of my earliest memories are of him at his typewriter, rattling off articles, reviews and, when I was six the novel *A Giant's Strength.* A large cardboard box arrived from his publishers, and the first copies were proudly lifted out. Each time a new book of mine arrives, I re-live that moment.

The success of *The Power House* gave Dad an American publisher in Viking, and when I was about seven his editor came over. Ben Huebsch was big and friendly, and when we met at the Athenaeum he handed me *Diesel Electric 4030,* describing a run from New York to Buffalo from the driver's cab. For months I could not be separated from it, and I still remember chunks of the text. The Athenaeum impressed me too, and when around 1988 George Jones proposed me for membership, I felt deeply honoured. I have lunched friends and contacts there, attended the occasional talk dinner and researched in its library, and when I reached 60 it seemed the natural place to hold my party; a repeat when I turned 75 came unstuck when I was "pinged" for Covid days before. I have met some fascinating people at the Athenaeum, from the coroner who had nipped in for lunch before deciding whether to reopen the inquest into Jimi Hendrix, to the stylist Julie Harris who won an Oscar for Julie Christie's outfits in *Darling.*

Dad finished *A Giant's Strength* as he moved to UCL to research into ageing, leading to his next book, *The Biology of Senescence.*

Researching whether long-lived animals had long-lived progeny, the only comprehensive record for any species was for racehorses, and he pored through two centuries of the Stud Book on the Tube before deciding the answer was a lemon - having attracted the attention of short men with bow legs who thought he had cracked the secret of form. They were wasting their time; I don't think he backed a horse in his life.

Of his 40 or so books, I was closest while it was being written to *The Biology of Senescence*; the question of how long animals live has always fascinated me. I marvelled at how fast he turned out page after page – in an age when if you wanted to make changes you had to crumple up the sheet and start again. Lacking four fingers didn't slow him down - though writing this I realise I only use one finger of my left hand and a couple on my right. Those years watching Dad at his desk made me type like a policeman.

As he and Jane got together, the romantic thread for my mother that had run through his wartime poetry evaporated. He abandoned his intensity for an overtly physical flippancy which unsettled her; she was not the most tactile of people. The first fruit was *Come Out To Play*, a tale of the disastrous consequences when a scientist named Goggins releases an aphrodisiac called 3-blindmycin into pre-swinging London; Goggins was a self-portrait, and his muse Dulcinea was, if not Jane, then the woman he would have liked Jane to be. Dad delighted in depicting a stuffy establishment loosening-up, much as he was.

Sex In Society was a more populist treatment of themes he first addressed after the war in *Sexual Behaviour in Society*. This time the tabloids took notice, after Marje Proops accused him on television of encouraging teenage promiscuity by suggesting responsible boys would take a condom with them to a party - advice he had certainly never given me.

Almost a decade later, in 1972, came *The Joy of Sex*, whose un-academic and quietly humorous approach reflected the changes in society and his own life over that time. Had *Joy* appeared earlier, its frankness would almost certainly have got it banned. Dad and Jane had produced a photocopied *Our ABC, By John and Jane*

Thomas in the early '60s, but didn't imagine they could publish it. Over those years, too, Dad's relationship with Jane had intensified, while his times at home with my mother were less frequent ... though he hesitated to make the final break.

Dad's connection with UCL was weakening, too; Haldane and Medawar had gone, and his research into ageing had run its course. Had there been a Cambridge chair in gerontology then he would have gone for it like a shot, but the discipline had not evolved that far. He was also spending more time in California, relishing the loosening-up of West Coast mores.

He claimed to have written *The Joy of Sex* in two or three weeks, but to my recollection it took several months - though much of it was already in his head. He insisted he was not *Joy's* author but its editor, partly to acknowledge Jane's role but primarily because he feared being struck off for "advertising" – a sanction then rigidly enforced by the General Medical Council.

The mix of erudition and humour that gave *Joy* its unique flavour was his, but the brand was the creation of James Mitchell, co-founder of the publishers Mitchell Beazley. I took an instant dislike to James, yet it was his nose for a successful product that turned a "how to" book into a global best-seller (at least 9 million, the bulk in the first three years). It was he who saw the potential for a read-across from *The Joy of Cooking*, with sections on sauces, pickles, main courses and the like. But Dad brought it to life.

At the heart of how *Joy* came to fruition was the struggle to find a way of illustrating it without "dirty pictures". Just about everything was tried, even Morph-type plasticine figures, before the artistic team came up with its iconic solution: drawings of the "bearded man" and his partner in the act. Realising that clinical photographs of specific sexual acts would offend, they hit in near-desperation on taking the pictures, then converting them into line drawings. The air of tenderness that made *Joy* work was created because the couple who volunteered to be photographed were Charles Raymond, one of the artists on the book who normally painted roses, and his charming wife Edeltraud, who got him through the positions with Teutonic efficiency. They are a devoted couple, and generations who have learned from *Joy* owe them a lot. The warmth in the pictures emanated from them – the team were working in a freezing garret during a miners' strike.

Dad told me enough about how *Joy* was developing for me to realise it was going to be special, but living in Sheffield as it took shape during 1971-72, I didn't hear much about the process until I met him and Jane for a curry before watching Sheffield United at Chelsea – Tony Currie scoring the winner. I got a full account years later when Peter Kindersley, Mitchell Beazley's art director who went on to found Dorling Kindersley, came to dinner. Apart from the problems over illustrating the book and the triumphal solution, his main recollection was Frankfurt Book Fair, with publishers from all over the world stampeding for the Mitchell Beazley stand.

Though conceived in Britain, *Joy* has a mid-Atlantic feel; James Mitchell realised American sales would be crucial, and his author was increasingly in California. Moreover as publication of *Joy* would be followed closely by Dad divorcing my mother, marrying Jane and settling in the States, he had no desire for an intrusive media launch in Britain. So the launch in the autumn of 1972 took place in the States; the first in Britain came only with the 30th anniversary edition.

Joy went straight to the top of the *New York Times* bestseller list, stayed there 11 weeks and was in the top five well into 1974. It leapt cultural barriers around the world, selling most copies per head in Australia and 80,000 in France. It sold well throughout the Hispanic world, and there was a successful edition in Japanese. It has been translated into some 30 languages, though there are gaps: eastern Europe has largely gone with the English text, prudery in parts of Asia resulted in some editions not being illustrated and growing Islamic conservatism has ruled out an edition in Arabic. But *Joy* achieved acceptance worldwide - except perhaps from the Trobriand Islanders, whose practices Dad singled out as particularly unusual.

The publication of *Joy* didn't change my life; indeed it almost passed me by. Dad sent me a copy, but while my Sheffield colleagues were aware of this huge bestseller in America – which did go on to sell heavily in Britain – you can't tease a 26-year-old as you can a teenager. A few other people made the connection, and I'm sure Bill Tadd's handing me stories on porn at the *Telegraph* had something to do with it. But even in Washington, with *Joy* still selling heavily, hardly anyone mentioned it, whatever they may have said behind my back.

My involvement only began 19 years later, after Dad suffered a brain haemorrhage and stroke early in 1991 with a revised edition imminent, then Jane died soon after it appeared. His literary affairs – of which *Joy* was the most lucrative but not the most time-consuming – devolved to me, and with Corinne I worked with Mitchell Beazley to deal with outstanding matters and keep the brand alive. At the time, Mitchell Beazley was headed by the young Simon McMurtrie (he now runs Direct Wines, having published Hugh Johnson's wine books). He gave *Joy* a further 15 years, with sales tailing off - which proved pretty accurate.

We worked with a series of heads of Mitchell Beazley – some with clout and imagination, others without – to keep *Joy* moving. They had no strict need to consult me - Mitchell Beazley (now Octopus) held the copyright, though Dad received royalties – but unfailingly they did. Dad retained an input, once spotting something in the fine print of a contract that I had totally missed.

He had twice made minor revisions to *Joy* and was content to let it putter along, as his focus by then was on writing poetry and trying to get his unpublished novels into print. Patrick Walsh, a literary agent not long out of Cambridge whom I had got to know, made valiant efforts to place these, but the novels' themes (the interaction between Indian mysticism and Western culture) had a whiff of the 1970s about them. Patrick admitted defeat - and went on to represent J K Rowling.

I did get an illustrated edition published of Dad's translation from Sanskrit of the *Koka Shastra*, a cousin of the *Kama Sutra*; it sold in Germany, but bombed in Britain. There was also a slim volume (I hate the phrase, but it was) of verse written before his illness, titled *Mikrokosmos*; excerpted in the *New Statesman,* it sold 250 copies - after which its publisher got out of poetry. To promote it, Dad gave a full-dress interview to the *Independent* – the only one in the final nine years of his life. He played mind games with the journalist, and some of his comments greatly upset my mother.

Mitchell-Beazley did their best to keep *Joy* fresh. They produced four "pillow books" of excerpts, similar in format, if not content, to the Beatrix Potter series. We had high hopes for these, but they didn't sell. *Joy* was also adapted for CDi, an interactive medium pioneered by Philips that didn't catch on.

More promisingly, there were approaches from film-makers about producing a video. The problem was that the movie rights for *Joy* had been sold to Paramount, whose *The National Lampoon's Joy of Sex* had used the title but left the content unmined. Years before, Mitchell Beazley had sent someone to ask Paramount to revert the movie rights; they were given a tour of the studio, but got nowhere. Letters went unanswered, but the video makers needed a response.

In the end we stopped off in Hollywood en route to a holiday in Mexico to call on Paramount ourselves. Thanks to Tom Clarke, then Arts Minister, we got in to see the head of Paramount TV; he was encouraging, but attempts to follow up hit a brick wall. I eventually rang the head of the studio: he thought I wanted him to re-release the *National Lampoon* movie, and when I told him we merely wanted clarification of the video rights the conversation ran into the sand. Several times after Dad's death in 2000 film makers showed interest in a biopic, but further approaches to Paramount – even from the BBC – hit that wall.

These abortive movie projects had a valued by-product. If the film makers couldn't reference the book, might they show an image of Dad with his words voiced-over? This led to our commissioning a bust of him from the sculptor Anthony Stones. The sittings gave my father – who knew about sculpting technique from his friend Reg Butler – a new interest; if the finished product didn't capture the Alex Comfort of his prime, this was because three strokes had imposed a rigidity on his features. Tony went on to do a bust of young Alex, producing a work of power, sensitivity and insight.

If it had been left to Dad, there would probably have been no further update of *Joy*. But not long after he died Jane Aspden, one of the most enterprising heads of Mitchell Beazley, proposed a 30th anniversary edition. I didn't feel qualified to make great changes, but as I read through it on holiday in France I could see where modifications were needed. Interrupted when a pine cone fell straight into my wine glass, I made tweaks to prevent *Joy* jarring in the new millennium. "Girls" became "women", greater note was taken of disability, and Dad's assertion that Middle Eastern men preferred fat women was excised. A few points he had mentioned to me went in, as did extra turns of phrase of his that I remembered. I would have liked to decant into *Joy* the one-third of *More Joy of Sex* that still seemed relevant (it has not worn as well as the main title), but couldn't, as Crown still offered the sequel in the States despite its stridently 1970s tone and minimal sales.

In September 2002 the anniversary edition was launched at the Café Royal, with adverts on the Tube paid for by leading booksellers (W H Smith contributed, then showed reluctance to stock it). Mitchell Beazley invited me to meet their sales team, and I was deluged with requests for interviews. The very first, with the *Guardian,* forced me to choose between promoting *Joy* and my role as a special adviser; I had hoped to be with Helen a few months longer. Sadly, despite all Mitchell Beazley's hard work (most other publishers are notoriously bad at selling books) the new edition sold modestly.

In 2007 Jane's successor David Lamb asked the agony aunt Susan Quilliam to bring *Joy* into the 21st century. They couldn't have made a better choice: she has a breadth of knowledge Dad would have applauded, a comfortable writing style – and for me the plus of being based in Cambridge, only yards from the garret where four decades earlier I helped produce *Varsity*. Sue expanded *Joy*, added all kinds of fascinating but relevant information ... and stayed so faithful to the tone of the original that I couldn't see the joins.

In the summer of 2013 Stephanie Jackson, Octopus's best publishing director to date, called me with startling news. Columbia Pictures were going into production with a movie starring Cameron Diaz and Jason Segel in which a couple whose marriage has gone stale find a copy of *Joy,* make a tape of themselves acting it out, then panic as through a chapter of accidents it goes viral. Ironically, this was roughly the plot Dad had originally suggested to Paramount.

Paramount, approached by Columbia, had done some digging and discovered that under a quirk of US copyright law their US – though not global – rights to *Joy* had expired because Dad had died months inside a 28-year time limit that would have confirmed their ownership. (For the same reason Mitchell Beazley's own US rights to *Joy* had also expired back in 2000, a situation Stephanie hurriedly rectified). So the US rights were now mine.

Columbia were relieved when I contacted them: shooting was about to start, and without my permission they would have had to use a different how-to book. They made me an offer; I consulted a showbiz lawyer, then wrote back asking for a little more plus – at Jeanette's urging – two tickets for the premiere. The cheque from Columbia just about paid for our wedding.

In July 2014 we flew to Los Angeles and booked into the hotel where the post-premiere party for *Sex Tape* was to be held. In the early evening we headed for the Regent Village Theater in the 1930s centre of Westwood. A street had been cordoned off for the U-shaped red carpet down which the stars would parade for the photographers and TV interviews. We collected our invitations from a table on the pavement, then crossed the road onto a shorter red carpet and entered the theatre to cheers from a youthful crowd. We were handed boxes of popcorn and bottles of water and directed to our seats. Next to us were the proud parents of the 11-year-old boy playing the couple's son, who must have grown up fast making the movie.

Fifteen minutes behind schedule, and without any introduction, the lights went down. The big difference from an ordinary night at the cinema was the audience's reactions; every so often a one-liner would trigger guffaws and frantic applause from some part of the theatre, as people recognised their own contributions. And everyone stayed to make sure they were on the credits.

Outside, amid the crowds, a line of black SUVs waited to take the VIPs to the party, but the rest of us covered the 600 yards on foot –

no joke for those in Jimmy Choos. Back at the hotel we teamed up with Rosie Pearson, a casting agent we had met earlier by the pool, and toured the party area. At the back of the restaurant was an inner sanctum featuring a double bed with "Sex Tape" pillows. Around it were little tables labelled "Miss Diaz' party" and so on, for first the cast, then the production team and furthest out the movie's financial backers. As it filled up Rosie – who had her boyfriend and 96-year-old father in tow – grabbed the cast members and made introductions. She got me a handshake with Jason Segel – who was trying to talk to someone else – then an enjoyable chat with Rob Corddry, who with Rob Lowe was the other main male character. Cameron Diaz was, sadly, now sealed off and Rob Lowe came and went before we could say 'Hi'. But we did meet several of the production team, and left the party well pleased just after midnight.

Next day we called at Paramount, to thank them for creating he opening and alert them to possible new projects that might require their sanction (as well as mine). Quite a few were on the table, but two – an educational TV series, and a biopic about the making of *Joy* from a British team well known in Hollywood which seven years on is now in development – stood out. When I mentioned apropos the premiere that Jeanette had been an extra in *Cleopatra,* our hosts walked us over for a private view of the studio "archive". Paramount had recently stopped making its own costumes and jewellery, but kept the best: Tom Hanks' running shoes and Robin Wright's dress from *Forrest Gump*, Will Ferrell's suit from *Zoolander* and so on. The curator showed us a tiara won by four leading ladies from the 1930s to the '50s, staggering Egyptian costume pieces dating back to the '20s and James Earl Jones's lion skin from *Coming to America*. Outside we crossed a car park covering the tank that doubled as the Red Sea for *The Ten Commandments*; its far wall was the one Jim Carrey bumped up against at the end of *The Truman Show*.

Being an only child, I was a bookworm and at ten I discovered Arthur Ransome's *Swallows and Amazons* series: for me, the children's outdoor life of sailing, map-making and piratical adventure had a special magic. Ransome had covered the Russian revolution for the *Manchester Guardian,* marrying Trotsky's secretary who spent the rest of her life trying to stop him writing children's books. (Another of Trotsky's secretaries was Fred Zeller, a friend of Magritte, whose *La Citadelle du Désert* hangs in our dining room.) My favourite Ransomes were *Pigeon Post*, set in the Lake District, and *Secret Water,* mapping a tidal inlet behind Walton-on-Naze. I persuaded my parents to take me there one weekend, then discovered there was a programme about Ransome on and asked them to undo their arrangements. They must have thought it a terrible pain.

My most intensive burst of reading came when I was fourteen and off school for several weeks, tackling all Thomas Hardy's novels at one go. This was deeply depressing, as their common theme is that we are fated to make the same mistakes over and over again. Worse still, Hardy was right.

My own first book was about a railway: the Mid-Suffolk Light which for half a century until 1952 meandered eastward from the Norwich main line to the village of Laxfield. It was meant to go further, but the money ran out. Dad had told me about the line and its dozens of level crossings, with steadily fewer gates as trains eliminated them. In my teens we passed through Laxfield and found the old wooden station still intact. I got in touch with the Oakwood Press, producers of branch line histories, and had an encouraging reply from its proprietor, Roger Kidner. I researched the gaps in my story in British Railways' archives at Royal Oak, and eventually sent him the manuscript for a 32-page booklet. To my astonishment, he published it; only years later, researching his obituary, did I discover that Kidner had started Oakwood as a schoolboy.

I was 17 when *The Mid-Suffolk Light Railway* appeared, to approving reviews in the *Railway Magazine* and *Country Life.* Over the years it has grown, through one reprint and two further editions, to 144 pages, and sold more than any other book I've written despite its narrow appeal. It is fatter now because of further research, the publication of a far more comprehensive history by Peter Paye which obliged me to make some corrections and additions, and the welcome fact that a preservation society has reopened a short stretch of the "Middy". I joined the society, and helped raise the money for the sole survivor of the J15-class engine that ran on the line – and used to shunt at Loughton - to revisit the restored section. The day I rode on its footplate was very special, even though a swarm of flies, disliking my yellow shirt, forced me to strip off in the car park.

At Cambridge I tried with Keith Reader and his friend Doug Levy (now Gabriel Donleavy) to write a history of pop, and people in the industry were surprisingly helpful. EMI's artists-and-repertoire man Norrie Paramor took us through the Cliff Richard era, but went quiet when we asked why Helen Shapiro faded. I had a riotous hour in the Radio Luxembourg studio with Jimmy Savile, who proved also a mean cartoonist (there were no rumours about him then). I was overawed by a pneumatic receptionist at Pye Records, touched base with my Trinity contemporary Jonathan King, and had a fascinating conversation on a train with an inebriated Chris Curtis of the Searchers. Royston Ellis, who had written a paperback on the pop scene before decamping to the British Virgins (who, he said, just would not leave him alone) took the time to answer a questionnaire. By the 1966 World Cup Final, when Doug came over to watch the match, it was shaping up pretty well.

Getting published was another matter. The surviving extracts now look rather academic and detached from the "swinging Sixties", but so was much of the subject matter. We felt we had a saleable commodity, but after patronising letters from publishers about this "not being the right time to comment" our enthusiasm flagged as exams approached and the book went unfinished. I felt we had let our informants down, but if any of them reads this I can assure them we were serious.

The second book I actually finished was again about Suffolk: a history of Dunwich, in the 13th century England's fifth largest town but now a village of barely 100 souls. The seat of a Saxon bishop, it became a thriving port and commercial centre; then most of it was eroded away – a large part during a horrendous storm in 1287 – and its harbour silted up. Its last medieval church went over the cliff a century ago.

My mother's interest in nearby Aldeburgh took us to Dunwich, and when divers investigated the seabed offshore and published their findings I felt there was a book to be written. I started my research in 1974 with a trawl of those shelves at Havengore, then returned to Cambridge, poring over precious 16th-century texts in the University Library. I visited the fascinating Dunwich Museum, drank Adnams in the last surviving pub, and stood by the ruins of the friary - relocated as the cliff edge crept nearer - and the last two gravestones of old Dunwich, trying to picture what the town had looked like. I picked the brains of Stuart Bacon, leader of the divers, and Kenneth Riches, retired Bishop of Lincoln and a family friend, who lived close by.

I had the material I needed when I moved to Washington, and in quiet moments there produced a manuscript. Steve Barber was supportive; he had a Thames barge, the *Ethel Ada*, moored not far away at Snape. I must have realised the book wasn't yet good enough, because after a couple of rejections I put it away. I worked on it sporadically over the years as new facts came to light – including, most excitingly, the discovery in Norfolk of 12th-century coins from the fabled Dunwich mint, proving it had existed. By the time I joined the *European*, computer graphics had reached the point where the chief artist could supply the maps I needed, and it was ready to do the rounds again. Patrick Walsh suggested a couple of publishers; to his embarrassment one returned the manuscript the afternoon I delivered it.

Eventually the Lavenham firm of Terence Dalton took it on, with me putting up half the cost. *The Lost City of Dunwich* was published in 1994, attracting a friendly review in the *Times* from my old *Telegraph* colleague Daniel Johnson, and sold steadily; by around 2003 I had recouped my investment, though in terms of work done I reckon I made 2p per hour.

After the Montreal Olympics, I had a call from Jim Coote, the *Telegraph*'s athletics correspondent (sadly killed soon after in a plane crash in the Alps). He was putting together *Olympic Report '76*, by the paper's Montreal team, and needed a chapter on events around the Games to complement the specialists' accounts of track and field, swimming, equestrianism and the like. It was easy to write, putting in all the colour there had not been room for in my news reports.

It was another decade before my next attempt at co-authorship: *The Tunnel: The Channel and Beyond*. Though my contribution was just 20,000 words and the book sank without trace, it was a milestone in my life. For it was then – 1987 – that I bought my first computer, enabling me to make corrections on screen and submit a flawless manuscript. It was a change my father never got round to. I did not imagine my Amstrad had any potential use other than word processing; the Internet and e.mail were for me years in the future. Nor was software installed; each day I had to reprogram the machine with primitive XyWrite floppy discs - losing 2,000 words the first evening because I didn't realise I had to save my copy. With a dot matrix printer I could also print it out - almost invisibly when the ink ran low – on sheet after folding sheet of computer paper, with the holey strip at each side laboriously torn off.

When Patrick Walsh told me in 1990 that Cassell were interested in a political dictionary, I did not realise what an undertaking it would be. They wanted a comprehensive but tongue-in-cheek companion to *Brewer's Dictionary of Phrase and Fable*, and by Jove they got it - 693 pages! In two years I managed to research a compendium of political definitions, historic events, potted biographies, famous quotes and trivia, and get it into publishable form. I carried everywhere a binder of embryonic entries, trawling through biographies, books of quotations and reference works in taxis and between meetings to make my *Brewer* as authoritative as possible. For American content, Rick Lidinsky was marvellous at finding obscure pamphlets about the evolution of the Stars and Stripes or niceties of Congressional procedure.

The book needed an authoritative foreword, and I was honoured when John Major agreed to contribute one. It was a rush to finish it for the start of 1993, after which I felt immense relief - tinged with sympathy for the book's editor, a lady in Kew whose husband was rugby correspondent of the *Guardian*. She asked me to change or clarify remarkably little.

Gordon Brown had given me plenty of encouragement, and through his PA Sue Nye (his gatekeeper when prime minister) he agreed to sponsor a launch at the Commons. When the invitations went out from Cassell I was mortified: they gave the title of the book, the location and time and the fact that Gordon was sponsoring the event ... but neglected to name the author. Cassell also had to be prodded to reimburse Gordon for hiring the room.

I was delighted by a glowing review from John Grigg in the *Spectator,* and disappointed by a nit-picking one in the *Guardian* from Roy Hattersley. I had a former colleague primed to write one for the *Telegraph*, but it fell foul of a supposed house rule against reviewing reference books. I did several radio interviews and a spot on Sky, who forgot to mention the book. *Brewer's Politics* became a talking-point among politicians - one minister took a copy out to Hong Kong for Chris Patten - and sold passably well, though not covering a handsome advance. In due course it went into paperback, enabling me to correct some errors and bring it up to date, and for a time, I like to think, it was a standard work.

There were dilatory exchanges with Cassell over a decade about a further update; my own preference was for a slimmer *The Language of Politics,* more dictionary and less encyclopaedia. I had pretty well given up when Iain Dale, the genius for publicity who had founded Politico's publishing house, commissioned a completely new edition. Cassell were happy to surrender the rights, but had lost the disks, so I had to type out the whole thing over again – spotting in the process many flaws I would otherwise have missed. I dropped a few arcane entries and eliminated some duplication, but New Labour and the Clinton and Bush administrations had added a lot to political language and, rebranded *The Politics Book,* my blockbuster grew to 911 pages.

I wanted to invite Gordon to write the foreword, though our paths had long diverged, but Blairite friends persuaded me to approach Number 10. I heard encouraging noises, but no reply came, time ran out and *The Politics Book* appeared in 2006 foreword-less.

By now, Iain had sold Politico's to Methuen, to build up a war chest for fighting a seat (he lost). My editor Sean Magee – best known for his books on racing – had high hopes for *The Politics Book*, but while Methuen even got my book into Harrods and loads of review copies went out, there was no follow-through. What promotion we did went off at half-cock and just as I started signing copies at the Labour Party conference, Tony Benn collapsed ten yards away. After a short pause he simply carried on talking, but by the time the paramedics arrived, another author was signing their new book.

The Politics Book was the second Iain Dale commissioned from me. In the wake of my media training work, at home and in Zambia, he had suggested a paperback on handling the media. I had much of the material in my training notes, but the scope ran wider: advising community groups on getting their local paper interested, and individuals on how to react if confronted by the media – something I personally have never been comfortable with. The book didn't take long to write, but by the time it was finished I had become a special adviser.

I consulted Ian Gordon, head of the Scotland Office, and was cleared through civil service channels to publish, but when Number 10 heard about it on the political net, warning bells rang. In the wake of the Jo Moore affair, they feared a book on media handling by a SPAD might include embarrassing advice on "burying bad news". So I was told to hold off until I had left government ... and in 2003, six months after my departure, *How To Handle the Media* appeared. The launch at the much-lamented Westminster Bookshop was memorable for tricks Alex pulled off with golf balls bearing the image of Iain Duncan Smith.

Once Iain Dale returned to publishing with Biteback, he commissioned me to write *Surrender: How British Industry Gave*

Up The Ghost, 1952-2012. This chronicled Britain's abdication of its global lead in manufacturing; much of the story came from my own experience, and my extra research into industries from buses to batteries proved deeply depressing. Timed to coincide with the Queen's Diamond Jubilee, I felt *Surrender* was a winner, but astoundingly there was almost no publicity; had Andrew Adonis not taken an interest as he began a review of Labour's industrial policy for Ed Miliband, it would have sunk without trace. A year later, rebranded *The Slow Death of British Industry*, the paperback edition fared better – largely because Biteback had taken on a new PR person. Appearing on TV with Joan Bakewell was one highlight; another was half an hour on air with Andrew Gilligan, largely discussing our mutual interest in buses. There was also a flurry of American interest after a positive mention in the *New York Review of Books*, which has led to other, lucrative, work.

For my next book I went back to railways, a little-known Midland Railway branch which is now Transport for London's planned West London orbital route. The manuscript was ready when I found that Ivan Stewart, a former signalman on the line, had produced privately a handsome coffee-table volume; the book will now appear as a joint effort.

I was already working on it in 2013 when Theo Steel told me the famed transport publishers Ian Allan were producing a trilogy covering British Rail's passenger sectors - InterCity, Network SouthEast and Regional Railways - and asked if I was interested in helping with the last. The enterprising railway manager Chris Green, creator of ScotRail and Network SouthEast, had written the first two, and the author of the Regional book was to be Gordon Pettitt, general manager of the Southern Region in the 1980s and, in retirement, a great help to the Bluebell. After the Southern he had taken on BR's Provincial sector, a ragbag of lines that had averted closure, and completed its transformation into the highly enterprising Regional Railways. Working with Gordon - and with Theo, Chris Green and Chris's ex-railway brother Alex - was a pleasure. In the lounge of Gordon's house at Woking, interspersed with refreshments and gardening tips from his charming German wife Ursula, we plotted the shape of the book and trawled through papers from his distinguished career.

By that Christmas I had loads of material on my laptop, and in the quiet moments of my Antarctic cruise I crafted three draft chapters. During the first half of 2014 we interviewed around 40 present and former railway VIPs, as the story fleshed itself out. For me the highlights were sessions with Paul King, an academic and company doctor brought in by Gordon to make Regional Railways utterly cost-effective, and Jim Cornell, BR's final chief civil engineer who later helped create Network Rail after the Railtrack fiasco. Each had run Regional Railways for a time, and had a first-class mind. I emerged with not only a range of policy and technical insights and some marvellous anecdotes, but a full contacts book and a very high regard for the people who run our railways.

The book was Gordon's; he did much of the writing and his priorities were the ones to follow. He is a gifted and civilised man, a hard worker despite bouts of infirmity, and very easy to work with. The couple of disagreements we had on the structure of the book were amicably resolved on a trip to the Bluebell, of which Gordon, to his immense pride, had been invited to be President. Within 18 months we were going through Alex Green's selection of photos and reading the proofs, with Theo and Chris devising a marketing campaign. With great generosity, Gordon arranged for the Railway Children charity to benefit. When it came out, *The Regional Railways Story* won good reviews from people in the business, and sold pretty well.

26: A word on defence

It may seem an irony, a betrayal even, for the son of a pacifist to have worked for a hawkish newspaper, in Whitehall during the build-up to the Iraq war, and in the defence technology industry. But my views are my own and I am ready to answer for them, just as my father was for his.

I'm not sure what made Dad a pacifist, but I am certain of when. After a year at Highgate when everyone was supposed to join the Officer Training Corps, he founded a "Peace Society". It was 1934, when fear of another Great War produced the "Peace Ballot" and high pacifist votes in by-elections. His pacifism was not shaken by early evidence of Nazi intentions, though he read *Mein Kampf* and in 1936 visited Nuremberg on a school trip; he told me it was hard to take early Nazi atrocity stories seriously as the public had been told during the First World War that the Germans were melting down Belgians to make margarine. He came to know intellectuals who had fled Nazi Germany, but one of his best friends was a Sudeten German poet badly treated by the Czechs. His mother certainly knew the score; she kept the postcard of Hitler he sent from Nuremberg in her bureau "in case it ever comes in useful". Grandfather firewatched during the Blitz from the roof of County Hall and organised cover for London's schools. One man volunteered to watch one in Hackney he'd been trying to get demolished for years; Grandfather told him to look the other way, provided the building was empty.

The loss of his faith after war broke out strengthened Dad's pacifism, though many who stayed in the Congregational Church were as convinced of the war's wrongness. My uncle Stephen confided when I was up at Cambridge that he now believed he had been wrong to refuse to fight; it takes a brave man to say that. Dad's wartime writings were uncompromising on the evil of conflict, and pushed the envelope of protest to the limit. Despite his disability, he insisted on appearing before a conscientious objectors' tribunal to put his views on record. He proved his physical courage by turning out to treat casualties from air raids and VI and V2 attacks.

Most of my friends had fathers or uncles who had been in uniform, but only later did I learn that Dad had a cousin – Joe Gardiner - who had killed a German with a spade at Arnhem (the German had a flame-thrower), and another – John Fenner – killed in action with the RAF. His first cousin Ken Comfort commanded a detachment of West African troops who had to be sent home from Burma with sunstroke.

My mother only mentioned in passing that her office in Bethnal Green had been flattened by a V1 while she was out on her lunch break. It was years before I learned that her brother-in-law, Jimmy Doyle, had been killed at Arnhem on his first mission as an Army medic when his field hospital took a direct hit. And I was in my teens by the time Auntie Alison married John Coals, who had landed on D-Day plus 4 and was the sergeant outside the house when Himmler committed suicide. By astounding coincidence, I later met the officer who declared him dead; they must have passed at the gate.

Over breakfast – a near-monologue from Dad punctuated by the radio and his opening the mail - I absorbed his involvement in pacifism, as a writer for *Peace News* and the like. It had its limits; he remarked of several dictators that it would be a shame if they died in their beds. When I was ten and British troops occupied Suez, he was one of the first to get out and protest, driving down the High Road with the car door open shouting: "Kick the bastards out!" and persuading local bus crews not to strike. (He was also very concerned for our postman when he was called up). At one meeting Dad was heckled vociferously by two women from the League of Empire Loyalists, until he told the audience (in the words of a TV advert of the time): "The question for you is ... which cat is the grandmother?"

Not everyone who was against Suez joined CND when it was founded in 1958 – Nye Bevan, to the surprise and hurt of many on the Left, insisted Britain could not go "naked into the conference chamber". But Michael Foot, Canon John Collins and many others moved on from one campaign to the other ... and so did my father. The authorities had long regarded him with suspicion – in part at the urging of George Orwell - and he became convinced our phone was tapped. Reckoning to hear a loud click when he picked up the receiver, he would say before contacting the operator (we didn't have a dial phone then): "Good evening, Inspector. And I hope your piles come down."

CND meant Aldermaston: the marches spanning Easter weekend which the first year took a few hundred protesters from Trafalgar Square to the Atomic Weapons Research Establishment west of Reading, and thousands in the opposite direction thereafter. We marched near the head of the procession; at the height of New

Labour, Jack Straw would remind anyone in earshot that he and I had marched together. Each evening there were big meetings – I stood outside one in Slough as Michael Foot and Fenner Brockway raised the rafters – before the marchers hunkered down in church halls and we went home. The march culminated in a rally, the first in a field at Aldermaston, later ones in Trafalgar Square. When Norris and Ross McWhirter arrived at Aldermaston to barrack the marchers, an unpacifist element tried to overturn their car. Years later I lunched Norris at the Commons and found him charming, though unrepentant. My most vivid recollection of the Trafalgar Square rallies is of Michael Foot making a passionate speech in a cloudburst.

Locally a thriving CND grew up, involving our GP and a largely middle-class bunch of professionals and Labour activists. In our garage, Dad made a dinosaur suit with a Dexion frame to be strapped round the person inside, with a placard reading: "Too much armour. Too little brain. Became extinct." He also made the suitcase-sized transmitter for a pirate radio station started by militants who became impatient with CND. It broadcast from the fringe of Stevenage New Town, breaking into BBC television at the closedown; its call sign was the opening notes from *Do You Hear the H-Bomb's Thunder?* I'm not sure many people heard it, but for years I had an Ordnance Survey map marked with the area of Stevenage it targeted.

When the Committee of 100 was formed, Dad was among its leaders. Its intention was to sharpen the campaign through Gandhi-like civil disobedience; at one of its protests he heard an Irish demonstrator tell one hothead: "If you don't start being non-violent, I'll thump you." In September 1961 the Committee called a demonstration in Trafalgar Square, defying a ban from the Ministry of Works. When the police intervened, they sat down. Dad was arrested, along with the philosopher Bertrand Russell, then 89; they shared a cell overnight in Brixton before being taken to court. He refused to be bound over and was sentenced to a month in Drake Hall open prison, Staffordshire. I thought his action self-indulgent, though I defended him at school where I was nicknamed

"Jailbird". He spent ten days working in the prison garden before paying up and coming home. That Christmas he sent cards to every nuclear disarmer still in jail – and plants to the warders.

In 1966 Michael Randle and Pat Pottle, former colleagues from the Committee of 100 who should have had more sense, asked Dad to help spring the Soviet spy George Blake from prison. He told them to forget it, but they went ahead and spirited Blake to what he regarded as freedom in Moscow. Dad kept their confidence, and years later had a visit from a *Sunday Times* reporter who had worked out most of the story. He chose to be hazy in his recollections, and a needlessly incriminating piece appeared.

Dad's pacifism ruled out my having toy guns ... a disadvantage when I played cowboys and Indians with John and Glen Coyle. He also barred me from Peter Thwaite's birthday outing, to see *Battle of the River Plate*. There's hardly a shot fired, but to him that was not the point. Fortunately I wasn't policed too closely, and in our final year of school together Peter, David Roberts and I spent Saturday afternoons at the Majestic, South Woodford watching films like *I Was Monty's Double*. If anything has corrupted me, it hasn't been war films.

When I got to Highgate, part of me wanted to conform and join the Combined Cadet Force, but I did not want to let my father down. I took the middle way, spending two years in the Couriers, who tore around Hampstead Heath in sports kit. When too old for Couriers I briefly joined the handful of rebels who swept the Chapel, then joined the Band, which was semi-detached from the Corps; the moustachioed bandmaster, rumoured to date from the Boer War, made me an almost competent Second Cornet. Practicing in Kyffin Williams' Art School among canvases that must now be worth a fortune, we played salutes like *Scipio,* the intermezzo from *Cavalliera Rusticana,* the march of the Middlesex Regiment (which still puts a spring in my step) and, if we were lucky, *Colonel Bogey.*

There was a minimum of square-bashing, to get us up to pace for Annual Inspection, plus occasional coach trips to Pirbright to fire blanks at mushrooms. The only bind was the uniform. Getting your brasses to shine was a chore for everyone, as was spooning polish over your boots to smooth the bumpy toecaps. But while most of the Corps had khaki belt and gaiters, ours were white. It is hard to blanco a belt white and leave it looking smart, and well-nigh impossible to thread the newly-cleaned brasses over it without smearing the belt and having to start again. But with National Service ending, we would not have to go through the bull in real life. War came closest in October 1962, with the Cuban missile crisis. Playing football at Highgate when Kennedy's ultimatum to the Russians to turn their missiles back from Cuba expired, we shook hands before the kick-off in case we weren't around at the end.

The *Daily Telegraph* used retired officers to cover their own services, among them Air Commodore Teddy Donaldson who had broken the world air speed record in a Meteor *circa* 1948. The great thing about them, I found working on the night news desk, was that they did what you asked instead of arguing the toss. Nevertheless every *Telegraph* reporter was expected to have a working knowledge of the subject, and my shortcomings were revealed when I had hurriedly to produce a piece about the SAS and got everything wrong except its location at Hereford.

In Washington I was surrounded by professional Cold Warriors and politicians, generals and journalists "thinking the unthinkable". I quickly learned about mutually assured destruction, throw-weight, MIRVs and the like, disarmament negotiations with the Soviets, the hardware used by the US forces (and items we were trying to sell them) and the flashpoints, such as Korea, that could trigger Armageddon.

I witnessed stunned expressions as Rolls-Royce landed a Harrier in the car park at Dulles Airport, and in a combat exercise over North Carolina I watched Harriers in service with the US Marines; I would have been mortified to know this was just about the last aircraft we would manufacture ourselves in an abject national loss of nerve. Out on the road, we dictated our stories to copytakers in St Louis, whence it was telexed to London. As I filed on the exercise, I could sense my copytaker getting interested. When I told her

McDonnell Douglas would be building Harriers under license, she said: "I must ask my husband about that. He works there."

In deepest Virginia covering a miners' strike, I encountered the legacy of Vietnam full-on. I got talking in a bar with an ex-Marine who was finding it hard to hold down a job, couldn't get what he had experienced out of his system and was really only happy with his guns. He was just my age, and as I got over a sore head from the beer and Bourbon the next morning, I realised that had I been American, that could have been me.

I also joined a NATO press trip to Fort Bragg, home of the Green Berets. They wanted to demonstrate how much they had learned since Vietnam, showing us unarmed combat "with lethal blows omitted", a psychological warfare operation with loudspeakers bellowing "Come out, you're surrounded!" in Russian, a display of shelters for survival behind enemy lines - and animal traps that looked very similar. The Green Berets cooked us lunch from the wildlife they had caught during a 24-hour exercise. A giant Hispanic sergeant prepared us tea made from sassafras roots (bearable), plus possum, fox and frog, cooked on a wood fire and served in foil. The frog tasted like chicken, the possum was stringy and the fox tough as hell, but in the best journalistic tradition I went through the card. Back in London days later, I went down with salmonella. When eventually I crawled to the doctor's and he asked what I had been eating, all he could say was: "I'm not surprised."

Back at Westminster, Labour was going unilateralist again; the likes of Michael Foot had been in at the birth of CND but now Tony Benn joined them. From the Tories, I learned about British military tradition. Lord Carrington told me of the time the Shah was briefed on a tank we were trying to sell him. Watching it put through its paces, the Shah turned to a cavalry general and asked: "How fast does this thing go?" Unhesitatingly, he replied: "About the huntin' pace of the Beaufort, Your Imperial Majesty."

The early Thatcher years were dominated by her determination to slim down the Royal Navy. When Keith Speed, the Navy minister, resisted, she changed the structure of the MoD so the individual services were no longer championed by a minister. It didn't end the infighting, which carried on at senior brasshat level with each service leaking that any piece of kit wanted by the others was overpriced, unnecessary or unworkable. It also heightened the parliamentary campaign against the cuts, and particularly the plan to pay off the ice patrol ship *Endurance* - Britain's only naval presence near the Falklands - led by Speed and Labour's former naval persons Jim Callaghan and John Silkin.

The Government's plan to replace Polaris with the far more destructive Trident nuclear missile had a special resonance on Clydeside, near where the nuclear subs would be based, so became an issue in the Hillhead by-election of March 1982. Mrs Thatcher told that weekend's Conservative Central Council in Harrogate that Roy Jenkins' capture of the Tories' last seat in Glasgow had been due in part to Trident. On the train back the SDP's Ian Wrigglesworth, who had been in Hillhead, told me she was right, and when I lunched one of her speechwriters on the Monday, he said that was the message they had wanted to get across.

I had always found John Nott a bit like a member of some austere cult. Though he'd been an officer in the Gurkhas he had little sympathy with the military, and was forcing through heavy cuts. I was in the Members' Lobby hours later when Nott bore down on me, waving his arms and shouting. I remember his manner rather than what he said – George Galloway is the only other politician to have ranted at me like that – but the upshot was that Mrs Thatcher had never attributed the loss of Hillhead to Trident and I shouldn't fabricate stories on such an important issue. When I managed to interject that Number 10 said I had pitched it right, that made him angrier. He wheeled on his ankles and stormed off.

Four days later, Argentina invaded the Falklands. Nott must just have heard that the invasion force was on its way and there was nothing he could do to stop it when he spotted me in the Lobby. Realising he was about to be blamed for a national humiliation, he vented his frustrations on me. The invasion did humiliate Nott, who only survived a dreadful performance in that Saturday's emergency debate because Mrs Thatcher couldn't afford to lose him as well as Carrington, who honourably resigned. Nott struggled through the war, hung on for a few months, then went into the City, where he was paid unaccountably large sums of money.

I strongly supported the recovery of the Falklands; I had been fascinated by the islands ever since the retrieval of Brunel's *Great Britain* some years before. But I can't say I had a good war. I knew Carrington's successor Francis Pym quite well and covered his meetings with Alexander Haig over the Peruvian peace plan, which doves hoped would avoid bloodshed. I sounded out Labour MPs on the strength of anti-war feeling, finding them deeply divided. But as the crunch neared, I collapsed in the office with viral flu and was ordered by Peter Eastwood to take a holiday. By the time I got back, matters were close to resolution.

Not too late, though, for me to see Bernard Ingham embarrassed by a particularly crass example of MoD spin. Bernard one day briefed us – in good faith - that the RAF had carried out a leaflet raid on Port Stanley. This was reported on the World Service, only for word to filter back that the weather had been atrocious and no planes had flown. Bernard was outraged, and the MoD, already a global laughing-stock with its non-informative daily briefings from the "I speak your weight" civil servant Ian McDonald, suffered a long overdue shake-up to its PR operation.

During the airlift from Ascension Island, an RAF Hercules was reported to have landed in Brazil after developing engine trouble. I can disclose here that it was being flown by a Luftwaffe major based at RAF Lyneham on an exchange. Before they landed the German, fearing a diplomatic incident between Brasilia and Bonn, told his co-pilot to take over and field any questions. He stayed mute and Germany was spared an awkward situation; the crew were speedily extracted by Concorde. I heard the story from the major himself in Cape Town, where he had gone in 2008 to dive with Great White sharks.

The Falklands gave rise to Tam Dalyell's campaign to prove that the Argentine cruiser *General Belgrano* - a survivor of Pearl Harbor - posed no threat to the Task Force when she was torpedoed with the loss of 323 lives, because she was steaming away from the islands. Mrs Thatcher had been briefed otherwise, and stuck to her guns. Tam – convinced the ship was sunk to forestall that Peruvian peace initiative (in fact communicated to London just afterward) - secured the final Commons debate before the 1983 election on the *Belgrano*; I found Tory MPs searching for white coats in which to escort him from the Chamber. And his last question before retiring as Father of the House in 2005 concerned ... the *Belgrano*.

After the conflict Ted Rowlands, the former Foreign Office minister criticised by Mrs Thatcher for revealing that during a previous standoff we had been reading Argentina's diplomatic telegrams, told me of visiting the Upland Goose, until the conflict Stanley's only pub. Its landlord, Des King, was, he observed, "the kind of landlord you'd travel 7,000 miles to avoid".

A major hardware issue of the day was whether the RAF should have the Nimrod airborne early warning aircraft (an updated Comet) or AWACS, the early-warning Boeing already in service with the US Air Force. The order meant a lot to British Aerospace, and to GEC who were supplying the avionics. Jim Prior was now chairing GEC, and with speculation rife that Nimrod's detection systems had run into trouble and ministers were about to switch to AWACS, he gave several of us a glowing account of the plane's progress and capabilities. After my piece appeared, someone involved in the trials rang to tell me that on a recent flight Nimrod's radar had picked up two targets: a tanker crossing the North Sea at 1,400 mph and the bowl of its own lavatory. Soon after, the MoD ordered AWACS. (A new generation of Nimrod would be cancelled in 2010, years behind schedule, with £3 billion spent, and not a single plane in service.)

In 1986 I covered Mrs Thatcher's visit to the British Army of the Rhine. The picture of a Rommel-like Maggie in the turret of a tank on Luneberg Heath has become iconic. But running alongside as her Challenger blasted eastward was a half-track carrying the Lobby and a posse of elderly German defence correspondents. You knew what they were thinking: "If only we'd had *her!*"

I have other snapshots from that trip: a visit by colleagues to the Kit Kat Club in The Hague ("They were still trying to get the wrapper off at 3 am", one reported), and discovering that Britain's Rhine Army PR man was a German baron who had joined our forces to get more soldiering and more time on a horse. But one overshadows them all: a night in barracks at Rheindalen when the *Mail's* Bob Porter launched with rich Walsall tones into an unexpurgated rendition of *Eskimo Nell*, unaware that the Garden Girls who accompany the Prime Minister everywhere were beyond the partition.

Whenever British governments were contemplating military action, Tony Benn, Tam Dalyell and, with more authority, Denis Healey would portentously assert that it would end in tears. They were wrong about the Falklands and wrong about the Gulf War, so when the invasion of Iraq was mooted it was tempting to assume they were crying "wolf". I thought we should have ousted Saddam Hussein in 1990, but realised why we hadn't: John Major and George Bush senior were warned that their Arab partners would pull the plug if they moved on Baghdad, RAF crews were repulsed by the experience of bombing troops who didn't fight back and, most important, no-one knew where Saddam was.

The realisation that the Americans were going in whether we liked it or not filtered through Whitehall after the 2001 election. Tony Blair had concluded that we had to join them if Washington was to continue treating us as a trusted partner. However nobody here could see a connection between Saddam and Al Qaeda as George W. Bush did, indeed quite the opposite. And this time Iraq's elite forces were expected to resist, their fanaticism repulsively captured in BBC footage showing members of Saddam's intelligence service tearing a live wolf to pieces and eating it. Moreover in the Gulf War more British servicemen had been killed by the Americans than by the Iraqis, and there was no confidence things would be different this time (they weren't; a British major told me the Americans fired on his camp every day despite a gigantic Union Jack over it).

Then there were the weapons of mass destruction. I was a SPAD until days before the less dodgy of the two Government dossiers on Saddam's WMD capability was published, in September 2002. Nobody doubted he had them; why else would he go to such lengths to thwart the UN inspectors? In fact he had given up his chemical warfare capabilities (and worse), but was keeping up the myth to cow his people. And although no minister in my hearing disclosed Cabinet secrets, they came back from each meeting shaken by the intelligence reported. So, like many, I could see a case for going in, capturing the WMD (which Saddam had previously used on the Kurds) and getting rid of a thoroughly nasty regime.

It was plain that Bush (or rather Dick Cheney and Donald Rumsfeld, the forces behind him) would go in whatever the world thought, largely because Saddam, in J R Ewing's words, had been "mean to my Daddy". The more hawkish Washington became, the less chance there was of Britain persuading France, let alone Russia or China, to sanction an invasion in the Security Council. France did, we understood, have a naval force standing by, but Washington was so arrogant with Paris that President Chirac withdrew it. When Tony Blair did persuade Bush to go to the UN, its resolution was far less than he wanted, so he went ahead anyway ... with Blair obliged to follow suit.

I supported the war with a heavy heart, but remain convinced the concerns over WMD were sincere. To my mind removing Saddam was justifiable; it was the Pentagon's insistence on binning the State Department's plans for what should happen next that landed Iraq with ongoing bloodshed. I do not believe discussion in Cabinet was suppressed, as Clare Short claimed when she resigned; from what I heard no-one else could get a word in edgeways. Nor do I feel I was deliberately lied to: it was a classic case of poor intelligence being believed because pretexts were sought for action.

When, later, the affair of the "dodgy dossier" and the apparent suicide of Dr David Kelly generated a host of conspiracy theories, I was disinclined to believe them. It was plain the BBC's Andrew Gilligan had overstepped the mark in saying on air that the

Government had deliberately distorted the facts, but I could see how it happened. As a reporter I have made that kind of misstatement, but I have had a sleepless night afterwards and gone into the office expecting a rocket. That didn't happen, which was why the Hutton Inquiry was right to censure the BBC. Nevertheless, some people in Whitehall got off lightly.

By the time we went into Iraq I had joined the defence technology company QinetiQ to set up its government relations operation as it was spun out of the MoD – and for more than three years I revelled in working alongside some of Britain's brightest scientists. QinetiQ is based on the complex at Farnborough where Concorde was developed, with major sites at Malvern, Boscombe Down and Portsmouth and a host of other laboratories, proving ranges and so forth, some strictly commercial and the rest operated under contract for the MoD. Its chief executive, later chairman, was Sir John Chisholm, an engineer from the private sector and racer of classic cars. His enthusiasm, technical knowledge and entrepreneurial flair converted a ragtag of near-geniuses in superannuated huts into a FTSE 250 company without losing its reputation for excellence.

When QinetiQ was floated, the Armed Forces Minister Adam Ingram teased me about the packet I must have made; but as a consultant I didn't qualify for shares. With hindsight, the MoD should have driven a harder bargain with Carlyle, the American private equity firm who took the principal stake in QinetiQ until flotation. Equally, I suspect senior figures at QinetiQ were embarrassed by the millions they made. But this was not the only instance of the taxpayer being denied by short-termist pressure from the Treasury for a quick sale, and financial ineptitude at the MoD.

I was hired for QinetiQ by Andrew Jeacock, a supreme practitioner of aerospace PR for whom I had done media training at Royal Ordnance. Andrew was at his best during QinetiQ's attempt to keep Concorde flying when British Airways decided it was no longer economic; it failed because in a few key areas the rights rested with

Airbus, who didn't want it to happen. After I had been there a year Andrew was replaced by Nicky Louth-Davies, who arrived from MORI full of ideas, and is the best boss I have worked for outside newspapers.

My role, working out of the press office, was to construct a relationship between the emergent company and departments other than the MoD, plus leading politicians and the 30 or so MPs with a QinetiQ operation in their constituency; in a couple we were the largest non-public sector employer. Most important was to formalise links with the DTI, having inherited close technical co-operation but little on the policy and business relations side. Plugging into the DTI team liaising with defence contractors brought senior civil servants and ministers to see us, culminating in the Science Minister Lord Sainsbury coming to Malvern. It enabled QinetiQ to get across to government the importance to local economies of contracts it was bidding for. It helped us engage with the Regional Development Agencies to which responsibility for strategic R&D had unwisely been devolved. And it created a channel for troubleshooting, when things happened which the Department should have known about - or when QinetiQ's competitors tried to get the DTI to give them a seat on the company's Board.

Dealing with the DTI I worked closely with QinetiQ's Dolores Byrne, a red-headed Irish physicist determined to make science popular. Much of our collaboration concerned securing funding for aerospace research programmes we were working on with BAE Systems, Rolls-Royce, Airbus and others. After an iffy start to a new system for allocating grants through the regions, the DTI set up an Aerospace Innovation and Growth Team (AEIGT), which set much-needed priorities. One of its prime movers, Lord Broers, former vice-chancellor of Cambridge University, told me how when his family emigrated to Australia in 1948, Don Bradman's Ashes-winning team were on the ship and gave him the best cricket coaching a schoolboy could wish for. In our meetings, AEIGT was a cause for amusement: Dolores couldn't help pronouncing it "eejit", the Irish for "idiot".

In my dealings with the MoD, I was careful not to trample on existing relationships. However MPs were still trying to question ministers about things that had become commercial matters for QinetiQ - and the welfare of goats submerged (unharmed) in our diving simulator at Gosport in lieu of naval ratings. MoD officials were still providing answers when they shouldn't, and we devised a procedure that clarified their responsibilities. I also intervened with the MoD when we were unsure whether ministers might have political or ethical concerns about work we were negotiating to take on. I had a quiet word with one of Geoff Hoon's SPADs, who would touch base with the relevant minister. These contacts upset some brasshats, but otherwise there was a risk of a done deal backfiring politically.

Through me, QinetiQ submitted evidence to a wide range of inquiries and consultations, ranging from the formulation of Gordon Brown's 10-year science strategy to Select Committee inquiries. We had to decide whether there was anything to be gained by giving evidence or some good reason not to, and which of our experts should provide the information. I would knock it into shape, run the draft past whoever our expert was, then submit the final version to Sir John, as he would be invited to give evidence if the committee wanted to hear more. On seven or eight occasions in my time, they did.

Sitting in on parliamentary proceedings relevant to QinetiQ, I had one hair-raising escape. The *Times* carried a lurid story on our capabilities in transport security on the day Alistair Darling appeared before the Transport Select Committee and its fearsome chairperson Gwyneth Dunwoody, with whom I'd had the odd run-in as a lobby correspondent. I thought I had switched off my mobile, but just as Alistair started criticising an unnamed defence contractor (us), I felt a vibration and heard the strains of *Crazy Frog* emanating from my pocket. Terror of the consequences spurred me to switch off in nanoseconds, before the sound could register with Gwyneth.

There were individual MPs to be briefed on the company's situation generally, the need to halt the slide in defence R&D spending –

which has continued - and our reasons for tapping into America's far larger defence budget. Gerald Howarth was a double target as our MP at Farnborough and a Conservative defence spokesman. I also kept Robert Key, the Conservative covering Boscombe Down, Michael Spicer (Malvern) and Mike Foster, the Labour MP for Worcester who had many constituents working at Malvern, in touch. Because so many QinetiQ sites were in the countryside, we had mainly Tories to brief even when Labour had a three-figure majority. I also arranged informal dinners at which Sir John and senior executives ran through issues of the day with Labour, Conservative or Lib Dem MPs. They took an enormous amount of organising, by me and the chairman's PA, and with the Lib Dems we managed to hold only one. But the format worked well, and over rack of lamb at Shepherd's I think we opened a dialogue.

Our most contentious local issue concerned noise and vibration from the artillery range at Shoeburyness, east of Southend: 32 secure square miles of farmland and marshes, with the village of Foulness at its heart. Redundant trains are stored there, and it briefly housed Hitler's Mercedes. It is home to marvellous bird life despite the sporadic bangs and thuds as weaponry is tested. Yet while the family in the clapperboard cottage next to the giant gun barrel – and the people of Southend - hear very little when it is fired, it resonates miles away to the east.

People as far away as Clacton and Margate became convinced that activities at the site were damaging their homes. Consultants we engaged assured us the level of vibration could not be bringing down ceilings or making dogs sick as was claimed, noting that 40% of the complaints concerned times when the site wasn't operating, but we were given a hard time when we tried to explain this to a meeting in Herne Bay. I came away suspecting houses in North Kent must be jerry-built, but after a second meeting on the Essex coast when a retired builder detailed damage for which there could be no other explanation, I began to wonder if the properties of air and water in the arc to the east of Southend needed reassessing.

My time at QinetiQ was a unique opportunity to learn about the technologies its scientists were pioneering, in the footsteps of their predecessors who invented radar. They were not always spectacular – one nanopowder looks very like another - but there were some showstoppers: the ion drive developed for a mission to Mercury, the radar system to prevent a re-run of the Concorde disaster by spotting the tiniest piece of runway debris, and my favourite, the integrated waste management system for warships. The idea of "green" warfare may offend some, but the world's navies are now treaty bound not to endanger marine life by dumping rubbish overboard. At Gosport a small QinetiQ team devised a system of pipes, filters, macerators and an incinerator to segregate the waste produced on board into nine types, treat them all and end up with almost drinkable water and a cupful of harmless powder a day. The implications are immense, as the average warship has to dock every few days to offload binbags and pump out sewage, and a variant of the system is now in use. One problem emerged: sailors wash their hair so often that the filters became clogged, and rotating blades had to be retrofitted.

Although QinetiQ's Farnborough site is no longer connected to the airfield, I had a front-row seat for the 2004 Air Show. I'd never been to it before; Dad tried to take me when I was small, but mistakenly made for Farnborough in Kent. The highlight for me was getting Alex, then ten, into the cockpit of a Eurofighter and QinetiQ's jet fighter simulator, from which he commanded pilotless drones before inadvertently shooting himself down. A USAF B52 bomber flew all the way from Nebraska to make a low pass over the show, but buzzed the non-operational airfield at Blackbushe by mistake, causing havoc at a car boot sale. No wonder they bombed the wrong side in Afghanistan.

What was once the showcase for Britain's aircraft industry is now at best an opportunity to show how we contribute to European or transatlantic consortia in which we punch below our weight. By contrast the Paris air show at Le Bourget is orchestrated to highlight the latest products of Airbus, Dassault and the like ... though having missed a meeting there because of gridlock caused by roadworks, I feel they could learn from us on the ground.

27: Boring for Britain

My mother treasured her schooldays in Folkestone, and often went back there. A family friend, Sidney de Haan, owned the Hotel Rhodesia on the Leys and I stayed there with her, playing with Sidney's son Roger. Sixty years on, Roger has turned the Hotel Rhodesia into the Saga travel and insurance empire and sold it for hundreds of millions, reinvested in Folkestone to bring back its great days.

The clifftop offered a panorama of Folkestone harbour with its ferries, the Channel and, on a clear day, France. That view sparked my interest in the Channel Tunnel, a project that seemed a pipe dream until Ted Heath adopted it to prove Britain's commitment to Europe. Then, at the Road Research Laboratory with Sheffield councillors, I saw a demonstration of how cars and lorries would be loaded onto shuttle trains for the Tunnel. The exercise was basic – a handful of vehicles driven in and out of box-like structures representing wagons – but for me the idea became real. Work began, then early in 1975 Harold Wilson's government cancelled the project. I took the decision personally.

In 1978 British and French Railways proposed a single-track low-cost "Mousehole", and despite understandable fears by the French that we might cancel again and isolationist opposition in Britain, a fixed link (not necessarily a tunnel) crept back onto the agenda. The issue increasingly came up in my dealings with politicians, notably Norman Fowler and Labour's Peter Snape, with whom I spent a happy afternoon at the TUC Congress playing Space Invaders in the bar. Rival schemes were promoted and in 1981 Mrs Thatcher (provided no British taxpayers' money was involved) and President Mitterrand committed themselves to a link. Then several expert reports questioned the economics of any such project, and during the 1983 election I heard Mrs Thatcher say in Dover (where opposition was understandably strongest) that she didn't see it happening.

By now, though, the debate was being driven by heavy hitters like British Steel's Ian MacGregor who saw an opportunity. Promoters advocated a bridge, a tunnel and a combination of the two, with Mrs Thatcher believing motorists should be able to drive through. The ferry operators responded with Flexilink, a campaign as crude as it was effective: a typical poster showed rabid animals and garlic-breathing Frenchmen stampeding out of the tunnel. Much play was made of how a tunnel would be unsafe ... until 180 lives were lost when the *Herald of Free Enterprise* sank off Zeebrugge.

Most combative of the ferry operators was James Sherwood, the larger-than-life American who would revive the Orient Express, develop a chain of luxury hotels and own the stylish GNER rail franchise until his Sea Containers conglomerate hit the buffers in 2006; my Baltimore friend Rick Lidinsky became Sea Containers' vice-president in Washington. Sherwood's conduit to the media was Maureen Tomison, a flame-haired former *Glasgow Herald* lobby reporter who took no prisoners and had an endless supply of anti-Tunnel stories. Though we got on well I held back a little in print, and felt vindicated when, overnight, Sherwood abandoned his opposition to a tunnel and launched "Channel Expressway", a tunnel through which traffic and trains would alternate in "flights", being "swept" of stragglers in between. The scheme looked crazy to me, but won the attention of Nicholas Ridley, Transport Secretary, just as negotiations came to a head. Ridley was open with me on many things, but was determined to say nothing that might compromise a deal involving not only Mrs Thatcher but the French. The choice narrowed to EuroRoute – a bridge-tunnel combination favoured by the French - and Channel Expressway; the conventional rail tunnel, rebranded Eurotunnel, seemed out of it. But at the decisive meeting Ridley and his French counterpart deadlocked, and Eurotunnel emerged the compromise choice. Sherwood unashamedly went back to declaring tunnels unsafe.

Mrs Thatcher and Mitterrand awarded Eurotunnel the concession in January 1986, and three months later the Bill authorising construction was presented to Parliament. Opponents mobilised, and there were procedural hurdles: had the Bill not squeaked through the Standing Orders Committee on the chairman's casting vote, an entire year would have been lost. After a comfortable Second Reading, it went to a Standing Committee who heard hundreds of objections at Westminster and over four stormy days at Hythe, with firefighters and seafarers making ever more extravagant claims of disaster. Some memorable exchanges concerned what became Waterloo International station. Peter Snape could not resist telling objecting locals there had been a station at Waterloo since 1848 so it was a bit late to start complaining, while Ken Livingstone's GLC claimed Waterloo would not offer adequate facilities for gays and lesbians. A bemused British Rail press officer told me: "I think it's something to do with our having closed the Gents."

Around this time I was asked to collaborate on a book about the Tunnel by Bronwen Jones, an enterprising engineering journalist who would later (as I have mentioned) make waves in South Africa.

She wanted 20,000 words on the politics and history of the project, to go with chapters on financing, tunnel technology, the rail aspects, the environmental impact and so forth. Bronwen wrote the technical chapters herself, and her fiancé, Peter de Ionno, the financial section after one City journalist told her: "Why should I do this for peanuts when a merchant bank will pay £2,400 for one article?" (this in 1987). I realised then that I was in the wrong business.

Bronwen's elderly father was a director of the *Observer* with family ties to Lloyd George, and a true eccentric. Arriving at their home in Thanet to find it festooned with "Beware of the Dog" signs (there wasn't a dog), you got used to your host wearing a teacosy on his head, a blowfish hanging in the lavatory, and Chartist posters framed on the wall. In his workshop were Ramsay MacDonald's briefcase, a fine collection of political mugs ... and his own coffin, lovingly prepared.

The Tunnel – The Channel and Beyond was published that autumn just as Eurotunnel was floated on the stock market (coinciding with the hurricane and Black Monday, and being bailed out by Robert Maxwell). I bought some shares, losing more on them than I made from the book, which was not marketed. Yet I kept up with the project, and two decades later would produce a book of my own.

The 1987 election – with the Bill almost through – yielded me one Tunnel story: the fury of Michael Howard, then a newish MP for Folkestone, at anti-tunnel comments from Alan Clark, whose Saltwood Castle was close to the Cheriton terminal. Though a Plymouth MP, Clark characteristically saw nothing wrong with speaking up in mid-election with Michael fighting a strong Liberal challenge.

At Eurotunnel's temporary headquarters at Victoria, Alastair Morton, the volcanic South African without whom the Tunnel would not have been completed, had replaced an ineffective leadership and there was a new sense of determination. I got to know Alastair quite well – once sharing his helicopter from Battersea to Calais to check on progress – and suffered only one of his legendary tongue-lashings, when after another visit the only thing I got into my paper was a piece on precautions against rabies. When years later I interviewed him during his bumpy stewardship of the Strategic Rail Authority, Alastair was helpfulness itself; he died months later.

Soon after that election I left the Lobby to write leaders, with transport one of my specialities. Eurotunnel was striving to raise capital in the face of a spoiling campaign in the City from Flexilink, and I got to know several agreeable Eurotunnel spokespeople: Alison Porter, Simon Storer (with whom I would work in media training) and Tony Guterbock, the company's evangelical head of community relations. Tony devoted years to the Tunnel before becoming Lord Berkeley and heading the Rail Freight Group - whose formation I had triggered when the waste disposal firm Shanks & McEwan complained to me about BR's abysmal service. Soon after, Eurotunnel moved into the former Salomon Brothers offices over Victoria Station – now home to the *Telegraph*.

By the time the Tunnel opened in 1994, I had moved from the *Telegraph* to the *Independent on Sunday* to the *European* to the *Daily Record*. With each I kept up with events; a dedicated telephone line carried weekly updates on the rate of tunnelling. One story that reached me was the launch of a "Mile Deep Club", embarrassingly for the management by two male construction workers.

In March 1991, three months after British and French tunnelers had broken through and shaken hands, I joined the first press trip through the tunnel. It wasn't today's high-speed transit; we took 5½ hours in narrow-gauge colliery manriders. We gathered at a Folkestone hotel (not the Rhodesia), then on site were given high-visibility clothing, pit boots and helmets, searched for matches and issued with tokens and life-preservers. Then it was down in the lift to the marshalling area beneath Shakespeare Cliff from where construction trains shuttled to the boring machines or, increasingly, into sections being fitted-out. We travelled for 15 jolting and noisy kilometres in near-darkness to the first of the two great undersea crossing chambers, via the service tunnel rather than one of the larger running bores from which this cathedral-sized cavern had been hollowed out, then accessed the chamber through a muddy passageway dug out by hand. Then it was back to the manrider for 10 kilometres more to the end of the British section, where the track ended ... except for a few weeks when the systems were joined, enabling Prince Philip to pass through and a few mining locomotives to be transferred.

Beyond the border marked by a metal grille, a cairn of champagne bottles showed that the French did not ban alcohol from the workings; there was also a relaxed attitude to smoking. While we operated our end like a coal mine, the French ran theirs like a nuclear power station, a gleaming console at Sangatte controlling their construction trains contrasting with the basic mechanical signalling run from Shakespeare Cliff. Seven workers died excavating the British section, but only one at the French end despite conditions being more difficult.

The French manrider took us through less murky tunnels to a lift accessing the ground level complex at Sangatte, where we showered and were taken to a country hotel for dinner. There we were presented with certificates that we were among the first to travel through the tunnel; mine is no. 211.

Parliament approved the tunnel on the understanding there would be no high-speed link to it; commuter-belt opposition to such a line (to a terminal at White City) had helped kill the previous scheme. But with Eurostars due to use existing lines through Kent, Mitterrand's scathing comment about the tunnel being the flight and the British end the runway was justified. The French were building their high-speed line from Paris to the tunnel (justifying the cost because it also went to Brussels) and within months of work starting on the tunnel, BR proposed their own.

The four alignments first suggested provoked fury from locals, not least because one had already been built on; it was claimed the route had been plotted on someone's kitchen table. Meanwhile Cecil Parkinson, now Transport Secretary, was considering which consortium should build it; in the end he rejected them all, buying valuable time to get things right. For me at the *Independent on Sunday*, there were rail link stories aplenty, talking to Parkinson's SPAD Elizabeth Buchanan on Saturdays when she could break off from grooming her horse.

BR originally planned to run Eurostars beneath south London to an underground terminal at King's Cross, part of a grand redevelopment designed by Richard Rogers, and this was sold to me by the project team - among them Jeanette whom I first met at this time. But there was pressure from councils in east London, the Arup consultancy (for which Maureen Tomison was now lobbying) and, crucially, Michael Heseltine, to shift the route east through Stratford to regenerate the Thames Gateway. BR were in an impossible position; tasked with evaluating all the options, they felt inhibited from promoting their own when their project leader Gil Howarth briefed us over breakfast at the Waldorf. At the height of the intrigue Richard (now Lord) Faulkner, whom I first met when he was helping Peter Shore's Labour leadership campaign and was now working for the BR chairman Sir Bob Reid (II), told me BR would go for the Arup scheme. Richard was some way ahead of Reid, who was still committed to the original route and was furious when the story appeared, telling me he assumed the story came from Arup. Finally, to the dismay of the King's Cross team, Heseltine persuaded the Cabinet and the route through Stratford to St Pancras was adopted, despite the Bill for the original project being almost through Parliament. Ironically, Eurostars have never called at what is misleadingly titled Stratford International.

The process of fitting out and commissioning the tunnel dragged on, and interest charges racked up alarmingly. Eventually I was able to walk with the Scottish Select Committee into the tunnel entrance, with track laid and overhead wires up. The Queen and President Mitterrand formally opened the Tunnel on 6 May 1994, the first HGV shuttle ran between Cheriton and Coquelles on 19 May (almost a year late), and the first Eurostar on 20 October.

The first ever direct train from London to Paris was a PR disaster; even my semi-congratulatory story for the *Daily Record* was headed "Le Coq-up". Eurostar management rejected advice to have a spare ready; the train failed at Waterloo and it took an hour to get a replacement, adequately stocked with food and drink, from the depot. Despite having lost its path over congested lines through south London, the train recovered 13 minutes to register the then-astonishing time of 2hrs 49 mins from Waterloo to the Gare du Nord. But the reputational damage was done, and even a stupendous buffet lunch off the Champs-Elysées could not compensate.

Nevertheless I felt a sense of wonderment. Previously you crossed the Channel with everything in view; now the sea lay above us and we trusted to the integrity of a 51-kilometre man-made tube. Time and distance blurred as we sped between featureless concrete walls; it took several transits to tell where in the Tunnel one was by the change in the sound and feel of the ride as each crossover chamber was passed. The 20-minute passage in the comfort of Eurostar contrasted vividly with that jolting 5½-hour manrider transit three and a half years before (today it is simply the part of the journey when you can queue at the buffet without missing the view). And on the French side the train accelerated to 186 mph, to jubilant announcements over the intercom.

During my brief stay at Politics International, the client I had most to do with was London & Continental Railways. The Government had just awarded LCR the franchise to operate the British end of Eurostar and get the Channel Tunnel Rail Link built, imagining – on the basis of traffic forecasts which Alastair Morton later told me French Railways had inflated to justify their own high-speed line – that profits from Eurostar would finance the building of the link. Eurostars to Paris or Brussels from Glasgow and Manchester were planned, plus overnight trains from these cities plus Swansea and Plymouth to Germany and the Netherlands. Even before the advent of budget airlines the economics of these were dubious, and by the autumn of 1996 – when I was telling old Sheffield contacts they would soon be able to catch a Eurostar from Doncaster - the chance of their running was receding fast. The specially designed sleeping cars were eventually sold to Canada at a thumping loss to the taxpayer.

With a stock market flotation in prospect, the Bill authorising the link on its way through Parliament and public interest in Eurostar considerable, LCR was a fascinating client. Its chairman was Sir Derek Hornby, father of the author of *Fever Pitch* and no relation of the Frank Hornby who pioneered model trains - though he was presented with several Hornby Eurostars during his tenure. Day-to-day control lay with Adam Mills, a Eurosceptic entrepreneur who had come from National Express, and Nick Wakefield, a banker with very different instincts. The CTRL side, Union Railways, was run by John Armitt, whose leadership and integrity would pull Railtrack out of the mire and transform it into Network Rail, and get London's Olympic stadium built. Jeremy Candfield had come from Whitehall to head LCR's corporate affairs, and Theo Steel, a gifted and experienced railwayman, was in charge of planning; both became friends.

It became increasingly clear that Eurostar, though gradually picking up business, was not a pot of gold. I also discovered that LCR had upped its bid for the franchise at the last minute by £200 million. Moreover members of the consortium - notably National Express and Virgin – were divided over whether to go for high-priced business traffic or "bums on seats". Neither strategy could bridge the gap.

The strains came to a head after a fire on an HGV shuttle train on 18 November 1996 severely damaged one bore of the Tunnel. Eurostar faced a credibility problem when services resumed a few days later, and it was Richard Branson who – with National Express terrified he would go off-message - summoned the media to Waterloo and reaffirmed his faith in the product. The passengers came back.

With the CTRL Bill yet to complete its passage, I felt relief when Bill Deedes told me he and fellow peers from Kent would not be causing problems. Bill's gripe about Eurostar was that it sailed through Ashford station half-empty as commuters waited to board their slower, overcrowded trains to London. It would have been easy for incoming trains to pick up rush-hour passengers, but the Home Office and Customs and Excise were adamant this would create a security risk. They were never able to explain how a terrorist could bomb the Tunnel after the train had passed through it, or why Eurostar was at risk when trains had operated between Belfast and Dublin throughout the Troubles without border checks. There was also the distraction of Central Railway, an attractive-sounding scheme for a freight route from the Tunnel to the North using the trackbed of the old Great Central. LCR feared Central Railway would undermine the CTRL's economics, but also had discovered that between Ashford and the Tunnel it would overlap the alignment Parliament was approving for the Link. I organised a dinner where Sir Derek explained to wavering MPs why they should give Central Railway, in that form, the thumbs down. The scheme was overwhelmingly rejected – though one of our guests voted for it.

One glory of LCR's portfolio is St Pancras Station, now magnificently revamped as Eurostar's terminal, and above it St Pancras Chambers, a Victorian hotel which became railway offices. It was Sir Derek's dream to turn the then-derelict Chambers back into a hotel, as has now happened. LCR had some of the public rooms restored and staged a few events there. One – a transport conference – sticks in my mind, as I was writing Sir Derek's speech and learned a valuable lesson. Knowing who was to introduce him, I started the speech with a sentence of thanks. Imagine my embarrassment when the batting order changed at the last minute, I couldn't get to Sir Derek when he arrived, and he began by thanking someone who wasn't on the platform. Ever since, I have left the person delivering a speech to make the opening pleasantries off the cuff.

I was back in the Lobby when, at the start of 1998, John Prescott made the dramatic late-night announcement that LCR had hit the buffers. The flotation had been dropped, the cost of the CTRL was rising, Eurostar's revenue projections were down and on the eve of the election Sir Derek and Adam Mills had tried to meet

Conservative ministers to secure more cash. When the meeting did take place it was with Prescott, who told them the party was over.

No other parliamentary journalist had followed the LCR saga closely. So once Prescott finished I was briefing deadline-facing colleagues on what had gone wrong, and the outlook for Eurostar – which Prescott was ready to renationalise pro tem – and the CTRL. Prescott negotiated a new formula which more or less stuck: Eurostar continued under a new consortium (minus Virgin) and the CTRL (re-christened High Speed 1) was completed in 2007. Prescott lamented the expense of the never-used night trains, and Parliamentary watchdogs would criticise the amount the government put in to ensure completion of the line, wrapped up as a subsidy for high-speed commuter trains. But it happened, and Prescott deserves the credit.

Around that time, Jane Kennedy of the Oakwood Press suggested I write a comprehensive book about the Tunnel, aimed primarily at railway enthusiasts. I had kept my files updated, but needed to do more research; this included my first passage through the tunnel by car shuttle train (Alex, then five, put on his snorkel and goggles), and a trip to check out Lille station, compliments of Eurostar. LCR unaccountably vetoed my use of any of their photos, but I managed to plug most of the gaps. I was now at QinetiQ and its TopSat satellite had just taken a high-resolution photograph of the Thames Crossing from 430 miles up. QinetiQ's Space Division were happy to let me have a photo of the CTRL's path across Essex; in return I assured them that a scar across it was the new railway and not some flaw in their camera.

By the time my book went to press, Phase 1 of the CTRL had been completed. There had been a shareholder revolt at Eurotunnel, and disruption as asylum-seekers housed on the former Tunnel construction site at Sangatte tried to storm freight trains in the nearby Fréthun yard. With the French authorities half-hearted in tackling the problem, rail freight through the Tunnel was at times halted altogether as Iraqis and Afghans heading for Britain forced their way onto the trains and even surged into the Tunnel itself.

I was at the Scotland Office when whisky exports to the Continent became a casualty. I got a call from the freight operator EWS requesting a meeting, and the company's planning director brought in a video which he showed to an incredulous George Foulkes. Shot by one of EWS's drivers, it showed the migrants inside the yard looking for hiding-places on trains - and those who had failed being taken back to Sangatte for their lunch in French security vans. George fired off a note to David Blunkett, who eventually got results ... though only after Lionel Jospin's Socialist government was voted out and Nicolas Sarkozy as Interior Minister took action. Sadly, the problems would recur with a vengeance in 2015, and rail freight through the Tunnel has never really recovered.

The Channel Tunnel and Its High-Speed Links was published in 2006. I didn't think of a formal launch until my old *European* colleague Mike Maclay suggested I approach Invest In France. It was an inspired idea; they were keen to highlight the Tunnel as an incentive to increased British investment across the Channel. The stars of the launch were Sir Robert Malpas, former chairman of Eurotunnel, and David (now Lord) Freud, the Warburgs banker turned social security minister whose book, *Freud in the City,* entertainingly chronicles the collapse of LCR.

Taking advantage of a Eurotunnel staff reunion to promote the book, I was enrolled in the Triangle Club, comprising the engineers who made the project happen and other Chunnel pioneers. As well as a superb annual brunch at the Landmark Hotel – formerly the headquarters of BR – the club each year visited northern France ... through the Tunnel of course. Our first trip was coincidentally booked for D-Day weekend; we passed Pegasus Bridge as the veterans were forming up, and reached Arromanches just as the band struck up the *Marseillaise.*

28: Last words

Back in 1995, Simon Heffer asked me to write Tony Benn's obituary for the *Telegraph*, as they would need one eventually and had nothing ready. I put together around 5,000 words, then trimmed it to 3,000, the most there would ever be room for. There was a lot to cover, from Benn's first (non-political) speech aged six at Sir Oswald Mosley's house, through his attempts to renounce his peerage, to his radicalisation, his defeat by a whisker for the deputy Labour leadership and his still rebellious old age. When he died nineteen years later, updated over time it made a fascinating read.

Churchill was the only person ever allowed to read their own *Telegraph* obituary, but I was anxious to get Benn's family facts correct, so I ran my text past his daughter-in-law Nita Clarke, an old union contact of mine (a fixture clash sadly kept me from her wedding) who later worked for Tony Blair. Nita enlightened me that Stansgate in Essex, from whom Benn's father took his title, is not an ancestral pile, but a prefabricated Edwardian building.

That commission led to others: Shirley Williams, Roy Mason and Winifred Ewing were my next, the last still with us at the time of writing. And my sporadic reappearances at the *Telegraph* – by then at Canary Wharf under the editorship of Charles Moore, whom I had first known as a young leader writer – opened up other parts of the paper. I wrote a feature on a Hertfordshire landowner determined to grow Britain's first truffle, a financial piece on Bristol & West's mishandling of one of my father's investments, a motoring feature on what happens if you fill your diesel car with unleaded (my fee covered the cost of fixing the car) and features for advertising supplements, until they were abruptly discontinued. I courted controversy with a comment piece describing how Alex, then three, was encouraged at his nursery to draw pictures of mosques ... and a column after hounds killed a fox outside my Oxfordshire window. There was no sign of the huntsmen until a former Master of Foxhounds, who happened to be a friend, came up the drive, said: "I was hoping it wasn't you", and put the fox's entrails into the pocket of his Barbour.

The argument in Parliament over hunting was at its height, and I was not taking sides; I personally felt it should continue, but with a curb on abuses everyone knew were happening. Yet inevitably readers jumped to conclusions. A vicar told me I should be ashamed to bring up my son to support hunting (Alex had seen what happened before I did) and another MFH wrote that the hunt should get its act together. I did not name the hunt; they had just been in the *Mail* after killing a cat in a nearby village, and I had no wish to make matters worse for them.

One piece I wrote for the health page brought, unnervingly, a call from Sean Connery. I had always suffered from short sight, diagnosed at seven when I couldn't see the writing on the blackboard; when tested, I couldn't even see the big letter at the top of the optician's chart. From then – apart from a tiresome experiment with contact lenses in the 1990s – I wore glasses. Then, in 2003, I plucked up the courage to have the defective lenses in each eye removed and artificial ones inserted. The operation, under local anaesthetic, wasn't painful, though injecting the anaesthetic behind the eyeball causes discomfort. It worked, though I had a scare when I woke up next morning, switched on the television and the screen was blurred; an orderly told me they were having trouble with the aerial.

Arriving at Moorfields for a pre-op consultation, who should I see but 007 and his wife; I guessed she was the patient. I didn't interrupt them, but when I wrote up my experience I mentioned they had been there. I was out viewing flats when my mobile went and a voice said: "This is the *Telegraph* switchboard. I have Sean Connery for you."

Having covered Scottish politics I knew Connery wasn't the easiest of men, and prepared to say I hoped I hadn't intruded into his privacy. But he was very friendly, commiserating on the fall of Conrad Black before explaining that while he didn't have a problem with what I'd written, his own eye man felt my surgeon David Gartry, rather than he, had been credited with solving the Connery ocular problem. He wanted a correction, which was tricky as there wasn't really anything to correct. After consulting the *Telegraph*'s ombudsman I called him back to suggest a brief letter for publication; Connery's first reaction was "You're trying to fob me off", but he agreed to think about it. Calling again I got his wife, who told me: "Don't worry, I'll sort him out."

When my father died in March 2000 several papers asked me for a memoir, but I had no doubt where my loyalties lay; the double-page spread appeared in the *Telegraph* (I had made a point of not looking at the obituary they had ready). Though he had suffered three strokes and been in a wheelchair for nine years, the end still came as a shock. As on most Sundays, he came over by ambulance from his nursing home the other side of Banbury. The conversation was a bit one-sided as he had difficulty getting his words out, but when weeks before I'd asked him the name of Hercules' horse, he had shot back: "Pegasus!" This time I told him about a newly-discovered species of dinosaur. The ambulance returned, he was wheeled in and they drove off. Late that afternoon, the matron rang to say he had had a heart attack and was on his way to hospital, but we shouldn't hold out much hope. Corinne and I drove to the Horton, but he was already dead. When I saw him, he was at peace. After his funeral, on land near Cranbrook he and Jane had donated to the Woodland Trust which was turning from scrubby orchard to young forest, I felt ready to say my piece, though I knew this would be difficult for my mother who was declining fast. The day he died, she was due to have a blood transfusion; her home cancelled it, and that afternoon she wrote me a sympathetic if characteristically distant note. By the time for her next transfusion, four weeks later, myeloma had caught up with her, after deeply troubled final days. I had arranged to hold her funeral tea at her beloved Debden House, but couldn't bring myself to tell her.

The Barclay brothers replaced Black at the *Telegraph* when his grandeur caught up with him. Editors changed too: Charles Moore gave way to Martin Newland, John Bryant, Will Lewis, Tony Gallagher (one of the best), and several since, currently the much-liked Chris Evans. And the *Telegraph* moved again, to offices over Victoria Station, its fourth headquarters I have worked in. At times I have put obituaries almost on hold, but when other work has gone quiet I've been grateful to successive obituaries editors, most recently Andrew McKie, Harry de Quetteville and Andrew Brown, for commissioning them.

I have also enjoyed being in the office at times of high drama: the MPs' expenses scandal; the banking crisis of 2008, when a baffled Jeff Randall told me: "I never imagined I'd come into the office wondering if Citigroup would still be there"; or the sudden closure of the *News of the World* over phone-hacking.

The major papers all keep "stock" obituaries of leading personalities, which need to be regularly updated. To date (September 2021) I have had some 630 obituaries printed in the *Telegraph*, with a larger number ready for use. I also did a few, shorter but better paid, for the *Financial Times*. Many of the ageing politicians I first wrote up in the mid-1990s are still alive, so having me write your obit seems a good form of life insurance. And I still have hundreds of former ministers, MPs, peers and the like to work through. At first I simply decided who was old or interesting enough and asked if they were needed; then I drew up a definitive list.

The most interesting politicians for me have lived broader lives. Wing-Commander Ernest Millington, who precipitated the break-up of Churchill's wartime coalition by winning a by-election for the socialist Common Wealth party while commanding a squadron of Lancasters, was one; Anne Crossman, widow of the diarist and Labour Cabinet minister Dick another. Her obituary gave me the chance to tell a story I heard from the veteran dockers' MP Bob Mellish. Crossman had invited him down to Prescote Manor to see how the other half lived. They encountered a cow with its feet sticking up in the air, and when Mellish asked what was wrong with it, Crossman told him: "They always sleep like that" - only for the cowman to interject: "That one be dead, zur."

I have obituarised Whitehall mandarins, diplomats, Eurocrats, trade unionists ... plus the odd scientist, businessman, railway preservationist and sportsman. My obituary of Derek Dooley was a personal tribute to a footballer of talent, courage and integrity. Dooley died between my ordering his autobiography – written with my *Morning Telegraph* colleague Keith Farnsworth – to start work on his "stock", and its arrival. Special too was Donald Michie, the pioneer of artificial intelligence and a colleague of my father's at UCL. Weeks after I finished, Michie died in a car crash with his equally distinguished ex-wife, Anne McLaren.

Chance led to my producing the last word on the classicist sculptor Arnold Machin. Features had commissioned a piece from me on Machin's portrait of the Queen on our stamps, the most reproduced image in history with maybe 200 billion sold. I interviewed Machin over the phone about the way he achieved the clear-cut yet slightly shadowed profile that since the late 1960s has been a constant in a changing world. Then I was told the piece wasn't needed. However Machin, well into his 80s, had told me he was in and out of hospital, so I rewrote it as his obituary. When months later he died, the *Telegraph* carried a detailed insight into his technique, from the man himself.

Writing obituaries obliges you to confront your own mortality – something I first traumatically faced at 24 watching *Citizen Kane*, and which has occasionally woken me in a cold sweat ever since – but keeps it in perspective. Most of my subjects are years older than me, and the fact that my exact contemporaries are around no. 500 in my "to do" list is reassuring. When someone my age or younger dies I regret the promise unfulfilled, rather than imagining I am next. I realise, though, that many obituaries I write will be in the system long after I have gone.

The *Telegraph* has come from behind to earn its reputation for fascinating obituaries. Until the mid-1980s few ran to more than a dozen paragraphs, fewer still were accompanied by a photograph, and many fascinating people were dismissed with a one-paragraph "nugget". There was a cabinet of obituaries long since set in type, on yellowing galley-proofs; usually written early in a person's career, they were mostly useless. One described a former minister as "the happiest man in the House of Commons", when everyone at Westminster knew he had battled against clinical depression. Bill Deedes' patience ran out after the paper ran an obituary of Diana Dors, carrying the byline of a long-dead member of the staff, which omitted most of her career. The cabinet, though, survives; not long ago I removed an obituary prepared for someone who died in 1953.

Under Max Hastings, new technology and the end of union power brought larger papers, and soon the *Telegraph* was delivering the menu of eccentric colonial types, war heroes, clerics, female aviators and lion-tamers which now makes such a compelling read. Even the advent of photographs was not without pain; our assessment of a West Indies cricketer lost credibility because the photo was inadvertently reversed to show him batting left-handed instead of right.

It's alarmingly easy in writing about one person to mention another you wrongly assume is dead. The *Telegraph* "killed off" the footballer Tommy Lawton several times in its news pages, usually through a reference to "Fred Smith, who played for Notts County alongside the late Tommy Lawton". We did the same regularly for Cecil Beaton, in a different context, and the violinist Max Jaffa. It reached the point with Beaton where, on receipt of his latest complaint, our most glamorous reporter was despatched with a magnum of Krug and a bunch of flowers. We also inadvertently terminated one of the wives of Baron Blixen, in the obituary of another of his spouses (not Karen). It turned out that this lady, by then 96, read the *Telegraph* daily in a Guildford nursing home. A reporter sent down to pacify her returned with reminiscences that made a marvellous read ... with enough left over for a colourful obit when she did die months later.

Every newspaper has carried the obituary of someone who is still alive. Mark Twain was an early victim, remarking that "reports of my death have been greatly exaggerated"; and I recall the *Times* killing off the cricket commentator Rex Alston. The *Telegraph* in recent times has only committed this ultimate faux pas twice, once with the folk musician Dave Swarbrick (who amazingly didn't mind) and once when the obituary of a peer known to be on his deathbed was readied, only for another with almost the same name to die. The risk is greater now papers can hurry out breaking news online just by someone pressing a button – but meticulous efforts are made to check.

The obituary with the greatest fall-out appeared early in Max's editorship, while I was on the leader writers' desk just across from the obituaries staff (then tiny, and today little larger after rounds of cuts: three full-timers plus the odd freelance like me). The wife of Lord Stevens of Ludgate, short-fused proprietor of the *Express*, had died, and our obit dwelt on the colourful early life and explicit writings of this former Hungarian countess. It was a riveting read.

Unfortunately Conrad Black was meeting Stevens that morning to finalise the agreement for the *Telegraph*'s new plant on the Isle of Dogs to print the *Express*. Stevens was incandescent to read in Black's paper a hatchet job on his just-deceased wife's morals; he arrived in ballistic mood, and a few noughts came off the price.

Black was livid at his company's finances being damaged by an article in its own flagship paper, and unleashed his anger on Max. Though his instinct was to defend his staff (reprimanding them in private), Max knew that this time the paper had to wear sackcloth. He administered an almighty rocket to those involved, and dictated a grovelling apology.

A couple of times, insights from me into the foibles of the dead have been discarded in the interests of taste or diplomacy. One concerned that senior Conservative MP who was reported to the Chief Whip by Commons secretaries for having a woman into his office to thrash the daylights out of him. Bill Deedes agreed we shouldn't run the story, but I felt it fair to tell it in his obituary, though it would have caused some upset. Silenced then, I see no reason to name the politician now. The other involved a Labour MP with a successful career outside politics. I couldn't find out what he did in the war, so I rang Tam Dalyell, who knew him well. Tam told me, then added: "The one thing you should know about Jack is that he and Julia (neither name is real) have one of the closest marriages in politics." Maybe so, but the MP was also a notorious Lothario who had celebrated his 700th conquest in Annie's Bar. I consulted my tabloid counterpart Simon Walters, whose advice was: "Why not split the difference and call it 350?" I did not feel the man's widow would have been any less upset, and again editorial caution prevailed.

Relatives, school friends or shipmates often believe an obituary should provide credentials to convince St Peter, rather than be honest. It has never been the *Telegraph's* policy to go looking for shortcomings yet if, as was the case, a bishop was renowned as "the rudest man in the Church of England", or an author had based his reputation on a blatant piece of plagiarism, an obituary should give at least a hint. Moreover, the grief of bereavement can these days trigger a complaint to the watchdog IPSO from over-touchy offspring. Yet for every complaint from outraged relatives or friends, there will be a call asserting that the deceased was an even bigger shit than we had dared suggest.

Telegraph obituaries, unlike those in many papers, do not carry bylines. Each writer has a speciality – military types; City, society and racing figures; Catholics, scifi writers – but it would be unwise to jump to conclusions about the authorship of any. The obituaries of political giants like Jim Callaghan, Tony Benn, Denis Healey and Geoffrey Howe have been mine, but many, including Lady Thatcher's, have been the work of others; equally plenty of non-political figures have had their *envoi* written by me.

Preparing an obituary, I first go to *Who's Who* (if the subject is in it, and many are not) for the basics: their date of birth (which even a few men annoyingly omit), parentage, spouse(s), children, education, working history, books published and honours received. I also take a side glance at Wikipedia, but try not to rely on it. I then ask the *Telegraph* library for their cuttings. Originally these were kept in the building, but now everything is stored at Wigan, our librarian collecting what is needed every few weeks.

Until the mid-1990s every person mentioned in the paper had references to them meticulously clipped; then only the more prominent articles were kept, and in 2004 the practice was halted. Fortunately these cuttings remain a marvellous resource if you don't need them in a hurry. With Sir John Gilmour, a much-decorated Conservative MP whom Helen stood against when young, we could report that he rowed for Cambridge in 1931 but was dropped the next year with a loss of form that turned out to be appendicitis. My source was cuttings from the *Morning Post*, which the *Telegraph* absorbed in 1937.

You can go through cuttings like a bank teller, pausing when something jumps out at you to add flesh to your story. But for details about anyone active since, say, 1997, you log onto an electronic "retrieval system", which obliges you to read every single article in case it turns out to be of use ... a very time-consuming business. For this reason, I tend – except for the most obvious candidates – to concentrate on people whose careers were over by the late 1990s, and do more recent research online. Eventually my successors will not have cuttings to draw upon, and many obituaries of today's politicians will lack those extra touches.

Reworking Geoffrey Howe's obituary (first written by a predecessor in 1988) involved going through 30 packets of cuttings; with projects that size you would get stale if you stuck to one subject, so I generally have three on the go. Before you ask: you are paid for obituaries when they are written, not when the person dies.

Despite the riches in the library, there will always be gaps to be filled. Over-90s have often had an interesting war, and if they have won, say, an MC, one of the contributors who write our service obituaries will be asked to find out more. With MPs, where there are gaps in our own files (often because a colleague borrowed the cuttings years ago and didn't return them) the fall-back is Andrew Roth's *Parliamentary Profiles*, which gives you every cough and spit of each MP's career, and personal details not found anywhere else. Andy, who died in 2010, was a US Navy intelligence officer cleared in the secrets trial that triggered McCarthyism, who settled in London where he pioneered the documenting of MPs' business interests. The copious files he amassed in his garage at Cricklewood are now in the Bishopsgate Institute - and a very useful last resort.

Obituarising politicians is relatively easy; so much is on the record. I also have known many of the people I write about, and include anecdotes I can vouch for personally. My colleagues must usually rely on friends and relatives of the deceased, who even if they are pleased to help sometimes have flawed memories. Actors are a particular headache, as you need more than a list of the plays or films they appeared in, the reviews usually providing little personal colour. One can easily fall foul of family politics: the children of one wife frequently try to airbrush out the offspring of another. Occasionally, too, informants have an agenda of their own; one falsely claimed the subject of the obituary as a convert to their own faith. Yet many bereaved people give generously and patiently of their recollections.

Many friends and relatives expect to see an obituary within days of a death. This is usually not possible. Even if the passing of someone well worth commemorating has been announced through the news agencies or the family have sent in a paid death notice – we scan them each night before publication - you cannot conjure up an obit in a flash. Although the *Telegraph* has some 3,500 ready (the BBC by comparison has 350), the vast majority are compiled once the person has died (or we have been alerted that they are in extremis). Thorough fact-gathering and checking are required, with care taken not to miss out important areas of someone's life by rushing things; our obit of one man with a colourful war record failed to mention that he had also drafted the Beeching Report. Furthermore people with must-have information are not always easily located.

If a former prime minister or film star dies, we have something ready and clear the page to use it. But celebrities don't die at carefully-spaced intervals; like buses, there can be long gaps, then several come along: March is the worst month for this. If several die on the same day, we can now publish them all online, reaching the bulk of our audience, and hope to catch up in the following day's paper.

Three months after someone dies is normally the cut-off point; astonishingly, some informants wait up to a year before letting us know and are surprised to be told they've left it too late. There are, however, rare exceptions: with a pioneer woman aviator who was buried in a pauper's grave on Majorca, it was three years before anyone realised she had died.

Atypical too was the demise of Andy Cunningham, who as regional secretary of the General and Municipal Workers' Union and a key Labour figure ran Tyneside until he was jailed in 1974 for taking backhanders from the Yorkshire architect John Poulson. In 2002 I put an obit together, despite nagging doubts over whether he was still alive: he had disappeared from *Who's Who* and the entry for his son, the blameless Labour minister Jack Cunningham, made no reference to a surviving parent. Over time I assumed he had died, then one quiet day in October 2010 I happened to check his Wikipedia entry - finding a note that he had passed away that June. The Labour Party couldn't confirm his death, his union's office was closed, and I couldn't find a death notice in the local paper; I was bracing myself to ring Jack Cunningham himself when my colleague Roger Wilkes tracked down a neighbour. She confirmed that he had indeed died, six days after his 100th birthday.

The obituary appeared four and a half months after his death – leaving Tyneside's papers to wonder how they had missed the demise of a towering figure in the region. In the meantime the Cunningham family had been able to bury their father with privacy and dignity. What still puzzles me is who put the date of his death onto Wikipedia, and why.

When the pressure of high-profile deaths slackens, as it can in the summer and autumn, there is a lengthy backlog of obituaries ready for use. In the meantime, we receive regular calls from the fan clubs of socialites, QCs, surgeons or academics, pressing for their inclusion or waxing indignant that we have not used them when they have been in the *Times*. Our criteria, however, are our own.

The obituaries editor has much to consider when deciding which two, three or even four obituaries to use. Are any so important that they cannot wait? Are the available pictures interesting enough? How do we keep a balance, between say bishops, female novelists and airmen? (First-rate DFCs and MCs are still dying at a rate that makes it hard to do them justice).

I must be a borderline candidate for an obituary in the *Telegraph*, as not everyone who has worked for the paper is acknowledged and I haven't made it into *Who's Who*. But to give an idea of our style, I have tried my hand at what might appear if there were room. You can find it at the front of this book.

Printed in Great Britain
by Amazon